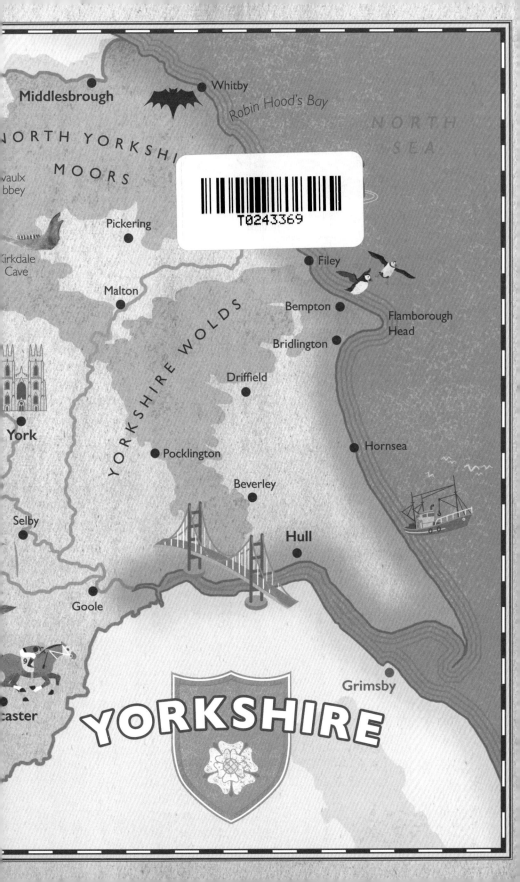

NOW THEN

Also by Rick Broadbent

Looking for Eric: in search of the Leeds Greats

The Big If: the life and death of Johnny Owen

Ring of Fire

That Near-Death Thing

Endurance: the extraordinary life and times
of Emil Zatopek

NOW THEN

A BIOGRAPHY OF YORKSHIRE

RICK BROADBENT

ALLEN&UNWIN

Published in hardback in Great Britain in 2023 by Atlantic Books,
an imprint of Atlantic Books Ltd.

10 9 8 7 6 5 4 3 2

A CIP catalogue record for this book is available from the British Library.

Hardback ISBN: 978 1 83895 736 0
E-book ISBN: 978 1 83895 737 7

Printed in Great Britain by CPI Group (UK) Ltd, Croydon CR0 4YY

Allen & Unwin
An imprint of Atlantic Books Ltd
Ormond House
26–27 Boswell Street
London
WC1N 3JZ

www.atlantic-books.co.uk

For my brilliant mum

CONTENTS

Prologue:

DIGGING UP THE PAST

'Do you want it all?'
One thing to remember when exhuming the ashes of parents is to always take your own casket. Not having done this sort of thing before, Mum and I had arrived unarmed at the black iron gates of Tadcaster Cemetery, squeezed into a triangular plot of weary grass between a graffitied wall and the road to the breweries.

The original casket had long since rotted away. The cemetery man sighed, walked into his sooty black office and emerged with a cloudy coffee jar. My dad had put on some weight in the last few years of his life, and I could not help wondering whether it would be big enough.

'Well, as much as you can manage,' I answered, and after removing the stone tablet and some turf, he started scooping up mud and worms.

It was 2011, 25 years since my dad had died of a heart operation gone wrong, and it was time to move him. His sons had all gone south through work and love and gravity. Now Mum had gone too, so it seemed wrong to leave him there in Yorkshire beneath a slab of unseen stone, growing ever smaller in tandem with the cemetery man's to-do list. He had always wanted to end up in Cornwall, the venue for what felt like all our family holidays, several hundred miles away. I was sure he'd miss things like the Angel in Tadcaster, even if I remember it as a barren pub tinted grubby brown. Whatever time of day you went in, there would be the same faces with personalised tankards and personalised seats, taking it personally. It was like the scene in *An American Werewolf in London*, in which overseas visitors walk into another Yorkshire pub, and Brian Glover, that gruffly affable wrestler-turned-actor, throws a bad dart and growls, 'You made me miss.' It was great.

'Do you want the stone as well?'

Mum and I exchanged puzzled looks. We had not anticipated taking the tablet that covered what, as it turned out, was not his final resting place. 'Well, yes,' she said. I nodded. Then I contemplated picking the thing up.

''Evee, in't it?' Cemetery Man said.

'Yes. Slippy too.'

''Ang on.'

He went back into his office and emerged with a Tesco carrier bag, which he wrapped around the corners so it looked like we had a huge pizza. I lifted it and staggered to Mum's old Honda Civic, the rust blossoming in the rain. I let it drop into the boot, and the suspension roared with the pain of a wrestler flattened from the top rope.

'Don't forget this,' Cemetery Man said, and handed me the coffee jar.

'Thanks.'

'Better go. I've got an eleven o'clock.' He sounded like a businessman rather than a man who mowed the lawn and sometimes cut back the long bits. He lived on the edges. He was the man who tended borders. Grumpily. He seemed the perfect fit.

From that moment I started to think about the Yorkshire we had known. It felt like a severing of roots, and leaving again made me reconsider. I loved the place but had sometimes loathed it too. Now its uniqueness hit as hard as a Leeds United hooligan behind the Lowfields Road terrace in the 1980s. All points mattered – north was the posh bit with people who ate game, wore tweed and went to Ripon races of an afternoon; west was the land of mills and honey, an industrial landscape leavened by David Hockney and his paintings of naked Californians; south was steel and Sheffield and Jarvis Cocker wiggling his bum at Michael Jackson; east had gone west long ago, leaving an aftershock that would come to be known as Humberside, and then the East Riding of Yorkshire, or something.

Not long afterwards, we stood in a West Cornwall car park by Lamorna Cove at the wits' end of England. I thought back to nights at home, in the Falcon where my best friend lived and painted Monet's *Poppy Fields near Argenteuil* on his bedroom wall; to John Smith's, a bag of scraps, vinegar on cut lips, dodging quarry lorries, Ilkley Moor, light and shade, life and death, Dad then and Dad now. We opened the coffee jar at the end of the Cornish valley and chalked our names on a rock that we would forget in the years to come. Mum added a shot of whisky for the journey. I took my dad in hand again, but the ashes were damp and heavy, and almost decapitated the seagulls below us. This curious substance plummeted like a brick, but we at least scattered the scavengers. And though we were now bound to this other place, it was at that moment that I pondered whether, in this life or the next, you ever really leave Yorkshire.

I recalled that distinctive greeting when you met friends: 'Now then.'

That summed it up. The past and present bottled in a dirty jar. Yorkshire – there is no better place.

But ...

More years passed, and I became older than my dad had ever been. My kids were now older than I was when he died; 51 and 17 were the numbers. That sort of stuff makes you think. The cemetery stone is down the bottom of our Dorset garden. *A Very Special Man*. Mum and Dad always wrote 'ILA' on their Christmas and birthday cards, and while it could have stood for Interstitial Lung Abnormality or the Idaho Lacrosse Association, I guessed it was I and Love and Always. Or close. But I never asked. In another year I would have lived in Dorset for 19 years, as long as I managed in Yorkshire before going to see what the south was all about at a university that didn't bother with interviews. I decided I had to go and look again. As my dad became ever more distant, I wanted to go back and find out what had helped make him what he was, and what made Yorkshire a place that had been victimised and stereotyped since the days of William the Conqueror and beyond.

We all know the tropes – Geoffrey Boycott incarnate, whippets, flat caps and fat heads, folk singers gambolling about Ilkley Moor without appropriate headgear – but why is this God's Own Country? After all, Sutherland Shire in Australia and Kerala in India have also claimed the mantle, while the Nazis published propaganda taking issue with the USA using the term in the 1940s. In England, one origin story has Jesus visiting with his great-uncle, Joseph of Arimathea, who was there to buy Cornish tin; this version also has Jesus as a model for the legend of King Arthur, so perhaps Cornwall is God's Own Country. Or County. Which is it, anyway?

A few other questions buzzed. Why, now that our family had left for good, did I feel the pull to return? And can you ascribe communal characteristics to a place that has a bigger economy than Wales, more people than Scotland, and includes three of the UK's largest cities? Can you distil some sort of familial traits from the creative breadth of a region that spawned TV programmes as diverse as *All Creatures Great and Small* and *All Creatures Great and Small* the remake? I'm joking. I know it's wrong to stereotype Yorkshire folk as tough-talking tykes with an unreconstructed view of the world, and I know that at least some of my old friends have long been aware that *Les Misérables* is not a dour northern comic. But I wanted to scrape away this scabbing and find out the raw history of a place that claimed to have given the world its first football club and England its last witch-burning. I wanted to know if Yorkshireness was even a thing any more, and whether that mattered in a shrinking world; and I also thought that, just maybe, if I went backwards, I might feel closer to my dad.

Bill Bryson started his book about going home to America, *The Lost Continent*, with the line: 'I come from Des Moines. Someone had to.' But I have always sensed that exiled Yorkshire folk's pride in the Knaresborough Bed Race grows in direct proportion to the likelihood of them never having to attend it. So I decided to bin the rose-tinted binoculars and regress, to look at Yorkshire past and present. Basically, I wanted to know if we had made a mistake by chucking Dad off the Cornish coast.

As Yorkshire is so large, multifarious and unmanageable, I decided to break down this account into sections. Inevitably, themes and characters run from one chapter to another like geological seams, but I decided this was my best chance to get a grip on an unwieldly past rather than trying to cover everything chronologically. I apologise for the many missed-out bits. History is a selective edit, and this is a personal attempt to separate myth from massaged memory and reality from perfumed legend. I hope that by weaving these strands together, some sort of tapestry will emerge, even if, come the final reckoning, it does not say 'Home Sweet Home'.

It was a journey of rediscovery that I tried to make with a broad brush and broader mind. Some of the things I would learn about, revisit and revise included the Sheffield Outrages, *Wuthering Heights*, the fire at York Minster, the miners' strike, Ted and Sylvia, Kaiser Chiefs, the Yorkshire accent, *Kes*, republicanism, Davids Batty, Bowie and Hockney, wool and Wilberforce, the tragedy of sport, the 'Four Yorkshiremen' sketch, the M1, M&S, ferret legging, the Ridings row, the most controversial poem ever written, and bitter. Lots and lots of bitter.

1

OUTSIDERS

We just thought people in Yorkshire hated everyone else, we didn't realise they hated each other so much.

David Cameron, prime minister, 2014

In 2021, the Yorkshire Society issued a report into the future of the region. The survey answers were to be expected: people overwhelmingly saw themselves as from Yorkshire, not England; twice as many respondents would vote for a Yorkshire parliament than against it; a quarter said, yes, they could see Yorkshire being an independent country. Part of this is down to a superiority complex and part to the scars and suspicion of outsiders, southrons and offcumdens. Yorkshire welcomes you with terms and conditions and an understanding that just because you're paranoid doesn't mean they're not coming for you.

Aliens and zombies

Before heading back to Tadcaster, the brewery town set between Leeds and York where I grew up (someone had to),

I dug around in some archives. I came across one story that seemed to sum up the perceptions that outsiders have of York- shire, namely that people there are suspicious of them. It was the spring of 2012, and as the rest of Britain was warming up for the Olympic Games in a southern city called London, a town councillor in the Stakesby ward of Whitby went the extra mile to prove that people from Yorkshire were, as many had long suspected, different.

Tradition dictated that denizens of Yorkshire were mean, blunt and marinated in beef dripping, but Simon Parkes felt the other-worldliness went deeper, even past the perennial calls to turn the nation's largest county into a republic. Councillor Parkes maintained that he had been adopted by a nine-foot-tall green alien and had been for a life-altering spin in her spaceship when he was only eleven. He elaborated in a series of internet videos, but had grown weary of explaining himself by the time the national media got wind of the tale. 'It's a personal matter and doesn't affect my work,' he told the *Guardian*. 'People don't want to talk to me about aliens and I'm more interested in fixing someone's leaking roof or potholes.' The mayor of Whitby said he was 'completely in the dark', but added generously that everyone was entitled to a private life. Effortlessly shifting perspective, Councillor Parkes then gained the support of Whitby's townsfolk by turning his extraterrestrial parenthood into a parochial issue. 'I get more sense out of the aliens than out of Scarborough Town Hall.'

Of course, as everyone in Whitby, Scarborough and the wider Wolds knows, everyone's a bit funny when you get past Woodall Services, but it was an undeniably fresh take on the status of the outsider. This distrust is an age-old fact rather than fantasy, and if you get a few minutes, I heartily recommend looking through the Tripadvisor reviews for Wharram Percy, a deserted medieval village between York and Scarborough, and drink in the disillusionment you will find: 'The angry farmer that lives next door decided to come out and scare us off by shooting his shotgun in the air for some unknown reason. I won't be visiting again unless I have a police escort and a decent bulletproof vest. Can only recommend this place to someone who either doesn't care about their life or would like to commit suicide. It's a no from me.' Or: 'There was a boarded-up farmhouse and the remains of a church but not very much more to be seen. Disappointing couple of hours. Won't be back.' A more optimistic poster suggests: 'May be of interest to aficionados of cross-country hikes and lumpy meadows.' But the gist is undeniable, and the bottom line comes from the definitively blunt subject heading of another review: 'You can see why it's deserted'.

Why it is deserted has been a long source of debate. What we know for sure is that by 1086, William the Conqueror had confiscated Wharram, and the Percy family, best known for the less controversial village of Bolton Percy, near York, came to control the settlement, lumpy meadows and all. Southerners paid little attention until the 1960s, when an archaeological dig unearthed 137 human bones. This was a good haul by any digger's standards, but those archaeologists must have been a slightly apathetic bunch, as it was not until 2017 that a team from Historic England and the University of Southampton looked closer and an ugly truth emerged. The bones were not just graveyard relics but had also been burnt and mutilated with axes, swords and knives. It was deduced that this had been an attempt to stop the corpses rising and wreaking havoc on the good, if undeniably violent, folk of Wharram Percy. Lingering malevolent life forces in individuals who had committed evil deeds when properly alive was big back then, when the preferred way of dealing with a revenant – or zombie, in modern parlance – was simply to dig up the corpse, dismember it and then have a good old sing-song round the campfire.

In his twelfth-century hit *Life and Miracles of St Modwenna*, Geoffrey of Burton insisted this behaviour was commonplace. He wrote of two men rising from the grave in another village and, despite the not inconsiderable burden of having coffins on their backs, proceeding to terrorise villagers, who developed a tendency to be found dead the following morning. This was before Agatha Christie, and so the villagers did what any decent medieval person would do and, ignoring parish council protocols, started to rip out the hearts of the undead. Severed heads were placed between the legs of the corpses in a final act of indignity, although in hindsight it was generally accepted that dignity was probably not at the forefront of a zombie's warped mind.

I had visited Wharram Percy a couple of years before deciding to write this book, and could not help but think that Historic England had not played on this in the same way that the more mercenary entrepreneur might. There is no zombie gift shop, no black or blue plaques, not even a café selling headless beer. In fact, there is no evidence of the walking dead at all. It is basically a field exercise. Perhaps Historic England deserves credit for this. History owes as much to imagination as to fact, and if you sit in the lumpy meadow between the lake and the cemetery, it is not hard to envisage a dark night and some flaming pitchforks.

Many people will recognise that Yorkshire. For them it is a small-minded place, like one of those interview rooms in the detective programmes where you can see in but they can't see out, and no doubt these critics would warm to another theory, namely that the mutilations were down to a fear not of revenants, but outsiders. This seemed plausible to me, but Alistair Pike, professor in Archaeological Science at the University of Southampton, dismissed the idea. 'Strontium isotopes in teeth reflect the geology on which an individual was living as their teeth formed in childhood,' he began in an assessment in the *Yorkshire Post*. 'A match between the isotopes in the teeth and the geology around Wharram Percy suggests they grew up in an area close to where they were buried, possibly in the village.' The professor did admit that this had caught his team of isotope testers off guard; they had feared this was Yorkshire, imbued with the spirit of Brian Glover, baring its teeth to newcomers. 'This was surprising to us as we first wondered if the unusual treatment of the bodies might relate to them being from further afield rather than local.'

We know the village was deserted not long after 1636. Skeletal scientists, archaeologists and historians wondered if it was down to this ghoulish past, or perhaps the Black Death. Eventually they deduced it was sheep. In the post-medieval period, common land was closed off by walls and ditches, and the price of wool meant landowners turned away from arable farming. Across Britain, settlements succumbed to depopulation, and families who had lived by the plough were rendered useless. They left, and for the living, the dead and the disgruntled of Tripadvisor, there would be no coming back.

Who do you think you are?

2 November 2022 is a historic date, and I take a drive over to Langton Matravers, near Swanage in Dorset. This small

village is set in the heart of the Purbeck Hills. You could easily call it God's Own Country. Here today is where the three norths will meet for the first time over Britain. Three norths? you ask. Well, yes. There is true north, which is the direction of the lines of longitude that go to the North Pole. Grid north caters to cartography and nods to the fact that maps are flat representations of a curved surface. These norths merge two degrees west of Greenwich. Then there is magnetic north, which is where your compass points, though unhelpfully it changes due to variations in the earth's magnetic field. Indeed, it has been moving up to 30 miles a year, according to the British Geological Survey. Leeds University scientists have also found that two competing magnetic blobs on the earth's outer core have caused magnetic north to move from Canada to Siberia. Now, for the first time in British mapping history, the three norths have chosen Langton Matravers as their meeting place. This sounds confusing. The most northern place in Britain today is just off the South West Coast Path. The one man I see as I reach the village sounds equally confused when I ask if he's here for the three norths. 'No,' he says. 'I'm waiting for the boilerman.'

If the north is confusing as a single entity, Yorkshireness can be just as baffling. Is it a thing, and if so, what? In 2016, researchers from the Ancestry genealogy website said they had analysed the genetic history of two million people and concluded that Yorkshire had the highest percentage of Anglo-Saxon ancestry (41.7 per cent) in the UK. This translated into headlines about Yorkshire folk being the most 'British' people going. Whether you saw this as cause for celebration may have depended on how you felt about Anglo-Saxon pursuits such as wrecking French market squares before kick-off and empathy levels for migrants risking their lives in overcrowded Channel dinghies.

The Angles came from Angeln in northern Germany. The Saxons were Germanic coastal raiders. So who do we think we are? Well, the Neanderthals made it back to Britain via the Doggerland – a land mass connecting Britain to Europe, and not what you think – but the weather meant it was sporadically occupied. Indeed, given there was a catastrophic Ice Age, modern Britons can all be regarded as immigrants, with the first people to travel north being reindeer chasers, as suggested by 12,000-year-old cave art across the border at Cresswell Crags in Derbyshire. DNA testing enabled researchers such as Alistair Moffat, of Yorkshire's DNA project, to study Y chromosome lineages passed from fathers to sons. He found Yorkshire people were, indeed, different. The most common chromosome lineage across Britain was officially R1b-S145, which the researchers called Pretani, a derivative of a Greek word meaning 'tattooed people'. The Ancient Britons were Celts and were around during the Iron Age, which started around 800 BC. Their origin story has been disputed, but one theory is they may have originated in France. Moffat said this Pretani lineage was present in a third of British males, but in Yorkshire the figure was much smaller; according to Moffat, more than half of its Y chromosome came from groups he labelled Germanic, Teutonic, Saxon, Alpine, Scandinavian and Norse Viking. This compared with 28 per cent across the rump of Britain. Basically, Yorkshire people were actually more western European and southern Scandinavian than the rest of the UK.

Back in 2007, an article in the *European Journal of Human Genetics* offered more pause for thought. A team from Leicester University had found the hgA1 chromosome in an 'indigenous' British male, which suggested a west African origin. The researchers said seven out of eighteen men carrying what they called 'the same rare East Yorkshire surname' had the hgA1 chromosome. 'Our findings represent the first genetic evidence of Africans among "indigenous" British, and emphasise the complexity of human migration history,' they wrote.

The researchers did not name the men, but the *Mail on Sunday* found one. He was John Revis, 75, a retired surveyor living in Leicester. He had responded to a newspaper advertisement looking for people who had researched their own ancestry and would be willing to give DNA samples. He said he was flabbergasted, and friends at his bowls club were shocked. 'At least now they can say they have got one more ethnic-minority member,' he said.

An African presence in Yorkshire was not a new concept, even if the genetic trace was. In 1901, a skeleton was found in Sycamore Terrace in York on the site of an old cemetery. It was clear that the woman, aged around 20, was of some social standing, due to the jet and ivory bangles and the glass necklace and earrings found with her. She became known as the Ivory Bangle Lady, a woman of Roman Britain, but it took until 2017 for her origins to be more scrupulously addressed. By measuring chemical markers in her bones and teeth, Dr Hella Eckardt's team at Reading University deduced that the Ivory Bangle Lady was of mixed heritage and partly North African descent. This was significant, as it went against the idea that slavery alone was responsible for the first black people in Britain. Some found this curiously hard to take, and the Yorkshire Museum faced a vitriolic backlash for stating as much in a blog. It responded:

'Let's be clear, Roman Britain and Roman York were diverse places with people from all over the empire mixing together. Romans were not all white, male soldiers. Anyone who suggests otherwise is factually incorrect.' They might have added that Septimius Severus, one of York's Roman emperors, was Libyan.

However, one of the Leicester researchers thought the most likely cause of the Revis African lineage in East Yorkshire was the slave trade. Slavery was abolished in most of the British Empire in 1833, but that did not stop it elsewhere, or the victimisation of those who looked different. In 1904, the Bradford Exhibition, designed to champion the textile industry, featured a village in which spectators were invited to gawk at 100 Somalis and their chief as they threw spears and shot arrows. More than two million people came to watch. A team of Somali children defeated a local ladies' cricket team, and the chief's newly born daughter was named Hadija Yorkshire. Such human zoos were common at the end of the nineteenth century, but some people were less able to cope when black and Asian people settled and did not move on.

There were riots in 1919 as the immigrant population became the spittoon for anger over a lack of post-war jobs and housing. The arrival of the *Empire Windrush* in 1948 brought people from the West Indies who filled the gap in the labour market and helped to rebuild Britain. Boats from Africa also arrived, although mass immigration was a thing of the fifties. South Asian migrants also moved to the UK, with many settling in West Yorkshire, but they too suffered as industrial problems were turned against them.

In 1981, the racial tension boiled over and riots broke out around the UK. In Chapeltown in Leeds, much of the focus was on the damage and mayhem rather than the causes. 'Inside the trouble areas coloured youths were seen touring around in cars,' said the *Yorkshire Evening Post*. 'Police believe CB radios were being used to help the rioters slip the police net.' *Leeds Other Paper* was more sympathetic. It told of how in the preamble to the riots, three white youths attacked a black youth in broad daylight; of white women working in a 'black-owned chip shop' being called 'n*****-loving bitches'; of a gang of skinheads singing racist slogans.

There were riots in West Yorkshire, notably in Bradford, in the 1990s, and then the devastation of 2001, when more than 1,000 young people clashed with police. Tension had already been high across the north, but the juxtaposition of a gathering of the National Front and an Anti-Nazi League rally in Centenary Square ended violently. Estimates of the damage published in the media ranged from £7 million to £27 million. An inquiry by Lord Ouseley, former head of the Commission for Racial Equality, was conducted before the riot; the report, published afterwards, painted a picture of segregated communities, and said that neither all-white nor all-Muslim schools did enough to preach understanding.

Bradford's reputation was the collateral damage, but that was a minor thing compared with the fault lines caused by housing, education, drugs and discrimination. As had been the case with race riots 20 years earlier, deep despondency and distrust of civic leaders were raging undercurrents. Bradford, where my family hails from, is now one of the most deprived areas in Britain, with half the children in Bradford East and West living in poverty between 2015 and 2019. That's half. It is clear Yorkshire has still got serious problems.

It's not where you're from, it's where you're at

So said Sheffield singer Richard Hawley at a gig in Leicester in 2007, after a few people in the audience roared with delight when he name-checked his home city. He had a point, but to understand modern Yorkshire – a place that both Bill Bryson and England football manager Gareth Southgate chose to make their home despite being from Des Moines and Watford respectively – you do need to know where it came from. Yes, it was a lump of ancient volcanic rock, once a desert, then an icy wasteland, and yes, it drifted up from Spain with the rest of Britain, which is ironic really, now that Britain goes back to Spain every summer to celebrate sunburn and the olden days. There is a Mesolithic site at Star Carr, a few miles from Scarborough, and Neolithic burial mounds to the east in the Wolds, but the heady depths of Yorkshire archaeology came in the 1830s, when a man called Michael Horner lost his dog in a cave at Langcliffe Scar, high above Settle in the Yorkshire Dales. He crawled into a hole in search of the missing canine and found bones and coins and a variety of man-made objects. Not knowing the history of Wharram Percy, he was not in the least fazed by this. The place was soon subject to intense excavation, with the artefacts found including the fossilised bones of hippos and elephants, dating back some 130,000 years to a time before tanning booths. It would even grab the attention of Charles Darwin, who helped set up the Settle Cave Exploration Committee, and if by the 1890s geologists were squabbling over finds, with one, James Geikie, calling another, William Boyd Dawkins, a 'nincompoop', Victoria Cave helped our understanding of the creation of Yorkshire.

Other finds have suggested that what would become Yorkshire was first inhabited by people around 9000 BC. Tools were found that showed these first Yorkshiremen and women were hunter-gatherers, fishers and farmers. If we can trust these treasures, they seemed particularly keen on making flint harpoons and preserving fish scales.

Then, in 2017, an Iron Age chariot and horse skeleton were found in a field in Pocklington, some 12 miles to the east of York. This news was of particular interest to me, as in the mid 1980s, when I was 19, I had spent a year working on a two-man newspaper called the *Pocklington Post*. The news agenda had been so limited that a golden wedding could be guaranteed to make the front page; an Iron Age chariot was off the scale. I feel sure we would have given it an extra column.

Nowadays, Yorkshire – or more accurately that little slice of misplaced Surrey called York – is synonymous with the Romans. It was part of their empire from AD 71 to around 410, but prior to that, the Brigantes had lived peacefully enough under their queen, Cartimandua. After the Roman invasions of AD 43, she seemed to be behaving diplomatically enough, although this has alternatively been interpreted as devious treachery. Certainly, in handing over the British resistance leader, Caratacus, to the Romans, she ensured favour from Rome but revulsion from others.

However, it was when she divorced her husband, Venutius, and took up with a mere servant, Vellocatus, that her fortunes really turned. There are no known Brigantes historians, so it was left to the Roman scribe Tacitus to provide a skewed version of events. He claimed the royal house was 'shaken by this disgraceful act'. In addition, Cartimandua had used 'cunning stratagems' to capture her ex-husband's kinfolk, and people were 'stung with shame at the prospect of falling under the dominion of a woman'. Yorkshire's warrior queen was no Boadicea.

A domestic issue grew into wholesale battle that was settled only when the Romans sent their crack fighting force, the IX Hispana, to help the queen. The upshot was the Romans were now in Yorkshire and found it to their liking. When Venutius revolted again in around AD 69, the Romans were distracted by other troublemakers, and Cartimandua was evacuated to Chester. The great queen of the north then disappears from history, although it is believed she had a fortress at Stanwick St John, way up north to the west of Darlington. Shortly afterwards, the IX Hispana conquered the Brigantes and built a wooden fortress that they set about turning into the tourist attraction of Eboracum. 'Be harmonious, enrich the soldiers, scorn all others,' said Emperor Severus on his deathbed. Many in Yorkshire still abide by part of this sentiment.

Eventually the Romans got bored and went off to start wars and introduce better healthcare to other corners of the Empire, so that by the end of the fifth century, the Angles got their chance to have a go. York then became the capital of Eoforwic and Edwin of Northumbria stretched his wings to conquer Elmet, which included the prized assets of what would become Leeds and Hallamshire. Then came the Vikings and Ragnar Lodbrok, sometimes known as Raggy Shaggy Breeches, who tried to introduce conscription in Northumbria and, according to legend, was duly tossed into a snake pit for his trouble.

Undeterred, the Vikings renamed York as Jorvik, thus paving the way for mass queues for the eponymous centre, which opened in 1984 to considerable fanfare, with articles in the national media and rave reviews about how even the smell of manure was authentic. With no way to verify the truth of this, the imagined whiff of Viking dung lingered over many a dinner party in the Georgian town houses of Bootham in the late eighties.

The history of Yorkshire is one of blow-ins, or 'offcumdens', of migration and ensuing conflict. The creation of the county as a single entity can be attributed to the Vikings, too, with their three ridings. A riding was a thirding, and so there was North, West and East but no South, although Winifred Holtby did write a compensatory novel, *South Riding*, in the 1930s. The ridings lasted until 1974, when the Local Government Act played more havoc with identities. Parts of the North Riding, including Middlesbrough, were now in Cleveland, others in County Durham. Hull and Goole went to Humberside, Sedbergh to Cumbria. People went mad.

The Danish influence endured, and then in 1066, Edward the Confessor, England's penultimate Anglo-Saxon king, died and all hell broke loose. I will get to elements of Yorkshire's magnificently bloody history elsewhere, but suffice it to say here that King Harold (Godwinson) beat a Norwegian army, also confusingly led by a king called Harald (Hardrada), at the Battle of Stamford Bridge, just outside York. The Norman invasion was the next problem, and Stamford Bridge morphed into the Battle of Hastings, which was really the Battle of Battle, where all Hal broke loose and William the Conqueror became King of England.

The north, unsurprisingly, did not take the Norman Conquest well, and rebelled, which led to the scorched earth campaign that would become known as the Harrying of the North in 1069–70. Simeon of Durham, a monk and a scholar, damned William thus: 'It was horrific to behold human corpses decaying in the houses, the streets and the roads, swarming with worms. For no one was left to bury them in the earth, all being cut off either by the sword or by famine. There was no village inhabited between York and Durham – they became lurking places to wild beasts and robbers.' Domesday Book, commissioned by William lest we forget, recorded that 75 per cent of the population of the region died or fled during this period.

Orderic Vitalis, an Anglo-Norman chronicler and later a health spa on the ring road, bought this version and wrote an account decades later: 'The King stopped at nothing to hunt his enemies. He cut down many people and destroyed homes and land. Nowhere else had he shown such cruelty. This made a real change. To his shame, William made no effort to control his fury, punishing the innocent with the guilty. He ordered crops, animals, tools and food be burnt to ashes. More than 100,000 people perished of starvation. I have often praised William in this book, but I can say nothing good about this brutal slaughter. God will punish him.'

In 2014, Rob Wright sat in a hall in York and contemplated the daunting task in front of him. The academic was midway through a lecture series intent on restoring the reputation of William the Conqueror. This rewriting of history is an important cornerstone of progress, but as he looked out at the audience, he must have known he was up against it. After all, others claimed that William's Harrying of the North could reasonably be classed as genocide. Dr Wright took a deep breath and argued that William would not have had enough men to cause the carnage he had long been accused of. 'William did crush a rebellion with force, but we shouldn't forget what the Normans did for us,' he opined. This sailed dangerously close to Monty Python asking what the Romans had done for us too, but Dr Wright pressed on. 'Not least bringing the culture of Christianity to our shores.'

A few abbeys were scant compensation for some, and by the end of his series, Dr Wright concluded that he was unsure whether he had managed to change any minds. 'It's hard to make people listen,' he admitted. 'I guess a villainous reputation with all its blood and gore is much more interesting than the truth.'

Sócrates' shin pads

Reputation can be both carved in stone and a fragile thing, but the Harrying of the North is scarcely the sort of historical tale that would foster a love of outsiders. Ancient tales can become passed-on truisms over decades and then centuries, and it is possible to develop a perverse pride in old prejudices.

Not long after deciding to write this book, I went to see Simon Clifford, a maverick and eccentric Yorkshireman who made a million from creating Brazilian Soccer Schools in a flat above an Italian café opposite where my father used to work in Briggate, in Leeds city centre. Simon was middle-aged now but looked younger. He had long, well-kept hair and gave short shrift to anyone who thought small. Prince William had called him 'tenacious' and 'a force of nature'. He seemed to know everyone and had eclectic tastes. In his garage you could find Luke Skywalker's original landspeeder and football manager Brian Clough's old desk. Simon also did the football choreography for films such as *Bend It Like Beckham*, *The Damned United* and *The English Game*. When his Brazilian soccer schools were gaining success at the turn of the century, he asked Lego for £20,000 sponsorship and they gave him £2 million. His story is remarkable by anyone's standards.

A former primary school teacher, he began coaching waifs and strays at a school snubbed by society. 'I sat them down and made them watch a film about the great Brazilian players. I said, "This is Pelé, this is Zico and this is how we're going to play. We start Thursday."'

He became renowned, and mocked, for focusing on tricks and skills, but eventually got a job at Premier League club Southampton. Then he bought his own club, Garforth Town, in the eleventh tier of English football – whose ground was round the back of the dentist's where a man with a drill and dense nasal hair had terrorised me as a youth – and said he would take them into the Premier League with his methods. He was good at speaking about Yorkshire and how what he had done could not have happened anywhere else. 'People here are open-minded,' he said. 'They accept anyone as long as they work hard.'

'They all thought you were mad, though, didn't they?'

'Yes, but I *was* mad,' he said. He was all passion. 'I was like Rambo, I never drew first blood, but if you underestimated me then I would take you on – whatever the odds.'

I had known Simon since 2004, when he pulled off quite the coup by bringing Sócrates, one of the world's greatest footballers and former captain of the Brazilian national team, to Yorkshire to play a cameo role for Garforth Town. I watched that match with split loyalties, as I was in awe of Sócrates' way of playing – elegant, erudite, hairy – but I had also once played for that day's opponents, Tadcaster Albion. I could not help thinking that it was a long way to come for five touches and thirteen minutes, and as he witnessed the heated touchline exchanges, the plummeting temperatures and the frenetic pace, Sócrates must have wondered what he had let himself in for.

He put on a philosophical front after his debut in the Northern Counties East top-of-the-table clash. 'The point is not to be playing football,' the 50-year-old Brazilian legend said. 'The point is Simon's project and I've fallen in love with it.' It was surreal. Leader of the globally loved 1982 side dubbed 'the beautiful team', Sócrates was a doctor-thinker who would write 'Democracia' on his golden shirt. He added that he would happily sit out next weekend's home date with Pontefract Collieries. 'The last time I played was so long ago I can't even remember,' he told me. Given that his cameo appearance raised the question of whether hyperventilation or hypothermia would get him first, his decision was understandable.

What could Yorkshire glean from Brazil?

'Creativity and the joy of playing,' he said as the Tadcaster manager shouted, 'Fucking hell, ref!' The heavily tattooed boss was clearly not enjoying the spectacle. This was brass-tacks football and Sócrates' presence was in danger of bringing the game into repute. None of those present could get used to seeing an all-time international great sipping coffee while wearing three coats, two pairs of gloves, a hat and a scarf. 'It's years and years since I saw snow,' Sócrates mused. These days football was just an interest – he busied himself with postgraduate studies and writing plays – but Simon said he would have made him take a second-half penalty had they not misplaced his shin pads and been forced to delay his substitution. The match ended in a draw.

I admired Simon. He had gatecrashed various worlds from football to film, brandishing psychedelic ideas, and was often regarded as an outsider. As I returned to Yorkshire and met him again, it felt nostalgic walking back past the café where he had once told me his plans to conquer the world. I looked across the pedestrianised street to the first-floor window where my dad had realised a more ordinary ambition. His accountancy office was now a Pilates and waxing studio. Dad was gone. Simon was still here. Yes, he had sold Brazil to the world from a cheap Briggate garret, but I wondered whether he could have done the same with Yorkshire.

2

WORKERS

There are mates of mine in Sheffield who think I'm a big ponce, but that's because of the acting I do, not because I live in London.

Sean Bean, actor, *Daily Mirror*, 2008

ndustry has been one of the cornerstones of Yorkshire's reputation. From the textile mills of the west to the steel and iron manufacturing in the south, the fishing and ship-building industries way out east and the coal fields straddling boundaries, the great communal trades have fuelled, fed and clad a nation. A source of pride and self-image, their post-war demise cut slashing wounds as part of the county died, never to be replaced by anything as meaningful.

The beer talking

An old school friend has posted a pre-Christmas message on Facebook. 'Would Tadcaster West revellers please refrain from pissing on the John Smith's baby Jesus on their way home this evening.' It is a quick reminder that Yorkshire is not immune to problems encountered in most other counties (although obviously not Dorset, which still dominates National Trust calendars and where people with thatched cottages most certainly have a portable ceramic chamber pot to piss in).

I grew up in a village called Stutton, just outside Tadcaster. There was a plot of grass across the road that was the scene of endless summer nights playing sticks, football and torchlight tig. A woman called Fag Ash Lil (it may not have been her real name) would periodically appear with a curled lip rippling beneath curlers in grey hair. If a ball landed in her flower bed, she would confiscate it and take it into her witch's lair, where we assumed she was boiling naïve centrebacks while she made tea for the Child Catcher. The assorted players would look furtively to the floor, searching for the last vestiges of bravado, and hope they would not have to go and knock on the door.

'Whatcha go and do that fo, Woody?'

'I din't mean to, did ah.'

'You menk.'

There was a rusting signpost outside our house that stated it was 14 miles to Leeds but only 13½ to York. This geographical nugget was buried by many in the village. York was okay for nice cafés and a sizeable scone called a fat rascal, and it had a modicum of class and culture. Leeds had grime and the Leeds United footballer Billy Bremner, but it felt more quintessentially Yorkshire, even if Bremner was from Scotland, and more suited to those growing up a short walk down a disused rail track from Tadcaster, a proud working town built on beer and one which, according to Facebook, is still spilling it.

The story of the Tadcaster breweries is old and angry. This is part of a proud tradition, or more accurately, a tradition of pride. The monks of Yorkshire were big brewers and drinkers until Henry VIII suppressed the monasteries in the sixteenth century. After the dissolute gave way to dissolution, Yorkshire remained a brewing stronghold, but trouble lurked at the bottom of the barrel. Take Masham, a pretty market town on the edge of the Dales that was invaded by Vikings who, when not burning the place to the ground, introduced sheep farming to the region. This bit is usually skirted over in the more bloodthirsty dramatisations. In the nineteenth century, Robert Theakston was a farmer-turned-pub-landlord. His son would build a brewery in Paradise Fields. It thrived and eventually was subject to a series of takeovers, but disgruntled family member Paul Theakston quit and set up next door. This became the Black Sheep Brewery, because that was what he was.

The family feud that most interested me was closer to home. In 2007, the *Oxford Dictionary of National Biography* decided to include John Smith, which the *Yorkshire Post* marked by writing: 'It's not just an exercise in making toffs feel good about themselves through their dead relatives.' It was noticeable to anyone who had ever had a full bladder in Tad that Sam Smith, owner of the adjacent brewery, did not make it into the dictionary, which was about par for a difficult family relationship.

In 1852, John Smith took advantage of Tadcaster's hard water and his father's money to buy Backhouse & Hartley brewery. Working with his brother, William, and nephews Frank and Henry Riley, he made it into a thriving business. When he died in 1879, the business was left jointly to William and Samuel, his other brother, who had a tannery business but no brewing experience. The will stated that it would then pass to their heirs. However, William had no heirs and the Rileys felt they were getting scant reward for their efforts. The seeds of discontent were sown.

William and his nephews shifted all the brewing equipment to a new site next door. This was not covered by old John's will. In 1886, William died and the new brewery was run by Frank and Henry. Samuel Smith Junior, now the heir in accordance with John Smith's will, was left with an empty shell of a building at the old site. He took legal action to retain the Old Brewery name and set up in competition as Sam Smith's. John's was the behemoth that would be taken over by corporate giants and supped by students in Wetherspoons all over the country. As for Sam's, the place became increasingly eccentric as time moved on.

John Smith's lorries were crammed with steel barrels and would power their way onto the high street and head for the motorways, but as kids in Tad it was common to see Sam Smith's white shire horses pulling ancient drays around town with a few wooden barrels on the back. They seemed to take pleasure in doing things differently, at least from the accursed John Smith's. In a matter of yards on the high street you had a battle being fought between modern life and nostalgia.

It was not quite that simple, but Sam Smith's has since taken its contrariness to controversial extremes. Banning bikers from pubs in 2017 was one thing, but closing a pub on New Year's Eve 2011 because the landlord was allegedly overfilling glasses seemed a novel way to dust down the old Yorkshire cliché about the thrifty tyke. In *The Spirit of Yorkshire*, published in 1954, the splendidly named John Fairfax-Blakeborough, a First World War major and author of more than 100 books, wrote: 'From very early days we find those born in the county of York lampooned on the one hand as half-witted country bumpkins, on the other as the shrewdest, most astute, sharp-witted keenest businessmen in the country.' Perhaps Edwin Sandys, the sixteenth-century Archbishop of York, was right when he opined: 'A more stiff-necked, wilful or obstinate people did I ever know or hear of.'

Humphrey Smith, a descendant of the original Sam, now heads the SS operation. Under his stewardship, a ban on foul language was implemented in his 200 or so pubs, mainly based in old mill, steel and mining areas of the north but with a few escapees. The *Guardian* quoted one landlord speaking on condition of anonymity: 'He walked into pubs unannounced – he does this a lot – and found people swearing. The managers were sacked on the spot. It didn't seem that fair. There are places Sam Smith's have pubs where the only language people speak is swearing.'

The same article claimed that Smith had a habit of dressing as a tramp and posing as a customer to monitor his pubs, though it is easy to imagine such a disguise falling foul of his own bar rules. Mobile phones are another no-no. The swearing ban was most offensive, however, and Steve, an HGV driver, could not comprehend its implementation. Other locals pointed out that 'jammy bastard' might creep out inadvertently during a game of cards. A builder might lament a 'bloody awful day'. One woman was so roused by the decree that she stood up and declared, 'I'll tell you what I think of the fucking swearing ban, it's a load of bullshit.'

In 2021, the comedian Joe Lycett visited Tadcaster and set up a pop-up pub at the bottom of Kirkgate, opposite the Old Brewery and next to where Radio Rentals had long since died. It comprised a barrel, a few chairs and one frothy pint. A Sam Smith's employee called the police, though the constable dispatched seemed more interested in meeting a celebrity than in upholding Old Brewery values. On his Channel 4 show, Lycett said that Sam Smith's was the perfect place 'if you love going to the pub but are not that interested in it being nice'. He also recalled the pensions regulator writing to Sam Smith's and receiving acknowledgement that their 'tiresome letter' had been received.

I think of Brian Glover.

This gruffness harked back to 2015 and the only time Tadcaster ever made the national TV news, when the Grade II listed eighteenth-century bridge collapsed as Storm Eva flooded the town. The bridge was the artery from east to west – and, incidentally, had a Sam Smith's pub at one end. Cut in two, the town needed a temporary footbridge in order to be reunited. The obvious site was on Sam Smith's land. The brewery refused. A waste of money, they said. It was just PR nonsense, they added. A piece in *The Times* later suggested that the Sam Smith's reaction was probably created by a bearded hipster working in a marketing agency in Dalston, but Tadcaster Albion was underwater and Yorkshire MP Robert Goodwill was 'irritated'. An alternative was found.

Stiff-necked, wilful or obstinate, perhaps, this all fitted with the wider image of Yorkshire. The bridge saga was emblematic of the divide between insiders and outsiders, of the generation gap, of old and new, stereotype and myth-buster.

To start at the beginning, I had to go back to Tadcaster again, and so before long I was standing at the west side of this same bridge. My mum used to work a few yards away, on the third floor of a red-brick building, for the British Heart Foundation. Just along the river stood the church I had not set foot inside since my dad's funeral in 1986. That was the year Diego Maradona beat England in the World Cup. I remember lying on the floor by the fireplace to get close to the TV set as the little genius heated his cauldron. My dad was in his green armchair behind me. Except he couldn't have been. My dad died in April and the World Cup was July. It is another false memory. It turns out there are lots.

Along the high street was what used to be Guy's café, a would-be bistro run by an effervescent Italian who was one of my dad's clients. The office Dad moved to from Leeds was just behind that, near the Angel, the Sam's pub that has white horses in the stables. It had all changed in one way and had stayed the same in another, yellow stone tainted brown by brewery smoke, no chip shop, no Guy's, but bricks and water, and ale fermented in slate vats at Sam's and steel ones at John's.

Up the road I came to the Riley-Smith Hall. I had recently seen a photograph in *The Times* of people doing ballroom dancing there as evidence of the UK's resilience during the pandemic. I had other memories. I was a callow teen in the 1980s with a part-time job for a freesheet called the *Tadcaster Extra* when I went to interview Big Daddy, a middle-aged wrestler from Halifax who was really called Shirley Crabtree and was long famed for wearing a leotard and beating superior athletes by hitting them with his blubber.

It was easy to dismiss wrestling as tacky, a coliseum for blue-rinsed pensioners to wave their false teeth at Mick McManus in Batley British Legion. It always seemed to be Batley when it was on ITV. The Queen liked it. So did fashion photographer Terence Donovan and artist Sir Peter

Blake. Greg Dyke, then head of ITV sport, did not, and pulled the plug on wrestling in 1988 because 'we were stuck in about 1955 and wrestling clearly wasn't a proper sport'. He had a point. It was vaudeville, *The Good Old Days* with Boston crabs, panto with teeth. In the flesh, the thing that was most noticeable about Big Daddy was the flesh. I asked him if wrestling was fixed. He sighed and said: 'The pain's real.'

Big Daddy's father was a rugby league player. His mother was a blacksmith's daughter. Shirley Crabtree was on the books of Bradford Northern rugby league club but got into fights and became a lifeguard in Blackpool. Then he turned to wrestling. His wife made a chintzy costume from their sofa and he made the *Guinness Book of Records* (for his chest size) and *This is Your Life* (for the other bits). He was a star. Was it fixed? Well, the year after we met, he did his trademark bellyflop on an opponent, Mal 'King Kong' Kirk, who it turned out had a heart condition. Kirk was dead by the time he got to hospital. Big Daddy, a moniker borrowed from the Tennessee Williams character in *Cat on a Hot Tin Roof*, retired six years later and became Shirley Crabtree again.

The demise of wrestling shows how trades can change over time. John Smith's is now owned by Heineken. The Tadcaster Tower Brewery, the third in the town, directly opposite the junior school, became part of Bass Charrington and then Coors. I once had a 'fight' outside the school gates. I was 10 and had tripped an opponent playing football at lunchtime. 'I'll get you after school,' said Damon Bainbridge.

I fretted all afternoon. I hoped he might forget, but I could tell by the looks on my classmates' faces that this was a near impossibility. They bubbled with glee and nonchalance at the camaraderie that came from anticipating a fight they

were not involved in. Politics is now based on this same principle. I did get a few sympathetic glances from friends during
history, but I could tell none of them fancied my chances,
and by the time I was outside the school, beneath the metal
spire, trouble was brewing. Sure enough, the chaotic mob
of schoolchildren parted like biblical waves, and there was
Damon, evidently fully recovered from his traumatic shin
injury and simmering with the intent of Jet and Shark and
Bremner. It was one of the scariest moments of my life.

He threw the first punch. It landed firmly on my head. His
seconds cheered. Then he stepped back, clutching his hand.
I was confused. Only later did we find out he had broken
his wrist. Technically, I had won. It could have been the
moment that elevated me to the rank of cool kids, but for the
fact I started crying. It was widely accepted that I had sullied
my reputation and the fight was declared a dishonourable
draw. The kids drifted onto their buses, disappointed. That
pain was real, too.

Llama drama

If Tadcaster was built on beer, the wider world of Yorkshire
was famed for other industries – cloth, coal, iron, steel, fish
and whale oil. I will look at some of these in the chapters
ahead when I get to their old strongholds, but the textile
industry is here in West Yorkshire, my first extended revisit.
The relics of these industries mark the landscape, from the
dark Satanic mills that William Blake saw as emblems of
industrial enslavement to the wool office that Bradford
writer and social commentator J. B. Priestley deemed 'the
very symbol of the prosaic' until he got old and nostalgic

and saw the romance in importing human hair from China and clippings from the belly of the camel.

Priestley, the son of a head teacher and a mill worker, wondered whether the city's wool men ever thought about the terrific adventures of the clothes they made, as they were exported to Finland and Spain, and concluded they did in private. I suspect they did nothing of the sort, but if the disused relics of industrialism now seem totems of local identity, wool was an industry that shed the ties of Yorkshireness. The trade became so important to England as a whole that Queen Elizabeth I issued a decree that said woolly caps must be worn on Sundays unless you were upper class. The aim was to bolster the wool trade and spare the toffs, although Elizabeth also issued numerous other proclamations on what people should and should not wear, while also overseeing the start of colonial growth. It may sound draconian and certainly interfering, but perhaps she was only concerned about young men falling on hard times and turning to crime to fund their damask addiction.

Such altruism is sadly gone, but had subsequent monarchs been so sartorially aware, we might never have had to witness the madness of the snood. The wool trade is now so interwoven in the imported polyester fabric of modern society that it has become an accepted part of our language. Phrases such as 'dyed in the wool' and 'pulling the wool over eyes' were born in it, the latter's origins most likely hailing from medieval fairs where brigands would tug at the wigs of the rich to induce a state of confusion and make it easier to relieve them of their purses. A tenter was a wooden frame used to stretch woollen cloth and stop it shrinking, while the nails driven into the wood were known as hooks. Hence the phrase 'on tenterhooks'.

The word 'shoddy' is also made from wool. When trade embargoes meant there was a dearth of wool to meet demand, Benjamin Law, an enterprising figure who now has a memorial in Batley parish church, created a rag-grinding process that effectively tore up material with teeth-layered rollers and then blended it with other wool. Two decades later, in 1834, another Batley man, Samuel Parr, created a recycled product with shorter fibres. This was mungo. Thus, Batley became proud of turning out shoddy goods, to the extent that William Smith could not hold back when it came to editing a book titled *Old Yorkshire* at the end of the nineteenth century. Of Batley he wrote: 'Its temples, though many in number and various in degree of merit, are neither the dwelling places of the gods nor the Hades of a lower race; they are not dedicated to the muses or to Apollo; they are dedicated to Rags! Batley was once, and not that long ago, a remote secluded village almost lost to the world. Now as a borough it is a huge commercial maggot that has fattened on vestural corruption.' Well, quite.

Not everyone was happy with the situation, as highlighted by one 'astounding Australian' attack on shoddy. Evidence given to a Royal Commission in 1905 claimed the Yorkshire shoddy makers were using rags from rubbish tips, hospitals and asylums. Newspapers of the time recorded a mill manager saying, 'The filthy cast-off garments from all the reeking dens of the civilised earth are gathered.' Yorkshire was accused of not killing off the germs from this diseased 'stench-laden foulness'. The mayor of Batley waded in and claimed the material was subjected to 220-degree heat and the dyeing process included sulphuric acid, which would kill off anything.

And anyway, waste material would make shoddy heavier and that would be costlier to export. The clincher.

Yorkshire's geography, with its peat hills, vast grazing land and more than 60 rivers (those draining into the Ouse, the Humber and the sea taught to kids by the vertical mnemonic SUNWAC, for Swale, Ure, Nidd, Wharfe, Aire and Calder), made it the ideal industrial setting, and the textile trade flourished. By the fourteenth century, monks found time to both honour God and make a fortune from tending sheep at the great Cistercian bases at Fountains and Jervaulx abbeys, to the south and north of Ripon, Yorkshire's smallest city. Flemish weavers came from Ypres and Bruges, and their skills raised the quality of cloth in the east of the county. Gradually they kept moving west, to Halifax, Leeds and Wakefield. Huguenots followed in the seventeenth century as they sought asylum from the French Catholic state, a fact that might incur the wrath of those clinging to dyed-in-the wool beliefs about out-of-towners. Bradford specialised in worsted cloth, Dewsbury in blankets, Wakefield in broadcloths.

Cloth halls were established for trading. Leeds got its first in 1711, in Kirkgate, in a direct attempt to wrest back trade from Wakefield. A second was opened in 1755, and then a third. This played host to some tremendous spectacles as well as routine business, with Italian aeronaut Vincenzo Lunardi descending in a balloon in front of 30,000 people in 1786. This was the sort of thing people did for kicks in those days. Lunardi was a man of noble descent and so would not be seen dead wearing shoddy clothes while descending in West Yorkshire, but he did manage to endanger the scruffy underlings on his jaunts in England by spilling sulphuric acid on them and somehow lifting off with a man entangled in one of his dangling ropes. It appears he was more concerned about his female passengers; he would be portrayed as a Byronesque figure whose high-flying groupie, Lydia Lovely, marvelled at the 'enormous swell of his balloon'.

Leeds clothiers who had not served a seven-year apprenticeship were not allowed to use the cloth halls and instead had to frequent what became known as Tom Paine's Hall, which was on the ground floor of the Albion Street music hall. Upstairs, the likes of Professor Anderson, hailed as the Grand Wizard of the North by no less a sage than Sir Walter Scott, could be seen pulling rabbits out of woolly hats.

The greatest spectacle of all to take place at the Leeds White Cloth Hall was the Circus Royal of 1858. Pablo Fanque, a black entrepreneur from Norwich, had long been famous as an equestrian manager and circus owner. He would become synonymous with Leeds, bringing the famous American dwarf General Tom Thumb to the city, and would also be the inspiration for the Beatles song 'Being for the Benefit of Mr Kite'. Fanque did indeed perform a benefit for the said Mr Kite in Rochdale, and John Lennon bought an antique publicity poster for it from a Sevenoaks antiques shop in 1967. Ten years before Fanque's appearance at the White Cloth Hall, his wife died tragically when a gallery collapsed as she watched her son tightrope-walking in the city. Fanque died of bronchitis in a pub in Stockport. He is buried on Leeds University campus.

Fanque was also a member of an organisation called the Ancient Shepherds, who helped pay for the funerals of poverty-stricken locals. This seam of philanthropy is often there in the retelling of the wool story, with the undisputed champion of do-gooders being Sir Titus Salt, lionised by Charles Dickens in his story 'The Great Yorkshire Llama'.

Young Titus was born in 1803 in Morley, a town in the borough of Leeds, and was sent to grammar school in the fat commercial maggot of Batley. He was the son of Daniel Salt, who had worked as a dealer of dyes and as a farmer before being lured by Bradford's status as worsted capital of the world. By 1850, around 60 per cent of the nation's wool was made in Bradford and the majority of the city's workers were working in the textile industry; as Dickens would write, it was the best of times, it was the worsted times. The worsted yarns were high-quality smooth material spun from long-staple wool, and made many in Bradford rich, but workers lived in poor conditions, with paltry, variable wages and no sanitation.

Even before the automatic power loom arrived in 1834 and rendered many workers redundant, the advent of machinery was fuelling the simmering dissent. One mill owner, William Horsfall, installed a cannon as a safety precaution against the Luddites, the secret society of disaffected workers intent on destroying textile machinery. The cannon was a good idea, but less sensible was going boozing at the Warren House Inn in Huddersfield one night in 1812. Four Luddites shot Horsfall on his way home. The *Leeds Mercury* offered a terrifically jaunty and gruesome account of the murder, describing how 'the blood flowed in torrents' and his thigh swelled 'to an enormous size'. Clearly this was a time when all manner of swellings were a journalistic preoccupation. Despite the fact that he died, he was at least 'in perfect possession of his faculties'. Every cloud. The *Mercury* also noted Horsfall's unremitting quest for justice over other attacks of machinery that had 'rendered him obnoxious to a high degree'. Three of the attackers were executed after a fourth, Benjamin Walker, turned informer and sought the £2,000 reward that had been offered.

Titus witnessed violence himself when two workers were shot dead at Horsfall Mills. He also developed an interest in social conditions and the Chartist movement, a working-class quest for political reform. It was a grisly period, with a benevolent government bringing in so-called reforms stating that children under 12 really should not work a jot over 48 hours a week.

Meanwhile, the Salts thrived. In 1833, Titus spotted bales of alpaca wool in a Liverpool warehouse. Nobody had any use for it, so he took it and found that it could be spun into the finest cloth when woven onto cotton or silk. He rose through the ranks and grew a fine beard that would, as with all men of a certain standing of that age, make him look like Dickens. This air of gravitas was no affectation. While Dickens was trying to come up with something to save himself from his debts, finally landing on *A Christmas Carol*, Salt was putting Rodda smoke burners into his factories to cut down on pollution from the chimneys. Other mill owners were nonplussed by this do-gooding; if workers got cholera from drinking polluted waters from Bradford Beck, then so be it.

Salt would not be deterred. He had become mayor of Bradford in 1848, and with other factories and the council not sharing his commitment to improving pollution and health, he decided to build a new town for his 3,000 workers a few miles away in Shipley. This became Saltaire, a land of hope and outside loos for all the 850 houses. There were public baths, shops, a church, a hospital and a library, every-thing that any worker could dream of other than a decent pub selling full measures and allowing people to swear while flagrantly abusing carrier pigeon rules.

If Salt's Christian streak would not run to a pub, people were nevertheless impressed. Georg Weerth, the German poet and drinking partner of Karl Marx, spent three years living in Bradford, but was not blind to its shortcomings. Leeds provoked coughing akin to swallowing a pound of cayenne pepper, and Birmingham was like sitting with your nose in a stovepipe, but Weerth reserved his harshest criticism for home. 'In Bradford, however, you think you have been lodged with the devil incarnate,' he wrote. 'If anyone wants to feel how a poor sinner is tormented in Purgatory, let him travel to Bradford.'

Saltaire, by contrast, was regarded as something of an industrial idyll by those who visited. Dickens loved the alpaca link, and waxed lyrical as he imagined Salt stumbling across the genesis of an empire in that Liverpool warehouse. 'Our friend took it up, looked at it, felt it, smelt it, rubbed it, pulled it about; in fact, he did all but taste it, and he would have done that if it had suited his purpose, for he was "Yorkshire".' Quite what Dickens meant by that is unclear. Was he talking about the peculiar culinary habits of Yorkshire folk, or their resourcefulness bordering on meanness? Or was it a backhanded compliment? Certainly, he seemed taken with the county at that time. 'There can scarcely be a more picturesque journey than that through the manufacturing districts of Yorkshire,' he wrote in what we can now regard as an early example of clickbait. He wrote of bold hills, gently undulating meadows, charming rivers and pretty villas, concluding that Yorkshire resembled an uneven grass plot stuck about with beehives. 'It is true the hives are rather smoky hives,' he added as a caveat.

This sense of disbelief that Yorkshire, and that wider landscape known as the north, could be a place of worth and interest was part of a snobbery that endures. The working class has long been romanticised as a downtrodden mass united by the shared hurt and steeped in the goodness of God's own earth. These were people working at t'mill and supping pints together. Even social reformers could indulge in poverty porn, it seems.

More than a century later, John Lennon would write 'Working Class Hero', spitting bitter words into the post-Beatles abyss about smiling and killing as you get to the room at the top. He wrote of the working class being fed through the same mincer later purloined by Pink Floyd in 'Another Brick in the Wall (Part 2)', but a working-class hero was still something to be. Lennon, with his millions, his Rolls-Royce and his apartment in the Upper West Side, still knew that. And so did Dickens.

However, a decade or so later, in the 1860s, Dickens had changed his mind. In his collected essays that became the book *All the Year Round*, he recounted a traumatic trip to Leeds that had such a debilitating effect on him that he wondered if he had got in the wrong carriage at King's Cross and ended up in Manchester. He went to the pubs, criticised the women and expounded on the demerits of shoddy trousers, which he said were not suitable for gymnastics. He went to a music hall and was treated to 'slap-bang' and 'kafoozlum' and 'um-doodle-day' before the act knocked his hat over his eyes and brought the house down. The town hall was the best in the kingdom but 'too fine' for such a place, and the mills looked like houses suffering from jaundice. 'It struck me as strange that a town which produces such fine soft glossy cloth, should be itself so rusty and threadbare.' In short, he thought Hull was better.

Salt's legacy has endured to the extent that coach parties now visit Saltaire to look at works by David Hockney and buy expensive plant pots. When statues were being toppled as the oddity of having slave traders on pedestals was justifiably questioned, Salt stood firm. A report to Bradford City Council by the Monuments Review Steering Group in 2020 was guarded. 'Our research has not uncovered any direct local links to slavery in our most famous historical figures,' it said. 'However, the wealth produced through slavery funded key aspects of technology in the Industrial Revolution and so forms the backdrop to our local story and should be recognised.'

A more undisputedly chequered legacy belongs to another great mill owner, Samuel Cunliffe Lister, who was born near Bradford in 1815 and later went by the stage name of Baron Masham, which sounds like the middle ground between a children's entertainer and an IPA. Another near-local, from the village of Calverley, he invented a way of making silk thread from waste and put his name to the Lister nip comb, a machine to separate and straighten raw wool. His real legacy, though, was Lister Mills, aka Manningham Mills, which was rebuilt after a fire in a suburb of Bradford in 1871. It boasted a 249-foot chimney that was said to have been based on St Mark's Basilica in Venice. One November day in 1873, Lister climbed the column with his mill manager and architects, smashed a bottle of wine in celebration and named the edifice Lister's Pride. The name was telling; the philanthropy of the time was firmly tethered to a pride that routinely saw the likes of Salt and Lister name buildings and streets after themselves or family members.

Lister Mills became the largest silk factory in the world, employing 5,000 people. It dominated the skyline as an exclamation mark. It has a distinguished and varied history, providing velvet for King George V's coronation and over 1,000 miles of parachute silk during the Second World War. When the business finally hit the buffers in the late twentieth century, the mill was remodelled as sought-after flats.

Good old Sam was well regarded by all, according to some historians, but he fell out with his business partner, Isaac Holden, over a row about the 1848 patent for the square motion wool-combing machine. He also fell out with his workers. Lister may have been big on building Wesleyan churches, but his decision to cut the pay of 1,100 silk and velvet workers by up to a third in the preamble to Christmas in 1890 led to strike action. He made little attempt to blow smoke up the collective backside of his staff and let his feelings be known in a letter to the *Bradford Observer* that December: 'That they have earned in the past not only good wages but very good wages, is certain, or the Manningham ladies, the "plushers" as they are called, could not dress in the way they do. Silks and flounces, hats and feathers, no lady in the town can be finer. No one likes better to see them comfortably and befittingly dressed than I do; but there is reason in all things. But what is the moral of all this? What I never cease to preach and teach – utter want of thrift. The women spend their money on dress and the men in drink; so the begging box goes round – it matters not what their wages are.'

Suggesting that workers flounced around spending money on clothes they did not need gathered pace when Harvey Nichols opened in Leeds in 1986. I would contend that part of the reason why Yorkshire folk bristled at features in broadsheet magazines about how the opening of the department store was symbolic of a changing county was down to the insinuation that the only way to get London's attention was by dropping their £85 gold lamé G-strings.

Back in the nineteenth century, Lister's hard-line approach gained approval from the local press. The *Yorkshire Evening Post* said: 'Mr Lister's letter, in which he referred to the women wasting money on fine clothes and the men on drink, has been severely criticised, but Mr Lister knew what he was talking about. The girls who go out to collect [donations for the strike fund] often do so attired in fur-lined cloaks and fur-trimmed jackets, with long boas reaching to the ground. And it is the girls who have to collect. The men prefer to "mouch" about with their hands thrust deep into their trouser pockets – excepting on pay day.' The strikers said workers in other regions were better paid. Lister and his supporters said relief pay to help those struggling workers was issued indiscriminately. A report by the strike committee countered the idea of women in fur coats and boas by talking of the starving, the naked and the shoeless, and of women travelling all across the north to help.

It was to no avail. Lister, his profits in danger from American import restrictions, would not give in, and he was aided by the city's Watch Committee, which stifled public assemblies. Strikers were denied poor relief if they refused to work, and by the fifth month of the action, most of them were out. Around 20,000 people attended a public meeting that March. By 13 April 1891, *The Times* was reporting, 'As was feared the disturbances, which commenced yesterday after-noon, became more serious during the evening, so much so that the throughout the whole night the town was one scene of disorder and uproar. The military had to be called out.'

The Riot Act, demanding that the crowds disperse or face action, was read by the mayor, and at 9.05 p.m., 106 members of the Durham Light Infantry arrived in the town centre armed with 40 rounds of ball cartridge. They drew their bayonets and charged, but that was ineffective, so the police waded in with batons. *The Times* concluded, 'As a result of this evening's violence many were injured and 10 men arrested.'

The textile industry was not unionised at the time, and the impact of the strike would lead to the creation of the Bradford Labour Union and then the Independent Labour Party. Lister would get his park and statue, and the Italianate column still stands as a monument to the 'plushers'.

Steel city

Steel was – and is – another great industry, and Sheffield was both capital and kingdom. Initially, the city was famed for cutlery, which referred specifically to things that cut. Forks and spoons, therefore, were flatware. Three processes were involved: the forging from steel bars, the grinding by foot-worked treadle, and then the attaching of the handle. The independent cutlers were artists as well as artisans, known as little mesters because that was how locals pronounced master, and had their own workshops dotted around the city. Chaucer would reference the Sheffield knife as early as the fourteenth century in his *Canterbury Tales*, and the craft lasted until 2021 when Stan Shaw, referred to as the last of the little mesters, died aged 94. He had been seen creating at Sheffield's Kelham Island Museum almost to the end, 80 years in the trade, old man and boy.

Sheffield had it all. Seven rivers provided water power, and wood and charcoal could be harvested from the land.

Quaker Benjamin Huntsman revolutionised the industry in the mid eighteenth century when he realised that clay crucibles used in glass-making could cope with far higher temperatures than the ones in brass foundries. His process was a practical success but not a commercial one, at least not initially and not in Sheffield. Instead, he exported to France and Germany, who then sent his products back to Sheffield, where locals tried and failed to get these imports banned. Now the Sheffield manufacturers were in peril. At the time, Huntsman had no patent, so unscrupulous rivals tried to find out his secrets, with one even disguising himself as a tramp and asking for shelter in order to glean his methods.

Huntsman's breakthrough was one of the significant staging posts in Sheffield history. More than a century later, Henry Bessemer unveiled his converter, which was a means of making steel by using oxygen to purify pig iron. This was truly revolutionary and facilitated the mass production of steel for industries such as the railways, which had hitherto been forced to put their faith in more unreliable iron. You can still see one of these great mechanical leviathans outside the Kelham Island Museum.

By the 1860s, Sheffield's steel production had risen to 80,000 tonnes a year and was no longer restricted to cutlery. The population spiralled from 46,000 in 1801 to 110,000 in 1844. This was repeated elsewhere. Middlesbrough's growth was perhaps the most astonishing of all, spiralling from 25 people (and one farm holding) in 1801 to 90,000 a century later. The town was dubbed Ironopolis, but as well as it providing a third of the nation's iron by 1860, you can find 'Made in Middlesbrough' stamped on the steel arches of the Sydney Harbour Bridge, while the industrial explosion also made the region a proud part of the north-east's booming shipbuilding trade.

A success story, then? Well, Friedrich Engels had already published *The Conditions of the Working Class in England* in 1845, although since it was in German, most of Yorkshire had to wait until 1887 to read it for themselves. It gave a grim assessment of Sheffield as a place of teenage prostitution, underage drinking and more immorality than 'anywhere else'. And if they weren't being immoral, these kids were lying in the streets and fighting dogs.

The grinders, with their revolving stone wheels to sharpen blades, are given this assessment in Engels' book by one Dr Knight: 'Their complexion becomes dirty yellow, their features express anxiety, they complain of pressure upon the chest. Their voices become rough and hoarse, they cough loudly, and the sound is as if air were driven through a wooden tube. From time to time, they expectorate consider-able quantities of dust, either mixed with phlegm or in balls or cylindrical masses, with a thin coating of mucus. Spitting blood, inability to lie down, night sweat, colliquative diar-rhoea, unusual loss of flesh, and all the usual symptoms of consumption of the lungs finally carry them off.' Blimey.

Just as interesting were Engels' remarks on violence within the labour movement. The Sheffield Outrages, as they became known, hit their peak in 1867, when publicity about attacks led to Royal Commissions in both Sheffield and London. At the time, trade unions were unofficial bodies using subscrip-tion fees to help workers if they were sick or on strike. The unions were a means of defence against unscrupulous bosses, but they also went on the attack, literally, and co-workers were also targeted. If you crossed the union or were consid-ered 'obnoxious to the trade', the repercussions were severe.

In 1860, a saw-grinder named James Linley was shot in the head in the Crown Inn. An elderly woman was killed at home by a canister of gunpowder meant for a neighbour. Horses were maimed. Tools were stolen and only replaced when the worker fell into line. Bosses who introduced equipment unapproved by union men would also be in danger.

The Sheffield Commission offered immunity for information, and so William Broadhead, secretary of the Saw Grinders Union, took advantage to avoid prosecution and confessed to ordering the murder of Linley, who had offended the union by keeping unlawful apprentices. The commission heard a grinder named James Hallam explain that Broadhead had knocked him down to a share of £15 for the killing. He also said he had only meant to hurt Linley and ensure he could no longer work, but his aim through the pub window was a bit off. Broadhead admitted to throwing gunpowder, paying for other crimes and signing threatening letters 'Tantia Tope', the name of a leading mutineer in the 1857 Indian rebellion against the British East India Company. Spared conviction by the rules of the commission, he went to America, but returned to Sheffield to run a pub and a grocer's. He died 10 years later from what contemporary reports called 'a softening of the brain'.

Breathing lessons

Of all the industries where danger, toil, community and injustice have always sat close to the surface, deep coal mining is perhaps most synonymous with Yorkshireness. We will get there too, but the industry was obviously never the preserve of the county, with Wales, Nottinghamshire

and the north-east among other strongholds. In 2017, Public
Service Broadcasting, an art rock group, devoted an entire
album to the industry and the effect on communities as the
pits closed and miners gathered on picket lines. The band
leader, J. Willgoose, Esq., emails me some answers to questions. I ask about soundscapes and landscapes and how the
album finishes with the Beaufort Male Choir from South
Wales. 'The machinery and industry have gone by that point
and all that's left is the humanity,' he writes. The enemy
within, as Margaret Thatcher branded these miners in the
1980s, were left outside, snow on the ground, London police
shipped in to taunt them with five-pound notes and talk of
Spanish holidays. This was real life not the utopian image of
Yorkshire as reimagined by Salt. Nobody from St Martin's
College wanted to sleep with these common people, as
Sheffield indie rock band Pulp would have it. These working-
class heroes were, as Lennon had prophesied in his song, still
'fucking peasants'.

Worst of all was what happened over in Hebden Bridge,
in the Calder Valley, a picture-book place with a past
hidden from the tourist trail. In keeping with Yorkshire's
troubled relationship between authority and the workforce,
this is the site of Britain's biggest industrial disaster. Yet
not many people know about it. Acre Mill was plain and
ordinary on the outside – run of the mill, if you like – when
it opened in 1859. It made wool and cotton and then, in
the 1930s, filters for gas masks. The irony of this would
be a tragedy.

After the war, Acre Mill used asbestos to make other
products, such as rope and lagging, for its owners, originally
named Cape Insulation Ltd. It was a successful business, with
its 600 happy workers rewarded with organised outings and

secure jobs. Then they started coughing. Lungs and hearts had been quietly savaged by a carcinogenic substance, and people would die for decades.

In 1971, Richard Creasey, a producer from ITV's *World in Action*, drove to Hebden Bridge and saw the red-brick factory looming ominously into view through the rain. He spotted a man approaching and told him he wanted to find out what was going on inside. 'It's a death mill,' the man replied. Creasey grabbed a hessian sack that was leaking blue asbestos and took it to a lab, where rumours were confirmed. The subsequent film showed that Cape had breached safety regulations. Former workers spoke of dust everywhere and of breaking windows to gain some ventilation. On his website, Creasey says that *World in Action* bosses were so anxious about being sued that they had lined up a replacement programme for that night. He adds: '*The Dust at Acre Mill* went out on schedule. Not long after my informant had died.'

Another film was made in 1982. Alice Jefferson only spent nine months at Acre Mill but developed malignant pleural mesothelioma. She died a month after filming wrapped on *Alice – A Fight for Life*. Between the two films, a report found that by 1979, 12 per cent of the 2,200-strong workforce had developed 'crippling asbestosis'. It gained some media attention, but it was a never-ending disaster, with people suffering for years, so there was no definitive, headline-grabbing death toll. In 2006, six decades after taking over at Acre Mill, Cape set up a £40 million compensation fund. 'Cape's management did not set out to deliberately kill anyone,' said a spokesperson. The payouts would start at £5,000.

Blue asbestos was banned in the UK in 1985.

It is a shocking and largely unknown history. Cape moved on and Acre Mill was knocked down. A memorial plaque was erected in 1990. It was vandalised. In 2013, another was unveiled at Pecket Well, on the 'tops' above Hebden Bridge. The pleural plaque lingers on.

3

WRITERS

To be provincial – particularly Yorkshire – and working class has been trendy since the fifties.

John Braine, author, *Writing a Novel*, 1974

Write about what you know is one of the oldest maxims in teaching creative writing (unless you are doing science fiction, historical novels, books anthropomorphising animals or obviously anything involving murders) and hence it is no coincidence that there are themes of entrapment in many of Yorkshire's most lauded works. For a county oft portrayed as near-perfect by its denizens, its writers have fought a contrary battle, one way or another, to get out.

50 swear words

Another day and I find myself in another graveyard. I don't feel great about this. I think insiders probably think outsiders are a bit of a macabre bunch and that hanging around old tombs is a sort of educated but more pretentious form of fandom. Instead of lurking by stage doors or stalking Taylor Swift on Twitter, these people go to churches and scurry around the moss and erosion to find the last resting place of decayed lives.

It is February 2022, and I do three graveyards today. The first is up in Beeston in Leeds, high on a plot that drops as a depressing sigh down to Elland Road, home of one of the most reviled football clubs the world over. I used to go down this hill with my dad to watch Leeds United in the 1970s and 80s. People dubbed the brick and corrugated iron a cathedral, but it was a godless place too, and on those heavy, black bright nights, a congregation of the condemned would head to the next shift at a different pit of doom. There were riots, venom and the National Front outside the gates. I once saw a dart sticking out of the side of a Manchester United fan's head. Pitch invasions were common, but you got seduced by the noise and the tallest floodlights in Europe, like a flaming back four of Lister towers, breaking from the tedium of mediocrity to watch some poor sod shinning up a silhouetted skeleton to change a bulb.

I am in this cemetery because it is where Tony Harrison's parents are buried, beneath a gravestone that was once aimlessly daubed with a swastika and 'Nazi'. It is a personal choice, and I know a timeline of fans of the Brontës, Priestley, Ted Hughes, David Peace, Alan Bennett, Wole Soyinka, Barbara Taylor Bradford, Simon Armitage, Helen Fielding et al. will disagree, but the two most seminal works in my personal canon of Yorkshire literature are *A Kestrel for a Knave* by Barry Hines and 'V' by Tony Harrison.

The former is famous partly because it was turned into the film *Kes* by Ken Loach and people prefer films to books nowadays. In the introduction to my copy, Ian McMillan, the

Barnsley poet-cum-cultural-custodian of them parts, writes:
'If you're from Barnsley like I am, then *A Kestrel for a Knave*
is your defining myth, your Domesday Book, your almanac
and your pocket diary. It's your *Moby Dick*, your *Great
Gatsby*, your *War and Peace*, your *David Copperfield* and
your *Things Fall Apart*.'

I will get to Kes, but 'V' made the bigger impact on me. I
was 17 when it was published, and it was born of the nasty
side of Leeds United, the north–south divide, racial rip tides,
and the alienation-cum-subjugation of the working class.
It has remained searingly relevant. In this graveyard, Tony
Harrison imagined a conversation with the skinhead who
had desecrated his parents' grave.

> *This graveyard stands above a worked-out pit.*
> *Subsidence makes the obelisks all list.*
> *One leaning left's marked FUCK, one right's marked*
>   *SHIT*
> *Sprayed by some peeved supporter who was pissed.*

It is a long poem. There are 112 verses. It rhymes, which is
often frowned upon in literary circles. It is bleak, too, about
the boredom of sameness and the fear of difference. It is a
poem about limiting thought, which is something Yorkshire
has wrestled with as arduously as Big Daddy flagging on
his corner stool. Harrison is a poet, but he comes from this
land, a place of division – hence the ambiguous title – and
unremitting conflict. It's versus and verses, Leeds United v.
the rest, black v. white, the miners v. Thatcher. I also took V
to mean V-sign, just like on the *Kes* poster, with Billy Casper
sticking two fingers up to his brother, his teachers and the
man running the careers talk.

'V' is as scathing an exposition of social inequality as anything Dickens managed when he got home from his northern jaunt, Harrison admitting that the skinhead with the aerosol is like the poet with his pen. Both writers. Both angry. But nobody noticed any of this when it first came out in 1985. That's because it had a lot of swear words in it. Loads of them, in fact. Those swear words had magic in them. It was a sort of mucky alchemy. The swear words also made it infamous. 'V' was an underground text for edgy arty types, but before long everyone seemed to know about it.

Bloodaxe Books published 'V' as the miners' strike ended. For many in Westminster, the return to work was the ultimate symbol of the establishment's victory over grubby oiks. They'd harried the north again. Bloodaxe, based in Northumberland, did not expect to do much business. It was a poem, for heaven's sake. But then Richard Eyre, later the director of the National Theatre, made a film of it, with Tony Harrison standing in the same graveyard where I am now, and Channel 4, at the time a byword for filth, agreed to screen it.

Over Mary Whitehouse's dead body. Whitehouse, the self-appointed moral guardian of British sensitivity and the perennial president of the National Viewers' and Listeners' Association, was outraged.

Eyre had moved on and was working on another film when a make-up assistant walked up to him one day on set and merrily told him that he had made the front page of the Daily Mail. 'FOUR-LETTER TV POEM FURY', raged the headline. 'Outraged MPs last night demanded an immediate ban on the screening, which will unleash the most explicitly sexual language yet beamed into the nation's living rooms.'

Naturally this piqued the interest of those who had previously felt poetry was a bit, well, dull and inexplicitly sexual. We had done the war poets at school, and I remember an unusually urbane classmate arguing with the teacher about whether the war might have ended sooner had the front line not spent half their time writing this guff.

When it was revealed that 'V' had 50 swear words, including the XXX ones, the deal was sealed. I saw another boy reading it at school. Given that he was a nihilistic figure who carried a Stanley knife and liked to throw sharpened compasses across the common room, I would have assumed he was more likely to go down the skinhead route than indulge his poetry fetish. It seemed Tony had hit on something, although for a while the fury outweighed the filth.

MPs lined up to denounce the slip in standards. What was the world coming to? They missed the point that the world had already come to a pretty horrible cul-de-sac in large swathes of the north. They didn't bother with the meaning of the poem, just the medium. Lives were being ruined by the pit closures, but when Harrison chose to dedicate the book to Arthur Scargill, the president of the miners' union, it was as if he had invoked the spirit of Stalin and was going round sixth forms armed with a balalaika and some vodka chasers.

Then the *Independent* only went and published the poem in full. Mary Whitehouse was on the bat phone straight away. The paper published her complaint. 'The four-letter word, referring as it does to sexual intercourse, has within its very sound, let alone context, a harshness, even brutality, that negates and destroys the nature of the love, sensitivity and commitment which is or should be its very essence.' Or as Wordsworth might have said, 'Lyrical Bollocks'.

The controversy raged and wailed, but Eyre's film was shown in 1987 and the world did not end. Indeed, the Channel 4 duty officer's report from the night of the screening, later reprinted by Bloodaxe, is a hoot.

Mrs F. Complaining about the plan to tx. What will young teenagers think, you aren't allowed to put this sort of thing in the newspapers so why is it on TV. Advised that 'V' had been published in full in the *Independent*. Rang off.

Mrs H. Born and bred in a mining village. Isn't there enough sadness in the world without showing this?

Mrs F. (Dane End) Foul language unnecessary.

Mrs H. (London) So-called obscene language totally necessary.

Mr Y. (London) V good.

You take what you want from poetry, like most art. Mary Whitehouse took offence. I took the optimism. Beneath the dirty words and depressing set-up, Tony was talking about erasing some of the graffiti and leaving United, a celebration not of dirty Leeds but of a joined-up society.

Outside this graveyard, social media is at war with itself, Russia is at war with Ukraine, Yorkshire Cricket Club is at war with change. I email Bloodaxe and then Tony Harrison, but he is not well and is unable to speak. I want to let him know that some of us old teens still regard him as a towering figure and that his words lasted. I get a lovely reply from his partner a few days later. 'Tony sends his regards to you + is very pleased to know how much his work has meant to you over the years. I've told him he is still very much a "towering figure"!' The self-deprecation of that exclamation mark only makes me love 'V' more.

The Bell brothers

With apologies to Tony, Beeston is not the spiritual home of Yorkshire writing. That is Haworth. This is the wild west, a town atop a hill with a steep cobbled street to meet biscuit-tin criteria and just enough green fields to separate it from the bad breath of Bradford. Haworth is now a tourist destination and the sort of place Americans come to celebrate their lack of culture. It is best witnessed with a brass band playing in your head. On the day I visited, a grubby-faced urchin was pushing his rusty bike up the hill, pursued by scurvy and a Victorian plod. Well, it might have happened.

People go to Haworth for one reason. This is Brontë country, which is enough to get it its own brown sign. People go to the parsonage where Charlotte, Emily and Anne wrote novels under the pen names Currer, Ellis and Acton Bell because the very idea of women writing books of this nature would have been a scandal in the mid nineteenth century. Since their pomp, the Brontës have been appropriated as Marxist, feminist and Yorkshire icons. Pilgrimages are common. Busloads of people walk up and down these cobbles in search of a broken ankle, and in the gift shop you can buy almost anything with the Brontës' faces printed on it. Candles do well, the books less so. I buy a fancy edition of *Jane Eyre* and the assistant literally gives me a Brontë stamp of approval on the title page. I flick to the opening passage: 'There was no possibility of taking a walk that day.'

The *Guardian* once hailed this as one of the 10 best opening lines in history. I could take the walk out onto the moors to Top Withens, where a windswept Emily purportedly got the inspiration for *Wuthering Heights*, but it's a four-hour hike and it's brassic. Instead, I honour the sentiment of Charlotte's opening and duck into Cobbles and Clay, a classy-looking café on the high street.

You might think Haworth would be the kind of place where they'd serve up pie and chips for brunch, or a scone (rhyming with gone, not bone) if you're lucky, but Cobble and Clay is bereft of Brontë memorabilia and cliché. I have a halloumi stack, and Debs, my wife, has shakshuka. It is perfect preparation for voyaging back into the past with wider eyes.

Tripadvisor is good at sniffing at Haworth and its ilk. Tourists travel there because of the Brontës and then bemoan the fact that shops and cafés have cashed in on the Brontë association. You overhear people debating whether it's authentic, but you don't really want the tour guide to be puffing opium while you pick the scabbing off your smallpox. Haworth is not unspoiled because like the rest of Victorian England it was already spoiled. It is now a pleasant, satisfied town, though, and not harmed by calling things the Brontë Hotel and Wuthering Arts. It looks like a town with more pride than prejudice, although we might remember here that Charlotte had no time for Jane Austen. 'Miss Austen is not a poetess,' she griped with inherent stiff-necked, wilful obstinacy.

Nowhere celebrates the spirit of the Brontës better than Wave of Nostalgia, a shop with a window to warm the heart of any frozen moor-bound heathen. 'Our shop is themed on strong women,' says its website, and it is, with novels old and new, and knick-knacks championing the suffragettes, feminism and LGBTQ rights. It is lilac, lavender and unique. As I look at the cardboard suffragette in the window, three teenagers come gambolling up the hill arm in arm, laughing hysterically.

'Bloody hell, Rachel, why are we shouting?' says one.

There is a brief pause for thought.

'I don't know,' shouts Rachel.

Admittedly, the Black Bull's delighted boast that this was where Branwell Brontë used to drink is a slightly insensitive claim to fame given that the tragic Brontë brother ended up dying young, undone by his addictions to alcohol and laudanum. I wonder how long the pub waited after his passing in 1848 before they started chalking his association on the specials board. But the Brontës' legacy is remarkable, and the parsonage, now a museum, is worth a visit even if Tripadvisor seems inordinately obsessed with the lack of toilets. Hey, folks, in the old days they had no sanitation at all, so at least this bit is authentic.

When I was there, contrary to some cyber-whingeing, the staff could not have been friendlier, and the displays are informative and even revelatory for those whose interest had waned by exam time. You do have to go to the car park if you need the toilet, but the possibility of a walk and a bit of contemplation is no bad thing given that the themes of the Brontës' lives have often been reduced to the triptych of love, death and sexism.

Their father, Patrick, was born in County Down and went to Cambridge University. After he took holy orders, he worked in Essex and other Yorkshire parishes before arriving in Haworth in 1820. His wife, Maria, died soon afterwards, and so his sister-in-law, Elizabeth, moved from

Cornwall to help look after the six children. Then two of his daughters, Maria and Elizabeth, also died, leaving Charlotte as the eldest, followed by Branwell, Emily and Anne.

They would cram a lot into their short lives. Constrained by roles as teachers and governesses, the girls were at a loose end come the summer of 1845, when Charlotte was 29, Emily 27 and Anne 25. A display curated by the current Poet Laureate, Yorkshire's own Simon Armitage, suggests what Branwell's room may have looked like around this time. It is a chaotic mess of letters, drawings, bedraggled clothes and spilt paint or booze. His career as a portrait painter would never take off, just as his poetry aspirations suffered a blow when he wrote a long letter and poem to Wordsworth, who was too busy cloud-watching to reply. Actually, it turned out that Wordsworth was disgusted by what he received, because Branwell had criticised a number of other poets, including Robert Southey, the then Poet Laureate.

Poor old Branwell. Holding a gun, he looks out of one of the paintings in the parsonage at a life of dwindling and ever-unfulfilled hope. In another reproduction of a painting, the more famous depiction of the three sisters, there is a gap in the middle where he has painted over himself. His exist-ence was literally blurred and brown. It is probably his most moving work. He grew increasingly frustrated that his letters to *Blackwood's Magazine* also went unanswered. 'Is it pride which actuates you or custom – or prejudice?' he wrote. 'Be a man – Sir!' You can imagine the *Blackwood's* staff thinking, 'Not him again.' He faded away.

Meanwhile, Charlotte did get a reply to her letter and poems sent to Southey. Although Southey has a reputation as something of a social reformer, it is also indisputable that he spent a good portion of time loafing about with Coleridge and not showing true enlightenment when presented with a letter from some West Yorkshire wannabe. Time has not been kind to his advice. 'Literature cannot be the business of a woman's life: & it ought not to be,' he said. He added that when Charlotte was more committed to her 'proper duties' she would be 'less eager for celebrity'. Charlotte felt this was a 'little stringent', but at least she got a letter.

The sisters knew they would need to hide their identities if they wanted a quiet life, given that the subject matter of their books was risqué. Charlotte's passion was one thing, the domestic abuse in Emily's *Wuthering Heights* another. Allegations of coarseness would plague them until Britain became truly coarse and realised that a bit of innuendo about Mr Rochester was no 'V'.

They first published a collection of their poetry under their pseudonyms, using money left to them by their aunt. It gained several favourable reviews and sold two copies. Charlotte's first novel, *The Professor* – influenced by her spell in Belgium, where she fell hopelessly, and lustily, for her host, the married Constantin Héger – failed to find a publisher, but she got one for *Jane Eyre*. At the same time, Emily was writing *Wuthering Heights* and Anne had finished *Agnes Grey*. The museum shows the room where the Brontës wrote and discussed plot lines. It is impossible to stand there and not picture three women knocking out classics at the table.

'Do you reckon this is any cop, Charlotte?'

'No, Emily, too rambling.'

'Well, you can talk. Yours is all sex, sex, sex.'

'What the hell is wuthering anyway?'

'God, it's chucking it down. No chance of a walk today.'

Reverend Brontë was surprised when Charlotte told him she had been working on a book, and he warned her not to waste money on the project. But *Jane Eyre* came out to promising reviews. 'It is better than I expected,' the reverend told his other girls. In fact, it did so well that Thomas Newby, Emily and Anne's hitherto apathetic publisher, rushed their books out in a tatty format with numerous grammatical errors. Nevertheless, the Bells became sensations, and the mystery over their relationship only served to fuel interest.

Charlotte/Currer, who emerges as the undisputed hero of the museum, kept the guessing game going as she corresponded with her publisher, George Smith. Newby, meanwhile, knew he was on to something good, and after publishing Anne's *The Tenant of Wildfell Hall*, he told an American publisher that all four books were by Currer Bell. Understandably, Smith was slightly miffed by this and wrote to Currer at the parsonage, seeking an explanation, prompting a mortified Charlotte and Anne to walk four miles in the rain to Keighley station, where they began the long journey to London. On finding the bookshop that was the mailing address she had been given, Charlotte invoked a tremendous sense of theatre, as recounted in Claire Harman's definitive *Charlotte Brontë: A Life*.

'Is it Mr Smith?' I said, looking up through my spectacles at a young tall gentlemanly man.
'It is.'
I then put his own letter into his hand directed to Currer Bell. He looked at it – then at me – again – yet again – I laughed at his queer perplexity – A recognition took place – I gave my real name – 'Miss Brontë'.

And so the mystery was solved. And they all lived happily ever …

Ah, sadly not. Branwell, whose misery had been exacerbated by a doomed love for a woman 15 years his senior, died in September 1848. When the affair was discovered, he had been dismissed from his position as tutor to the son of Reverend Edmund Robinson. He died from a broken heart. And tuberculosis. Charlotte's description of his death sounds bleakly callous. 'I do not weep from a sense of bereavement – there is no prop withdrawn, no consolation torn away, no dear companion lost – but for the wreck of talent, the ruin of promise, the dreary extinction of what might have been a burning and a shining light.'

Three months later, Emily died of tuberculosis. She was 30, more promise ruined. Anne also became ill, but soldiered on and took a last-chance trip to Scarborough. She died in May and was buried there on a hill overlooking the sea, possibly so the Reverend Brontë could avoid too many visible reminders of his heartache. Three siblings gone in eight months. Only Charlotte was left, and she would go on to write *Shirley* and *Villette*, get married to her father's curate and die when pregnant, aged a mere 38.

The fight to unmask Currer Bell was a great literary mystery. It was initially felt only a man could write about such violence, evil and sex. Some thought the sisters were brothers, or perhaps a husband and wife. By the time *Shirley* came out, most careful readers, especially those with knowledge of the Spen Valley and thinly veiled local influences, had concluded that Bell was a woman. In the *Edinburgh Review*, philosopher and literary reviewer G. H. Lewes criticised the coarseness of *Shirley* and the inferiority of female creativity. 'The grand function of woman is and ever must be Maternity,' he griped. He should get to Wave of Nostalgia. The poet Elizabeth

Barrett Browning believed that a governess at Cowan Bridge School had written the novel, but said the 'half savage and half free-thinking' evident in *Jane Eyre* meant she could scarcely be a model governess.

The debate highlighted the gender orthodoxy of the time, and although George Smith knew Charlotte's identity – and before long, so did her literary hero, Thackeray – it was her own wish to salvage her sisters' fading reputation that finally blew the Brontës' cover. She said she would write a preface to new editions of *Wuthering Heights* and *Agnes Grey*. This took the form of a mini biography of the sibling story. Of Emily she wrote: 'Stronger than a man, simpler than a child, her nature stood alone.' Anne, she said, had a constitutional 'taciturnity'.

The battle for the legacy has been fought ever since. Elizabeth Gaskell, an eminent author herself, wrote the first of countless biographies of Charlotte, published just two years after her death and the source of much conjecture thereafter. Writing in the *Guardian* around 150 years later, journalist Tanya Gold gave a scathing assessment. 'Elizabeth Gaskell is a literary criminal who, in 1857, perpetrated a heinous act of grave-robbing.' Her thrust was that Gaskell had taken the author of 'the dirtiest, darkest, most depraved fantasy of all time' and transformed her into a 'sexless, death-stalked saint'.

That article made for a good read. Charlotte was a 'filthy bitch, grandmother of chick-lit, and friend'. She was randy, rude, lustful and the master of 'dribbling, watchful and erotic prose'. Gold ended up wanting to burn down the parsonage, which was perhaps going a little far, but she had a point in saying Gaskell had tried to rescue Charlotte from a flesh pit of doom by presenting her as an introverted spinster.

I walk through the graveyard where Branwell, Emily and Charlotte are buried. There is another grave here marked only with 'JS 1796'. This refers to James Sutcliffe, the last highwayman to be hanged. His crime was feloniously assaulting John Wignall on the King's Highway in the West Riding and stealing 60 guineas. He was laid to rest just by the Black Bull. Branwell probably urinated on him on the way home.

I go into the pub and picture Branwell looking like Poldark and telling some bored farmer about his latest poem. I feel some long-distance sympathy. You can buy ales celebrating each of the Brontës here. Anne's is blonde with big traditional flavours, which sounds vaguely smutty. Charlotte has a fruity start, which could be a book review. Inside the museum I'd been fascinated by a letter from one of the Bells to her publisher lamenting her poor punctuation, and to discover Emily had trouble spelling in her school years. A hoppy ending would have to do.

This lesbian polymath

Does environment inform writing? It is easy to think it does from the moors of Haworth. The Brontës' books were wild and raw and different. Okay, maybe not *Agnes Grey.* But the texts are more nuanced and open to interpretation than decades of dreary teaching in schools have suggested. For example, there is very good reason to suspect that Heathcliff was envisaged as a black or mixed-race character. This comes in part from the actual text, with him being referred to as 'a black villain' and 'a dark skinned gypsy', and having skin 'as dark as though it came from the Devil'. Nelly also

suggests that a good heart could help him to a bonny face
if he were 'a regular black'. Egyptian? A Spanish Moor? It
may not matter and it is possible to take literature too literally, but it is worth remembering that while we may think of
the Brontës operating in a slightly rougher and more windswept Austen-esque landscape, they were also well aware
of slavery's links with the quainter parts of the Yorkshire
Dales. Indeed, Emily and Charlotte had spent time at school
in Cowan Bridge, part of Lancashire but close to Dentdale
in north-west Yorkshire where Edmund Sill had made a
fortune from a Jamaican plantation worked by hundreds of
slaves. Sill is buried in the graveyard in Dent and is known
to have kept slaves at his home. He even posted a reward
notice in a newspaper for the return of a runaway. Research
by historian Kim Lyon also found that the Sills adopted a
'foundling' called Richard Sutton and kept him with slaves.
Eventually he is rumoured to have had a relationship with
their daughter, Ann. Another story has Ann falling for a
black coachman, to the horror of her brothers.

Mr Rochester's first wife, Bertha, is locked in the attic and
has a mad, drunken Creole mother. Critics of the Brontës say
their feminism did not extend to all women and they peddled
stereotypes too. Whatever the truth of Emily's inspiration,
there is little doubt that parts of the sisters' story have not
always been highlighted in traditional teaching.

In his letter to Wordsworth, Branwell had riffed on the
theme of 'secluded hills where I could neither know what I
was or what I could do'. The Brontës upset people, just like
Tony Harrison did. Dirty Leeds. Filthy bitch. You could find
plenty of writers who did not go through this, but a battle
for acceptance is on every shelf in the library of the National
Coal Mining Museum, and in the re-daubed 'Tories Out'

and 'Scargill' graffiti on the railway bridge down Orgreave Lane near Rotherham, the scene of a landmark conflict in the 1980s. It is there in the beautiful evocations of a northern life in Alan Bennett's work. Unspectacular hard times summed up by Bennett's killer line about his childhood: 'Had I known it would become fashionable I would have enjoyed it more.' The lack of pretence or embellishment is part of Yorkshire DNA.

More scandalous than Bennett's diaries were those of Anne Lister, an antecedent of Samuel Cunliffe Lister. These were so far ahead of their time that the author wrote in a 'crypthand' code comprising Greek, Latin and algebraic symbols. Lister was an extraordinary woman who ran Shibden Hall in Halifax, owned a coal mine and travelled the world. She did this while clad in Johnny Cash funereal garb, a nineteenth-century woman in black dubbed 'Gentleman Jack', and she secretly wrote close to 8,000 pages of diaries, making Samuel Pepys look like something of a slacker.

Pepys was good on plagues and fires, but what made Lister stand out was that her diaries include detailed descriptions of sex, love, affairs, emotions and venereal disease. Only after her death in 1840 did a relative, John Lister, crack the code; scandalised by what he read, and by Anne's lesbianism, he duly hid the diaries behind a panel at Shibden Hall. John Lister also happened to be gay but was not about to leave his closet in that unwelcoming age, and when he died in 1933, the property passed to the Halifax Corporation, later Calderdale Council.

The diaries resided in council archives for years, and Anne might have remained hidden away for ever but for a 50-something graduate called Helena Whitbread, who rediscovered the diaries in 1982 and realised their significance. Initially frustrated by the painstaking nature of the decoding, she found she was reading a remarkable story of self-identification in an era when lesbian was not a word. The ensuing *I Know My Own Heart* was a landmark compilation of Lister's diary entries. The *Sunday Independent* called it 'a Rosetta Stone of early lesbian life'. Another volume followed, and *Gentleman Jack* became a hit TV biographical drama penned by Sally Wainwright, generally regarded as a chronicler of northern grit, which is southern code for 'set in the north'. Like many, Wainwright was unimpressed by the traditional template for a classic novel in which the leading woman is desperate to find a man. It was empowering not only for the LGBTQ audience but for anyone feeling trapped or unable to be themselves. Wainwright said that one agoraphobic woman had written to her after watching the TV adaptation, and had found the courage to go out. She also pointed out that her own upbringing in West Yorkshire had only made her want to get out. 'I felt that if you were different in any way, you just couldn't survive.'

A few days after my trip to Haworth, I get a reply to the email I had sent to Laurie Shannon from Northwestern University – which is in Illinois rather than Manchester. She is the chair of the Anne Lister Society, and tells me, in italics, that '*This Yorkshire landowner and lesbian polymath also happens to be the author of an emerging masterpiece in the English literary tradition.*'

On the TV I watch Wainwright's *Happy Valley*, about strong, sarcastic women and idiot, violent men. The revolution is now. And then.

Slack work, lad

Maybe it is Laurie's email or maybe it is driving down rural routes, but I find myself pondering that idea of being caged in, pigeonholed, denied your true self by social norms. I think of Billy Casper, the downtrodden hero of *A Kestrel for a Knave*. He briefly finds an escape from daily drudgery by looking after a wild bird. Billy couldn't care less about school or the bullies because when Kes flies, he feels free, or at least sees the possibility of it. This being the mining belt of Barnsley, his brother Jud, a man without the wit to think of escape and destined for a life down the pit, kills Kes when Billy doesn't put a bet on for him at the bookmaker's. His mother is so battered by this life of no expectation that she sides with Jud. It was a tenner after all. It sounds a lot like the narrator of 'V', finding a way out through words. Billy found his way out through a bird. Now it's in the kitchen bin. No wonder he is forever sticking his fingers up.

I have arranged to call Ian McMillan. 'I'm just having a cup of tea,' he says, but he is happy to talk. 'It was the first book I'd read where we weren't being taken the mickey out of,' he tells me in a soft Barnsley accent of ebb and flow. 'Like Tony Harrison says, "We're the ones Shakespeare gives the comedy parts to." When I was a kid, I read Billy Bunter and Biggles and I thought these people talked like me. Years later I realised how stupid I'd been. But in *A Kestrel for a Knave*, they *did* talk like me. I walk past people today who look like Billy Casper. It's set in a place like ours, which is seen as marginal, somewhere available but hard.'

Barry Hines came from Hoyland, near Barnsley, and wrote about class and social problems. *A Kestrel for a*

Knave was published in 1968, the year I was born. The film adaptation is often remembered for Brian 'You made me, miss' Glover's showboating turn as PE psycho Mr Sugden. You laugh when Sugden takes the ball off Billy and then throws it at him.

'What wa' that for, sir?

'Slack work, lad. Slack work.'

But the bullying turns darker when Sugden makes Billy stay in the freezing shower. Even the other boys plead with him to let Billy out. An earlier exchange with the sadistic teacher might be an indictment of an education system or plum-voiced levelling-up speeches from 2021.

'Well don't blame me then.'

'Of course I'll blame you, lad. Who else do you expect me to blame?'

Ian, a well-known poet once billed as 'Les Dawson for the Beat generation', used to work alongside Hines at Sheffield Polytechnic, where Hines was the writer-in-residence. 'It was amazing how he approached writing,' he says. 'He'd turn up at nine o'clock, take the dog for his walk and then sit down and start. Sometimes he'd come out and ask me something like "If I were in a pub and you were going to buy me a pint, which side would you stand on?" He'd go off and write a bit more and then come out again. "If I said 'ey up' to you, would you say 'ey up' back or summat else?" He was authentic, was Barry.'

Hines wrote lots of books, including ones about the demise of the coal and steel industries, but he was stuck with *Kes*, like it or not. McMillan says most people in Barnsley still claim to have been in the film. 'They'll say, "I were in background in the football match." I say, "You weren't even born when it were made."' It has become Barnsley's equivalent of the Sex Pistols playing Manchester's Free Trade Hall. If you weren't there, you wished you were.

Ian is a worldly wordsmith. He presents on BBC Radio and has made a living from poetry since 1983, but he has always lived in Darfield. South Yorkshire is not known as pretty. It's got disused mines and disowned towns, terraces the colour of a drunk's bulbous nose. Brass bands play and the wind blows hard too. When a town like Barnsley tries to dress up, it gets the mickey taken out of it, the comedy parts.

This reached its zenith, or faux-Italian hilltop at the very least, in 2003. Remaking Barnsley suggested the place could become a sort of Tuscan hill town. Everyone laughed, but Will Alsop, a maverick architect best known for letting his imagination loose on Peckham Library, had a vision on the M1. 'I'd never been before,' he said. 'I was a Barnsley virgin.' His idea was to make Barnsley beautiful, turning it into a sort of walled hill fort modelled on Lucca on the River Serchio, the birthplace of Puccini rather than Dickie Bird and known in Italy as Arts Town. This was down to government plans to deal with 10 per cent unemployment and the loss of identity after Barnsley Main Colliery ceased production in 1991 by repainting the north with a Renaissance feel. Yorkshire Forward, the regional development agency, had £150 million. Alsop's eccentric dummy model was a work of art itself, like Lego on drugs, featuring a ferret and a fighter plane, and his enthusiasm was infectious even when mildly insulting.

'It sounds harsh, but at the moment I can't think of one thing that would bring people to Barnsley,' he said, before reconsidering and adding that 'It can boast a world-class angling team.' Alsop, a provocateur with a vampiric rock-star mien, said that he had been to a market in Valencia where you could buy all manner of cheese and oysters while a brass band played. He lingered on the last bit in case we had not noticed: Barnsley was already a third of the way there. And although a letter to the local paper deemed it a 'crackpot grandiose scheme' and one wondered what Arthur Scargill, born in nearby Worsbrough, would have made of this type of regeneration, it was hard not to yearn to see Alsop plough on with plans to erect a giant halo above the town centre to light the way ahead.

This radical scattergun could not be contained by Barnsley alone, and he turned to Middlesbrough too, promising a Rubik's Cube cinema and a tower block modelled on Marge Simpson's bouffant. Then Yorkshire Forward went backwards and bust. Alsop died in 2018, but even if there was no halo, Barnsley did at least tart itself up a bit. And in dreaming of escape, he was following a long line of Yorkshire realists.

Billy Casper does not fit in because he is different. He does not want this life of strict limits and toxic masculinity. Ian knows Billy's people but says Darfield Lower County Primary School was actually an inspiring place. 'We had singing, dancing, art and music and poetry. I thought I could do that. I encourage people now because I was always encouraged. I got published in magazines and was doing clubs and then I went to North Staffordshire Poly because my mam and dad expected me to. I didn't work very hard, though, and got a job on a building site. When I started out, they said, "Wev heard tha's got a degree." That became my name. "He's here – Deg*ree*", with the emphasis like that. My mate worked there too and he was doing cello at the Northern School of Music so they'd pretend to go on strike. "We're not having cellists and we're not having poets – we're off." I got it every day, but I found people very supportive.

They always thought I'd write about them. Someone would have a bag of crisps – "put that in yer poem".'

He gets called a professional Yorkshireman. This can be a badge of honour and a source of irritation. In the *Yorkshire Post* in 2019, writer Anthony Clavane said: 'Professional Yorkshireman is a label lazily applied to anyone born in Broad Acres who has made it down south. Any man, that is. For some reason it doesn't apply to successful women like Jodie Whittaker, Judie Dench and, well, the Brontës. It is a form of insult and implies the chap in question is dour, has a penchant for flat caps and whippets and constantly prattles into a microphone about the wonders of God's Own Country.' In other words, Geoffrey Boycott.

'I think it's fascinating I get called that,' says Ian. 'I'd rather be a professional Yorkshireman than an amateur Lancashireman, but I never fathom what they mean. I think they try to define us. "Brussen", in South Yorkshire, means we're a bit oppositional, a bit loud and a bit determined, always taking the other point of view. I think we are like Texas, bigger is better. My mate Tony Husband, the cartoonist, says when two Yorkshiremen start talking, they very quickly start talking about Yorkshire in comparison to whatever everyone else is talking about.

'"What time is it?"

'"Ten past three."

'"But quarter past in Yorkshire."

'That sort of thing.'

Kes is about categorising too. It is about the education system that fails those who fail the 11-plus. They are never going to amount to anything and they know it. So do we. It is brutally sad. A bird does not really offer a way out but it offers a moment of difference. Like Ian says, this Yorkshire is hard. It is unforgiving. Brussen. Like in 'V', creativity is beaten out of people.

The last of 'V''s 112 verses imagines the poet's epitaph on his tombstone

Beneath your feet's a poet, then a pit
Poetry supporter, if you're here to find
How poems can grow from (beat you to it!) SHIT
Find the beef, the beer, the bread, then look behind

Barry Hines didn't leave Yorkshire, but he did move to a nice part of Sheffield. Dr David Forrest, from the University of Sheffield, where Hines's letters, papers and unfinished writings are housed, says it was a struggle. 'Hines cared about what coal miners think, but he was living in a well-heeled area and struggled to reconcile that. There was a tension there. He was in this new world and so was disconnected from the miners' strike.'

Hines wrote about the view from the ninth floor of the arts tower at the university. Nobody else could see much in it, although Will Alsop would have dressed it in tinsel and put in some blow-up palm trees. Although Hines did much more and wanted to take a wrecking ball to stereotypes, there was a 'grim up north' aspect to his books, which showed how ideas about Yorkshire and the north were often constructed without beauty.

Sport is also key to his work. Forrest says football was 'a transformant working-class art' and Hines was drawn to the footballers who defied categorisation, the number 10s. Other great Yorkshire works also consider the disconnect between art and physicality. David Peace's epic novel *The Damned Utd* told of Brian Clough and his revenge mission against

Leeds United. Bold and as blistering as a Clough half-time team talk, it did not meet with all the players' approval. One of them sued. Similarly, an abiding image from *This Sporting Life*, David Storey's great novel about rugby league and more, is of the central hero, Arthur, as 'a great ape on a football field'. Storey's own battle with the machismo and categorising of old Yorkshire stemmed from the death of his brother, aged six, after a fireside boxing match with his miner father. This was broken Yorkshire. It was 1940.

In his book *The Uses of Literacy*, published way back in 1957, Richard Hoggart, son of a Yorkshire boilermaker and an orphan at 10, says the working class sees the world through the prism of them and us. 'The solidarity is helped by the lack of scope for ambition.' There was talk of Billy Casper getting a job in a zoo at the end of *Kes*, but it was a contrived ending at odds with all that had gone before. That got binned too.

Ted and Sylvia

The idea that you can get on in the arts world even if you're born into a modest working-class community had really gained ground when Ted Hughes became Poet Laureate in 1984. It is why I am on the road to Heptonstall, 10 miles south of Haworth. To get there from the east, you take the Burnley Road, towards the unforgiving slag heaps of Lancashire. You drive through a place called Friendly. An enterprising journalist for the *Huddersfield Examiner* once decided to see if the place lived up to its name. 'It's unremarkable in its ordinariness,' said the man at the chip shop. The landlord at the Copper Cow said he had one client who was an absolute arsehole, but the writer concluded: 'Friendly is friendly. I would say averagely friendly for a place of its size in the Calder Valley which is itself a fairly friendly place.' I drive on.

I get to Mytholmroyd and stop. This is where Ted Hughes was born in 1930, in a soot-stained end terrace on Aspinall Street. Local schoolchildren created storyboards of *The Iron Man* to mark the village's most famous son, but I suspect they would have rather done drawings of Iron Man the Tony Stark superhero. Anyway, Mytholmroyd does not overplay its hand. Hughes lived in the Calder Valley for his first eight years but was not enamoured. While its influence remains in poems, notably his 1979 *Remains of Elmet*, it was a melancholy place mourning a devastating death toll in the First World War; indeed, William Henry Hughes, Ted's father, was one of only 17 men from his battalion to make it back from Gallipoli alive.

War cast a pall over Mytholmroyd and Hughes. 'Nothing quite ever escapes into happiness,' he wrote. He chalked a skull and crossbones on a terrace wall. The Mount Zion chapel on the other side of the street blocked out light in one direction, but he could still see Scout Rock – his spiritual midwife, as he put it – looming large above all. In this village there were no roads north or south. You were stuck. Hughes's love of the natural world was cemented in those years, but dead men and animals also played their parts. In August 1938, he moved to a South Yorkshire mining town called Mexborough, and then to Cambridge.

Down this eastbound road is Hebden Bridge, on the banks of the Calder, the stuff of calendars for those who have never heard of Acre Mill. It still has soot on the old mill walls, but it also has a girl and a bicycle tattooed onto a whitewashed stone canvas in the centre. It is quaint and vibrant and has a surfeit of culture. Hughes wanted to get out, but other writers come here in their droves now. So do artists, hunt sabs, ex-punks, yoga gurus and socialists. It became renowned as a LGBT haven before the Q was added, and is like a big arts commune. If you want to spend an afternoon in Yorkshire debating the relative merits of quinoa and lentils with a Free Palestine protester, this is your slice of organic lemon drizzle heaven.

I drive through until a sharp turn up a hill so vertiginous that it almost falls back on itself. This is the ascent to Heptonstall, which is less arty but proudly forbidding. The weather up here can be condescending. In 1847, the thirteenth-century church of St Thomas a Becket was mortally wounded. The west face of the tower fell. The church was left to feel sorry for itself. It took seven years to build a new church. Now there are two, the old and the older.

As stated at the outset of this chapter, my tombstone tourism seems a little macabre, but I wander around the stones flat on the ground and lined in green, looking. Sylvia Plath was American, but she married local boy Ted in 1956, a few months after they had met. She wrote *The Bell Jar*, an autobiographical novel detailing the pain of suffocating expectation, and committed suicide a month after its publication when she put her head in the oven in her flat in Camden. The creative partnership, disintegrating marriage, Hughes's affair and the alleged emotional abuse, and worse, have fascinated fans and scholars ever since. Both sides have passionately argued their case in the poets' absence.

Plath suffered from depression from an early age and tried to take her own life before meeting Hughes. Like her protagonist in *The Bell Jar*, she also underwent electroshock therapy. Scholars debate their respective merits as writers, with one theory being that Plath grew jealous of Hughes's fame. Yet she was the one who would receive a posthumous Pulitzer, and they were both plagued by misery. Six years after Plath's death, Assia Wevill, Hughes's Berlin-born mistress, who had escaped the Nazis by fleeing to Palestine, also gassed herself. Life grew darker than anything Scout Rock or Mount Zion could manage.

It is 11 February 2022, and by coincidence, this is the fifty-ninth anniversary of Plath's death. I walk through a gate at the rear of the church and see a few people gathered in what seems like the grassy overspill. An old man with white hair, a stick and a vaguely bored look is leaning on a headstone. Two women, one in a fine black overcoat and a younger one in cream anorak and jeans, are standing a few yards ahead of us by the grave.

I chat to the old man, whose name is Stuart. 'I live round the back there,' he says. 'I come here and help people find the grave.' He comes every day of the week, apart from Friday, when he visits his sister in a care home. I ask if he likes poetry. 'Oh no,' he replies as if I had suggested he liked drowning puppies in the canal.

It turns out Stuart knew Ted Hughes's father, though. 'A real gentleman,' he says. 'He ran the tobacconist, sweet shop and travel agent in Hebden Bridge. He sold me my first trip to Switzerland. Cost £25. Two weeks' wages.' Stuart tells me that his own uncle used to live on a farm nearby and survived on goose eggs and pineapple chunks. 'Needless to say, he didn't make his seventieth birthday,' he adds. His father was the local mayor. 'Several times.'

The two women approach. The one in the overcoat is called Jessica Lawrence. She tells me that she had been doing a creative writing course half a mile away at Lumb Bank, the former mill owner's house bought by Hughes in 1968, when she found out where Plath was buried. 'I ran straight here,' she says. She began to study the people who visited the site from all over the world. Sometimes suicide notes are left on the grave, but she says the pilgrimage has often helped people make pivotal changes in their lives. Some have even turned back from the brink. Her dissertation was about the therapeutic benefits of being here. The younger woman is an American studying comparative literature at Oxford University, which seems apt as the proxy battle between Hughes and Plath rages on.

The headstone reads 'Sylvia Plath-Hughes', but the 'Hughes' has been defaced. This is common practice. Jessica says she hopes to be on the panel for the forthcoming Plath festival, which may clash with the Hughes one. It is a never-ending domestic squabble.

Hughes hated this and what he called the Plath Fantasia. In 1989 he felt compelled to write to the *Guardian* to point out that he and Plath had never divorced, and he addressed the headstone issue head-on. 'If I had followed custom the gravestone would have borne the name Sylvia Hughes, which was her legal name, the name of her children's mother. I took it into my head to insert the Plath after Sylvia because I knew well enough in 1963 what she had brought off in that name and I wished to honour it.' He added that the riveted lead lettering of 'Hughes' had been removed four times; this was more than 30 years ago. The north Devon pebbles that he left around the grave had been stolen. He asked those seeking a signpost to the grave to feel 'the horror of what it will be when Sylvia Plath's grave becomes one more trampled Disneyland toy in the

Northern Cultural Theme Park'. I can't help thinking Ted might not have liked Haworth.

Offcumdens

I leave the pilgrims because I want to find one other grave-stone back near the church. It takes more looking. There is no Stuart for this. Nobody is confusing 'I shut my eyes and all the world drops dead' with the log flume. Nobody has been saved by visiting it and I don't feel there is a dead poets' society frowning at me from the past. But I know that some-where down there, beneath Heptonstall, which stands like a broken lighthouse atop a Heathcliff hill, Shane Meadows, the much-lauded kitchen-sink director, is making a TV series about the man under the stone. It is a slab that provides the first line to a story of murder, organised crime, beastly shenanigans in the woods, wonderful words like bittersnike, and betrayal in the murk below Mytholmroyd. And here it is. David Hartley. 1770. Hanged in York and planted here.

The man to tell the tale is nearby. I drive a short distance and knock on the back door of a row of fine terraces that have paused for breath on the long descent into Hebden Bridge. This is the home of Benjamin Myers, a writer from Durham who won the Walter Scott Prize in 2018 for *The Gallows Pole*, his novel about David Hartley and the Cragg Vale Coiners; and Adelle Stripe, a writer from Tadcaster who knows more than most about fighting.

There is a connection. My mum used to get her hair done at Adelle's mum's salon by the River Wharfe in Tadcaster, close to the bridge that was washed away in the great flood. Angela Stripe was a force of nature. Bold and brave and brassy in a warm way, she never breezed in, she hurricaned. I worked for her briefly as her part-time bookkeeper in the holidays, locked in the back room while gossip raged over the curlers, the intoxicating breath of hairspray and innuendo clouding the mirrors. I didn't last long, but I liked Angela. Adelle tells me her mum was brought up in a prefab in Withernsea after Hull was bombed to high heaven in the Second World War. Hence the painting of a prefab on the landing wall. 'It's why my mum was so bling,' she says. 'She grew up with nothing. She wasn't going back.'

Adelle's new book, *Ten Thousand Apologies*, has just made the *Sunday Times* best-seller list. It is a biography of a dysfunctional rock band, the Fat White Family, but it is also a story of immigration and unforgiving Yorkshire. Michelle, mother of Lias, the lead singer, met Bashir, from eastern Algeria, in a nightclub called Johnny's in Huddersfield. Michelle's father was a miner at Woolley Colliery and a member of the Communist Party. The miners' strike of 1974 saw him standing on the picket line, and he was forced to shoot rabbits with a catapult to feed his family of seven. Waste coal from Emley Moor Colliery was the only way to warmth. Michelle's brother fell onto a circular saw while working for a farmer, and lost his arm. The farmer's wife picked it up and put it in a freezer in the pantry. The community rallied round to buy him a bionic arm, but he wasn't bothered. He stuck the false limbs from the NHS in the garden as bizarre decoration.

Michelle got pregnant at 18 and lost her job at the mill because of morning sickness. Nurses in the birthing suite were unsympathetic due to her being unmarried, and hours after the birth, a social worker arrived and recommended that she give up the baby because he was mixed race. She refused.

Lias was her second child. Drugs, debauchery and mental illness followed, but there was a poignant reunion with his mother years later when she was living in Scarborough, looking over North Bay and dreaming. He told her she was too nice to junkies on the street. She said she knew. 'Because I wonder how much their mothers worry about them.'

It is fair to say Adelle is drawn to those on the margins, the non-obvious heroes of extraordinary living. Hence her enduring affection for Andrea Dunbar, whose story is one of those remarkable Yorkshire tales ignored by guidebooks. Her parents worked in the textile trade, and she survived on the Buttershaw estate in Bradford, rough enough for her gift of total recall to be a curse. Two years after leaving school, in 1979, she had a daughter with a taxi driver, but domestic violence led her to a hostel in Keighley. Miraculously, a script she had been working on in green biro on a large pad was passed to a writer, and a year later, *Rita, Sue and Bob Too* was performed at the Royal Court Theatre.

It concerned two teenage girls and their affair with a married man, and became a 1987 film that shocked. Thatcher's Britain with her knickers down. Mary Whitehouse was not a fan. Again. Nor was Andrea, who thought director Alan Clarke had wrecked the ending and put the emphasis on the philandering man rather than the bond between the two girls. In writing stories, she was telling tales. This was what was left of working-class life for those on the Buttershaw estate. It was not UNESCO World Heritage sites like Saltaire, or happy mill workers.

Andrea Dunbar died at 29, like Anne Brontë, and has a plaque on her former home and a painting in a grey underpass, but she is largely forgotten. The same goes for Cragg Vale Coiner David Hartley. The Calder Valley, later frequented by Ted and Sylvia, was also the habitat of Hartley and his melancholy band of reprobates, who thought nothing of robbing Peter to pay themselves.

Clipping and coining was a way of making counterfeit money by filing the edges of gold coins and adding the shavings to a base metal. Because much of the money in circulation in the eighteenth century was old and faded, the slight reduction in size would generally go unnoticed. Hartley arrived in the Calder Valley in dubious circumstances from Birmingham and came to run a large organisation comprising disgruntled weavers, farmers, clothiers and innkeepers.

More Soprano than Brontë, the means of survival was to intimidate everyone. You can see why Shane Meadows might like the story. This is England. As Myers writes in *The Gallows Pole*: 'No chains so strong, no cell so small, no noose so tight to kill us all. Cross the coiners and dig your plot.'

The Coiners coined it in until a gang member called James Broadbent – I know, I'm not proud – turned King's Evidence for 100 guineas. Not long after that, William Dighton, a tax collector, had Hartley arrested. The coiners tried to get him released when Broadbent recanted, but to no avail. So they did the next best thing and shot Dighton.

Enter Lord Rockingham, a two-time prime minister from Rotherham, who was ruthless in his pursuit. In April 1770, facing the endgame, Hartley came clean and admitted that Matthew Normanton and Robert Thomas had murdered Dighton. On 28 April, he was taken to York and hanged, because for all its finery the city still liked a good picnic on the Knavesmire, that old marshland where they now hold horse races instead of executions. The year after Hartley's death, it is claimed some of his band were at the Union Cross pub in Heptonstall when a man named Abraham Ingram suggested he would inform against the murderers. He had his neck locked by red-hot tongs and was plunged into a fire while his breeches were filled with burning coals. Centuries later, a plasterer at what was now the Cross Inn knocked through a wall and an ancient fireplace was unveiled. The pub now has a Coiners Suite and proudly advertises itself as a romantic setting with open fires.

'Up here hardly anybody is from Hebden,' says Adelle. 'The old families are few and far between. We're blow-ins. Offcumdens. It's like London. When you live in London, everyone is from somewhere else and that's what makes it in a way. It's less like Yorkshire here, but' – she hikes a thumb – 'go to Old Town up there and the pub is full of farmers.'

This seems to be the dilemma for many in Yorkshire. We want the best of the past but softened with mod cons. 'I like it here because I lived in London,' says Ben. 'I didn't want to move somewhere I was considered a total freak because I was a writer. I didn't want to get my head kicked in.'

There is a Pop Art poster on the wall with the words 'Piss Off' in large letters. Some might think this encapsulates modern Yorkshire, unwelcoming but in a nice frame. Adelle says it is a joke because of the footpath by the window outside on which people tend to stop and stare.

'Have you had your head kicked in?' I ask Ben.

'Yeah.'

Adelle adds, 'If you grow up an outsider in your town, you're not going to go back. It's failure.'

'Go back on your own terms,' Ben corrects.

'Yes, that's true. Lots of people grow up in small towns but don't want to go back, but this place is outward-looking. I like the escapees. They bring an insight. There are these people with bourgeois upbringings in London and their family are musicians or artists or theatre designers. Andrea Dunbar didn't have that. That's why her work is really important. She never left but she got out because she managed to have a creative life, which wasn't expected of a person like her.'

Ben excuses himself to take the dog out. Before long, his book will be a BBC series. For a while he chased rock stars around the world as a music journalist, but he found it was more interesting to watch deer than bands. The reason he is here is because he saw a programme about Ted Hughes on *Countryfile*.

'Yorkshire is a complex place,' says Adelle over a cheese and tomato roll. 'People have this idea of it being everyone down the pits voting Labour, but there are loads of working-class Tories in Yorkshire, bloody loads of them. Yorkshire is 100 places. You've got Richmond, which is incredibly wealthy, estates where there's extreme poverty, the anomaly of Saltaire, and the green corridor north of Leeds from Headingley to Roundhay to Harewood and East Keswick, where all the footballers live.'

Later, I drive down the hill into the centre of Hebden Bridge and park up. I soon find myself drinking a mani-cured latte in the square. Christine Drake, 74, who once campaigned at Greenham Common, is staging a one-woman protest by a lamp post, four days a week. Walkers who have arrived after drinking in the scenery straddling the Rochdale Canal may be mystified by this activism. And it has not always been peaceful. One council official tried to rip down her display, and cut her arm in the process. 'Blood everywhere,' she told the *Morning Star*. The police said she had brought it on herself. When one of the coffee shops in the square complained that her graphic photographs were disturbing customers, she replied that they bloody well should be disturbed.

She became involved after seeing Gaza being bombed on TV. It's a long way away, hard to fathom in the peace and tranquillity of a sleepy day in Hebden Bridge, but Christine goes to Palestine every year, meeting with a dozen volunteers in a secret village, working as an international observer and helping with the olive harvest. I watch her as I drink and nobody stops. I think of Michelle and Adelle's line about worrying mothers.

4

MINERS

It is clear then that the work a miner does and the wage
he receives both express concretely his status as a man
and as a member of his profession.

Norman Dennis, sociologist, *Coal is Our Life*, 1956

British coal mining can be traced back to Roman times,
but it was the late eighteenth century that led to the
King Coal boom as the boys from the black stuff
provided the power for steam engines to turn growth into a
revolution. At the time of the miners' strike in 1984, there
were 56 Yorkshire collieries, but the closure of Kellingley
in 2015 signalled the end of deep-pit mining in Britain. The
interim was devastating.

That sentimental feeling

In the spring of 2022, I go to Orgreave, or what's left of it.
Like Acre Mill, it is not easy to find, and those who worked
here are also scarred. Many of Yorkshire's bloodiest battles

are pointed out by crosses. X marks the spot at Towton, near Tadcaster, where more than 50,000 Yorkist and Lancastrian troops met on a snowy Palm Sunday in 1461. X also marks the spot of the Battle of Marston Moor, where the Royalists were routed by Oliver Cromwell in the Civil War in 1644. There is no X at Orgreave, though, just crosses to bear and a festering bitterness about one of the great miscarriages of justice in British history. You can go down Orgreave Lane, imagine the pitched battles, maybe even read Helen Mort's poetry –

A stone is lobbed in '84,
Hangs like a star over Orgreave

– but the life and soul of Orgreave, and the visible markers of what the lawyers called the 'worst public order offence in the history of this country' have been razed to the ground.

The colliery closed first. Then the coking plant. It led to violent clashes between the police and pickets during the strike in 1984. After the bloodshed, the arrests, the rozzers by the Rother and Thatcher's ensuing 'victory', followed by the final extraction of millions of tonnes of spoil, the site became the Advanced Manufacturing Research Centre. The spoils of failure. Orgreave as it was in the 1980s is no more. The Orgreave Truth and Justice Campaign continues to battle for justice, but governments try to ignore them. This lost pocket of Yorkshire in the borough of Rotherham might be a figurehead for the history of coal mining.

Coal was mined in the Bronze and Stone ages. In the sixteenth century, the Dean of York got a patent to purify pit coal and 'free it from its offensive smell'. This was the advent of coking, which is effectively cooking coal to 1000 degrees

Celsius to leave a high-carbon fuel, akin to making charcoal from wood. Coke was used in blast furnaces to turn iron ore to iron, and so led to a shifting landscape. The Industrial Revolution, from around 1760 to 1840 – although the historians like to argue about dates, as time is all they have – led to a huge expansion of coal mining, moving from the shallow bell pits and horizontal drift mines to deeper shafts. The use of steam pumps and engines solved the problem of drainage from pits. Down, down, deeper and down. In turn, coal fuelled the steam engines that turned the machines at the textile factories, and the trains that transported raw materials and finished products. Titus Salt built Saltaire.

Progress did not make for a better life. At the start of the nineteenth century, William Blake had written about his 'dark satanic mills', even if he was actually referring to the Albion flour mills in Southwark, where steam power was driving traditional millers to the brink until the place mysteriously caught fire. A century later, J. B. Priestley described the road down into Sheffield as a descent into hell. From on high – by which he did not mean innate superiority so much as the big slag heap on a hill – it seemed that 'Sheffield, far below, looked like the interior of an active volcano.' Priestly marched on. 'The smoke was so thick that it made a foggy twilight in the descending streets, which appeared they would end in the steaming bowels of the earth.'

That was 1934. The peak for British coal production had come in 1913, with 287 million tonnes, but the figure was still 228 million in 1952. What would become known as the South Yorkshire coalfield, although it breached the boundaries of its name by stretching to Selby in the north and Wakefield in the west, became famous, but bituminous coal was 300 million years old and taking it from the earth came with risks. Firedamp, the flammable gas found in mines, formed in pockets in the coal, and contact with flames, from either pre-Davy-lamp candles or sparks from working the rock, could cause explosions. And so death and danger became daily hazards for those working unseen beneath the ground.

But in 1838, the wider public did begin to notice. This was because of what happened that July, when more than 600 men, women and children found themselves trapped at the bottom of the Huskar Pit outside the village of Silkstone Common near Barnsley. A raging storm had disabled the steam boiler and hence the pit's winding mechanism. A message was sent down telling the miners to sit and wait, whereupon, according to a contemporary newspaper report, 'darkness, terror and a dismal hubbub' prevailed. Fearing an imminent explosion of firedamp, a group of 26 children, aged between 7 and 17, decided to get out via the day hole, an alternative means of descent. They were scrambling to safety along the passage, some four feet wide and five feet high, when a torrent of water burst through an air door and drowned them all. It was the village's Aberfan, a disaster that damned a community. Joseph Garnett was one of those who helped to remove the mud-bound children. The *Sheffield Iris* newspaper recalled, 'He got hold of his own child, but could not get him out, there were so many upon him. He did not attribute blame to anyone.' George Garnett was nine years old. Eight of those drowned were under ten.

Thomas Badger, the coroner, addressed a hastily convened jury at the Red Lion in Silkstone at 4 p.m. He had already viewed the dead of Dodworth and then those at Thurgoland, and now he got to Silkstone. The *Iris* reported: 'It was a melancholy business. As the gentlemen went from house to house, sometimes taking the houses in succession, it seemed as if the destroying angel had visited the place, and scarcely left a house where there was not one dead. It was a most piteous thing to witness the grief-stricken faces of the men, the bitter anguish of the mothers, and the wailing of the children, as the Jury passed along, inspecting the bruised and blackened bodies. At eight o'clock, this formulary having been completed, and the Coroner and Jury having taken a slight and hasty refreshment, the enquiry proceeded.'

A verdict of accidental death was recorded. Now a slightly macabre monument sits in Nabs Wood, depicting two children emerging from the day hole. A few years ago, a paranormal investigator visited and said she detected mysterious activity. There was some obvious stuff – the usual rustling of leaves, disembodied laughter, and local reports of ghostly images of children playing hide-and-seek – but then she mentioned one thing picked up on her listening device that suggested she might be on to something. 'Piss off,' said a voice.

The disaster is also remembered via a stained-glass window in the local church and a song, 'Halt the Wagons' by Yorkshire folk singer Kate Rusby, which references the gift of children and a 12-hour shift.

Queen Victoria ordered an inquiry and Lord Ashley, a Tory politician and social reformer who would die from inflammation of the lungs, obliged. He even went down a mine. It was bad, granted, that six-year-olds were given the task of opening and shutting ventilation doors, thus risking firedamp accidents, and made to drag carts with chains bound between their legs and around their waists, but Ashley knew what would truly grab the public's attention.

He gathered testimony on working conditions for children and laid it out in his report. Poor Robert North recalled: 'I went into the pit at 7 years of age. When I drew by the girdle and chain, the skin was broken and the blood ran down. If we said anything, they would beat us. I have seen many draw at 6. They must do it or be beat. They cannot straighten their backs during the day. I have sometimes pulled till my hips have hurt me so that I have not known what to do with myself.'

In his speech to Parliament in 1842, Ashley made his feelings clear: 'Never, I believe, since the disclosure of the horrors of the African slave trade, has there existed so universal a feeling on any one subject in this country, as that which now pervades the length and breadth of the land in abhorrence and disgust of this monstrous oppression.' Yet he knew this might not be enough, and so he went for the jugular – which in Victorian times was locked beneath a chastity belt, probably made from the same iron created thanks to the child miners – telling horrified politicians: 'In the West Riding, it appears, girls are almost universally employed as trappers and hurriers, in common with boys. The girls are of all ages from 7 to 21. They commonly worked quite naked down to the waist and are dressed – as far as they are dressed at all – in a loose pair of trousers. These are seldom whole on either sex. In many of the collieries, whom these girls serve, they work perfectly naked.'

Victorian England could probably have coped with girls being part of an uncivilised underclass, down in the underbelly, working 12-hour shifts, bruised and bleeding, ragged and deplorable, but taking your top off was a true scandal. Victorian prudery won the day and the Mines and Collieries Act was passed. This ground-breaking legislation meant girls and women could not work underground, and the minimum age for boy miners was now set at 10. It was well intended, although some point out that it also led to an increased gender gap and the splintering of families, as women had to travel further to gain employment. In some cases, girls just disguised themselves as boys to carry on working.

And the tragedies continued. In 1857, an explosion at Lundhill, in Wombwell, South Yorkshire, killed 189, and in 1862, the Hartley disaster in Northumberland claimed another 209 lives. Explosions in 1845 and 1847 at the Oaks Colliery near Stairfoot, Barnsley, had already killed 76 men and boys, and in 1856, the workforce went on strike. It lasted 10 weeks. In 1864, the miners again went on strike amid safety fears, and once again they were evicted from their colliery-owned homes. Yet the worst was still to come.

On 12 December 1866, an hour from the end of the shift, another explosion ripped through the pit. The *London Illustrated News* described how those on the surface felt a 'tremulous motion' followed by a dull, heavy explosion that could be heard a mile away. Dense columns of smoke and dust were expelled as grey geysers, and in moments a thick black pall hung over the pit. 'Frantic women, terrified children and colliers from the neighbouring works, eagerly crowded round the place, in the utmost anxiety and despair.'

A rescue party found 18 men and boys suffering from burns and sent them to the surface, but the searchers were almost overwhelmed by the noxious gas. Then they came to 38 dead men and 20 horses in the space of 50 yards. 'Some had to be identified by a button, or a shoe, or some part of tattered garments,' said the *Illustrated News*. Twenty men were found with their arms linked as if in solidarity against the blast. Other bodies were found kneeling with hands clasped in prayer.

Thomas Woodhouse, the mine's engineer, was in London when he received a telegram. 'The Oaks Pit is on fire. Come directly.' He sent a man named Parkin Jeffcock instead. When Jeffcock arrived, he went down the shaft to try to ventilate the pit and sent word to the surface that the mine was heating up. A thermometer was lowered to check the temperature. Another explosion. More panic, wailing and hopelessness. A cage was lowered soon after, but as expected, it was empty when it rose. Jeffcock was among the 27 members of the rescue party added to the death toll. One of those who had got out had left his coat on the floor of the shaft. Now he saw the dismembered sleeves blown into the air before becoming wedged in the headgear, the imposing winding tower sometimes known as the gallows frame

The Oaks was burning. This truly was a dark satanic mill, a volcano, the steaming bowels of the earth. A village had been ruined, its menfolk all but wiped out. And then, at around 4.45 a.m. on 14 December, a couple of men at the pithead heard the signal bell ring. There was someone alive down there. A flask of brandy was lowered, and then two men, John Mammatt and Thomas Embleton, descended into the hellhole. There they found Samuel Brown, dazed but conscious. Remarkably, he survived where 361 did not.

The miners' union said it needed £3,000 to help the widows and orphans and it would be a drain on their resources. Queen Victoria asked to be put down for £200. But in the mining communities, where death and degradation had always frayed the ragged seams, life went on. In these darkest days, a spirit of defiance and community formed as igneous rock.

More than a decade later, Mammatt, one of the heroes of the rescue, gave evidence to a Royal Commission into mining accidents. He was asked if it was hard to overcome 'that sentimental feeling' when he visited the Oaks now. 'For a few months there was that feeling, but it has quite died out,' he said. 'We sometimes come across some bones; we did the other day and we sent them up to the top, but nobody claimed them, and they were buried. There was only a skull and a piece of leg.'

The man who climbed out of Yorkshire

Andy Cave was born in mining country in 1966. His mother told him, 'No bairn of mine is going down that shit-hole.' The shit-hole in question was Grimethorpe Colliery, in the borough of Barnsley. His great-grandfather had worked down the Monkton pit and his great-uncle was the National Union of Miners (NUM) branch secretary, but Andy was different to many boys who grew up in nearby Royston. When Monkton closed, his father got a job at Grimethorpe, made famous by *Brassed Off* in film and proudly militant in real life. Andy wanted to go down t'pit, but he also did Latin American ballroom dancing in the old miners' gym, later Tassel's nightclub, and he liked reading. Even when he had got out of mining and was carving out a career climbing mountains in the Himalayas rather than working the subterranean rock in Yorkshire, he knew there was something about mining that was hard to define. It was more than a job. In his autobiography, *Learning to Breathe*, he wrote: 'From Émile Zola to D. H. Lawrence, it was as if the effect of extracting coal in return for one's wages always caused more than a mere geological tension.'

We meet in the David Mellor Visitor Centre in Hope Valley. This is Derbyshire, and no, not that David Mellor. This one was a designer from Ecclesall, in Sheffield, whose work you will see most days – if not his cutlery, then the traffic lights and bus shelters that became the British standard. I ask Andy about his dancing. 'We didn't boast about it because it was quite a macho culture,' he says. Nevertheless, even at Grimethorpe there was a secret library, hidden behind a steel girder, where he found a dog-eared copy of prison break epic *Papillon* next to the porno mags. He chose Henri Charrière's story and perhaps did not realise that the seed of his own escape was germinating.

He rode motorbikes and, like Billy Casper in *A Kestrel for a Knave*, would look for eggs; birds would often nest in disused mining buildings. One of the curiosities of Yorkshire's mining belt was the way it mixed the industrial and natural worlds. Priestley marvelled at this in another age, as did Andy in the eighties. 'Between Barnsley and Sheffield you have the slag heaps up top, the associated industries, but most of it is underground, and there was all this farmland around,' he says. 'My own street was bordered by a railway line at the top and farmland. That's what I looked out on. At that time family holidays were all in Skegness or, on the one time we got exotic, Paignton; that was *really* out there.' He also liked to climb trees and buildings. One escape up the doctor's surgery ended in a police cell marked with NUM chiselling.

His father put his name down for a job. Andy began on the surface, until finally, on 6 September 1983, he went underground. 'My dad worked on the surface and his dad was killed underground,' he says as he nurses his coffee, the traffic lights in the café forever red. 'I don't think they got any compensation back then. I imagine mining is a bit like war, with the main difference being you don't get medals in mining – quite the opposite. On the surface there was quite a bit of immaturity, but underground it was hardcore and very easy to lose an arm or a leg.' In his book he recalls characters like Big D, who once held him down in black sludge up top and burnt a cigarette into his cheek. There was only one way to escape.

Life was cheap and softened by gallows humour. One man was hit by highly pressurised fluid from a broken pipe; the story went that the fluid had entered his anus with such force that 'he now shits in a bag'. But beneath the veneer, all sorts of fears coalesced. There were stories of ghosts, but just as frightening was the prospect of gnarly veteran Old Moffa pulling out your pubic hairs if you farted in his presence. It was buttock-clenching fare, but the mine also looked after its own if you were injured at work.

'It's the speed of the first descent I remember,' says Andy. 'There were 120 men in a cage, 3,000 feet, the only light from cap lights but most have them turned off so it's pitch black, down a shaft almost 100 years old, built by navvies, every so often a flash of horizontal white light from men working another seam, maybe you stop to let someone off, and a voice says, "Watch out for the ghost of someone who's been killed."'

Down 3,000 feet, and then maybe another 3,000 on foot to the face. Men would be lengthening the tunnel on both sides. 'Think of a letter M and the legs of the M are being advanced and the top half of the M is the coal being cut,' explains Andy. 'If you cut the coal, you let the bit behind you collapse, like cream being taken out of a Victoria sponge. That job is called the ripper. It's hot down there too. Men would be working in their underpants, drilling, exploding the tunnel, advancing the coal, with us behind them with haulage ropes, shovels and conveyor belts.' It was expressly forbidden to ride the conveyor belts, with decapitation in the dark one industrial hazard, but everyone ignored that.

Andy tells me he was claustrophobic, and he means both literally and socially. Miners sometimes drank in neighbouring villages because it got too much to stay local, long shifts with the same faces and then showering with them, drinking, playing darts, pulling women, going to the football. 'It was just hard,' he says. 'I would not have survived another 20 years. It would have just broken me. But when I was broken, they would have given me a job on the surface too.'

Richard Hoggart, the academic who penned *The Uses of Literacy*, wrote of accepting that life is hard, of dull fatalisms like 'if you don't like it, lump it', of the pointlessness of 'kicking against the pricks'. He said, 'T. S. Eliot says somewhere that stoicism can be a kind of arrogance, a refusal to be humble before God: working-class stoicism is rather a self-defence, against altogether being humbled before men. There may be little you can do about life; there is at least something you can be.'

So Andy Cave, with a vague yearning for something out there over the farmland, took his lunch, or snap, of pilchards in vinegar, picked up the metal box with its emergency device for turning carbon monoxide into carbon dioxide, affording you two hours to escape, and went underground.

At the same time, his new hobby was taking up more of his thoughts. When a climber named Paul, who had mentioned he was part of a mountaineering club, had fixed some problems in their council house, Andy had nagged him to take him along. Finally, he got to Wharncliffe Crags, north of Sheffield, the place where rock climbing was born in the UK and where the Dragon of Wantley is said to roam. It may be a tall tale, but the dragon was sufficiently famous for Dickens to reference it in *David Copperfield*.

Andy was smitten. He began to idolise Walter Bonatti, the great Alpinist whose own dreams had been sparked by Jack London, Herman Melville and Ernest Hemingway. 'When I started climbing, people would mention these places I had never heard of – the Himalayas, Peru, whatever. I went to Barnsley library and for some reason it had an incredible array of climbing books. I began discovering England, Wales and Scotland, started doing all these iconic routes, learning to read maps and compasses. I didn't think of myself as an athlete, but I was working towards it. I was used to discomfort and grew a few muscles. I was good at working as a team, good at sussing people out.' He also remembers, aged 16, getting changed after work one day and one of the old-timers looking at him and saying 'What a waste of a fucking life.' There was dignity in doing a job, binding the community and being brave, but it was a hard and oppressive life.

And then, in March 1984, the miners went on strike.

The Battle of Orgreave

It was not the first time. In 1969, Yorkshire's miners had gone on strike to protest the hours and poor wages for surface workers, but it was also a reflection of the growing disillusionment as pits began to close. That was when Arthur Scargill came to prominence, breaching his confines at Woolley Colliery to become a significant union figure, imbuing the dispute with a wider political idealism; he once had tea and cake with Nikita Khrushchev after all. For many, this was the start of a more militant approach by Yorkshire's miners. And Scargill, who had become one at 15 and a member of the Young Communist League at 17, craggy face, flinty vowels and defiantly chippy, was their man.

In 1972, there was another strike, caused by the breakdown of wage talks between the NUM and the National Coal Board. It went to a ballot, and miners voted overwhelmingly in favour of action. The highest percentage of those voting to strike came from South Wales and Yorkshire.

On 3 February that year, Freddie Matthews, from Doncaster, was on the picket line at Keadby power station near Scunthorpe, when a non-union lorry mounted the pavement and struck him. More than 5,000 people attended his funeral, and a Labour MP warned of a new Ulster forming in Yorkshire. A few days later, around 2,000 pickets went to a coking plant in Saltley in Birmingham. Their numbers were swollen to 30,000 by sympathetic workers from other industries. This was more than a miners' strike; it was class conflict laid bare, Hoggart's them and us, but without the un-idealism and passive stoicism he said were the bedrock of working-class living.

When the seven-week strike ended with a new pay deal, the Conservative cabinet emphasised the violence of the clashes between pickets and police, which had been fuelled by Matthews's death. The Cabinet Office Briefing Rooms (COBR) were set up to deal with national crises, and there was the strike-breaking unit being planned at an RAF base in Scotland, comprising hundreds of trucks, with the aim of breaching the picket lines.

The three-day week followed at the bitter end of 1973 as Edward Heath's government responded to a landscape marked by flying pickets, who travelled to boost the ranks in non-local areas, while the mainstream media, with the notable exception of the *Daily Mirror*, rounded on the miners. Another strike was called in 1974, followed by an election that led to a hung Parliament, Heath's resignation and the return of Huddersfield pipe-chomper Harold Wilson as prime minister. The miners were seen as local heroes by many in the north and Midlands, but one cabinet minister had been unimpressed, saying that the government should continue to fight the unions and not call an election, in the hope that the 'Who governs Britain?' slogan would be enough to tempt those frustrated by the strikes. Her name was Margaret Thatcher.

By the time Andy Cave was discovering climbing in 1983, the number of miners had dropped by 75 per cent from 1922 to around 200,000 but there were still 56 collieries in Yorkshire. Wilson retired in 1976 and was replaced by James Callaghan, and then Thatcher assumed the throne in 1979. The pace of decline in the mining industry accelerated in the early years of Thatcherism, as she saw in Scargill all that was wrong with British industry – monopolised trade unionism, the danger of industrial action holding a country to ransom, the welfare state propping up inefficient industries. Scargill became president of the NUM in 1981. War was inevitable.

Central to this was the Ridley Plan, which was the government's secret way of dealing with nationalised industries; at least it was secret until it was leaked to *The Economist* in 1978. It stated that one way to defeat the unions would be to 'provoke a battle in a non-vulnerable industry where we can win'. Workers were described as enemies and disrupters. Documents referred to past pickets as 'the Saltley coke works mob' and recommended a large mobile police squad to deal with troublemakers.

The signs were ominous as the government began talking up nuclear power as an alternative to coal. One study suggested 90,000 jobs could be lost by 1990, and on 6 March 1984, the National Coal Board (NCB) announced the closure of 20 pits. Scargill correctly predicted that the long-term plan was to shut more like 70 and that Thatcher had ordered the stockpiling of coal to deal with the inevitable strike. Miners walked out at Cortonwood in South Yorkshire, and other pits swiftly followed. Flying pickets were sent to Nottinghamshire, where support for the strike was weaker in the absence of a ballot. The police mobilised. 'There is nothing paramilitary about our operation,' said David Hall, president of the Association of Chief Police Officers. And so it escalated. The M1 was blocked. Scargill's wife, Anne, was arrested for wilful obstruction. Polls said most miners would strike if it went to a ballot. There were arguments about whether cutting off the coal and coke supply to the steel industry would amount to damaging a client that was already being savaged, and an agreement was struck to supply Scunthorpe steelworks with 15,700 tonnes a week. After an explosion at the plant, British Steel arranged to import coal from Poland and use non-union lorry drivers. Another order was made for coke from Orgreave, and news of that deal led to an increase in picketing at the plant.

Ian MacGregor had been chairman of British Steel when the government rationalisation programme saw 70,000 jobs shed between 1979 and 1981. Famous steelworks at Consett in County Durham and Corby in Northamptonshire had gone, and losses had been stemmed – financial ones anyway. MacGregor was now seen as the perfect man to turn his attention to the miners, and so he was made head of the NCB.

'I was young and immature and caught up in the idealism of it,' says Andy. 'I worked at Grimethorpe, the most militant pit around, a Scargill stronghold, and it was easy to think the strike was the way to go. It was not about wages, which people think it was, it was about keeping pits open. It was exciting at first, but it was different for my parents. They had to deal with the bills. I remember police horses running around and one of my dad's friends having a silver Ford Capri that was used for transporting flying pickets. It was weird because I'd go climbing. I had more time. Then I'd go home and it'd be soup kitchens, the butcher giving people things for free, somehow getting something from a charity shop for Christmas. It was amazing how people survived.'

Not everyone did. On 15 June 1984, a picket named Joe Green was knocked down and killed by a 'scab lorry' at Ferrybridge Power Station, the group of elephantine chimneys whose foul contrails always signalled my approach to home when journeying from the south. Three days later, miners gathered at Orgreave for a mass picket of the coking plant. Helen Mort would write:

Star of Orgreave, star of light, star
Of fucking royal shite. Westward leading,
Kids want feeding, guide us to your
Perfect light. One brings a half-brick,
One brings a shield, one brings
A truncheon, one a chain. Bearing gifts
We've travelled so far. God
Or fuck knows who we are. A man's foetal
Beside the railways tracks,
Anointment of blood.

Stan Orme, a Labour MP and energy spokesman, had done his best to get Scargill and MacGregor around a table, but now the time for talking had passed. 'It reminded me of *Henry V* with the armies ranged up on different sides facing one another,' he said.

It was Monday 18 June, the hundredth day of the strike. The scenes still shock. A policeman on a horse wields a bar at a woman in a red shirt with a chunky necklace who has been helping a stricken man by a stone wall. To protect herself from more bloodshed, she instinctively dives out of the way. A miner without his shirt is shoved against a car bonnet and beaten. A middle-aged man emerges from Asda with some cream buns. He is struck on the back of the head. He goes to pick up his buns. 'Leave them bastard things there!' shouts the policeman. Another man loses consciousness. When he comes to, he wonders if these are real policemen.

It is hot. Some of the pickets were playing football, but it is no longer a laugh. Tony Clement, the assistant chief constable of South Yorkshire, thick moustache, with the looks and patrician tone of a Captain Mainwaring from *Dad's Army*, describes the air as being black with missiles. He sends in the horses and later says in evidence, 'They were told to advance at a walk and then a trot. I wouldn't have been worried in the slightest if people had been trampled. I could not be held responsible if miners were silly enough to stay there.'

Clement sees Scargill go down. He says he slipped and hit his head on a sleeper. Another witness says he was struck with a long shield. Scargill goes to Rotherham Infirmary. Flying pickets are now fleeing and are told to get down a railway bank. It is steep and they stumble and tumble. Police stand across the top of the ridge. It is like a scene from a South Yorkshire western.

There were 6,000 police at Orgreave, with 345 in riot gear, and 42 horses. Fifty-five people were charged with riot, 40 with unlawful assembly, and more than 120 were injured. There were no half-measures. The government-led prosecution wanted life imprisonment, even for the man who had been arrested on his allotment and the one with a flask. The brutal policing and indiscriminate arrests were exacerbated by the cover-up. A year later, the trial of some of the accused miners began in court. The British public had already been swayed by the reporting by both broadcast and print media, causing long-lasting wounds and suspicion. After 48 days, the trial collapsed as it became clear that some of the police witnesses were reciting near-identical scripts. Michael Mansfield QC, the barrister whose CV would go on to include both the Birmingham Six and the Hillsborough disaster, called it the biggest frame-up ever. His hair jet black then, he faced a camera and spoke of 11,000 miners being arrested in a single year for political reasons. He asked if an entire community had suddenly woken up one day and decided to turn criminal.

One of the accused, Arthur Critchlow, was 26. He was filmed a year later for Yvette Vanson's evocative film *The Battle for Orgreave*. In it he says, 'They took me into a room with 24 convicts, sat me in chair with a number. In-between two chairs was a partition. I remember them leading my wife in to see me, her nose running, I can picture it like yesterday. That first visit I don't think we spoke. We just held hands and looked at each other. She was amazed as I were to find usselves in that position, still got stitches in my head, being treated as a criminal and beaten by police for, well, basically being on strike to save your job, it's a bitter pill to swallow and will be for as long as I live.' He stutters and wipes away the beginnings of tears as he says he has not told his children he has been behind bars. 'I'm sure when they're older and I tell 'em I was in prison they won't think I'm a convict like a thief, a rapist or whatever, think they will walk around with their head high.'

Others in the documentary are mystified by the vilification of a community. One woman looks at the camera and says, 'The one thing that upset me about Mrs Thatcher was when she called us "the enemy within". I've got a boy fighting in the Falklands, and he were on a frigate, and I've got a husband and son working down pit. I don't want one being a hero and the other being the enemy within.' For her, they were equally brave.

The prosecution and press portrayed the miners as a group intent on causing a riot. It was the 'rule of the bully boy', albeit bullies who were often topless and shorn of riot armour. Some wondered just how so many miners had been able to get to Orgreave. Had they been led into a trap?

The strike went on and stories have been retold and twisted. The Orgreave Truth and Justice Campaign (OTJC) is still fighting for the true story to be heard. At the end of the eighties, South Yorkshire Police paid £425,000 in out-of-court settlements to 39 miners, but there was no apology. The OTJC demanded a public inquiry. Prime Minister Theresa May said maybe. In 2016, Amber Rudd, the Home Secretary, eventually said no. After all, nobody had died. Just communities.

Parallels with the Hillsborough tragedy, which would claim 97 lives when fans were crushed at the FA Cup semi-final in Sheffield in 1989, were obvious. That happened about eight miles away. The police lied in the aftermath. An underclass was vilified. Miners and football fans were hooligans. The media ran their narratives, which morphed into stereotypes and worse. In the aftermath of that football match between Liverpool and Nottingham Forest, false stories were told. The bereaved fought for decades and said the police were to blame. Finally, in 2016, some 27 years on, a second inquest ruled the fans had been unlawfully killed due to failures by the police and ambulance services.

I walk down a deserted Orgeave Lane and imagine recent history. Then I take another trip to the library at the National Coal Mining Museum, looking through books and films and listening to recordings made by miners, villagers and policemen. There are so many fragments that remain with me. From all sides. One policeman explains the anxiety he felt when the van went into his own community, and how he asked to be left in the back. He had to live there too.

The bereft of Orgreave were left with their anger. Miners became a mass, a single entity, probably with unkempt hair, a tash, low education, an empty can and a flat football. Yet in every house there was a personal story. Many women felt their role in the strike made them more valued – they marched, they chained themselves to colliery gates, they held rallies. Nobody was telling them to get back in the kitchen now.

The miners were not all angels. How could they be? In a book by a women's support group, Rose from Featherstone said: 'I've had a rough marriage. He used to knock hell out of me – he put me in hospital once or twice. But since the strike's been on, it's all different. He cleans up now, washes up. I couldn't wish for a better husband and that's the God's truth.'

Ethel of Castleford felt like crying when she hurt her back and the Indian market trader who employed her daughter gave her a 12lb turkey and some frozen chips. She said she didn't think he would understand, but it was a fight for the marginalised.

One woman told the story of a car of flying pickets being stopped by the police. They said they were going to join their wives on holiday. The policeman pointed out that it was 5.30 a.m.

'It's a long way,' one offered hopefully.

The policeman asked to look in the boot, whereupon 'our lad' emerged from the rope and jacks and spanners. Quick as a flash, he scratched his head and said: 'I've been in there well over an hour and I still can't find that knocking.'

Himalayas

Andy was only a trainee miner and so received no money during the strike. His family got £17.59 a week from the Department of Health and Social Security. Andy tells a poignant story of his dad collecting potatoes in a plastic bag during a clandestine raid on a field. Police came with flash-lights, and his father fell, lying motionless for an hour. It is an image that reeks of sorrow and the stripping of dignity.

One night Andy went out and stood in the street, looking over wheat fields and glasswork chimneys, and thought of getting out. He managed it by climbing, but then came up against more divides. 'When I moved into a more middle-class world, I was seen as wild and savage,' he says. 'I used to spit a lot because I had seen people do that in Barnsley. Everyone did it in our village. I think it was because there was an almost Dickensian smog from the chemicals. I moved away when I was 20, and suddenly I didn't have a bad chest any more.'

His dad was once reminded he should not talk to a certain man as he was a scab who had broken the strike to go back to work, and the different beliefs of miners in Yorkshire and Nottinghamshire still remain in football chants whenever Barnsley play Forest; in Nottinghamshire, many miners continued to work, unthinkable to those striking. Andy himself fell out with his climbing friend, Alistair, who went back, deaf to the explanation of being engaged to Dee, the deposit on the house, the mounting desperation.

He slept rough in the Peak District and climbed with miners and unemployed steelworkers during the strike. Then, in March 1985, the miners went back to work. Andy went to university, and at 21, he cashed in his pension and went to Asia for five months. A year later, he was guiding in the Himalayas. In 1997, he was climbing Changabang, one of the great challenges of mountaineering. His friend Brendan Murphy tried to fit an anchor on a slope but had not bothered with ropes for what was going to be a quick and easy fix. Andy saw the avalanche 'so quietly and so softly' take Brendan like molten magma. He shouted his name into the night.

The risk and rewards of descents and ascents run through his parallel lives. When he decided to do a PhD on the dialect of a mining community, he finally found out how his grandfather had died. He was with his father, talking in a pub, when a man overheard their conversation and said he had been there all those years ago. Fred had got into a tub to get out of the pit, but 'someone had done a shit in it' so he moved to the front one. The rail had broken and when the tub came to the end, the metal skewered both tub and Fred. A policeman took his boots to Andy's grandmother, who passed out.

Andy became a renowned climber after that. 'By the time I went to university I had climbed in the Himalayas five times,' he says. Now he climbs, teaches, writes and does motivational talks for businesses. An hour from Leeds and Bradford, on the edge of the Peak District, is a land undiscovered by nowness, where Yorkshire's gritstone provides a grippy canvas with tricky holds, encouraging strength and guile. 'It's more poetic than climbing on limestone,' says Andy.

Coal had powered Britain. Made it. And it seems fitting that it should be Yorkshire's gold, because like the country, the substance is also frowned upon. Coal is outdated, a fossil fuel, and the mines and their stories are becoming fossilised themselves, covered by time and detritus. I recommend Jeremy Paxman's book *Black Gold* for those wanting an in-depth history. 'A midwife to practical genius', he writes, but the labour was long and painful, with gas and air explosions. Closure was one thing, abandonment another.

I thank Andy for his time and head back to the car, the border and Yorkshire. I put on *Every Valley*, the Public Service Broadcasting album with its mix of music and archived voices, including Richard Burton, who was from mining stock, talking of the 'arrogant strut of the lords of the coalface', the pride of the pre-mechanised worker. Another track has words from the 1971 advertisement 'People will always need coal', with its radio-friendly 'be a miner' jingle. Public Service Broadcasting are middle-class Londoners, but sometimes an outsider's voice adds a different perspective and comes to a subject free of heirlooms and baggage. I open the email from the band's leader, J. Willgoose, Esq, and look over the lines he has written. 'I think what made it even worse was the way miners had previously been lionised as great heroes, and that the wealth of the nation had been built upon their backs and through their efforts and sacrifice. The line in the second track on the record, "the people of Britain are building, hewing out from their native rock the foundation for the future", makes that very clear, as did the way they were portrayed as heroes during the Second World War. In the space of less than 40 years, for that to be turned on its head and for them to be demonised by the government as the enemy within, is a quite extraordinary (and extraordinarily cynical) transformation.'

I hit the road and the Beaufort Male Choir sings.

5

MINSTRELS

'Sheffield Sex City'

Song title by Pulp, 1992

Detroit gave birth to Motown, the Mississippi Delta to the blues and Liverpool to Merseybeat. Other genres were born of a borderless spirit or yearning, the cathartic anger of punk with its London clubs and Billy Casper fingers, and the New Romantics with entry open to anyone with frilly shirts and your mum's eyeliner. But Yorkshire? Where is its musical soul and what does it want?

Brassneck

I am off to Huddersfield. It is a big Sunday night in March: the 2022 Yorkshire Brass Band Championships. A smattering of shoppers are in the town centre, which aches with ennui, but down New Street, people in band uniforms, scuffed cases in their hands, hurry to and from the town hall, built with stone from nearby Crossland Moor and christened in 1881 with a concert by the Huddersfield Choral Society, conducted by Sir Charles Hallé.

The brass band is synonymous with Yorkshire but seems part of the past. This concert is taking place opposite the Global Diversity Hub and hen party venue the Rock Café, which is advertising a gig by Bash the Bishop. The tarmac between is a time warp.

There were more than 5,000 brass bands in Britain at their peak in 1895. These ranged from village bands, funded by public subscription or a rich local benefactor, to the works bands tied to industries and companies. There were also temperance bands, set up to spread the merits of tee-totalism, and the Salvation Army bands. William Booth, the co-founder of the Salvation Army, was initially sniffy about the purpose of these groups, but soon appreciated they had a galvanising effect. Indeed, in the 1880 Christmas edition of *The War Cry*, the Salvation Army's official newsletter, the change of tune saw him write, 'Not allowed to sing this or that tune? Indeed. Secular music, do you say? Belongs to the devil, does it? Well, if it did, I would plunder him of it, for he has no right to a single note of the whole gamut. He's the thief. Every note and every strain and every harmony is divine and belongs to us.'

The devil did not have all the best tunes, then. This was a sort of blues music for the Victorian age, and as Trevor Herbert wrote in his book *The British Brass Band: a musical and social history*, few things better 'focus the mind on the British working-class experience and the tension between continuity and change'.

The likes of good old Titus Salt saw the merits of having a band as a focus for his workers at Saltaire, and he set up a drum and fife band. This morphed into what is now Hammonds Band, originally the fabulously named Hammonds Sauce Band, due to their benefactor's day job. Colliery bands also grew up, funded by the miners themselves. They would be immortalised in the 1996 film *Brassed Off*, in which Tara Fitzgerald and Ewan McGregor used brass banding to fend off the ravages of pit closures. In the film, the band leader is played by Pete Postlethwaite, whose struggle to keep the band together is rewarded when they turn up outside his hospital window and play 'Danny Boy' while wearing miners' lamps. When they finish, they turn them off. That is supposed to be the end of the band, with the pit closing and a 4–1 vote for redundancy announced. It is a black comedy, featuring a glamorous romance and an uplifting denouement, with the band winning the national finals at the Royal Albert Hall to a triumphant fanfare. It is also dark, and involves the suicide attempt of a part-time children's entertainer dubbed Coco the Scab, and Postlethwaite, a stalwart of the brass-banding scene, admitting: 'I thought the music mattered, but does it bollocks! Not compared to how people matter.'

The story is based on real strife. Grimley is Grimethorpe, the village near Barnsley where Andy Cave worked. Like many others, the pit was its heart and soul. Over half the working population was employed there – more than 6,000 when absorbing mergers and those who travelled in. Then in 1993 it closed, and was rubbed from the landscape if not the memory.

The Grimethorpe Colliery Band was set up in 1917 and was a source of satisfaction. Three years after playing trumpet on the Beatles' *Magical Mystery Tour*, Elgar Howarth, a Cannock-born conductor, joined the band as their musical adviser. The band flourished, but it was *Brassed Off* that made them famous beyond the brass-banding world and its competitive circuit.

The real story began in 1992, at another Yorkshire Championships, this time at St George's Hall in Bradford. The band was due on stage at 6 p.m., but their solo horn player, Andy Armstrong, who was diabetic, had been rushed to Barnsley General after skipping lunch and suffering a hypo. It meant Frank Renton, the conductor, and Mark Arnold, the percussionist, had to begin frantically rewriting parts for first baritone and solo trombone. The band felt they gave a poor performance, and with all the other competitors yet to play, they sloped off to the pub, only for someone to burst through the door some four hours later and inform them they had come second and were off to the finals at the Royal Albert Hall.

A few days before the trip to London, Michael Heseltine, president of the Board of Trade, told the House of Commons that 31 pits would be shut. Grimethorpe was included on the list despite having 90 years of coal left. On the band's website, Arnold recalled, 'I listened in cold shock and nearly froze with fear when the words "Grimethorpe Colliery" were mentioned in the long list. It was like reading the "killed in battle" list on Armistice Day each year.'

The media descended on Grimethorpe, sensing the *Brassed Off* tale before it had even been written. Broadcast trucks parked up in the primary school car park, and then followed the band's coach to London. A crowd gathered and cheered the musicians into the Albert Hall. Renton then gave a speech, recalled by Arnold, which was more dramatic than Postlethwaite, with all his stage training, later managed. 'Win this contest not just for you and Grimethorpe Colliery Band,' he said. 'Win this contest not just for the 1,500 miners

at Grimethorpe and the village devastated by this announce-
ment. But win this contest for the 33,000 miners nationwide
who have just lost their jobs and may, just may, find a little
comfort in the knowledge that their band has triumphed
in the adversity that afflicts them all, and could just be a
glimmer of hope for a very bleak-looking future, whatever
they do from then on.'

Grimethorpe won. A year later, in 1993, the pit shut. A
year after that, the European Commission rated Grimethorpe
the poorest village in Europe. Unemployment spiralled to
35 per cent. Twenty years after the Albert Hall finals, the
population had dwindled to 1,831.

Now brass banding is like football, with principal
players signing for other bands, and a healthy dose of
rivalry, envy and skulduggery. Online forums accuse band
leaders of rewriting parts to make them too easy, of bands
bringing in ringers for difficult sections, of musicians
putting dusters over bells to make it easier to play the quiet
bits. This stuff matters.

There are 12 bands competing in Huddersfield. Black
Dyke, so famous that they even play Glastonbury Festival,
have already pre-qualified, so two places in the Albert Hall
are up for grabs. Outside, a man in band uniform, shirt
undone, talks to an old colleague.

'Why you playing trombone?'

'Our lass was going to do it, but she's just had a Caesarean.'

Inside, the lobby is buzzing. People flock to the wood-
panelled room housing the refreshments. Pieces of chocolate
cake are cellophaned. A few bandsmen are having a pint.
The first section – effectively the level below the Premier
League – has just finished, and now it's the big time. Sadly,
I have misjudged the format. Each band traipses onto the

stage in turn. The two judges are hidden in a curtained booth. When they are ready, they blow a whistle. The mystery band then plays. What I had failed to appreciate is that every band plays the same thing. It is called 'Contest Music' by Wilfred Heaton and it lasts 20 minutes. That is four hours of listening to the same piece. I look around the audience to see if anyone else has been caught out, but these are diehards, brass-band aficionados, or relatives. They are like a lower league football crowd, here not to be entertained but to endure. The devil's got all the short tunes.

The girl next to me asks who I'm here to see. I feel foolish as I tell her I've come for the whole thing. This is tribal. You nail your colours to the mast. She tells me her boyfriend is the principal cornet for the Brighouse & Rastrick. 'He's been practising for weeks,' she says.

The bands have drawn lots to see who goes first, and Brighouse & Rastrick are third on. Playing late is considered best because the judges might be demob happy at getting out of their fabric cage, but playing first means you can go to the pub.

First up are Rothwell Temperance. They are warmly received, blow hot and cold to my ears, and then slope off, knocking over a stand as they go, hours to wait until they find out that they are third and have qualified. The next band are Hatfield and Askern Colliery. Askern closed in 1991, but Hatfield made it to 2015, the year the death knell sounded and the last of Yorkshire's deep coal mines closed. A ringtone chirps and their conductor, wearing a brilliant walrus moustache, turns slowly and gives the audience a look of such withering disdain that three people check their ties and the rest their pockets. And now it is Brighouse & Rastrick. The girl next to me sighs and slumps into her seat.

The band play beautifully. The stages of the piece are working their way into my head by now, the thrill of charging trumpets and the purity of the horns. This is brass banding with the doors blown off, not your Hovis hill climb. It is nostalgic and it is also deeply melancholic, not least from knowing there are another nine bands to come, but I am on edge for the principal cornet. The conductor is a sharply dressed, whippet-thin man called Professor David King. He is a big noise in these circles. 'Is David King the messiah of banding?' asks one poster on the internet. It seems so. International Chair in Brass Band at the Royal Northern College of Music, he has the sharpest haircut to date, suave glasses, and a delivery that is somewhere between T-rex's tiny arms and Madonna's 'Vogue' video, until he cuts the atmosphere with a full-bloodied karate chop. It is performance art meets a nice day at the bandstand, and he laps up the adulation.

'I can breathe again,' says the girl next to me. I think she is talking about her boyfriend, but it may be that King's display has got to her as much as it has to the older women in the audience. At that very moment a pair of knickers is thrown on stage from the adjudicators' booth. Okay, I may have misremembered that, but it was rock and roll without guitars, Led Zep done by the medium of euphonium.

Others come and go, finished by Black Dyke, and even I can tell they are pretty good. They are also impeccably dressed. Some bands have looked like they are up in court, in their ill-fitting suits. Others have been going to a funeral. In their black kit with red and gold trim, Black Dyke look like they are going to war, which in a way they are. An online debate about the point of competition concluded that if you are from one of the top bands, it is all about the glory and death of your opponent.

Finally the adjudicators emerge from their booth. There is a tall man named Christopher Wormald, a member of AoBBA (the Association of Brass Band Adjudicators) – not to be confused with ABBA – who happens to resemble my old and violent Latin teacher; and Sheona Wade, a former BBC Radio 2 Young Musician of the Year, aka 'the voice of the tenor horn', which just seems the wrong moniker. Wormald puts his briefcase down by his seat on stage and proceeds to rattle some egos. He says that while he is the son of a proud Yorkshireman, he is 100 per cent Lancastrian. Bold. Only five of the bands were good and he talks in detail about the mistakes. Bolder still. I cannot help feeling that in critiquing the overblowing cornets, he is blowing his own trumpet, but all this pales as he gives the results in reverse order.

There is an audible gasp when Brighouse & Rastrick are named as the band in sixth place. I am glad the girl next to me has left. This is the first time they have failed to make the finals since 2009. Grimethorpe come fourth, then Rothwell, with the remaining qualifying place going to Hammonds behind winners Black Dyke.

Hammonds celebrate wildly in the hall, at least the ones back from the snug at the Head of Steam. Later a brass band reporter will write that Black Dyke's principal cornet played a solo that 'rose and fell like a leaf on the wind, the final chord dying in the ether'. The judging, however, was dismissed as a bit rubbish. King had led his troops to a 'complete under-standing and execution' with considered, artistic solos and only ephemeral moments of unease. Robbed.

Outside, three Brighouse fans are walking alongside me. 'Don't know what they were listening to,' says one.

'Ah well,' replies another. 'Worse things happen at sea.' The looks that kill say this is not so.

The hard life of Yorkshire industry and the windswept landscapes lent themselves to music. Booth was right. Music lifts the soul and unites places. Brass banding highlighted that tension between continuity and change, tradition and the need to throw off the guide ropes, the inward and the outward.

To the outsider, brass banding is something to which stereotypes can be tethered, and there is some truth in the bands' fight for survival reflecting their communities. When the *Yorkshire Post* visited post-Brexit Grimethorpe, supposedly regenerated by big government grants, they found plenty of people disgruntled over the number of immigrants bussed in from Leeds and Sheffield to take the factory jobs that were meant to replace the ones at the colliery. 'We are second in line for everything now,' said one. 'We are the foreigners.' Wherever you stood, it was all about alienation.

The trudge through the grudge

Folk songs and sea shanties were also born from the working practices of Yorkshire. One of the most enduring Yorkshire folk songs of all is 'Scarborough Fair', which is named after the 45-day medieval trade bonanza that drew merchants from all over Europe. The song became famous in 1966, when Simon & Garfunkel combined a version with their own 'Canticle', on their album *Parsley, Sage, Rosemary and Thyme*. It was a hit and was revived again on the soundtrack to the 1967 film *The Graduate*. However, if you think folk music is all Aran jumpers and beard-growing, the history of 'Scarborough Fair' is imbued with a controversy to knock spots off feather dusting.

The song as we now know it deals with a man issuing impossible demands to his lover, such as searching for a dry well in which to wash a shirt. She in turns asks him to reap the land with a leather sickle. This domestic misery is assumed to originate from 'The Elfin Knight', a Scottish folk song in which the devil threatens kidnap unless his victim can complete certain tasks.

Paul Simon learnt the song from Martin Carthy, an English folk singer well known in London's folk clubs. Carthy had constructed his version after reading a book called *The Singing Island*, compiled by Peggy Seeger and Ewan MacColl, a glum singer and communist who was monitored by MI5 in the 1930s and later became father to pop singer Kirsty MacColl. Ewan MacColl had become aware of it after a retired lead miner named Mark Anderson had sung it for him, reportedly at his Northumberland home in the 1940s. This caused a stir as recently as 2014, when a Bishop Auckland MP said that while Simon & Garfunkel had made millions from their recording, the stonemasons of Teesdale, where the song originated, had made nothing.

Meanwhile, Carthy was aggrieved that Simon had borrowed his arrangement. His music publisher sued, and got $20,000. Unbeknown to Carthy, however, the settlement involved him signing away the rights to any future royalties. He grew bitter at Simon, calling it 'the trudge through the grudge', a resentment that lasted decades. Then he learnt that Simon & Garfunkel hadn't got rich from the song after all. His own publisher, the one who had represented him in the lawsuit, had allegedly copyrighted the song. In 1998, Simon rang Carthy and asked him to play on stage with him, and they stood together at the Hammersmith Odeon and sang 'Scarborough Fair'. Nobody seemed too bothered that

Bob Dylan had also borrowed the song's refrain and used it in 'Girl from the North Country'. All of which goes to show that there's nowt so strange as folk.

Don't they teach you no brains?

It has always fascinated me that music can be associated with specific locations. Not everywhere, though. The tension between continuity and change runs through Yorkshire music, but there has never been a distinctive theme, which perhaps reflects the vastness implicit in the county's Broad Acres nickname. Indeed, for a 1980s teenager, Leeds and York seemed destined to be musical vacuums. Sure, there was the Wedding Present, achingly angsty blokes in black with abrasive guitars and acerbic gripes about not having a girl-friend. It was easy for fans to identify with them, as I did, but the lack of a geographical axis for Yorkshire music seemed to be borne out when they stuck a picture of Manchester hero George Best on an album cover and started making Ukrainian folk songs.

But there has been a rich music culture in wider Yorkshire. Janet Baker was the pre-eminent mezzo-soprano of post-war Britain, and if the works for which she became famous had no local links, the story of her being talent-spotted during mass at York Minster in 1953 was a distinctly Yorkshire tale. It led her to Ilse Wolf, a professional soprano, and contact with an eminent teacher, and that subsequent breakout from the straitjacket of a parish in Doncaster to make it in London was a template for unknown wannabes to follow.

From the Sisters of Mercy, with their drum machine, to Def Leppard, who miraculously took hormonal hair rock to the world despite their drummer losing an arm in a road accident, music has been a get-out clause. Artists like Paul Heaton and Tracey Thorn cut their teeth over in Hull. The Housemartins' *London 0 Hull 4* album put regionalism in the album title, although Heaton said the 4 referred to being only the fourth best band in Hull. One of the superior outfits was Everything but the Girl, comprising Hull University chums Thorn and Ben Watt and named after a slogan on a local furniture shop.

Hull also gave David Bowie his Spiders from Mars, the group best remembered for Mick Ronson's guitar and the 1972 *Top of the Pops* performance of 'Starman' that engaged, enraged and even scared a few. Ronson was recruited in Hull by old bandmate Mick Woodmansey, but he was not initially enamoured by Bowie's psyche-delic androgyny. Woodmansey would tell journalist Dave Simpson that Ronson needed convincing about the satin suit and peroxide hair. 'He packed his suitcase and went to the station. He said: "I'm a musician, I've got friends, I don't want them seeing me like that."' Bowie, an artistic genius and visionary, knew what he wanted, though. Ronson was the blunt, salt-of-the-earth northerner with the defiantly masculine personality he needed. Bowie's father was from Doncaster and the singer could do a good Yorkshire accent when asked. Bowie Snr had died young, in his fifties, and his son's recollection resonated with me: 'He just died at the wrong damn time, because there were so many things I would have loved to have said to him and asked him about.' But in Mick Ronson, Ziggy had his perfect foil. Music was never quite the same.

Yet as these trailblazers shocked and shook up the more mundane Yorkshire pews, there is no doubt that Sheffield has long been the heartbeat, or perhaps arrhythmia, of the county scene. I was entranced by the story of Joanne Catherall and Susan Sulley from the Human League, and how Phil Oakey, with his black anchor quiff, had seen them dancing in a club and on that basis transformed them from schoolgirls with normal looks and normal clothes into stars. It was not that most of us wanted to be famous in any way, but the idea that unusual things could happen was comforting. Sheffield was where the bulk of the magic happened. In the early twenty-first century, the Arctic Monkeys became megastars because they wrote good tunes, played fast, and peppered their songs with colloquialisms about taxi rides to Hillsborough in unabashed regional accents. When they won the Mercury Music Prize, they were like a younger, rougher Beatles. 'Call 999,' said frontman Alex Turner before he went off to the USA to lighten his roots. 'Richard Hawley's been robbed.'

Hawley, another Sheffield native and another Mercury nominee that year, looked like something out of the 1950s – he still does – but his songs, from beautiful ballads to guitar romps, mix nostalgia with modern Sheffield. His old mate Jarvis Cocker became an international star as the lead singer of Pulp, the wittiest and most withering of the Britpop bands. Cocker cannot sing as well as Hawley, or play the guitar like him. His mum voted Tory and for Brexit. Yet he is the perfect icon for the socialist republic of South Yorkshire, a magnificently pithy chronicler of hard times, grubby sex and dislocation. While Oasis were writing singalong anthems with banal lyrics on the other side of the Pennines, Cocker was doing 'Last Day of the Miners' Strike', although as arts journalist Kate Mossman wrote in an interview in the *New Statesman*, 'He was interested in perceptions of the north–south divide as much as the real thing.'

In that interview, Cocker says how he hatched a plan to escape the dole and, in turn, Sheffield, but he was still bothered by the place and his role in it, and, eventually, on the side of a student halls of residence on Boston Street. Asked to write something for the Off the Shelf festival in 2005, his words were to be reproduced in giant embossed letters fixed to the facade of the building. He said this overt display of showiness jarred with his idea of being from Sheffield so he thought he would compromise and write something inappropriate. Hence he talked of the future being forged within and someone getting trashed on cider. He wrote that when you melt, you become the shape of your surroundings, and then, as the pay-off, asked if they taught you no brains at school. Words and pictures. Cocker's huge yellow face is also on a wall by Kelham Island Museum in Sheffield.

His song 'Wickerman', which is now part of the A level geography curriculum, traces a journey along the River Don through Sheffield's shifting scenery. In his book of lyrics, *Mother, Brother, Lover*, he says the song was based on a real voyage with a friend in an inflatable dinghy bought from a jumble sale. They passed 'gypsy' children sledding down a weir in a bread crate. When the fog of factory steam enveloped them, he wondered if he was in a South Yorkshire re-creation of *Apocalypse Now*. Near Rotherham, they saw a man shooting fish with an air rifle and shouting, 'Stitch that, you bastard.' Then they made a pile of stones to mark the journey's end and vowed to carry on another day. They never did. The dinghy got a puncture. Cocker said it was one of the happiest days of his life.

His lyrics make references to Sheffield's 2p bus fares for kids; Tinsley cooling towers; the Yorkshire Ripper. Pulp had a rehearsal studio close to where miners and police fought the Battle of Orgreave. One day Cocker went to the Magna Science Adventure Centre in Rotherham and was fascinated by the model of the old steel works. 'It must be some kind of folk memory,' he mused. 'There is nostalgia, not for vibration white finger or lung disease, but for times when people worked together and there would be a result.' Years later, he would visit his mum for Christmas and go down the local caves, marvelling at how our ancestors might have made primitive music using sticks and bones and echoes. Indeed, the Malham Pipe, found during the excavation of a Bronze Age burial mound in the Dales, is made from a sheep bone and was long thought to have been a Bronze Age instrument until other researchers said it was probably post-Roman; stick that in your pipe.

Hawley was in Pulp for a while. He also nearly got very famous with his band Longpigs, but found his niche making critically acclaimed albums that were usually named after Sheffield landmarks. Coles Corner was a meeting place for couples, friends and lovers; Lady's Bridge was a Norman fording bridge built on the orders of the founder of Sheffield, the Anglo-Norman Baron William de Lovetot. The bridge was almost destroyed in the great flood of 1864, when the gas lamps lit a scene of horror as timber, furniture and logs boiled in the water, broke the parapets and, according to a contemporary report, rushed 'across Mr White's slate yard over the broad thoroughfare of the Wicker'.

Hawley still lives in Yorkshire. He turns down lots of interviews but has agreed to talk to me because it's not about 'fame and all that stuff', and he is very generous with his time and memories. 'I spent half of my life trying to get away and spent the other half trying to get back,' he says. 'When I did get back it was all gone. Lots of my mates went to

London and did the thing. Jarv went and it was life-changing for him. I think a person like Jarv could not have existed in Sheffield. It was too provincial for him. He once said this great thing to me on stage, when we were headlining some massive festival somewhere, and all these lads dressed up in casual gear were chanting "Yorkshire, Yorkshire". Jarv just looked at me and said, "It was only a few years ago that these people were chasing us down the street, calling us poofs and wanting to kill us."'

Why is Sheffield this music heartland and not Leeds or York or Middlesbrough? 'It's funny, that. I remember my dad telling me Leeds and Harrogate was where all the money went. I don't know if there's any truth in that, but the municipal buildings in Leeds are beautiful and Sheffield is aesthetically a horror film. They really fucked it up. Any time you go into the city centre you're taking your life into your hands. Seriously. But out of that edginess comes music because rich people don't make great rock and roll records. I think bands only have so many albums in them because the more remote you get from the place that inspires you the more wishy-washy it gets because you have nothing to say.'

Hawley did not have it easy. Born with a hare lip and a cleft palate, he came from a poor family rich in experience. His grandfather was a steelworker, a soldier and a musician. 'He taught me how to play chess and he taught me bits of musical theory,' he says. 'He was an amazing man. I still remember the smell of tobacco from his pipe, the ticking of the clock, slow, sharing a bit of Old Jamaica chocolate with the ship on it, just absorbing stuff. He told me, "The first thing to learn before you set out is that you might fail." I thought, "Thanks, Grandad." Then, when I started to get great reviews with my first band, he said, "Tha knows, son, reviews are no good to you." I asked why not and he replied, "Because if tha gets a bad one, tha don't want to get out of bed – and get a good one and tha head's that big tha won't be able t'get out fucking door!" That single statement stuck with me my whole life.' His parents told him he was no worse than anyone else – and no better.

In 1940, his grandfather was on the beach at Dunkirk. He had a violin he had bought in Paris. An officer told him to leave it behind. 'Grandad refused and the officer threatened to shoot him,' says Hawley. 'Then the officer asked if he could swim. "Aye, I can swim," he says. "Well, this lad can't and if you can get him to the boat, you can keep your violin." So Grandad swam to the boat at Dunkirk with this lad under one arm and the other out of the water holding his violin. Then he hid it under an army blanket and smuggled it back to the UK.' It is some story. 'It's in my bedroom,' he says. 'He got a medal for that.'

Hawley's first gig was at St Cuthbert's working men's club, playing guitar with a man named John Flats, who had a guitar, a drum machine and a mechanical pink rabbit. He went by the stage name John Steel. 'So everyone called him Stainless. I got up there when I was 12 and can remember the look on my dad's face.' His father, Dave, worked in the steelworks for 14 hours a day but was a Teddy boy in thrall to Gene Vincent and would still play guitar in the clubs and music halls by night. Hawley's uncle Frank was also a talented guitarist and played with travelling musicians including American blues artists like Muddy Waters, Sonny Boy Williamson and Little Walter. 'Uncle Frank and my dad took Walter to meet my grandma, who was the first ever staff nurse in Sheffield after the war,' says Hawley. 'They had Sunday dinner, but Walter only had one suit so he had to stick the tablecloth down his shirt so he didn't get gravy on it.'

Joe Cocker, the star singer with a voice so rich and thick that he could have been gargling on exhumed ashes, was Hawley's godfather – 'not because they were all in music, but because he fitted radiators with my dad'. Hawley's mother was a nurse and a singer, but they were all teachers too. Frank would show him part of a song – 'just enough to open up the cognisant part of my brain' – and then wander off to make a cup of tea, leaving him to work the rest out himself – 'you didn't get anything for free'. Another day his dad took him to his workplace in what was laughingly called light engineering and introduced him to the foreman. 'I know why he took me there. It was aversion therapy. I was given a tour of the factory and it was a terrifying place. I practised like mad after that, I can tell you.'

Hindsight is always clear and sharp, and Hawley is careful that his affection for these days does not become hagiography. I mention the line I heard him use in Leicester – 'It's not where you're from, it's where you're at.' I took this to mean you take your roots with you, but he says, 'It's also the opposite of that. It means your roots aren't important, it's where your head is. It's an old thing, almost a cliché. I don't know who said it first. It might have been Jack Kerouac or one of the old Beat poets. There are a lot of meanings to it, which is what attracted me to it. When I was younger, I was brought up with something called thigmotaxis.' Literally, that is a fear of physical contact, but Hawley says he means otherness.

His father told him that the only ways out of the industrial life were music, sport or boxing – 'he didn't equate boxing with sport' – and his grandad told him about the three things that governed Britain – 'money, land and power'. And then …

'I remember my dad running down Vickers Road. It was a weird thing because it was really sunny on our side of the street but on the other it was really pelting down, not drizzle. But the thing is there were no drops on the house windows. Dad had this light blue bomber jacket on. He was a union rep and he's running down the street and is using the *Green 'Un*, the sadly defunct sports paper, to keep the rain off his head. He came in, shook himself and said to my mum, "We're all out, then."' Strikes in the steel industry in 1980 would usher in a decade of change. 'I was about 12. I loved my dad and he had fear in his eyes. I can still see it now. I knew at that point that those plans of hers, Thatcher, did not include me and all those other boys and girls.

'I witnessed first-hand how my father was as ruined as a lot of men who had come home from the Second World War. They didn't just get dumped, it was a surgical destruction. They were damaged mentally. My mum and dad split up because they couldn't handle it any more.'

Some of Hawley's anecdotes and phrases sound like song lyrics. His musical heritage was a lifesaver because he says it kept him from 'sniffing glue and robbing cars', a parallel life encapsulated in Pulp's 'Help the Aged', Cocker's touching reminder that the only difference between generations is time.

After the best part of a decade on and off the dole, he admits he got lost when he made it. 'Suddenly I was going around in a chauffeur-driven limo, but the thing is, once you are sat there by the swimming pool in LA, you have very little connection with growing up in a council house. Music is a magic trick, it's creating something out of nothing. I have learnt that to do it you have to not be interested in baubles and peripherals.'

It was the same up the M1. Kaiser Chiefs became a hugely successful band and had the T-shirt that was part Yorkshire exceptionalism, part irony, saying 'Everything is brilliant in Leeds'. It's not in either city. 'When the pits closed, the drug dealers moved in,' says Hawley. 'It's not just south Sheffield – it's a modern plague.' The Kaisers' song was actually 'Everything is average nowadays', but that's not quite right either. 'When you demonise people, you make them like you want them to be – flat caps, whippets, a pint of warm beer,' he adds.

Hawley wrote an album that became a musical about families living on the Park Hill estate. The location is rooted in Sheffield's dark history. In 1981, J. P. Bean wrote a grisly book called *The Sheffield Gang Wars*, which depicts a rancid hotchpotch of unemployment, raw sewage, muck and brass being won by gambling at the Sky Edge tossing ring behind the estate. There had been gangs in the area in the nineteenth century, such as the Guttapercha Gang, named after a gum that created an igneous varnish useful for hardening weapons for street warfare. They were a disparate group using mafia tricks such as demanding protection money from small businesses. Later, the Neepsend Gas Tank Gang would rob miners and steelworkers on their way home from work. The gambling scene thrived under the rule of the George Mooney Gang, but a splinter faction, the Park Gang, sought to wreak vengeance on its followers. Mooney even had to barricade himself in his house and seek police protection before quietly fleeing the country. The gang warfare reached its nadir with the murder of William Plommer in 1925. As one contemporary report put it: 'The story of Plommer's death begins in a dark mean street in the slums of Sheffield, where grim shadows lurk in every doorway, and two or three street lamps shed a fitful light onto the pathway, making the passer-by shudder as he hurries home.'

Armed with pokers, razors, iron chains and even a bayonet, the Park Brigade set about Plommer, who died on his way to hospital. Spinks Fowler was later seen sitting in the doorway of a fish shop nursing a grazed hand. A policeman asked him what had happened. 'I hit him with a poker,' he boasted. When the officer said it looked like being serious, Fowler amended his boast to: 'Well, I did not hit him then.' He and his brother, Lawrence, were hanged at Armley Gaol in Leeds. It was an undeniably grim time.

Hawley's album, *Standing at the Sky's Edge*, was released in 2012. It was his angry record. 'Sheffield's gentle troubadour turns tough,' said the *Guardian*. 'What it boils down to is not ideologies,' Hawley says. 'It's individuals. The decisions corrupt politicians have made over decades have led us to this point, all the hideous zero-morals decisions made during a terrifying global pandemic, the appalling greed, pure naked pigs troughing. It's sickening.'

Yet he is still here, still proud of his heritage. He wanted his musical to be authentic and had to tell the musical's producers to put more jokes in. 'Sheffield's had a lot of grim shit happen to it, but I overhear the funniest stuff, close to gallows humour.' When his dad was dying, he told Hawley not to be crippled by grief and to make sure he finished his album. He added, 'Don't forget my beer and fags tomorrow.'

Hawley's son is now leaving to go to university. Like his own father, Hawley hoped for a bit of aversion therapy when his boy took a job at a joiner's in Neepsend, where his grandad had worked and where Hawley used to record.

His son needed to get up at 5.45 a.m. 'The thing is, he loved it,' says Hawley. He's leaving, but he knows where he's from.

Hawley is a good talker but likes to listen too. 'My guitar is my shovel and I dug a great big hole for myself, but I ploughed my own furrow. Is that a northern thing? I'm from the Deep South – deep South Yorkshire – but to be honest, we live in a posh part of Sheffield now with my ill-gotten gains, and I feel like a pirate bringing this stuff back from just writing songs. But where I was brought up, people were mad. Wonderful, eccentric people who will have had a part in who I am. I'm still a member of a social club. I go down there and sit with all these 70- and 80-year-olds and talk to them the same way I did when I was 12 when I sat with my dad absorbing all these old-bloke stories.

'My nan and grandad used to live on a road I passed every day on my way home. They'd be there in their chairs like two bookends. They were born on Duke Street during the gang wars, lived next door to each other and stayed together their whole lives. Only two things parted them – war and death. Every day, without fail, I would stick my head round that door, and you know what, I don't regret one single time I did that.'

Everything is average nowadays

One day in March, I sit down in the Hyde Park Book Club in Leeds, a boho arts venue in the shadow of a huge mural of Marcelo Bielsa, the Argentinian footballer manager who has just been sacked as the manager of Leeds United. Bielsa is a radical. His family worked in left-wing politics, and he likened the dangers of negative football to those of climate change. In a city whose ethos was money, winning and survival, he sat on an upturned bucket during matches, stressed the importance of beauty in football and challenged the fundamental principle of modern sport – that it is all about the results.

Simon Rix is a football fan and is not happy that Bielsa has been sacked. He also plays bass guitar in Kaiser Chiefs, the band he set up with old schoolfriends when their first one, Parva, was dropped by their record label. Kaiser Chiefs are named after the Kaizer Chiefs, the South African football club made famous by former Leeds captain Lucas Radebe, an amiable man who once told me about being shot in the back in Soweto – 'It was just flesh, it missed all the vital organs.'

Kaiser Chiefs are well known for being nice. That is not rock-and-roll enough for some, notably Boris Johnson, who used them as a way into a rant about Tony Blair back in 2006. The future PM wrote in the *Daily Telegraph* that they were the 'weeds from Leeds' and that the lack of actual violence in their best-known song, 'I Predict a Riot', was 'pathetic'. He went on, 'When I was a nipper it was standard practice for a rock star to start the evening by biting the head off a pigeon and throwing the television out of the window before electrocuting his girlfriend in the bath and almost drowning in a cocktail of whisky, heroin and his own vomit. The self-respecting British punk rockers didn't get up on stage and start whimpering about how they predicted a riot. They incited riots.'

I doubt Johnson ever listened to the song's lyrics. The Kaisers may never have been uber-cool, but that was Yorkshire. Indeed, years later, the county was so uncool that Johnson would ditch plans for the HS2 rail link to go to Leeds.

Rix tells me that before they made it big, the band had decided they were content with part-time jobs and playing to a core audience of around 150 people in Leeds and 50 in London. Playing the Duchess of York pub was a pipe dream. 'But when we were in the Old Chapel rehearsal rooms, we knew we had a big sound. We'd say, "This would sound good at Glastonbury." We pictured loads of people singing and waving. It's not very Leeds to think like that. The West Yorkshire thing was to have small ambitions, just play with your friends. But sometimes it's good to use the football analogy and go and get Bielsa.'

The biggest gig? 'Well, on paper, it would be a million, Live 8, on the streets of Philadelphia. We opened. On the Rocky Steps.' How did that feel? 'It was all right.' Global stars but synonymous with a city and its football club. 'We all used to live in Headingley or Meanwood and then gradually moved to London because of girlfriends and the music business, which is still there. But now most of us have moved back. Why? Because it's nicer? Better? I don't know. When you're younger, London is exciting, but you get older and you want more space, families, your football, the country-side, mum and dad.'

Their album *Employment* was huge. It sold millions, a multi-platinum classic. The world listened to lyrics about a night out in Leeds and a dead-end job in Leeds, to Yorkshire and English references, and to the word 'thee'. The Kaisers were made, but there had always been a work ethic to their success, guitars as shovels. The lyrics to another terrace anthem, 'Oh My God', were indicative of their pursuit of success. Ricky Wilson, the lead singer, explained, 'The verses are about the fact we've been playing together for such a long time and people think, "What's he doing? He's still trying to make a career out of music? It'll never work. One in a million people do it." But we still had the opinion that we were five of the people in a million, so we carried on.'

One founder member, Nick Hodgson, left, but other than that, they carried on. Old friends, memory brushing the same years, as Simon & Garfunkel would have it, sharing the same silent fears.

Rix does think about the hypocrisy of geography. 'We go to Sheffield, and they sing, "Yorkshire, Yorkshire",' he says. 'And I think, "We're from Leeds, you don't like us. If we were at Sheffield United, you'd be trying to kill us." It's weird. Bands will say they are from Manchester even when they're not. Like The Charlatans. I mean, some of them were from North Wales! But The Cribs are from Wakefield, so they're not part of the Leeds scene. And Sheffield is very different. Sometimes Yorkshire doesn't help itself. It's the "that's us, that's not us" thing. I don't know why Sheffield has produced so many bands, the same with Manchester, Liverpool. I think Leeds has always lacked people staying. You'd think it would be heaving with talent, but people spin off into the next big city. In the eighties, people who were linked with Leeds were not even from the city. Music was not a thing that people from Leeds thought you could be or do. And being an indie band from Yorkshire was about the least cool thing you could be.'

Others agreed. 'Lord, keep me away from Leeds,' said Kevin Rowland of the Birmingham soul revivalists Dexys Midnight Runners on 'Thankfully Not Living in Yorkshire, It Doesn't Apply'. Later in 2022, Leeds will anoint itself a culture capital, still smarting from being denied the official

European tag. A national poetry centre is planned for an old flax mill. However, the tone of Horsham-born comedian Harry Enfield in his sketch about an unreconstructed Yorkshireman in an office meeting is funny and a bit true: 'Don't talk to me about sophistication, love, I've *been* to Leeds.' In 2019, Liam Gallagher, the moping singer who was morphing into a middle-of-the-road pop star while affecting menace, got into a Twitter row with the Kaisers' keyboard player. 'It's naff c***s like you that give Leeds a bad name,' he tweeted.

Kaiser Chiefs don't care. They work hard, play hard. They are thicker-skinned and once penned the lines:

Never had a fight that we haven't lost.
We're not very tough or athletic.
Once I had a boxing champ in a headlock
And when he gets out, I'll regret it.

Self-deprecation allied to relentless ambition is their thing. It might be new Yorkshire's. Everything is not brilliant. Then or now. But something might be.

Jarvis Cocker became infamous when he interrupted Michael Jackson's performance at the Brit Awards in 1996. It was a distinctly weird display, with children fawning around a messianic Jackson clad in white and wings. Cocker, egged on by Pulp's keyboard player, walked on stage, turned so his back was to the camera and gave the whole thing the bum's rush. He kept his trousers up, but his wiggling was a tabloid storm. He was arrested and taken to Kensington police station. Comedian Bob Mortimer had been at the awards and went to the station to defend Cocker, despite being half-cut. His comedy partner and co-Yorkshireman, Vic

Reeves, stood outside with a sign saying 'Free the Jarvis 1'. Cocker said the incident had a poisonous effect on his life. He wasn't in it for the fame either.

'Killing Floor' on Ilkley Moor

For most non-tykes, the most recognisable Yorkshire anthem is not 'I Predict a Riot' or 'Common People' or 'Scarborough Fair'. Instead, it is 'On Ilkla Moor Baht 'at'. Down the ages this has been delivered with equal gusto by folk singers, Methodists and decades of drunks. The origins, though, reside in Kent.

Thomas Clark was an illiterate cobbler in Canterbury with a sideline in composing. Grateful for the help of a Cranbrook schoolmaster named John Francis, he wrote a homage called 'Cranbrook', which became a well-known hymn in the early nineteenth century, first attached to the words of Philip Doddridge's 'Grace, 'tis a charming sound' and then 'While Shepherds Watched Their Flocks'. According to Dr Arnold Kellett, a former mayor of North Yorkshire market town Knaresborough, indefatigable student of Yorkshire dialect and a survivor of five heart attacks, it was the influence of John Wesley, who advocated outdoor singing as a means of escaping smoking mills, clogged-up sewers and a diet of sheep heads and carrots, that led us to the version we now love or endure. Kellett wrote an entire book about the song, looking at all the origin stories and analysing the dialect, and concluded that the words were born on a Halifax choir outing to the moor in Victorian times.

Without hymn sheets, these rambles were a highlight for the members, starting at Dick Hudson's pub on Bingley

Moor. Kellett reasons that the accepted lyrics, 'Wheear 'ast tha bin sin' ah saw thee?' and 'Tha's been a cooartin' Mary Jane' and 'Tha's bahn' to catch thy deeath o'cowd', refer to off-piste activities. While Wesley promoted singing lustily, one member of the choir is said to have taken this a tad literally. In a clip still available on YouTube, Kellett stands on a windswept moor in his anorak, book in hand like a modern-day Wesley, and declares that a couple had wandered off for 'a bit of canoodling'. The man emerged from the heather without his hat, which may even have been a euphemism for trousers, and so was certain to catch a cold, die a death and be eaten by worms, and then by ducks from Ilkley Tarn, and in turn by us. It was, Kellett says, like *Hamlet*. Certainly the old prince does say 'A man may fish with the worm that hath eat of a king', but it seems a pretty harsh punishment for having the hots for Mary Jane.

In the 1980s, the local papers claimed that Mary Jane's skeleton had been found up on Ilkley Moor. They knew this because it had a locket inscribed with 'MJP'. It was a hoax, but facts often become besmirched over time. Ilkley Moor itself is actually only part of Rombalds Moor, and lives and breathes between Ilkley and Keighley in West Yorkshire. It is wild and rugged, a 300-million-year-old carboniferous swamp that was later moulded into millstone grit by Ice Age glaciers. I park up at the café by the Cow and Calf. I think it is a shame that Millstone Grit has not become the name of a legendary rock band, but music, romance and a hint of danger loom in this rock's history. It is said the Cow and Calf, a large outcrop and severed boulder, became separated when the giant Rombald stamped on the rock when fleeing his wife, who dropped her possessions to form the Skirtful of Stones.

I walk up to Ilkley Quarry, behind the Cow and Calf, a walled opening where trainee rock climbers get their first grips. A drone from another time zone is hovering above. A man follows it.

'Great thing,' he says. 'My mate's down there but he's got a bad knee so can't walk up here.' He nods to the Cow. 'I went up there once. Got stuck. Never again.'

Drones now provide spectacular views of the moors and mean you can always remember, even when semi-arthritic. 'Can't fly 'em near airport, though. Did that out of my flat window. It got turned over in wind and I lost it. Finally got it back and landed it on my bird feeders. Bloody 'ell.'

I think about the opening to Tim Binding's beautiful, part-factual, part-reimagined history, On Ilkley Moor, which in truth is far better than Charlotte Brontë's much-acclaimed line about not fancying a walk. 'Standing on the huge, lettered rock, the clink of climbers' chains at the back of him, the breath of other untutored scramblings fading as they make their way back down the grassy, bee-infested footholds, he can see, lying in that open valley at the foot of Rombalds Moor, the town where he first learnt the art of forgetting.'

Place leaves its mark on people, and vice versa. I stumble around the rocks, the cows, calves, monsters and other miracles of imagination. Many of these rocks are engraved with Victorian graffiti, each chiselled signature a memento mori of a visit to what was once a thriving spa town with its healing hydrotherapy waters. Charles Darwin was one of the visitors, recuperating here when On the Origin of Species was published in 1859, happy to get away from what he called that 'confounded' book that had half killed him. All the inscribers are now dead, all as immortal as their decisions about how deep to go with their marks. These rocks scattered around the Cow and Calf are a ledger. The moors endure, through climate change, erosion, war and revolution, and these people and their families are attached to this place and the hope they once planted here.

G Stead 1892
C Clark April 1904
T A Harris Hull 1889
E M Lancaster 1882

And then there are more recent ones:

Merritt 1977
Jesus is Lord – Turn to Him
Elaine & Jimmy

There are truly old carvings up here too. The most famous is the Swastika Stone on Woodhouse Crag, nine cups and then a flowing line forming an ancient swastika. It dates to either the Neolithic period or the early Bronze Age and so is possibly 4,000 years old, a mere itch compared with the ancient scratches found on mammoth tusks in Ukraine, but a reminder that the swastika was important to people long before it was misappropriated by the Nazis. The cup and ring design is thought to be associated with Thor's thunder, or the sun, or funerals. Even the iron railings around the stone cannot devalue its mystery.

It was also on this moor that Frederick Delius was believed to have been inspired to compose *On Hearing the First Cuckoo in Spring*, in which oboes, violins and clarinets mimic bird calls. Delius was one of those interesting choices as a favourite native of Yorkshire in that he could not wait to get out. He despised industrial Bradford and was delighted when he was sent to Florida in 1884 to loaf around on an orange plantation. From there he moved to Germany, Paris and Grez-sur-Loing, an artists' commune that he chose as his base to make life hard for his amanuensis, Scarborough-born composer Eric Fenby. In Ken Russell's dramatised version of Delius's life, *Song of Summer*, Fenby makes the mistake of telling Delius that he plays the organ to Laurel and Hardy films at Scarborough's Futurist Theatre. Delius is cantankerous, egotistical, blind, paralysed and syphilitic. 'English music,' he says at one point. 'Did you say English music?' He dresses in white, like Michael Jackson at the Brits.

Delius's parents were Germans who made good in the wool trade. They were part of an immigrant population that gave rise to Bradford's Little Germany district, known for its grand neoclassical warehouses, with Caspian House on East Parade home to D. Delius and Company. A carved sandstone grandfather clock and armchair have stood on one sloping street in Little Germany for 30 years. Passers-by often sit in the mill owner's chair and have their photograph taken. On the day I visited, someone had urinated in it and left a can of Foster's by the clock. You can see why Delius preferred Ilkley Moor.

One theory is that the teenage Delius wrote down the notation for a cuckoo after a walk on the moor but composed the actual piece when in France. He died there too, in 1934, but the authorities would not let him be buried in his garden. He ended up in Surrey. Hard life. Harder death.

I hear no cuckoos, just the drone and chunter of trucks, but can picture a pre-syphilitic Delius soaking it all in. The violinist Tasmin Little said there was 'an inimitable tone of rapturous regret' in his late work, possibly due to failing to find the child he fathered in Florida with an African-American woman. Others have talked about the slave songs he heard informing his work, but on Ilkley Moor he was on the cusp of adventure, and a quintessentially northern town.

Around a century later, on 12 March 1967, a van turned up at Ilkley's Troutbeck Hotel, a short journey from where I am now, just down Hangingstone Lane and Cowpasture Road. The party was shown to a small area at the back of the ballroom and started playing Scrabble and Risk. For the singer, James Marshall, this trip up north was an eye-opener. He was from Seattle in the USA, not Settle in North Yorkshire, and had spent four months in England trying to fathom the peculiarities of *Coronation Street* with his girl-friend, Kathy.

Cars blinked down the hill like the eyes of moor animals. Philip Edwards, who managed the Gyro Club in the Troutbeck, hoped to get away with not having a dancing licence for Sundays. It was a dour hotel, worn away at the edges, just faded, no glory. Edwards told the bundles of people that it was ten shillings to get in.

Mr Harvey lived a few doors down and was unimpressed by the cars and vans parked all over Crossbeck Road. He called the police. Sergeant Tom Chapman answered the call and drove to the Troutbeck. His report stated that there were 600 people in the ballroom and the capacity was 250. They began to pogo. Chapman asked the manager to turn off the record player. He went on stage, told people to leave and then went to ring for backup. 'I returned to the ballroom and found the beat group booked for the night had gone on stage and commenced the performance,' he reported.

Christine had made a purple catsuit with silver Lurex and bellbottoms. She and her friend Nadia had wangled their way into the dressing room. James Marshall looked at her and said: 'Hey, purple haze.'

The trio began with 'Killing Floor' but were interrupted by Sergeant Chapman. 'I went onto the stage, spoke to the leader of the group, whom I now knew to be called Hendrix. I told him the position and the action that had previously been taken and he stopped the music.' Hendrix then backed into the eponymous Marshall amps, and to the sound of deafening feedback, Chapman followed the wires and pulled the plug. On the lights. The howl carried on in the darkness like a remnant of a memory.

It took two hours for everyone to leave. Ilkley's unlikeliest night never really happened, and the police went undercover after that. They produced evidence of kissing, fondling, drinking and dancing. It sounded like a good night out, but would lead to a £155 fine for Philip Edwards and a change to his licence. Mr Harvey was satisfied. Two weeks later, in London, Jimi Hendrix set fire to his guitar.

The Yorkshire blues

In the 1960s and beyond, Champion Jack Dupree could most often be found in Ovenden, near Halifax. Kellett had said that Ovenden's Providence Congregational Chapel could well have been the starting point for the famous romantic trip to Ilkley Moor. The village seemed an odder destination for a blues pianist who had spent most of his early life in the Colored Waifs Home for Boys in New Orleans after his parents had been murdered by the Ku Klux Klan.

That was the same orphanage where the man sounding
the alarm call on the bugle each morning was called Louis
Armstrong. Young Jack would pound out his own notes with
one finger on the old piano in the shed, and after leaving
the home started to play in brothels and speakeasies for two
dollars a show, eking out an existence by also taking a job
as a pot-washer. He would go on to spend two years in a
Japanese prisoner-of-war camp, and then began fighting
with gloves after meeting Joe Louis, the world heavyweight
boxing champion, thus gaining the 'Champion' prefix, but
he quickly found that he was in another world of pimps and
parasites. He moved to Indianapolis and New York, and
recorded the popular *Blues from the Gutter* album, but he
grew weary with the racial divide and ventured to Europe,
where, after meeting his future wife, Shirley Harrison, he
settled in Ovenden.

Trevor Simpson, a local author and musical authority,
recalled that Jack Dupree was the first black man he had
seen in 1964 Yorkshire, resplendent in his sharp blazer and
utterly eye-catching from the personalised station wagon to
the gold tooth. Dupree would often talk about the stereotyping of home, and how he was a bluesman whereas New
Orleans was jazzland. One day a BBC man came to visit him
in Yorkshire, and Dupree played his barrelling background
as he imparted wisdom about pop music and life. 'They listen
to that racket and then it's finished,' he said. 'It dies because
it didn't have no story. People say white people can't feel the
blues they as crazy as hell. Anybody can feel the blues who
is human – we just don't have trouble the same way.' To
highlight the point, he added that a white man rejected by
his lover might think of murder. 'We don't think of murder,'
he explained. 'We think of going to get drunk and play the

piano and forget.' This gets to the heart of the meaning of music. It's whisky for the masses, aspirin for the soul. 'When you hear these blues playing it make you think way back and it's a bad life you think of,' he said. 'That's what makes good blues. But if you've never had no miserable life, you cannot do it. Nobody that never lived bad could make no good blues.' Every line a song title, he added, 'It's always a life story, it's not just playing.'

Champion Jack Dupree died in 1993 while he was living in Scandinavia. His ashes were scattered in the North Sea, but a plaque was put up in Halifax so modern mourners could gather together in Yorkshire and be forever blue.

6

ARTISTS

> I wanted to question everything I was presented with and
> prove it wrong. Not for any reason – just being awkward.
>
> Damien Hirst, Leeds-raised artist, *Yorkshire Post*, 2019

I f Yorkshire has sometimes struggled to finds its musical
voice, its art history is long and vivid. Inspiration was
found in the stunning scenery, but the art scene itself was
more radical, with a heart pulsing in the free thinkers down
at Leeds Art Club and beyond. From riverside painters to
well-dressed anarchists, the artists have summed up the
battle between parochial and broader landscapes. And as
they took Yorkshire to the world, they often found themselves constrained by it.

Lovers and romances

In March 2001, the *Guardian* announced, with lightly
stifled sniggering, that Hull University was planning to
launch a Yorkshire Studies course. It boldly proclaimed

that as from Monday, Yorkshire puddings and Wallace and Gromit would be going to university. This was media studies-lite and designed to get Middle England commentators choking on their vintage port. Mel B, Delius, flat caps and whippets would form part of the curriculum. The course founder, Dr Michael Paraskos, said it was pointless for Yorkshire to argue for its own parliament if there was no supportive cultural argument, but by then the sceptics had probably drifted off into a reverie about whether Baby beat Posh.

The very idea that people would want to study Yorkshire art, literature and history was an affront to any right-minded ad exec from Islington. It also fuelled the belief that Yorkshire people thought they were God's gift. It is an enduring problem. What's so special about Yorkshire that it merits its own degree course when Rutland hasn't even got a GCSE module? The county had long moved on from traditional barbs about meanness and hat-less frolics on Ilkley Moor, and by the new millennium was perceived as just being hopelessly in love with itself; still backwards, but bigoted and brash too. Anyone who loved the sound of their own voice was probably from Yorkshire, and if the county was only half as good as it thought it was, it would be twice as good as you, and if it wasn't, it felt it was and that was all that really mattered because it wasn't listening anyway.

Dr Paraskos believed that given that there were numerous courses catering to Welsh, Irish and Scottish studies it was not unreasonable to have at least one course for a place that was bigger than Greater London, but the mocking commentators were by then wrestling with the existential issue of why there wasn't a Mel A.

The good doctor went on the radio. He did not get far. Well, to the Midlands actually, where the presenter raged at him. 'I think he wanted to be a shock jock,' Paraskos tells me. The idea that Yorkshire would be an affront to others was interesting in itself and might have made a decent dissertation, but despite Paraskos's insistence that 'this is not like doing a degree in surfing, this is a very academic subject', positive interest waned.

Enter Fred Trueman, a leviathan of Yorkshire, the fast bowler from the cricket club, which has a sort of osmotic influence in a county where most people prefer football or rugby league, slowly working its way into your veins. Like religion for many, cricket is something that is there even if you are not that interested in it. Fiery Fred, though, was Yorkshire to the bone, uber-confident. He was discovered in Sheffield, where his trial ended with the coach pondering the 'two stumps sticking out of the net like herrings on a Grimsby trawler', took 307 wickets for England and then induced fear and loathing in the Home Counties with his *Indoor League*, screened on Yorkshire TV and responsible for bringing arm wrestling, darts and shove ha'penny into the nation's living rooms in the mid 1970s.

Incidentally, that show was created by darts commentator and former research assistant to the professor of Sociology at the University of Durham, Sid Waddell. I once visited Sid at his house in Pudsey, outside Leeds, and he told me a story that seemed in keeping with Yorkshire's nature and Adelle's 'Piss Off' poster in Hebden Bridge: 'I was in a duo called the Gravyboatmen and we played the South Bank Sporting Club in Middlesbrough, one of the roughest places in western Europe. Nobody clapped and my partner turned to me and said, "Let's fuck off." Unfortunately, his mic was on reverb and you heard this echo – "fuck off, fuck off, fuck off" – going round the hall. I was on to score with the girl on the door, but as we were thrown out, she shouted, "And never come back."'

The *Yorkshire Evening Press* went to get Fred's opinion on the Hull University course. Asked what distinguished Yorkshire people from the rest, he replied, 'Not many people like us.' It did not seem much, but he was soon doing that thing that outsiders hate: 'We do everything. There's everything in this county. It's the Texas of England, isn't it? We could be self-sufficient, with the oil and gas off the coast. We've got agriculture, we produce steel.'

The journalist also went up to Thirsk to seek the additional view of the son of James Herriot, the Sunderland-born vet who became famous for recording his rural adventures in a series of beloved books. Herriot was a pen name, and James 'Alf' Wight operated in and from his surgery in Thirsk in North Yorkshire. His son, Jim Wight, told the journalist: 'Yorkshire people seem to have a special pride in their past. My father always said the success of his books was down to the fact that people are living in a more technological, urbanised society, which is going faster and faster and faster.' Of course, the course never happened.

I meet Michael Paraskos in the Royal Society of Arts in London. He is an academic, art historian and author. The idea of that Yorkshire Studies course originally emerged from his belief that Yorkshire had something unique to say about art. 'In the 1910s and 1920s, Leeds is the centre of something very exciting,' he says. 'While London is looking to what is going on in Paris, Leeds is looking to what's going on in Munich. They want the spiritualism and the expressionism.

It's what's missing in Leeds.' It was the radical generation of the art anarchists, and central to it all was a taciturn figure called Herbert Read, who would have an important role in the life of Paraskos's father.

Read was a man of many parts – poet, publisher of T. S. Eliot, art critic, anarchist, war hero, Jungian psycho-analyst, Yorkshireman. He has largely been forgotten, but his name is in Poets' Corner in Westminster Abbey, and he co-founded the Institute of Contemporary Arts on the Mall in London. Born in Ryedale in 1893, he went to a school for orphans in Halifax while his mother worked in a Leeds laundry. He rose to prominence in London, but escaped to North Yorkshire, where according to his son, Piers Paul, the philistinism of his neighbours provided a balm as Read sought to escape the 'culture vultures'. He championed sculptors such as Barbara Hepworth and Henry Moore. He wore a Basque beret at the weekend and his wife wore clogs with six-inch soles while arguing with the secretary of the local golf club when their children made sandcastles in the bunkers. Paraskos, who was good friends with Read's youngest son, Ben, tells me: 'In a way he was this clichéd Yorkshireman and was sometimes referred to behind his back as a professional Yorkshireman. He would often say very little and just sit in silence. There is a story of him going to see Henry Moore, who shows him his new sculpture. Read wanders around and leaves without saying a word. Moore thinks, "God, he hated it." Then he gets a letter three days later asking for photos. But Read was a kind man too. And he was very kind to my father.'

Stass Paraskos was the son of a peasant farmer who moved to London from Cyprus in 1953 and started his new life in the UK washing pots on Tottenham Court Road. Then he moved to Leeds and worked in his brother's Greek restaurant, where students persuaded him to enrol at the Leeds College of Art. By 1966, he was teaching there alongside close friend Robin Page, an eccentric artist who had been part of the avant-garde Fluxus group in Germany and was now known for his 'happenings'. These included such things as handing out leaflets adorned with the words 'This leaflet has been handed to you by the artist Robin Page – now throw it away.'

Michael sips his coffee and says, 'Robin Page would do all these weird and wonderful and not so wonderful things. His most famous one was the final one he did. He was teaching at the art school and hated it, so the last Christmas he was there he decided he would lie naked on the town hall steps while students dropped presents on him from a great height. If he was still able to speak by the end, he would thank everyone.' Unfortunately for Page, there was a police station in the basement in those days, and he was told to go home.

Page helped organise an exhibition for Stass Paraskos in the college gallery called *Lovers and Romances*. It was a low-key affair until it was claimed a visiting school group had taken offence. Keen observers noted that in a corner of one painting a woman clearly had a man's penis in her hand. The artist was charged under the Vagrancy and Obscene Publications Acts and suddenly found himself at the centre of what is probably best not referred to as a mass debate about artistic freedom. Sandwiched between the Lady Chatterley and *Oz* magazine obscenity trials, it was a worrying time for Stass. He wrote to Read and asked for help. Curiously, Read said he would get Keith Waterhouse, the author of *Billy Liar* and later a writer for the *Worzel Gummidge* TV series, to defend him. Sadly, that never transpired but Read did speak on his behalf.

That trial made Stass Paraskos an international celebrity in the art world. Eric Taylor, the college principal, added insult to infamy by saying that only an uneducated mind could see anything wrong in the confiscated paintings. Under cross-examination, he said the work was very different to the 'dirty postcard type of thing'. Read was as good as his word and travelled from London to offer his input. He said the work could not be pornographic as that had not been the intention. Paraskos was still found guilty and fined a total of £25 for obscenity, the last artist to suffer that fate. 'He was in trouble,' his son tells me. 'He didn't know what was going to happen. He was an immigrant and there was a new colonial police force in Cyprus and you didn't want to deal with them – he thought it would be the same here. It meant he was forever grateful to Herbert Read for speaking up. Then, in the seventies and eighties, Read fell out of favour. People didn't want to be modern any more, they wanted to be postmodern, and he was attacked again and again. My father would not have any of that. He only remembered the kindness.'

Paraskos need not have worried. A bit of scandal did him good and he got an exhibition at the ICA, as well as teaching gigs. Michael would occasionally wonder if Robin Page had staged the entire thing, but his father was now featured in art journals around the world. I particularly like Michael's story of his father being quizzed by a panel of students. One student sat there with his arms crossed and announced that he was a Marxist-Leninist who was not going to listen to any bourgeois crap. 'Good,' said Paraskos. 'I am a member of the Cyprus Communist Party and have been campaigning against the British since the end of the Second World War.' That surprised them.

The idea that Yorkshire could be a hotbed of such scandal and free thought might go against the traditional grain, but it meant you could be a surrealist even if you dressed like Harold Wilson. Read's anarchic views would ensure he clashed with the Marxist idea that art was the product of a bourgeois society. He also said there was a biological wonder in the way we perceive things as we interpret them. Or as Michael explains when talking about his father: 'For me anarchism in art disrupts the expectation of the established status quo. Classic Marxism would say there is nothing to break out of, but anarchism at least suggests the imagination can make astonishing leaps into another possibility.' And so Yorkshire art does not have to mean pictures of Haworth high street. It can mean Herbert Read writing *To Hell with Culture*.

Read is a thread through the Yorkshire greats, endorsing Moore and Hepworth and living round the corner from them when they went to London. And in speaking up for an unknown immigrant, he showed you should not judge a book by its cover. In addition, if it were not for him, the Cyprus College of Art might never have been formed one night in an alcoholic fug in the Fenton pub in Leeds. Certainly it would not have a Herbert Read library. And nobody might have had the pluck to broach the subject of a Yorkshire Studies course.

Doodles

It's April 2022, and I go to see my mum. She is 81 and living in a nice small flat on the road towards Bournemouth Pier. It is a hotbed of gossip, and Mum says, with what I think is an air of contentment, that she sometimes gets referred to as 'that northern woman'. She still has the clipped vowels and verbal traces of her roots, even though she has lived in Surrey, and now Dorset, for 20 years. She still does not like Manchester United.

The man from the hospital is already there. Later I realise he is a consultant psychiatrist. Mum had a brain scan months ago now and we are waiting to find out why her memory seems more inconsistent these days. Some things are vivid and easily to hand, but the old days in Bradford and Shipley Glen seem to be lost in a cloudy amber.

The man says Mum did very well on the memory test. No surprise. She is an intelligent woman. Books adorn every surface in her flat. Folk tales, foxes, sport, Bill Bailey's birdwatching guide, Simon Armitage's *Walking Home*, a Yorkshire Shepherdess hardback, a tombstone Che Guevara biography, assorted Alan Titchmarshes. She says she doesn't like novels because she forgets what she has already read.

The bad news, says the doctor, is that the scan has shown a shrinkage of the brain. He diagnoses Alzheimer's disease. Once the words are out, months of talking, questions, wondering if it's the cholesterol tablets are lost. I look at Mum on the sofa and, ironically, a miasma of memories merge as a lump in my throat. My first thought, for some reason, is of watching from my bedroom window as she gets out of the car in 1986. She smooths her hands down her sides and looks at her friend Val. She is readying herself. Dad has been in hospital. The last thing he tells me: 'Your mum says you're worried. I'll be fine.' But he wasn't. She comes in the house and three boys came down the stairs. I can't remember the words, but I can remember the feelings. And so, in the same room where he had placed

Gulliver or Travels (I forget which guinea pig) on the green carpet and tried to revive its lifeless body with a pipette and a drop of whisky, we find out Dad is dead. I can't imagine how alone Mum felt at that moment. I'm glad I'm here now.

I look away and focus on more books. Banksy, Picasso, but mainly David Hockney. For Mum, Hockney has a special place. He is part of a past that is becoming harder to locate. More than ever, I want to take her back.

Hockney's parents, Ken and Laura, met on a Methodist ramble on a moor. That first day, they ended up at Bolton Abbey, in Wharfedale. Ken had his Brownie camera, with which he captured Laura and her friends for ever. The more I hear about Ken Hockney, the more I like him. A Charlie Chaplin fan, he often wore a hat and carried a cane, and according to Christopher Simon Sykes's wonderful book *Hockney: The Biography*, he was a dandy who would use toothpaste to clean the smog from the paper collars he had bought from Woolworths. He was uneducated and lived in basic poverty, but he was a free thinker, affected by his brother's gassing in the First World War and a conscientious objector by the second. 'Yellow Hockney' was painted on the doorstep of the house where he lived, defiantly, with his five children.

He was adamant his children should have the chances that he didn't and pushed them to study. It paid off when David got a scholarship to Bradford Grammar School. My mum remembers him being on the same bus as her sometimes, drawing doodles and passing them around. Occasionally she wishes she'd kept one, but the only Hockney we ever had was a poster of a print, and later, postcards of his Wolds work on the iPad.

David deliberately did badly at school so he would get shoved into art classes, which were seen as the preserve of the dim. 'There is no such thing as a dumb artist,' he would say a few years later. His future appeared to him one day as he watched his father working in his pram business, noting the thrill of seeing old items restored and marvelling at the draftsman's skill in producing a straight silver line on the frame. It was like Michelangelo, he reasoned. One pram was converted into a mobile art studio. He painted people, houses and a town red and blue as well as the more obvious brown. His portrait of his fidgety father was shown in Leeds Art Gallery in 1957, when he was 17. It sold for £10. He took his friends to the pub and spent £1 on a celebratory round for all.

Unlike Delius, Hockney did not seem to loathe Bradford, even if he saw a world outside. Art was about looking harder, he decided. In an interview with arts administrator John Tusa, he would later say, 'The way they teach drawing, or taught it then, you don't necessarily speak. What happened was, you would sit round a model, what you call a donkey, you know, and you would begin to draw, looking at the most complicated thing we see, another human being. And eventually after half an hour or so someone would come and sit down ... and then start perhaps drawing the shoulder that you'd been drawing, and you watched. And then you began to see they could see more than you saw. And you realised you weren't looking very hard.'

That might be the story of Yorkshire and its reputation. Look harder. Derek Stafford, one of Hockney's teachers at the local college, would reflect on his paintings of semi-detached houses: 'He looked at his own environment and

said, "This big city I may live in may be grey and black, a
dirty city, but there is magic in it if I look closely."'

It was also here that his puritanical work ethic was honed,
and when he ran short of money for paint, he would take
bets and jump into murky canals. Yet as Richard Hawley
had said of Jarvis Cocker, his town was too provincial to
contain him, and so he went to the Royal Academy of Arts
in London, where he was teased for his Yorkshire accent
and subjected to 'trouble at mill' mockery, but thrived
in a more bohemian world where other gay men existed
at a time when homosexuality was banned and he had
gained an early experience in a Bradford cinema. Now he
felt emboldened enough to put quite blatant messages in
his work. *The Third Love Painting* includes graffiti-like
phrases such as 'come on David admit it'. The figure in
Doll Boy is none other than Cliff Richard, who is identifi-
able by Hockney's code, 3.18, referring to Cliff's initials in
the alphabet. Hockney had a crush on the singer, who was
a British Elvis before becoming a sort of latter-day preacher
in C&A jeans. The word 'Queen' is falling from his mouth.

Where Ken Hockney would stand on his soapbox
around Bradford espousing the merits of communism, his
son considered himself an anarchist. This trait showed
itself early. On his school French examination paper, he
wrote that he had no knowledge of the subject and so
he had drawn some doodles instead. Sykes details how
the RCA initially refused to let him graduate because he
had deemed writing a 6,000-word general studies thesis
a waste of time. Realising this would reflect badly on
them, given that he was clearly one of their most gifted
students, they manufactured a face-saving miscount story.
The re-marked Hockney could not have cared less but did

seem to appreciate it was a big moment for his parents. His mum forever idolised him, even when he dyed his hair peroxide blonde and she heard neighbours sniffing about his perceived failure compared with his brothers. When he graduated, she wrote wistfully, 'Oh for the happy days when we all had so much fun at home again, but memory is a tonic.' It can be.

Hockney's reputation would grow and spread. In 1966, he went to teach in Los Angeles. He moved away from the abstract art of college days and said he wanted to depict the visible world. He became truly famous for *The Splash* after becoming fascinated by trying to capture something as intangible as water. Unsurprisingly, this is a painting of a splash in a swimming pool in front of a Californian one-storey house. Hockney noted the irony of spending so much longer on the splash than the building. Some people wondered who had jumped in. Others, including plenty in my vicinity in Yorkshire, would wonder what the fuss was about and conclude that a six-year-old could do that. It was, though, a moment frozen. Using a photograph as guide, this was a painting of memory rather than from it.

For many, Hockney will always be remembered as a man who painted nude Americans by the pool. *The Splash* sold for £23.1 million in 2020. This was small beer compared with *Portrait of an Artist (Pool with Two Figures)*, which sold for $90 million in 2018, a record for a living artist. The chief of Christie's in New York dubbed that one the 'holy grail' of Hockney's work. Art is not about money, well not all of it, and its value cannot be monetised, but even so, I do wish Mum had kept hold of those doodles.

Ken Hockney died in 1978, not long after his son had put his parents up in the Savoy so they could have easy access to his *Paper Pools* exhibition. David had flown back to California because his mother told him his dad was only in hospital for routine stuff related to his diabetes. Sometimes he would be seen staggering around Bradford, but Ken Hockney was a well-known man and people knew it was the sugar and not alcohol, and they would see him home. This time it was more serious. Hockney flew straight home after his brother called him at 6 a.m. In the *Independent*, he would say, 'My mother said, "Oh, you've come back to a sad house." In a way, at first, I was thinking of my mother more. Suddenly, a partner gone – they were about six months off their golden anniversary. My first feelings were to try and strengthen her.'

Another illness brought him home in 1997 and started one of the most celebrated Yorkshire art projects. Jonathan Silver had terminal cancer. Some 12 years younger than Hockney, Silver hated Bradford Grammar School but liked the school magazine and had the gall in the sixties to contact the former pupil to see if he would design a cover. They met at the Wimpy burger bar run by Silver's father and a deal was struck. It was easy to see why Hockney would be drawn to Silver. The son of a woman who ran a boarding house for Jewish refugees, he became a maverick entrepreneur, making a fortune from a clothing empire and trying, with some success, to drag the Swinging Sixties of Carnaby Street up north.

In the mid eighties, he upped sticks and went travelling around the world with his family for two years. 'We just accepted not going to school,' said his daughter, Zoe. On his return to the UK in 1987, he bought Salts Mill, which had finally closed the previous year, a victim of shifting times. His audacious plan was to turn it into a centre of arts and business in Shipley. Hockney was glad to help and sent 56 paintings. The old mill had once purred to the sound of 1,200 looms, boilers fired by 50 tonnes of coal a day, the metallic chug of trains on the Midlands line from London to Scotland, and men unloading raw materials from boats on the Leeds–Liverpool canal. Now it was derelict, but under Silver's guidance, it was soon hosting Opera North doing *West Side Story*. Tony Harrison recited his work there and now stands in a frame on the third floor in a thick black overcoat, a look of disappointment and, possibly, threat on his face, feet treading over books.

When Hockney returned home in 1997, Silver asked him, 'Why not come and paint Yorkshire?' He accepted the challenge. He based himself in Bridlington – what his sister Margaret called 'the seaside place for the poor' – and would paint the Wolds, a series of low chalk hills with valleys, sheep down below and crops up top, a topsy-turvy world stretching from Bridlington and Hunmanby in the north, where my Bradfordian grandparents had a bungalow looking out over a cold grey sea, down to Beverley and the northern bank of the Humber. He would take his canvases to Silver, stopping on the way to paint *Garrowby Hill* and *The Road to York Through Sledmere*.

Silver died later that year, followed by Hockney's mother in 1999. From 2004, he spent more time in Yorkshire, admitting to feeling alone and empty in LA. He started painting plein-air by the side of muddy roads in East Yorkshire. Sometimes he was captured on film. One day a car pulls up. 'Got a bit of decorating wants doing in the pub if you got a minute or two,' quips the driver. Another man, balding, in a yellow jumper the colour of dying light, wanders over and asks if he's ever been to America. He tells Hockney he lived in the house he is painting. 'I'll send you a copy if you leave your address,' says Hockney. After a pause, the man says he is off to watch the rest of the Test match. He doesn't leave his details.

Hockney worked from the attic of the house in Bridlington where his mother had spent her last years. Not everyone liked his Yorkshire world. One visitor to the 2012 exhibition at the Royal Academy suggested he had been eating magic mushrooms. The *Guardian* art critic seemed to think he had not had enough – 'garrulous, gaudy and repetitive with results low on emotion or depth'. Good for RA merchandise but not the walls. Hockney, passionate, prolific and with his soft Bradford accent not baked by California sun, could not have cared less. In time he would occasionally be portrayed as a grousing, forthright old man, sieving for stereotypes. The *Independent* asked if he was the grumpiest man in Britain. This was largely down to his anger at the smoking ban that had been introduced. 'Pubs are not health clubs,' he pointed out. He espoused an 'end bossiness soon' mantra, feeling that to ask for it now would be too bossy. The old Wesleyan chapel near his home had been turned into a skincare centre. 'At least when they built it they cared about souls,' he said. 'Now it's all about wrinkles.' It rankled.

He was still looking harder in his eighties. 'I was brought up in Bradford and Hollywood,' he said, referencing the cinema down the street where his father would laugh so hard at Laurel and Hardy that his false teeth would fall out. Now scores of Hockneys live in Salts Mill, a testament to roots and travel and imagination. Yes, it matters where you're from, but what also counts is where's your art.

Dirty etchings

It's not just Hockney who gets it from the critics. Art writers can often be grandiose masters, a bit like the music critic who decides which bands are edgy while quibbling about the temperature of the Sauvignon Blanc. Even the fifteenth-century effort on the walls of the Church of St Peter and Paul in Pickering, away to the east at the foot of the North York Moors, has been mocked. This shows religious scenes ranging from the crucifixion to the harrowing of hell, which is kind of a more upbeat Harrying of the North.

These images were whitewashed during the Protestant Reformation in the mid sixteenth century. It was a turbulent time with a boy king, Edward VI, and squabbling uncles seeking to assume power. Thomas Seymour offered the boy extra pocket money to curry favour but got carried away when he shot a spaniel during a botched kidnap attempt. He was executed. Kids, eh? That left the Duke of Somerset as Lord Protector, but unfortunately he was incompetent, and the Catholic uprisings saw him executed too. These were dangerous times now commemorated by bruised ice skaters at Somerset House each Christmas. Under Somerset, iconoclasm was king for a while and religious paintings were painted over. Anyone found hiding relics was also executed. Axes sold well.

Then, in 1852, during renovation work at the church, the paintings were exposed, much to the chagrin of Reverend Ponsonby, who would have slotted seamlessly into the sixteenth century. He wrote to the Archbishop of York saying the figures were, 'as a work of art, purely ridiculous', adding, 'especially in these dangerous days', a reference to the trend towards overturning the Reformation and reinstating old-time religion. God help us all.

The archbishop, befitting his role as patron of the Yorkshire Architectural Society, disagreed. He wrote back questioning whether obliterating relics was really in very good taste and suggesting Ponsonby did not 'meddle', at least not until copies had been made. Ponsonby, who was clearly a glass-half-full sort of scaremonger, took that as licence to knock off a few copies and then plough ahead anyway, so the paintings remained hidden until 1882 and another restoration of the church. This time Revered George Lightfoot was hailed a hero for bringing them back to life, although some sniffy critics said the new work had all gone a bit pre-Raphaelite, and what the hell were they thinking using beeswax and turpentine as a preservative because that was bound to attract dust and degradation. Nikolaus Pevsner, the eminent art historian best known for a 46-volume series on English buildings, hailed the vintage of the paintings, but added that they had been 'ruthlessly restored'. Still, given that many felt they were bad to start with, this could be seen as a good thing. In a lecture on Pickering's wall paintings, Kate Giles from the University of York said the series is unique because the scenes are in calendrical order. We can only imagine why Ponsonby seemed so keen to keep the wall covered up, but it would be no surprise if there were some dirty etchings up there.

The Strid

At the end of the eighteenth century, some 60 miles west of this great cover-up, it was not uncommon to spot one of the future greats of the art world sitting on a rock by the River Wharfe. Joseph Mallord Turner had an undeniably interesting life. The cockney child of a wigmaker and a mother who was committed to a lunatic asylum, he would end up living in snuff-addled squalor off a diet of milk and brandy spoon-fed to him by the mother of his illegitimate children. Street urchins dubbed him Puggy. Others favoured Admiral. This was some time after the Art Union of London simply called him a madman who lacked the education, manners and liberal feelings to be president of the Royal Academy. He liked Yorkshire, though, and produced sketchbooks full of his travels around the county, first visiting in 1797, when, according to a noticeboard a skimmed stone's throw away from the Strid Wood café, 'He made a quick and largely inaccurate sketch of Bolton Abbey.' Everyone's a critic.

He returned in 1808 and painted watercolours for his friend Walter Fawkes, a wealthy landowner and MP whose relative, York-based fireworks fan Guy, had tried to blow up Parliament in 1605. One of Turner's watercolours depicts Strid Wood, which is also infamous, and not only because of the £12.50 car parking fee.

The Strid is a deceptively deadly stretch of water on the Bolton Abbey estate at the bottom of the Dales. Walk down the trail between the oak and the ash, now joined by managed beech, sycamore and fir, and you might see a flycatcher, wood warbler or goosander, but you are best advised to keep your eyes on the path. The soporific hum of the Wharfe narrows to a noisier six-foot channel, and amid the dark trees, lime-green moss and browning leaves, danger lurks. We know this from the red sign that says: 'DANGER!' For extra effect it adds: 'The Strid is DANGEROUS and has claimed lives in the past. Please stand well back and beware slippery rocks.'

Some people can't help themselves and get too close. Others have tried to jump the gap and found it a chasm. It became a lover's leap and a dare, a site of doomed romance and ill-fated machismo. One YouTuber recently visited and said he used sonar to measure the depth at 63 feet. Whirlpools swirl, water is churned into a milky torrent, jagged rocks and underground caves lie unseen. I admit I used to be terrified of this place when my dad would bring us here, and Carolyn Roberts, former professor of the Environment at Gresham College, believes that fear was well placed. 'Vortices in the flow will trap bodies under the water close to the bed or sides. It's not a good place to play.'

The Strid features in Wordsworth's poem 'The Force of Prayer':

He sprang in glee – for what cared he
That the River was strong and rocks were steep?
But the Greyhound in the leash hung back
And checked him in his leap.

Dogs should not necessarily be kept on a lead, then, and poems can sometimes rhyme. The lost boy thus drowned, and his grieving mother, Alice de Romilly, bequeathed land to Augustinian monks to build Bolton Abbey and pray for him.

The Wordsworthian seal of approval gives the feel of a fable to the Strid, but newspapers have recorded deaths and near-misses for 200 years. 'Thrilling accident at the Strid', proclaimed the *Leeds Mercury* in 1857 with unseemly glee. An 1899 account of another mishap recorded an errant Huddersfield man trying to make it over the low crossing place. He slipped on a stone and fell into a 'boiling current'. The report went on: 'Fortunately, he kept his presence of mind, and whilst in the water asked one of his companions to hold out his hand.' It is reasonable to assume this was natural panic rather than presence of mind, but while the writer noted that the man did lose his hat, he was at least able to catch the train home that night.

There are sorrier tales: of Methodists gone mad; of over-cockiness (a Southport man, having made the jump, decided to jump back and perished); of 'more foolhardiness'; of a man who promised his mother he would not jump it and instead tried to see if he could straddle the divide – he couldn't. One of the most heart-rending accounts is a 1928 report from the inquest of Lilly Baines, a young woman who visited one day in a black hat and long blue fur-lined coat. She had tea at the lodge and insisted on going to see the Strid in pouring rain. A woman at the lodge named Sally Roberts was suspicious and went with her. However, Lilly broke free and jumped into the water, handbag and all. Her body was found a mile downstream. Her brother admitted she had been depressed because she had a job as a jeweller's assistant and had been told she needed to relocate to Birmingham. It was the third tragedy in as many months.

The 1998 deaths of honeymooners Lynne and Barry Collett on a day when the water rose at an alarming rate made the national news but did not stop the toll. Even those who were under the spell of the Strid sometimes fell. Arthur Reginald Smith loved the place so much he got married at Bolton Abbey. A renowned watercolourist who went to the Royal College of Art and was part of the Wharfedale Group, he illustrated *The Striding Dales*, Halliwell Sutcliffe's passionate account of his wanderings, published in 1929, and painted Bolton Abbey, the Wharfe and the Strid. Then in September 1934, he slipped. Police eventually found his easel and artist's bag by the riverside. They dragged the river to no avail and so called upon a part-time football referee from Richmond called Robert Brotton. The former army sergeant used a V-shaped copper-bound hazel twig to confirm his conviction that the body was snagged 50 yards downriver. When proved correct, he explained: 'I think I have an unusual power. I think that in me is a big store of electricity. If I carry some article of clothing from the dead person the electricity in my body has contact with that in the dead body, passing through my body and the copper wire. That makes the twig drop down.' Having recovered the body, Smith's family scattered his ashes – in the river.

Lauren Bacall gets star-struck

In 1981, an old man with two tufts of messy white hair nestling like heather on either side of a rocky outcrop sat in his studio. The cameras were rolling but he had not bothered to fix his loose tie and sunken knot. 'Yorkshire is something you can't get away from,' he said in his soft, unaffected accent. 'One doesn't want to get away from it. But unless you leave a place, unless you go and know something different, you don't know what it is.'

These words chime with me. It's a bedfellow of 'you don't know what you have until it's gone'. On the other hand, when you're a safe distance from the ills of a place, it's easier to forget them. Being from a place is about memory, however flawed, and I think that is the cruelty of

Alzheimer's. It burgles your old homes. I've already realised how support is lacking compared with those with other conditions. It seems cruel that those struggling to remember should also be so easily forgotten.

The documentary, *Henry Moore: Recollections of a Yorkshire Childhood*, was a loving one, made unsurprisingly by Yorkshire TV, which was suitably proud of one of its most successful sons. Henry Moore was by then considered the father of the modern art world, creating monumental works that had status and size. Biggest and best; this was Yorkshire exceptionalism laid bare in the form of a naked reclining figure. It was abstract but easy. Moore was the Castleford-born boy made good. And he was brave. He had served as a teenage volunteer in the Prince of Wales' Own Civil Service Rifles in the First World War and fought at the Battle of Cambrai. In a letter to his old art teacher, Alice Gostick, back in Castleford, he wrote, 'We had it very quiet the first few days but after that, things smartened up a little, we had a few selections rendered by the German big guns, the chief feature in them being the whizz-bang. The noise even during a small "strafe" is hellish.'

Moore's battalion was devastated by a mustard gas attack and he walked ten miles to a field hospital, whence he was sent home and started a long convalescence in a Cardiff hospital. When he had recovered, he went to Leeds College of Art and then, on an ex-serviceman's grant, the Royal College of Art, where he formed a great friendship with Barbara Hepworth, a middle-class woman from Wakefield who, like Moore, had been inspired by the Yorkshire landscape even as she left it. Her creative essence was distilled when accompanying her civil engineer father on his site visits around the Yorkshire Moors. Having a car, he was considered very modern as well as wealthy, and Hepworth would recall the juxtaposition of the 'granite sets, the steep hills of industrial Yorkshire' with the miner outside his ugly house or the scurrying mill girl sheltering from the wind. For Moore, this connection between the human and the land would lead to his monolithic figures growing from the very ground his father had mined. His mother would later lament him working as a sculptor, as she saw it as manual labour, and Moore himself would point out that he worked longer shifts than any miner. Like Hockney, he was a grafter.

An early inspiration was Adel Crag, a series of rock formations in the woods on the edge of Leeds. Moore would also visit Idol Rock, one of the extraordinary natural sculptures collectively known as Brimham Rocks close to Pateley Bridge in the Dales. Idol Rock is a huge lump of millstone grit dating back to the Ice Age, weighing an estimated 200 tonnes but balancing on the tip of a small stone pyramid base. For years people were told Druids had carved these strange shapes, which were given names like Dancing Bear and the Sphinx, but they were really forged by ancient rivers in times before beards and dinosaurs. Moore was smitten. So were the Bee Gees, the hirsute disco druids who featured Brimham Rocks in their video for 'You Win Again' alongside a black cat and some stills of dominoes; perhaps this was down to Maurice Gibb falling for a waitress at Batley Variety Club. Less enamoured were the five youths who pushed one of the balancing rocks off its pedestal in 2018 and watched it shatter on impact. In a moment they had shifted millions of years of history.

Moore always seemed the more iconic Yorkshire figure of the two great sculptors. That old film sees him recalling schooldays having fights with one arm tied behind his back, endless football matches in the colliery shadow, bunking off school to run to Pontefract Races and falling in a puddle. Both Moore and Hepworth sat on the Leeds table at the Royal College of Art and lived in a Hampstead colony. Hepworth would be something of a trailblazer as a posh, divorced working mother who had triplets with the artist Ben Nicholson. In the early 1930s, she was the first to produce the familiar pierced pieces that would also come to feature in Moore's work, making watchers wonder whether something was better than nothing. For a while, though, some critics just thought she was much ado about nothing.

The landscape she would become synonymous with was that of St Ives, that artists' colony and tourist trap in far-flung Cornwall, living and working in the lively light, and sniffing the smell of fish, until her death in a fire at her studios in 1975. 'Perhaps what one wants to say is formed in childhood and the rest of one's life is spent trying to say it,' she said. 'I know that all I felt during the early years of my life in Yorkshire is dynamic and constant in my life today.' Her early painting of Robin Hood's Bay on the North Yorkshire coast was testament to rootedness, and it was still a constant in the late 1950s, when a young, cocksure Yorkshire artist on a jolly in Cornwall heard that Hepworth lived nearby and knocked on her door, then asked if she could cash a cheque for £24 because he didn't have a bank account. Hepworth didn't know David Hockney, but she politely agreed to have it cashed by Newlyn Art School. Exiles stuck together. They still do.

Moore, though, would be famous first. Some were shocked by all those mothers and suckling babies because, well, it seemed a bit rude, to be honest. His wider artistic reputation was boosted by his dystopian wartime paintings of the Blitz, and then of miners at work at Wheldale Colliery, where his father had worked and decided his sons would not, but it was the reclining figures that made him. And as they grew bigger, bolder and bronzer, Moore's work began to spread around the world. Every city wanted a reclining woman to put in its park. The mayor of Toronto admitted his city was a 'hick town' until it got one. Lauren Bacall, the Hollywood star of *The Big Sleep*, had just made *The Shootist* when she visited Moore in 1976. She had already started to buy his work and was utterly starry-eyed at meeting the little Yorkshireman. 'There is no way possible to articulate my feelings after my visit to Much Hadham in Hertfordshire,' she wrote to him. 'Since then and my return to New York, I have thought and thought about that day. It was and will ever be a high point in my life.' First husband Humphrey Bogart was dead by then and unable to be offended, but divorced second husband Jason Robards was still alive. She went on, 'Some say it's dangerous to meet one's idols – but in your case, and this is true, you went far beyond expectation.'

That film about Moore's childhood does focus for a lingeringly long time on the legs of young netball players – this was not deemed bad form then, as it was all about form itself – but he seemed a bit embarrassed by this gushing from a Hollywood legend. Eventually he wrote back: 'I think of you very often and my conscience every now and then bothers me, for not having answered your letter – in fact your letter was overwhelmingly nice that I don't know to answer it – adequately.' Bacall had lots of Henry Moore pieces in her Manhattan apartment. Each had been on a long journey from the mind of a boy who learnt to use his hands when rubbing down his mother's arthritic back, through the landscape of industrial Yorkshire, and then on to 1 West 72nd Street, overlooking Central Park.

A few months after Bacall's death in 2014, her estate sold two Moore bronzes. Maybe they needed the space, or it could just have been that Bacall's custodians did not like them. Not everybody did. Indeed, the more popular Moore got, the more he became a figure of fun, and worse. It was as if he epitomised the Yorkshire ethos of everything being brilliant in God's country, a place with a sure sense of self but not much self-awareness. Moore was that Yorkshire braggadocio in monumental form. Hence, when he said in 1967 that he was prepared to gift £1 million worth of his work to the Tate Gallery, much was made of the proviso that it be adequately displayed and not buried in some dusty storeroom. Sir Charles Wheeler, former president of the Royal Academy, was first out of the blocks, pointing out that great works of today may be 'bronze oddities' tomorrow. After Harold Wilson, the prime minister of Huddersfield and other places, had pledged £200,000 towards an extension for the exhibits, others stepped forward. No fewer than 41 artists signed an open letter to *The Times*, complaining about the cost and size of the works, but mainly venting their grievance about Moore's reputation. 'Whoever is picked out for this exceptional place will necessarily seem to represent the triumph of modern art in our society. The radical nature of art in the twentieth century is inconsistent with the notion of an heroic and monumental role for the artist and any attempt to predetermine greatness for an individual in a publicly financed form of permanent enshrinement is a move we as artists repudiate.'

Anthony Caro, one of Moore's old assistants, went further in the *Observer*. 'My generation abhors the idea of a father figure and his work is bitterly attacked by artists and critics under forty when it fails to measure up to the outsize scale it has been given.'

Moore was hurt, but this sort of backlash would endure long after his death in 1986. Thirty years later, an op-ed in Columbia University's in-house magazine was beside itself at the proposal to install *Reclining Figure* outside the Butler Library in New York. It was a 'hideous sculpture', an 'offensive project', suggestive of 'a dying mantis or poorly formed pterodactyl', 'an idealisation of a chewed wad of gum', 'a war on our spirit', 'a monstrosity' and an 'arrogant middle finger to the world'. They didn't like it. Not suitable for their tiny strip of grass in Manhattan, they said. More than 1,000 students protested. Lauren Bacall was not around to fight back. In the end, they stuck it by the maths department.

That op-ed also referenced another phenomenon in the Moore saga, namely the theft of his works. 'The sculpture is so repulsive that when thieves stole Moore's original cast, valued at £3 million, they literally chopped it up and sold it for scrap,' it ranted. This was partly true, albeit it seems unlikely that the gang of thieves critically appraised their two-tonne haul before deciding to melt it down. In 2005, they had broken into the grounds of the Henry Moore Foundation in Much Hadham and used a crane to lift the 12-foot-tall statue onto a lorry. They were caught on camera, but the mystery endured. Romantics liked to think this was the work of an international art thief, probably with a moniker involving 'Fox', but the bosses at the Art Loss Register said the sculpture was not stolen to order. Jimmy Johnson, who had been accused of crimes ranging from murder to stealing a caravan but was best known for robbing stately homes, tipped off detectives that a band of travellers had taken it to a Dagenham scrap dealer. It then went to Rotterdam and possibly China. Caro and the Columbia students were presumably ruled out early.

It was one of many thefts. At one time, the Art Loss Register had 47 Moore works logged as stolen and unrecovered. One small sculpture did surface in a Sainsbury's carrier bag in a London taxi. A sundial and plinth were also stolen from Much Hadham and sold for £46, suggesting those thieves also knew little about the value of art. That one made BBC's *Crimewatch* and led to two men getting 12 months. Hepworth, too, became a target. Her *Two Forms (Divided Circle)* was stolen from a London park next to the South Circular. The chairman of Dulwich Park Friends said it felt like he'd lost a finger, but not the middle one that so offended New York students. This one hurt. 'A sickening epidemic,' said the council leader.

International art magazine *Apollo* even published an article titled 'The Long Tradition of Hating Henry Moore'. In 1995, the *King and Queen* on the Glenkiln estate in Dumfries were decapitated. Someone threw a brick at *Family Group* in Harlow. People, real and sculpted, were losing their heads.

Moore himself had become a pacifist after his wartime experiences and was a committed socialist with an interest in taking art to the masses. Hence his delight when *Draped Seated Woman* was sold to another London council back in 1962 for a knock-down £6,000. For years the oversized woman with a tiny head nestled amid three 17-storey tower blocks in the East End. Old Flo, as she became known, survived longer than the blocks on Jamaica Street, but different incarnations of the council fought each other. The mayor of Tower Hamlets said he wanted to sell the sculpture for £20 million to cover budget cuts. He was found guilty of electoral fraud. It ended up in Canary Wharf, ignored by cocaine-fuelled suits for years to come. All this angst was summed up by art critic Jonathan Jones, who opined that claiming Moore and Hepworth as great modern artists was plain daft. At least Hepworth was 'hard to hate', but neither was cutting edge. 'Modern art's true home was never St Ives or Yorkshire,' he concluded. 'Pretending that it was is complacent, insular and either intellectually dishonest or genuinely stupid.'

It seems a bit strong. Michael Paraskos has told me just how cutting edge Yorkshire had once been. 'There is a contradiction in the idea of Yorkshire culture,' he said. 'The culture may have conservative values, but it sees itself as not the same as cultures elsewhere. We might have to think of Yorkshire almost as a sense of difference.'

Moore and Hepworth could not get away from Yorkshire and so now some of their works are in the Yorkshire Sculpture Park, a vast collection set in 500 acres of parkland on the border between West and South and tucked alongside the M1. All sorts of artworks live here, from the pieces that grow from the ground to the ones standing in blissed-out incongruousness. Damien Hirst is over there, with his girl with the calliper and the charity box crowbarred. A unicorn has been flayed nearby. A depiction of a CIA detention centre is over the hill. Moore and Hepworth are here too, like old custodians but still provoking. 'I don't get it,' says one woman as she stands before the massive *Large Two Forms*. Like Hockney's teacher said, sometimes you have to look harder. Maybe even squint. I walk on until I get to the neon sign by Hilary Jack, by a lake, moulding Amelia Earhart's words into a clarion call.

NO BORDERS
JUST HORIZONS
ONLY FREEDOM

7

YORKISTS

York does not belong in Yorkshire, Northerners confirm

Headline on The Daily Mash, spoof website, 2022

Eboracum to the Romans, Eoforwic to the Angles, Jorvik to the Vikings and a good place for a booze-up to generations of stag and hen parties despite the 365-pub claim being an urban myth, what was sometimes called Yerk in medieval times is atypically pretty. It was made the capital of Britannia Inferior by the Romans (effectively the north), of Danelaw by the Vikings and even of England for six months by Charles I in 1642 (for Civil War convenience). A city of great buildings, conflicts and mystery, York is a badge of honour even though many in Yorkshire never go there.

The Wars of the Roses (or one rose and an antelope)

I lived by battlefields. If you left our house in Stutton and turned right at Fag Ash Lil's, walked down the hill and followed Mill Lane, you came to the beck. This was a brown stream that gently flowed under the road, a little oasis trickling through the onset of a wood that was often carpeted by bluebells. Every autumn kids would throw sticks at the horse chestnut canopies and splice open spiky flesh to find conkers. The more devious would then soak them in vinegar or bake them. Knuckles were rapped. Streaks spun.

We would look for water voles down by the beck. In the woods I never did see a badger, but the holes in the soft earth by knotty roots and the confused cries of dogs showed they were there in their subterranean labyrinth. It was a time when cars did not line the roads with carcasses or interrupt boys playing sticks. Rabbits would dart about the meadow beyond an ever-locked fence.

Yet it was not always that nice. The beck was Cock Beck. To the north it would turn right and flow into the River Wharfe in Tadcaster, but barely a mile to the south it ran alongside the Towton battlefield. It was here that it once ran red with blood, dammed by the drowned bodies of fleeing soldiers. It is estimated that in this field that looks down towards Saxton and up to Tadcaster, around 50,000 soldiers took part in 1461 in the bloodiest battle ever fought on British soil. The spillage was so bad that some claimed the blood fertilised the earth with iron and gave rise to the notion of a white rose flecked with red. The Towton rose was probably just a common form of *Rosa spinosissima*, and was the bane of a local farmer, who dug them up to annoy souvenir-hunters, but it summed up the thorny issue of making sense from the Wars of the Roses.

Generations of cricket and football fans believe the rivalry between Yorkshire and Lancashire clubs has an umbilical attachment to the Wars of the Roses, which lasted from 1455 to around 1487, although such conflicts rarely have definite endings. These folk are deluded. The Wars of the Roses might have become emblematic of a rivalry, of noisy neighbours and of a love of place, but the popular retelling has been so heavily spun that it is easy to become snared in a web of lies and medieval PR. The bare fact is that the bulk of Yorkshire was actually on the other side, fighting for the Lancastrians. This was not due to any great love of the House of Lancaster's schizophrenic king, Henry VI, but simply down to self-interest. Needs must. At its most basic level, the Wars of the Roses were a power struggle between the families of two sons of Edward III. John of Gaunt was one of them. His House of Lancaster had ruled for decades, but only after *his* son, Henry Bolingbroke (aka Henry IV), had usurped Richard II. The Duke of Clarence was the other, and the Yorkist claim was down to his daughter, Philippa, who had married into the powerful Mortimer family.

On Palm Sunday 1461, what was effectively a civil war had been raging for six years. Much of this was down to the enmity between the Duke of York, Richard Plantagenet, and the Duke of Somerset, Edmund Beaufort. With Henry VI suffering a complete mental breakdown in 1453, York was effectively in charge, and he used his position to put Somerset in the Tower of London. However, in these turbulent times of political machinations and power plays, Somerset was soon back in favour with Queen Margaret, possibly in the romantic sense to boot. Henry recovered in 1455 and York was cast out once more. He colluded with Richard Neville, the 16th Earl of Warwick – who would become known as 'the Kingmaker' – to strike back.

Somerset's death at the otherwise minor Battle of St Albans in 1455 meant the pendulum swung and York

(Richard Plantagenet), who had captured King Henry, was back in the ascendancy. The Act of Accord in October 1460 gave succession rights to Richard and his heirs. Queen Margaret was understandably unimpressed, and it all turned sour when her Lancastrian forces dealt a body blow with victory at the Battle of Wakefield two months later. York himself was killed and his severed head was adorned with a paper crown and set on Micklegate Bar, where a million York pub crawls have since commenced on a cobbled hill.

York's heir, Edward, Earl of March, inherited his claim to the throne, and for now, aided by Warwick, routed the Lancastrians at Mortimer's Cross and marched into London in March 1461 to assume the crown. The Great Chronicle of London stated: 'It was demanded of the said people whether the said Henry was worthy to reign as king any longer or no. Whereupon the people cried hugely and said, "Nay! Nay!" And after it was asked of them whether they would have the Earl of March for their king, they cried with one voice, "Yea! Yea!"' It seems a dubious way to determine a divine right, but it meant Towton was a chance to underscore the teenage Edward's fitness for the role.

It began badly for the Lancastrian army, headed by the new Duke of Somerset. The House of York was led by Edward IV, Warwick and the Duke of Norfolk, with the late Richard's brother-in-law, Baron Fauconberg, showing his military skill by utilising the strong wind to destructive effect. Thousands of his men's arrows flew into Lancastrian land and bodies. Blinded by sleet, they had no choice but to advance, and while the poleaxe was not ideal for hand-to-hand combat, they managed to shed some blood, but it merely merged with the snow to make movement hazardous. The Duke of Norfolk's troops then came around the foot of the plateau and struck the Lancastrian flank. Thousands were trapped in land between North Acres and Towton Dale. The Lancastrians' Lord Dacre was struck in the head by a crossbow bolt, and finally, after hours of combat, the Lancastrian line also became porous and then shapeless. Men fled a tripping, desperate path down the slope to Cock Beck. Sixteenth-century historian Edward Hall states that Edward said 'no prisoner should be taken, not one enemy saved'. Thousands were slain as a result. Some drowned. George Neville, the Lord Chancellor, wrote that the dead bodies would cover an area of six miles by three. Some Lancastrians made it to Tadcaster, where they were hunted down and made to drink Sam Smith's. The savagery was beyond anything that had preceded it and the heads of Lancastrian nobles now adorned Micklegate Bar.

We never went on a school trip to Towton. In fact, I don't remember anyone ever mentioning it. It was a small afterthought place. Maybe the bloodiest battle in history is not something to remember. Around 28,000 people are believed to have died that day, and it changed the rules of engagement. Warwick would change sides in one of history's great flip-flops, irate at either Edward's foreign policy or his marriage to a commoner, Elizabeth Woodville, and would briefly reinstall Henry VI on the throne before Edward and his brother, the future Richard III, drew on Burgundy's support and quashed the Lancastrians in Barnet, of all places. Warwick was killed. The following month, Henry's heir, also Prince Edward, suffered the same fate at the Battle of Tewkesbury, another bloody mess that inspired Shakespeare to open his play *Richard III* with the lines:

'Now is the winter of our discontent/Made glorious summer by this sun of York.'

Henry VI was then murdered, almost certainly on King Edward's orders and possibly by the hand of the future Richard III. After that, peace broke out. Edward saw out his reign in relative harmony, if you can overlook the small blip of having his turncoat brother, George, Duke of Clarence, murdered, supposedly by drowning the heavy drinker in a butt of Malmsey wine.

Edward's death from a stroke in 1483 led to one of the most scandalous and debated events in the history of the British monarchy. His son, Edward V, was only 12 but was now the rightful king. Or was he? Parliament was told to buy the story that Edward IV had already been betrothed to someone else when he married Elizabeth Woodville, thus meaning their children were illegitimate.

Richard, Duke of Gloucester, the late king's brother, was now an increasingly powerful figure. Edward V and his younger brother, confusingly another Richard and another Duke of York, were put in the Tower, supposedly for their own safety. Richard became king. The princes were never seen again, assumed murdered, with Richard the likely villain. Even by medieval standards of skulduggery this was something else, and it troubled the likes of the Duke of Buckingham, who joined Henry Tudor, the Lancastrian claimant to the throne, in rebelling. An alternative reading has Buckingham as the killer. Either way, Buckingham lost his head for this, but Tudor won the Battle of Bosworth in 1485, when Richard tried to engage his rival in hand-to-hand combat, only to become stranded in a bog. Outnumbered and, finally, outmanoeuvred, Richard III met his fate with a bravery out of kilter with historical appraisal. 'The bloody dog is dead,' says Henry in the last act of *Richard III*.

> *England hath long been mad, and scarr'd herself;*
> *The brother blindly shed the brother's blood,*
> *The father rashly slaughter'd his own son,*
> *The son, compell'd, been butcher to the sire:*
> *All this divided York and Lancaster.*

And so began the Tudor age

The Battle of Old Bones

More than 500 years later, a woman named Philippa Langley said she believed the remains of Richard III were buried in Leicester Social Services car park. The idea that he was somewhere around there was not new. Richard's body, 'despoiled to the skin', was trussed up and placed on a horse before being paraded through Leicester and buried in a friary, although some claimed it had been thrown into the River Soar. Langley was adamant. 'I knew I was standing on Richard's grave.' In an ensuing Channel 4 documentary, a historian points out there was a letter R on the tarmac, which gave credence to those thinking that whatever these people found, they might be a couple of ribs short of a full set.

Yet you have to credit Langley's persistence, even if certain scenes in *The King in the Car Park* are emotionally perplexing, not least when she is overcome when discussing putting the Royal Standard on a cardboard box containing what, at that point, may or may not be his remains. The looks on the faces of those with a scientific background, one clad in a white CSI boilersuit, speak volumes. Later, Langley is also upset that the bones are being raked over by another group of experts, although it is hard to know with any accuracy the right level of respect for exhuming some old villain you never knew.

However, in 2013, the University of Leicester confirmed that mitochondrial DNA evidence showed these were indeed the bones of Richard III. Cue an almighty fight for the right to bury him again. The university wanted him interred at Leicester Cathedral, in keeping with the archaeological idea that any excavation of a Christian burial should see the bones or body placed in the nearest consecrated ground. But some claimed Richard had wanted to be buried at York Minster. After all, he was significant as the pre-eminent northern nobleman of his time after assuming Warwick's land in Yorkshire and Cumberland. He also spent some of his childhood at Middleham Castle in Wensleydale and modernised castles and estates from Scarborough to Richmond. He effectively ruled Yorkshire long before becoming king, training to be a knight in the Dales, doing his best to fend off the downward salvos of the Scots, and fighting for York's particular rights. By 1477, he was calling a trip to York 'a homecoming', despite being born in Northamptonshire, and when he became king, he ensured the northern lands were exempt from the clerical taxation being levied in the south.

There was more to him being regarded as the only medieval king closely associated with Yorkshire. Not least by setting up the Council of the North, a sort of devolved powerhouse based in Wakefield and York. And perhaps most telling regarding his funeral plans – lest we forget, he was only 32 at the end – he set up a college of 100 priests at York Minster. Clearly this offcumden liked the place.

The Plantagenet Society, which claimed to comprise descendants of the king and included one man who ran a nightclub in Kansas, threatened legal action over the reburial location and said there had been a breach of human rights. 'Who do we think we are?' said one member in response to the scratched heads. 'We don't think we are anyone. We know who we are. We are the collateral descendants of Richard III and we speak on behalf of him. We know what he wanted.' The Secretary of State for Justice dubbed it 'this nonsensical case' as the Ministry of Justice's legal costs rose to £175,000.

The *Leicester Mercury* archives are full of indignation. Why was the university having to find £28,000 in legal fees to email a bloke from a Kansas roadhouse? How on earth could they countenance putting on a performance of *Richard III* in the cathedral grounds? Why did the new stained-glass window show Richard trussed up on a horse?

In 2013, a reporter from the *Mercury* went to York to see what they thought.

'He should be buried in York,' says Mike Howden, a market trader. 'Because he was the Duke of York.'

The writer points out he was in fact the Duke of Gloucester.

'Oh,' says Mike. 'Look, I'm not actually that bothered.'

Another trader, Gordon David, 64, adds, 'Leave him where he is, the poor bugger. He's had enough.'

The writer wears a Leicester City–Richard III hybrid shirt. He is biased but, not unreasonably, he points out that York's contribution to the Battle of Bosworth was 80 men who turned up late.

Richard stayed in Leicester and was reinterred in the cathedral in 2015 with a solemnity that makes me wonder whether we should have laughed on that Cornish cliff as seagulls scattered.

This tit-for-tat had echoed down the years. A 2015 report said Richard III had been worth £59 million to the local Leicester economy, and up in York one angry pensioner told the Dean of York she should 'burn in hell fires for ever' for not doing enough for the Yorkist case. He was fined £85 and admitted he'd had a drink. An attempt by online trolls to give low ratings to the Leicester visitor centre petered out despite a poster from North Dakota suggesting Madame Tussaud could have done better on a three-day bender.

Leicester had 34,477 names on their petition to Parliament for Richard to remain in the city. York only managed 31,134 for him to be reburied at York Minster. Case closed. There was a parade. It was no solace that Jack Greene of Coddington wrote to the *Mercury* to state that it was 'probably the most boring procession ever to have taken place on the streets of Leicester. One can't help thinking that York would have made a better job.'

Bad reputation

It was stuff and nonsense, but it told us something about tribal bonds and the paucity of good daytime TV. More fascinating than where Richard's bones should be is the attempt to reclaim the last Yorkist king from the villainous stereotype and medieval propaganda.

I contact Matt Lewis, the chairman of the Richard III Society, who says it started with scholars such as Polydore Vergil and Thomas More.

'In those days people did not write history in the way we recognise it,' he says. 'History was a branch of rhetoric and a part of political teaching. It always had to have a moral message. They weren't writing literal history. As C. S. Lewis said, "Rhetoric is the greatest barrier between us and our ancestors." Thomas More is writing about the idea of tyranny. He can't do that about Henry VIII or he will lose his head, but there's nobody to offend if you write about Richard. And every time you retell a story, you need a reason, so you make it nastier, stormier, maybe add a crime somewhere. The idea of Richard as an archetypal villain builds until it reaches a pinnacle with Shakespeare.' He has a point. In the opening monologue from *Richard III*, the eponymous villain explains he is not shaped for sportive tricks, and dogs bark at him. 'But I love the play and think Shakespeare might be horrified that we try to treat it as a documentary,' adds Lewis.

The end of the Tudors in 1603 had spawned a fashion for revisionism, and antiquarian George Buck was the first to write a scholarly defence of Richard, in the early seventeenth century. As for Shakespeare, Lewis believes his play was partly allegorical and that the hunchback villain was meant to make contemporary audiences think of Robert Cecil, the Earl of Salisbury, who was promoting James I as the successor to Elizabeth. 'If we believe Shakespeare was a recusant Catholic as people suggest, we can see him playing out a succession crisis in 1483 and applying it to the modern day. Cecil had curvature of the spine, and so when an audience in the 1590s sees this hunchback shuffling on stage and telling of all the dastardly deeds he is going to perform, I think they would have been elbowing each other.'

But why the obsession with a king who only reigned for a couple of years? Lewis says it is the sense of injustice. The society is not here to whitewash a reputation

but to do a serious investigation, although calling themselves Ricardians does suggest opinions may have been
preformed. Yet he says there is evidence that Richard was a
very different sort of person to the one we believe. Exhibit
One: when the husband of Katherine Williamson was
murdered in Barmby in the East Riding, the three guilty
brothers and their father went to Richard, then the Duke
of Gloucester, to serve and gain protection. They believed
the age-old convention of livery and maintenance would
cover them, effectively the rich looking after their mates.
However, when Richard heard the truth from Williamson,
he locked up the father and the brothers had to escape.
'Richard wanted to send out a message that he did not
want criminals in his affinity,' says Lewis. 'These were not
people he wanted to recruit.'

It hints at a basic level of decency, and there are other
cases of him championing the lower classes against their
superiors. On another occasion he supported a servant of
Cecily Neville, his mother, when a wealthy man tried to claim
her property. When the man said he had Richard's backing,
he received a letter telling him never to use the king's name
in such a manner again. 'He was defying the norms.'

This also extended to removing fish garths, enclosures
that noblemen put into rivers on their estates to catch fish
on an industrial scale. Richard not only got rid of these
from his own lands but also instructed other northern
nobles to do likewise, thus improving the spoils for the
rank and file downriver. Lewis says it is hard to see how
doing this enhanced his own status or brought him any
political leverage.

'We know from letters he wrote to bishops when he was
Duke of Gloucester that he was vocal about corruption. Part

of my interpretation of why people supported Henry Tudor is no one cared when Richard was doing all this in the north because he was only the king's brother, but the middling gentry classes in the south of England did incredibly well out of Edward IV's reign and suddenly they were finding it all shut down. They go looking for someone to replace Richard.'

According to Lewis's theory – and he accepts that that is all it can be – this is where the story of the princes' murders was invented. 'Go fight for Henry Tudor at Bosworth and you can't say "Can I have my corruption back?" You need a good reason for it and that could be the princes in the Tower. You need a chivalric cloak to throw over what you have done. "Oh yeah, those boys, nobody knows what became of them. I'll say it was because of them." I actually think Richard was socially progressive and might have made real changes. They are only theories. Other people will read the same stuff and say it's nonsense.'

Indeed, it seems remarkably timely that the boy king would go missing at a time when Richard was newly on the throne. Perhaps scepticism dictates that in an era of torturous ethics and casual killing for political ends, it is hard to reclaim Richard as a do-gooder.

I go walking across the bloody meadow of Towton. There are no roses today. We do know that the House of York used the white rose as their emblem in battle, but the Lancastrians did not widely use a red rose until later. Indeed, Henry VI preferred an antelope. Henry VII, however, saw the benefits of a decent logo and merged the white and red into the Tudor rose, thus underscoring his popular role as peacemaker.

This is a peaceful place now, with a few noticeboards and an old rugged cross. I walk on and try to follow the course of

Cock Beck, then climb back up the scorched slope and carry on to the graveyard in Saxton where Lord Dacre is buried. In 1861, a horse's skull was discovered nearby, varnishing the tale of him being buried upright on his horse. Then in 1996, 43 skeletons were found and studied at Bradford University, where the catalogue of injuries led archaeologists to deduce that ears had been cut off.

I pass the Crooked Billet pub, where my dad would occasionally call in for a game of cards and where the Earl of Warwick, whose heraldic emblem was a bear and ragged staff, was said to have set up camp the night before the battle. Nowadays it is trying hard to be a country pub in a time when drink-driving is frowned upon, but it is offering a Yorkshire pudding challenge. If you can wade through a three-course meal comprising a Yorkshire pudding and gravy, a giant Yorkshire pudding with sausages, jambalaya or chicken curry, and then a Yorkshire pudding stuffed with vanilla ice cream and sticky toffee sauce, you will make the wall of fame. It costs £16.50 and your health. The man behind the bar used to hand out the key for the car park Portakabin, which had a small exhibition – about the battle, not cholesterol.

The Battle of Marston Moor

The Wars of the Roses gave a nice but erroneous heading to a series of local feuds that spiralled into violence. The Yorkists' power was actually in the Welsh Marches and Shropshire. The seat of the House of York was in Northamptonshire. It was only Richard III who created the attachment to Yorkshire that gave free rein to half-cut sports fans half a millennium later.

We had moved to a house on a hill by a pig farm just before my dad died and I went south. After that, Mum moved to Long Marston, a few miles west of York. It was a nice white house with room for Mum's Gordon setter, Arnie. It was also a short walk away from Marston Moor. Towton was supposedly the bloodiest battle fought in Britain, and Marston Moor in 1644 was the largest since then. This time it was the Civil War, and the battle lines were clearer, the Royalists on one side and the Parliamentarians and Scottish Covenanters on the other. Or Cavaliers and Roundheads, if you prefer.

I go back and stand by another monument and another featureless field flattened as far as the eye can see by a portentous sky. We are 537 years away from Richard III's death, but a new film, *The Lost King*, is out about finding his bones. It is 561 years since the Battle of Towton, and the Palm Sunday Archers still muster once a month at the Crooked Billet to talk about old times and add a frisson of danger to the beer garden. It is 378 years since the Battle of Marston Moor, where ghosts still hover a mile from Mum's old house.

In the years between the two great battles, Yorkshire staged a rebellion in 1489 when asked to raise money to help Brittany in its own duel with France. Typically, Yorkshire folk did not see what it had to do with them. The Earl of Northumberland was killed. The rebels' leader was hanged. The north became a foreign field to the monarchy, and Henry VIII later exacerbated the divide when he dissolved the monasteries. In the late 1530s, the great North Yorkshire abbeys at Rievaulx, Jervaulx and Fountains were seized and stripped of valuables. More rebellions followed as discontent with the Tudors mounted, half-blind Robert

Aske leading the Pilgrimage of Grace in which large swathes of the Catholic north revolted, initially in York. Aske was sufficiently influential to meet Henry VIII and issued demands including a Parliament of the North, but soon found himself executed at Clifford's Tower in York.

Bigod's Rebellion took place in 1537, led by Sir Francis Bigod, who hailed from Scarborough and feared the king would seek revenge for the Pilgrimage of Grace. Bigod was actually a Protestant, but railed against the influence of theologian Thomas Erastus, who said Christian sins should be punished by the state. He was hanged for treason. Thirty-two years later, the Rising of the North began, and Catholic nobles conspired to replace Elizabeth I with Mary, Queen of Scots. Everyone knows Mary was executed, but the scattergun viciousness of Elizabethan reprisals has largely disappeared from standard history. More than 600 people were executed as the Dales were purged. Land and goods were seized, families ruined or killed, and a deep hatred spread in the fault line. This may have been the true origin of the north–south divide and a faithlessness in London-centric altruism that endures to debates about levelling up.

In her 1921 book *The King's Council in the North*, Rachel Robertson Reid calls the north a natural refuge of lost causes. They won some, they lost some, but Yorkshire has been a favourite venue for historic battles. Stamford Bridge, where King Harold saw off the Norwegian invaders in 1066 only to meet his fate three weeks later, is seven miles from York. The Archbishop of York himself raised troops to fight King David of Scotland in 1138 in what was known as the Battle of the Standard due to the consecrated banners on show. Others called it Northallerton, which is only 30 miles from York. The fourteenth century saw no let-up in the bloodshed, from Boroughbridge, where Edward II defeated his rebel barons (16 miles from York) to Byland Moor, where Robert the Bruce secured a significant victory in the Wars of Scottish Independence (23 miles from York), both in 1322. The first of the Anglo-Scottish wars came at Myton, three years earlier and three miles from Boroughbridge, when many religious men were cut down by the banks of the Swale. It was dubbed the White Battle due to the religious garments despoiled by blood.

Into the fifteenth century, and Henry IV ended the Percy rebellion at Bramham Moor just down the A64 in 1408. Then in 1642, King Charles I demanded access to Hull's mighty arsenal. Hull was not having this, and John Hotham, the governor of Hull, stood firm for the Parliamentarians. Effectively, this was the start of the Civil War. Even off the shores there was fighting, notably the Battle of Flamborough Head in 1779, in which John Paul Jones (not the one from Led Zeppelin) became a star of the American War of Independence, despite being a Scotsman who had killed a mutineer. Yorkshire, it is fair to say, liked a scrap.

By the time we'd got to the Civil War, between 1642 and 1651, Yorkshire, then as now, was not a homogenous entity when it came to allegiances. West Yorkshire was largely Parliamentarian, but many in the county were Royalist or ambivalent. That was not the case by the time Parliamentarian Sir Thomas Fairfax, aka Black Tom, marched across the Pennines and into Yorkshire in 1644 and occupied Selby. This was serious news for the Royalists, and the Marquess of Newcastle returned from the far north, where he was dealing with the Scots, to ensure York remained a royal stronghold. Fairfax and Alexander Leslie, the Earl of Leven, then began the siege of York.

When word of this reached King Charles I in Oxford, he decided to send in dashing nephew Prince Rupert. Handsome and headstrong, the Prague-born Rupert had already lived an eventful life. He had been jailed during the Thirty Years War, but had enjoyed enough privilege to become a decent tennis player, take up etching and engage in a passionate romance with his jailer's daughter. By the time he became a prominent figure in English history, he was known for both his savagery when it came to killing – which some have suggested was a mere cultural difference rather than a personality trait – and his pet white poodle, Boy, which Parliamentarians enjoyed claiming was a sort of witch's familiar. This, in turn, led to Royalist satirists mocking such superstitious hokum by arguing that Boy was actually a lady from Lapland who had transformed herself by occult means and had the gift of catching bullets in her teeth. Alas, this was categorically refuted when Boy was shot dead during the coming battle.

Rupert's skill meant he had waltzed through the north-west, drumming up support, and he raised the siege of York. Via an ambiguous letter from the king, Rupert felt he had orders not to settle at this and to defeat the allied army too. So while York was relieved in the military sense, he was not about to go south quietly. With two huge armies gathered on Yorkshire soil, a fight was looming, and so the Royalists and the allied besiegers met at Marston Moor.

Both sides were weary. The allied troops drank from puddles while the Royalists just got drunk. There was also bickering between Rupert, with his ego akin to *Blackadder*'s Lord Flashheart, and Newcastle, more senior, more cautious and a man whose wisdom had seen him employ a friendly poet as his artillery chief. Newcastle arrived on the field five hours late, and lost more time as he rounded up his crack infantry unit of 'Whitecoats'.

Despite the presence of 28,000 allied forces and 18,000 Royalists, the locals of Marston Moor were unaware of history forming in the morning mist. In his book *Prince Rupert*, Charles Spencer says one disgruntled farm labourer was told to get off the battlefield. When he asked why, he was told that a battle between the king and Parliament was about to kick off. 'Whaat! Has them two fallen out then?'

Initially Rupert seemed to have the initiative. He was in a good position with a ditch ahead of him and a hedge on one flank lined with musketeers. For several hours not much happened. Edward Lamplough, a nineteenth-century historian, claims this was down to a mutual awe at the significance of what was to come. Nevertheless, some fire was exchanged and Oliver Cromwell's nephew, Walton, was one of those to fall. Undaunted, Rupert tucked into his supper and Newcastle took solace in a pipe, meaning it was the Earl of Manchester's men who tried to cross the ditch first for the Parliamentarians, while 'Cromwell's magnificent cuirassiers swept forward to clear the same formidable obstacle and engage the enemy's right.'

Men were spread across a two-mile front and the allied infantry had some early success, only for the cavalry brigade that Rupert had put into reverse to trot forward and wreak carnage on the attackers. Not much fancying the mounting odds, Black Tom Fairfax fled the field for Leeds.

As the battle wound its savage way to a conclusion, it seemed Rupert might be on the cusp of victory, despite the efforts of Cromwell and his Ironsides. Rupert's failure to see it through has been variously put down to his impetuosity, his inability to act as a commander-in-chief and even his bloodlust. What we know with reasonable certainty is that he charged after the Scots cavalry, and this left the Royalist infantry exposed. As Lamplough wrote, 'Had Rupert succoured his centre at this stage of the battle he must have compelled the Parliamentarians to yield.'

Cromwell was wounded in the neck, but Leslie took over and saw off Rupert's men. Around 3,200 Royalists were killed compared with only 800 allies. Rupert saved himself by hurdling a fence into a field. Like the field, he was still full of beans. Newcastle, whose Whitecoats fought to the bitter, bloody end, was shamed by the north's defeat and did the decent thing and emigrated. Rupert suffered an even worse fate and went to Lancashire. He ended his days having an affair with a Drury Lane actress with whom he had a daughter called Ruperta. No, really.

The Civil War segued into Naseby, the beheading of Charles I and England the Republic. As Lamplough put it, 'The King's affairs never recovered from the results of this battle, and the royal cause undoubtedly received its death-blow on Marston Moor, when the last of the Yorkshire battles was fought.'

The wrath of God

Despite this penchant for violence, York is still a beautiful city. These days it is besieged by stags and hens, ghost tours, and teenage tourists who block the narrow medieval streets, not because Margaret Clitherow lived here and was pressed to death in 1586 beneath her own door for the crime of harbouring priests, which is grisly, dramatic and even inspiring, given that she refused to enter a plea to avoid her children having to testify and risk torture, but because the Shambles may or may not have been the inspiration for Diagon Alley in the Harry Potter books. So you can buy a wand here, or a ghost, or a York snow globe, but you can no longer buy dead meat fresh from the slaughterhouses in the back rooms that gave the bloody place its name, a shamble being a stool and then a table and then a meat market.

The centrepiece of York, though, is the Minster, and Neil Sanderson, who gives me a tour, is a fount of Minsterly knowledge. He is also the director of the York Minster Fund and needs to find £20,000 a day to run the building. For a money man, he has an appealingly boyish delight in the Minster's stories. He tells me that some sort of building has been on this site since 627, but it might have been over the way at St Michael le Belfrey. The story of a building moves on with William the Conqueror, who was crowned on Christmas Day 1066 by the Archbishop of York. 'It was the Archbishop of York because the Archbishop of Canterbury had been fighting against him at Hastings,' says Neil. A pause. 'And he had been killed.' Neil has a dry sense of humour that I feel would go down well on ghost tours if he didn't have to spend his time finding £7.3 million a year. As well as harrying the north, the Normans exerted their power by building big churches and castles. As Neil explains, 'The prevailing attitude was "Look at the size of this. God's on our side. You better behave."'

As William declined to say whether York or Canterbury was more important, the duelling archbishops proceeded to massage their egos and marshal their masons. It was the great British build-off. The oldest bit of the Minster above ground dates to 1220, but bits were added on thereafter. Indeed, if you enter from the west end and look down the vast innards, you see the door to the choir is not in the middle. That reflects the different stages in development and the whims of change.

The nave is a communal space where markets would have been held. The further east we walk, the holier it gets. Neil points to the pink hue on the pillars and says it is a stain from the 1840 fire. 'You can see the history in the stone,' he says, before turning me around and showing me the Heart of Yorkshire window. 'You see the heart in the tracery? That represents the heart of God. Then you see various lines of characters in the window: disciples, saints, bishops – you can tell bishops from the pointy hats – right down to where the current archbishop would enter. That's a direct symbolic link from God to now.'

We walk down the nave and look at the Kings' Screen, which is a row of statues of William and the 14 English monarchs following him. It is an interesting procession, culminating in the Lancastrian kings. It features Henry IV despite the fact he had the Archbishop of York beheaded out the back, which led to people making a martyr of him. Henry VI is there too; he also became venerated after his murder, and indeed his statue was removed for many years to discourage unseemly shows of worship. Even York Minster did not seem sure whether it was Yorkist or Lancastrian.

We turn left into the Chapter House, with its circle of carved stone seats. This is where the canons came to laud God and themselves. Each paid a tithe, and it was the same whether your area was large, like Masham on the edge of the moors, or the size of a domestic garden, like Dunnington in the city of York. Scandals about the dubious distribution inevitably ensued. Neil shows me a model of the structure of the Chapter House, which is almost 850 years old. 'See these spliced oak beams,' he says, pointing to the roof. 'Some of them weighed three tonnes and we have no idea how they got them up there. We know they got stone up there because they built stairs, but there was no craning technology.' It's a small miracle.

The door to the Chapter House dates from 1280. This raises the question of whether it should continue to be used and, therefore, damaged, or taken away and put in a museum. 'It's a door,' says Neil matter-of-factly. 'Probably the oldest in situ anywhere in the world. But a door.' Case closed. Gently.

We walk to the Great East Window. 'The most important piece of medieval glass in the country,' says Neil, and it is one of those wonders that goes unseen by millions of Britons. It tells the story of time, Old Testament scenes sitting in a row above the apocalypse cycle and historical figures. It was painted between 1405 and 1408, has 300 panels, and cost more than £11 million to restore over 13 years until it was bright and illuminating again in 2018. 'The Sistine Chapel of what was happening in the north of England,' says Neil, before pointing out the damned descending into hell. Inevitably, William the Conqueror is up there on show too, but the third row of Old Testament tales is blocked by the parapet and so is invisible from the floor and only there for professional pride and God's critical eye. It is hard not to be humbled by the craftsmanship and ambition.

A nearby carving on a pillar depicts a monkey with his paw doing something unmentionable to a pig. This is vintage satire about what the clergy does to the populace. It is crude, almost hidden, but graphic. And this is York Minster. It is more than just a building. It's an evolving history of a city, region and society. It is why if you look carefully in the carvings where the choir sit each day, you can see wooden cowboys. These are Victorian recarves and reflect the themes

of the day. There are Gothic arches, First World War memo-
rials and glass with oriental designs inspired by sights seen
on the Crusades. It is a fantastic trawl through time.

Outside, it is starting to drizzle. The windows do not
look much from the north side because they have protective
glazing on them. Condensation is a challenge, but so is age.
Some of the glass preservers think they should preserve the
preservatives because they are over 100 years old. 'No, it's
sacrificial glass,' says Neil, but it is a debate. Is something
worth saving just because it's old? God preserve us – and the
preservation orders.

Jonathan Martin was a troubled man with a colourful past.
Press-ganged into the Royal Navy, he served in the Battle
of Copenhagen in 1801 and later gained a reputation for
disrupting church services. He held the clergy in high regard,
and if they did not meet his standards, he was willing to take
the necessary action. Hence, when a magistrate questioned
him over whether he truly intended to shoot the Bishop of
Lincoln, he replied, 'It depends on the circumstances.' He was
committed to a lunatic asylum, but escaped. On 1 February
1829, he hid in the pews of the choir as York Minster closed.
Alone in the vastness, he piled hymn books together and
cut some tassels from the bishop's pew. Then he set fire to
his collection. The damage was extensive, and it is why the
magnificent woodwork in the choir is not as old as most
people think. Martin did not take much catching. He had
pinned rants warning of vengeance to the iron gates of the
choir, admonishing the clergy for their love of wine, roast
beef and downy beds, and warning, 'Your great minsters and
churches will come rattling down upon your guilty heads.'
Helpfully, he also included his address. It was a fair cop.

The trial was a sensation, as recorded in the 72-page report published that year. *The Times* felt it worthy of 8,000 words. Martin's brother was none other than renowned Romantic artist John, one of whose prints, *Belshazzar's Feast*, hung in the Brontës' parsonage, where Charlotte was profoundly influenced by its nightmarish quality. The eminent artist paid for Henry Brougham, a progressive lawyer and leading abolitionist, to defend his brother. Medical experts were brought in to attest that Martin was suffering from monomania and was influenced by his dreams. Martin told the court, 'I set fire to the Minster in consequence of two remarkable dreams.' One involved trying to shoot an arrow through the Minster door, and the other had a thick cloud descending on the Minster and his lodgings. 'From these things I thought I was to set fire to the Minster.' It was a stretch, and it took the jury only 10 minutes to find him guilty but insane. He was sent to the London asylum known as Bedlam and began to paint. Neil tells me lawyers often visit the Minster to see the scene where one of the first insanity defences was born.

But that is not the fire I remember. That happened in 1984, and was another sensation. It is why, after thanking Neil, I find myself sitting in a building not far from the Minster, in a first-floor workshop bedecked with drawings, plans and creative dishevelment. John David leads the team of stonemasons here. Maintaining the Minster is more than a lifetime's work, and there is a 100-year scaffold cycle, which means stone that is deemed resilient enough to last another century is retained. New limestone comes from a quarry by my old school near Tadcaster, and John likes to talk stone and how the quality can differ. 'Stone is an organic thing and varies from quarry to quarry. You will see some of the stone suffering now. It's the hardest thing to get right, but when we choose a block of stone you can see how it will weather in 300 years' time.' His work is all about the big picture, meshing the new to the old, trying to work out what the original builders did, frustration interspersed with eureka moments. Later, he takes me up the scaffolding to the roof and marvels at the intricacy of the work on one of the grotesques. These are what lay people may think of as gargoyles, but differ because they do not spout water. The respect for the original builders means the team of masons try to replicate what has gone before, but there is freedom in the carving.

On 9 July 1984, at around 2 a.m., John heard a knock on the door of his property on the Minster site. 'It was a very balmy night, one of those nights when you have the windows open because the air is still warm. I'd been to the pub round the corner but now there was this loud banging. I thought it must be kids messing about, so I went downstairs, opened the door and was ready to shout, but it was Barry, the landlord from the pub. He said, "The Minster's on fire."

'I went out and could see flames coming out of the gable end of the south transept. The leadwork on the roof was creeping back a bit. Fire engines were already arriving. After a few minutes I thought I should be doing something, so I went to the back of the Minster with my wife. Clergy who lived on site were already there. We started going into the building and saving anything valuable, even altar carpets. We put them in one of the buildings on Chapter House Street. One of the chief firemen was there and I remember him being worried because you could hear these thumps as the stone bosses fell to the floor.'

John's memories are still vivid. It was a night of trauma, recently relived when Notre-Dame caught fire and he went to Paris to lend his expertise and experience. In 1984, though, this was new. 'They wanted everybody out because the tower was working like a chimney and the flames started licking the arch between the south transept and the tower. We went outside again and watched. We could see the flames and I saw all these A frames start collapsing domino fashion towards the tower. I remember seeing a fireman whose jacket was covered in lead spots because he had been up on the parapet.

'The hours went by, and by four or five they were hosing everything down. At around 7 a.m. we were allowed to go back in, but I had to go to hospital. I'd been close to the doorway and I could hear things falling. I ran out of the way, but a stone bounced on the floor and a shard came off and cut my ankle quite badly. It's terrible really, but when I got to the hospital, someone said, "He's from the Minster", and I was taken to the front of the queue.

'People started speculating about the cause. There was talk of lightning. We'd heard reports from the YWCA hostel in the north-west of York where people had seen balls of it in the sky. I can remember it being so hot that outside the Dean Court Hotel there was a girl in a bikini because she'd been swimming. On top of the roof, we have lightning conductors, and I remember finding one on the floor and it was bubbled. It would not have done that just with heat, but lightning at high voltage? I thought it was a very good piece of evidence. I don't know where it went.'

Some 114 firefighters tackled the fire at York Minster. It united the city and those from far beyond. John remembers one man coming from Totnes in Devon to volunteer. People watched in tears as the roof collapsed. John, though, was already thinking about rebuilding.

'The support we got from the city and all sorts of people was wonderful. Everything was mapped where it fell. We removed the burnt timbers to trailers and they were all laid out on the floor at a local builder's yard in the same way they had laid in the transept so the archaeologists could carry on their work. There was talk of putting a steel roof in because it wouldn't burn, but the danger was it would buckle. Concrete doesn't last, so they went with oak, which doesn't burn much other than the outside, but lots of the bosses had death-watch beetle problems and had been stuffed with all sorts of filling, including newspaper.'

A building firm donated 10 wheelbarrows. Supermarkets provided crisps and orange juice for the workers. The masons waived their hourly rate. 'When you get a crisis, everyone mucks in.' The Archbishop of Canterbury, the old rival, arrived and looked at John, who was covered in ash, and said, 'God bless you.' 'That was nice,' says John. 'The Queen came to the stone yard during that time too. Margaret Thatcher came, which was funny because they gave her a hard hat with YM on for York Minster. But of course it was the time of the strike and YM also stood for Yorkshire Miners.'

The fire led the TV news and front pages and quickly developed into a theological row. As John and his team began their meticulous and never-ending work, the letters page of *The Times* sounded a furious backbeat. The controversy arose because three days before the fire, David Jenkins had been consecrated in the Minster as the new Bishop of Durham, after questioning literal interpretations of the virgin birth and Jesus walking on water.

Cue shock and awe. Dorothy Russell from Croydon wrote a pithy letter to *The Times*, aka the Thunderer: '"Just lightning," says the bishop dismissively. 'To those as old-fashioned as I, lightning is the wrath of God.'

The Archbishop of York, John Habgood, replied to the newspaper, asking, 'What kind of God do your correspondents believe in?'

It went on, but John and his peers just got on with making things better. His one regret is that he wishes he had gone home to get his old SLR Minolta. Barry, the pub landlord, took some black and white pictures, but John had a colour film in his camera. Some 37 years on, he is still here, preserving a building that lives, breathes, burns, floods, sings, changes and endures. It is Yorkshire's most famous building, but also a symbol of much that goes on in the county, regardless of gods and religion.

8

STEREOTYKES

'Ear all, see all, say nowt;
Eyt all, sup all, pay nowt;
And if iver tha does owt fer nowt –
Allus do it fer thissen.

Yorkshire motto, timeless

Few places are picked on with quite as much relish as Yorkshire. Politically and culturally it is lampooned until whittled down to a few core tropes. Hence those from Yorkshire are tight, blunt, taciturn, unsophisticated bigots who bathe in beef batter before playing the paper and comb in a disused mill. Some of the stereotypes have been manipulated by time, hence meanness has emerged from a 'Yorkshire bite' being a respectful reference to business acumen. From a grain of truth to sweeping, reductive gener-alisations, the line between stereotype and reality is now invisible. How did it come to this?

Living in a box

Yorkshire suffers for the same reason it thrives. It really does love itself. As I travel around, I see this in the people I meet in Leeds, Sheffield and Bradford, in the cafés, the clubs and conversations, on the terraces and the TV. It does so with unabashed glee while reserving the right to mock anything within or without its boundaries. Its superiority complex even extends to championing its inferiority.

This was picked up on in the 'Four Yorkshiremen' sketch that became synonymous with Monty Python but was originally performed by John Cleese, Graham Chapman, Marty Feldman and Tim Brooke-Taylor on the *At Last the 1948 Show*. In 1967. The premise was that four well-dressed Yorkshiremen would outdo each other with memories of their impoverished upbringing. One of the four is deemed lucky to have been brought up in one room, 'all twenty-six of us', with half the floor missing, because at least he had a room. He is put in his place by a man who lived in a water tank on a rubbish tip, and then by one of 150 in a shoebox in the middle of the road. 'Cardboard box?' asks another, and so it continues, a sort of down-and-out one-upmanship, about eating coal and poison and licking roads, working 29 hours at t'mill while fathers thrashed, bottled, sliced and strangled sons before dancing on their graves. 'But we were happy.'

It could, in truth, have been any working-class community, not exclusively Yorkshire, but Photoshopping old times is an enduring trait. Decades later, another comedy sketch tapped into Yorkshire's sense of self-worth. The Hale and Pace 'Yorkshire Airlines' sketch is a melange of stereotypes. Stewardesses say 'Ey up', cabins are split into working class,

where passengers feed fish and chips to whippets, and Alan
Bennett class, where people read the *Spectator* and get their
hair done. Gareth Hale is Captain Boycott, who will be
'flying at whatever height I like for as long as I like because
I'm the bloody captain'. In-flight entertainment involves him
sticking a ferret down his trousers. The punchline is that they
take off from Leeds-Bradford airport and return there. 'If it's
outside Yorkshire, it's not worth it,' he says.

It's a joke rooted in truth. There is an extraordinary clip
on YouTube showing violent ex-criminal Paul Sykes talking
about Wakefield. 'This is the best little city on earth,' he
says as he sups a cup of tea. 'How do I know? I've been
everywhere else. Nobody can tell me anything. I don't read
the *Daily Mirror* or the *Sun*, I go and have a look.' He
talks of having breakfast in Moscow and his tea in Wood
Street nick, of living in the forests of North America and
the outback of the Ivory Coast. Then he describes how to
deal with sharks in the Straits of Johor. 'Punch 'em right in
fucking earhole and they swim off.' It is funnier and sadder
than most comedy, but smacks of Yorkshire's belief that it
can do anything.

The stereotyping can niggle. Writer and broadcaster
Ian Clayton lives in Featherstone, near Pontefract in West
Yorkshire. He was there the day in 1983 when Featherstone
won rugby league's Challenge Cup. He hitch-hiked to
Wembley with his wife, Heather. 'I can't describe the joy,' he
says in his house, the town's old Gospel Hall. 'It's nostalgic
now. I look back and it's like a filmic memory. It made your
heart beat. There was a choreography about it all. Like a
murmuration of starlings. You know, how they all dance
in the sky, they don't seem to have any code but they know
how to do it. The movement of the players on the field, the

movement of shaking hands and slapping backs in the stand, the movement back north from London, the arrival of the conquering heroes down Wakefield Road into Station Lane.'

It was a romantic story, portrayed as miners from a little pit town climbing out of the ground to scale Andy Cave heights. It played to Hovis deliveries, cobbled streets and Yorkshire porn but not in a *Rita, Sue and Bob Too* way. 'But the thing is, the reason we won the cup was nothing to do with the romanticisation of coal miners coming out of the pits. It had nothing to do with old-fashioned values and tight-knit communities and people washing each other's backs. It was just extremely professional sports people who knew exactly what they were doing.'

The TV commentator that day, Ray French, portrayed Featherstone as a dour side, all northern grit and grime, but they liked him better than Eddie Waring, the avuncular commentator who is best remembered for saying 'up 'n' under' and for laughing about dipsticks on *It's a Knockout*. League fans chanted about sending Waring to Vietnam. Some 10,000 signed a petition calling for his dismissal from the BBC because of what writer Dave Russell called his 'pantomime portrayal of northern life'. In his book *Looking North*, Russell quoted a critic who said the BBC's use of Waring served to 'fuel the feeling that there was an anti-northern bias, a view that has had currency ever since 1895'.

The Hale and Pace sketch played on Yorkshire's navel-gazing, and from what I have told you so far, you might think Clayton is one of these parochial types, operating from the past and refusing to believe there might be a future over the slag heap. He is anything but. He once moved to the Isle of Skye because he wanted to see eagles, and he talks me through the pictures on the wall. 'I bought that off a Mexican hippy in San Francisco. That's from Tibet. I worked in China as a visiting scholar in creative writing. That's the Kremlin, 1961. See the angle. The photographer put the camera on the floor and ran the wire up his trousers.'

He puts the kettle on. 'Featherstone is a complicated town,' he says. 'It isn't Castleford, even though it's three miles down the road. Sometimes I have more things in common with places that are 300 miles away than three. It's like when the BBC refer to the north or to Yorkshire. Yorkshire? What could we possibly all have in common? I went to Poland and smelt things, tasted things and touched things that were far more akin to Featherstone than I would find in, say, Harrogate.'

Things happen in Featherstone that do not adhere to stereotype. Clayton is part of the CAT Club, an acronym standing for Classic Album Thursday. A group of friends started it, meeting in a wooden shed to listen to an LP. They started getting a few guest speakers in. One of them was Howard Marks, a notorious drug smuggler who did seven years of a twenty-five-year sentence and coined the name Mr Nice after buying a passport from a convicted murderer of the same name. They paid him with a bag of grass and a bottle of bourbon, but house rules meant he had to smoke outside.

If there is a fascination with the past, the same goes for our perception of it. Memories don't only fade. They also merge and shape-shift. They get out of place in the filing cabinet and the leaking sap of the family tree blurs chronologies.

I pop in to see Mum. That northern woman. She has been writing down a few notes of people, places and things. She has written a list of Yorkshire celebrities.

Alan Titchmarsh
Jessica Ennis
Judi Dench
The Owens from *Our Yorkshire Farm*
Alan Bennett
Herbert Sutcliffe
Fred Trueman

She has added, contentiously, 'All Yorkshiremen are very softly spoken – not shouters.'

It is May 2022, and Bradford has just been named the UK City of Culture. The title invites mockery, but it will lead to investment and show Bradford has a creative core. I say we should go back to Bradford, to Shipley, to the space left by the demolished Alma pub that she grew up in. I am not sure if it is good news for her. She says she has a strange sense of déjà vu now, but it's not like remembering, more foreshadowing, of feeling you knew this was going to happen. The various places in Bournemouth all look the same. She has started having bad dreams, too. It might be the tablets. Meanwhile, the papers are carrying a story about a breakthrough for those with Alzheimer's. It is based on a short press release from a Japanese pharmaceutical firm and a US biotech that say trials have shown a slowing in cognitive decline. It is the sort of story that offers hope but no timescale. Others urge caution. I'd urge the opposite.

I read another note she's written: 'That'll do. High praise. Remember that was what my dad said when I achieved 5 O levels – not well done or that's very good, but that'll do.'

When trying to fathom stereotypes, it's as well to go to the past, because that is where they were forged. George Orwell was the India-born great-grandson of a Jamaican plantation owner and served time as a Burma policeman. He also had an interest in social conditions in Britain, and before he was writing about pigs in dystopia, he studied the north, which, given that we once lived by that pig farm on an exposed hill, might amount to the same thing. The result in 1937 was *The Road to Wigan Pier*, which most people think is all Lancashire, but Orwell hopped over the Pennines too, and even visited Grimethorpe.

He knew what to expect. 'When I first went to Yorkshire, some years ago, I imagined that I was going to a country of boors,' he wrote. 'I was used to the London Yorkshireman with his interminable harangues and his pride in the supposed raciness of his dialect ("A stitch in time saves nine", as we say in the West Riding), and I expected to meet with a good deal of rudeness. But I met with nothing of the kind, and least of all among the miners.'

Instead, Orwell said he was treated with an embarrassing kind of courtesy. 'No one showed any sign of despising me for coming from a different part of the country,' he added. Place snobbery, he deduced, was not a working-class characteristic. He then added a crowd-pleasing turn when he recounted a car journey with a friend in East Anglia. 'Of course, most of the villages in Yorkshire are hideous,' said his pal. 'But the Yorkshiremen are splendid chaps. Down here it's just the other way round – beautiful villages and rotten people.'

It's the language of love, love

The West Yorkshire accent has just been voted the third sexiest in the UK. This comes after the wider Yorkshire accent, which is obviously not a thing, had previously been voted the second most motivating. This, in turn, followed the survey that found the Yorkshire accent was the friendliest in the UK, while way back in 2008, Bath Spa University said it was the most intelligent-sounding. The Brummie accent was associated with stupidity, and helpfully, a reporter in the *Guardian* noted that famous Brummies included Enoch Powell and Ozzy Osbourne. Which goes to show that academics spend an inordinate amount of time doing inane surveys.

Anyway, another survey is out and shows that there is 'accent prestige' in British society, just as there was half a century ago. The Speaking Up report found that 41 per cent of university applicants from the north were concerned their accent could affect their ability to do well in the future, compared with 19 per cent from the south. Why anyone would be prejudiced against friendly, motivating, sexy brain-boxes is anyone's guess, but there is probably more truth in this than in most of the surveys.

The Yorkshire Dialect Society deals with this stuff and was founded in 1897. It acknowledges that there is no single dialect, but a diagonal isophone drawn across the county from north-west to south-east a century ago provides a useful split. Above the line, which roughly equates to North Yorkshire and what was Humberside until 1996, there is a stronger Scandinavian influence. Below the line there is a stronger Midlands one. Yet anyone who travels around Yorkshire knows accent and word use are inconsistent and ever-changing.

Ian McMillan highlighted this when he did a segment for a TV programme with Stephen Fry. The hermetically posh Fry meets McMillan by a railway map, whereupon the

poet explains the differences. In Leeds they drop the t and
lengthen the e; in Hull they talk of a band called the Stern
Rerses; in Barnsley the accent is harsher, which McMillan
says may be down to the coldness of the wind and a subsequent unwillingness to open your mouth; in Chesterfield,
over the border, his auntie talks of her semi-detached arse.

Old Norse and Old English clash and merge, but the status
of the accent is the source of division. Ever since Lord Reith
decided that Received Pronunciation (RP) was the language
of the BBC, thus aligning it with the country's public schools
– it was even named Public School Pronunciation by London
phonetician Daniel Jones in 1917 – regionalism has been
a thorny subject. Reith said he wanted a style of English
that would not be laughed at anywhere in the country, but
the BBC still let Wilfred Pickles in. Unashamedly Yorkshire,
Pickles was a huge radio star and was even allowed to read
the news on the BBC Home Service during the Second World
War, although this was deemed partly down to a desire to
confuse any listening Nazis.

RP began to die when inverted snobbery grew in popularity. The Beatles spoke in some weird northern tongue,
and a place at Eton was not deemed the zenith for all.
Eddie Waring got a job. Regional accents became trendy.
Nevertheless, in the summer of 2021, more researchers
from Cambridge and Portsmouth universities sounded very
pleased to declare that northern accents could be dead within
45 years. They had used data from a 1950s study of English
dialects and compared it with 50,000 recordings from 2016.
Basically, southern pronunciation of certain words was
already replacing northern ones. What was more, dialectal
variations were also fading. The study added that the words
in most danger of being homogenised by the south were strut,

thawing and singer, which most of the north could probably cope without unless describing Mick Jagger's garden pond in early spring.

What is perhaps more worthy of study is why some people mollify their accent when they move south and exaggerate it when they go home. Presumably it is simply an innate desire to fit in. So, we hear that regional accents are out and then in and then out again. It's a linguistic hokey-cokey (or hoekay-coekay) as language evolves in the space of a car journey and even a sentence, let alone 45 years, by which time Cambridge University will probably be doing Yorkshire Studies and nobody will be happy.

King of the Ferret-Leggers

Twenty years after Orwell had given up on finding Wigan Pier, Richard Hoggart would talk of the working class's closed-in attitude. 'One is reminded of Tess of the d'Urbervilles moving from one valley to another and seeming, to herself, to move from one country to another. The contrast is not so acute, but the working man in this instance is nearer Tess than he is to the city solicitor who runs out seven miles for a round of golf. For plenty of working-class people a bus journey to relatives halfway across the county is still a matter for considerable thought and upheaval.' Especially now they're cancelling half the routes.

Yet even when Hoggart was working on *The Uses of Literacy* in the mid fifties, certain ideas were changing. 'Whippet and greyhound breeding seems almost dead except in a few mining areas or for commercial purposes,' he wrote. Canaries were right out now that miners did not have a need for them, but pigeons were still hugely popular. 'The Hulton Survey [a readership survey that split Britain into five socioeconomic groups, with an annual income for the head of each household ranging from £250 to more than £1,300] suggests that bird-fancying is more popular with working-class people than with any others.' Indeed, half a million pigeon fanciers in Great Britain went to clubs based in the local pub and paid annual subs of a pound each. Birds were released from cane baskets by railway porters, and 'the owners, flat-capped and with an eye cocked upwards and a stopwatch ready, wait for their pigeons to come softly out of the Saturday dusk'. That was the 1950s, but I know how it felt, because a racing pigeon once stopped in our garden. It was ringed and did not seem to want to move, so I put some seed and water out for it and let it sleep in the shed. It stayed for a few days, hobbling around the garden, and then, without warning, it regenerated and flew off. It was all a bit Billy Casper, but at least my bird was back out there.

Animals have played a pivotal role in the oversimplification of Yorkshire, although nobody much mentions the hares tearing around the Yorkshire Wolds, the red squirrels in the Dales, the red kites released from the Harewood estate between Leeds and Harrogate in 1999, or the puffins clinging on at Bempton's cliffs to the east. No, it's ferrets that are the animals synonymous with the brass-tacks paganism of these simple-minded folk.

Never was this more lucidly imagined than by Don Katz, founder of audiobook publisher Audible and a renowned American journalist, once rated just below Bruce Springsteen in New Jersey's pantheon of most influential figures, when he merrily suggested writing a story about ferret-legging for manly American magazine *Outside*. And so, one day in 1983, commission in hand, Katz arrived in Barnsley, which he hailed as 'home to a quarter-million downtrodden souls'. He failed to resist a bit of gentle accent-lampooning, and was given directions to the old pit cottage where Reg Mellor, king of the ferret-leggers, lived.

The ensuing article is a hoot. Mellor is portrayed as a manically practical man with a hardness hewn from mines and wars, topped off by a military moustache. 'Any more questions 'fore I poot a few down for ye?' he offered.

Asked if stuffing ferrets down your pants ever led to a few nips and tugs, he helpfully dropped his trousers, but despite his peculiar prowess, he was not about to leap to the defence of these animals. 'Cannibals, things that live only to kill, that'll eat your eyes out to get at your brain.' Basically, not ideal pet material.

Katz went on to paint Mellor as a man of curious manhood as he boasted of lasting longer with loaded trousers than anyone else. '"Why," Reg roared again, "I had 'em hangin' from me tool for hours an' hours! Two at a time – one on each side. I been swelled up big as that!" He pointed to a five-pound can of instant coffee.' Given Reg's age, Katz suggested that the risk to family life was less of a concern. The response was Boycott-esque. '"Are you sayin' I ain't pokin' 'em no more?" Reg growled with menace. "Is that what you're meaning? 'Cause I am pokin' 'em for sure."'

This fabulous furball fare stemmed from Reg marching around the moors with his ferret-lining while on hunting missions. A BBC clip shows a presenter, still clinging to his RP delivery, watching him feed liver to his ferrets. 'Now then,' Reg says. He admits the ferrets do not enjoy it, but he sees it as a challenge. At which point he grimaces and swears, and the camera cuts to the presenter saying, 'It was at this point that we had to abandon filming.'

Nasty things, land piranhas, with an appalling history of derring-do and dangling-down. The *Illustrated London News* in 1896 did not mess about with its appraisal. 'There is little doubt that there are some animals which to a certain extent have the faculty of corrupting human nature. Boys who nourish ferrets in their bosoms are hardly ever respectable.' This seemed a stretch, in a figurative rather than ferret-enhancing manner, but the writer was not finished. 'Familiarity with these animals produces not contempt but a certain similarity of character.'

Nevertheless, the penal and penile codes seem in harmony in not blaming the ferret. It is, as ever, people that are the problem. Reg knew this from bitter experience, and in 1981 the papers recorded his retirement. Even the *Aberdeen Journal* saw fit to record this sporting landmark, headlining it 'Ferret Fiasco': 'The uncrowned king of ferret legging Mr Reg Mellor has decided to give up his unusual and sometimes agonising sport. Reg (71), of Honeywell Street, Barnsley, who regularly puts ferrets with razor-sharp teeth down his trousers, had just survived 5hr 26min in a performance at a charity gala when the organisers started to dismantle the stage. "I packed in and went home. I never even got a letter of thanks," said Reg who has also been a soldier, steeplejack, steel erector and miner.'

The origins of ferret-legging are disputed. The Scots have laid claim, if not particularly vociferously, given that it is a patently daft hobby, and it is widely believed that the Romans used these mustelids for hunting and introduced them to northern England, thus providing an addendum to the question 'What have the Romans done for us?' Genghis

Khan was also an avowed fan. Shakespeare talked of the firk and ferret in *Henry V*. Surprisingly, this was not a pub.

Ferrets are still good at catching rabbits. And there have been persistent attempts at domestication, with crueller owners sewing their lips together and removing their teeth. Like skunks, they can issue pungent smells via anal glands. This means they are sold de-glanded or ignobly de-scented.

The rules for ferret-legging are simple: these abominable beasts must have all their teeth and must not be drugged. Similarly, Reg and co. must not be drunk. Katz noted that Reg's best technique involved putting the ferret's head in his mouth. 'Some very big Yorkshiremen stood around us in the pub. Some of them claimed they had bitten the heads off sparrows, shrews and even rats, but none of them would compete with Reg Mellor.'

Katz won an award for his article and named a collection of his work *The King of the Ferret Leggers*. Reg died in 1987. Few have been bitten by the bug since.

I come across a newspaper interview with Stan Richards, an actor famed for playing Yorkshire stereotype Seth Armstrong in what was then *Emmerdale Farm* before the escalating drama of plane crashes, underage sex and serial killers made the producers kick the farm suffix. 'He's a miserable old stirrer,' says Richards of the poacher-turned-gamekeeper who made his name. He adds that he went to see Reg for advice on how to handle ferrets, and makes an astounding comment. 'Those contests where blokes put ferrets down their trousers are a big joke,' he says. 'It turns out that where it's dark and warm, ferrets go to sleep. That's why you can put one down your trousers and still remain a man!'

It's a fix. A fraud. I think of a middle-aged man named Shirley Crabtree sitting across from me in a dusky back room at the Riley-Smith Hall, sweat making bloody pools on his leotard. Sometimes even the pain isn't real.

Professional Yorkshiremen

Howard H. Smith, lead singer with thrash metal band Acid Reign, originating from Knaresborough, was in Lille for New Year with friends a couple of decades ago. As they marvelled at the window of a patisserie, with its cakes and chocolates arranged in displays of sugar lawns, he said in an exaggerated Yorkshire accent, 'Yeah, but they 'ant got any effing pasties, 'av the?' His friends looked at him aghast and in awe. 'Where did that come from?'

It continued as a running joke. In another saccharine palace, Howard said, 'Three mushies, three Spam fritters, no salt, watching me heart.'

Back in London, he went back to doing part-time stand-up comedy. 'I was on a bill one night and there were six of us, and I realised we were all white, all male, all with at least some material on relationships,' he says. How could he differentiate himself? 'I remember it clear as day. I went down to my local Oxfam and got 90 per cent of the Keith outfit that I still wear now – coat, cap, scarf. I came back, took some pictures and practised the voice. I did the same set I'd been doing for three months but did it dressed up as an old Yorkshireman. This contemporary opinion coming from a grumpy northerner put a twist on it. I was never going to get the same reaction delivering that stuff like Keith does.' And so Keith Platt, professional Yorkshireman, was born.

Howard has been doing Keith for years now. People often come up to him after shows and say they know someone just

like that. He wonders whether he will morph into the character at some point. 'For over 10 years I glued a moustache
on, and then in lockdown I got used to not shaving and now
I've got some heavy stubble. It's the first stage, but Keith has
always been 69. Some of my friends describe me as grumpy
now. They would call me a cynic. I'd call myself a realist.
Which is probably pretty cynical. The older I get, the more
I recognise the world is becoming a place for people who
aren't me. I used to be all over innovation, but nobody is
making anything with me in mind. Youth is for the young.'

He admits he makes noises when he sits down, but fights
against age and Yorkshire stereotypes by saying he wants
to squeeze every drop from every day. Then he gives in and
rants about electric scooters. 'They haven't got lights, insurance, helmets. I've already had a 12-year-old kid plough into
my car on his bike because his mates told him to ride on the
pavement but hadn't told him they'd taken his brakes off.
They can eff off.'

As a professional Yorkshireman, Keith/Howard has
considered the clichés and the half-truths. He does not think
Yorkshire has its own humour other than there being no
sacred cows. 'All cards are on the table and everything is a
target, but I do think we laugh at our own pig-headedness.'

Loving Yorkshire increases with distance. Howard talks
of his old girlfriend who was from Skye and worked in the
Gaelic department at the BBC. 'She was *very* Scottish. She
called the police the polis. But we went to the Yorkshire
Dales and she said, "I could cheat on Scotland for this."'
His best friend was of Greek Cypriot heritage. 'He was
olive-skinned so he got loads of grief at school in the
eighties. He left Harrogate to go to university and has never
lived in Yorkshire since, but he still considers himself a

Yorkshireman and has more of an accent than me. He went back for a birthday and was driving around the Dales and his wife put her hand on his leg and asked, "Why are you driving so fast?" And he realised he had regressed to his 18-year-old self, thrashing his old car around those lovely twisty-turny roads.' It's an interesting thought that memories can actually make you regress in behaviour as well as emotions. At which point Howard admits he would love an electric scooter if he were young and would probably not bother with insurance. In terms of time, if not place, people forget where they come from.

The list of Yorkshire comedians is long. Frankie Howerd has a blue plaque in York but left for London when young. Michael Palin was born in Sheffield and penned a love letter to it in the *Spectator* in 2021. Sagely, he started it: 'I was born and raised in Sheffield, a proud steel-making city which drew much of its energy from a sense of under-appreciation.' Leeds-born Ernie Wise was half of the best-loved comic duo of all, and if he had to play second fiddle to Eric Morecambe, at least it was a Stradivarius.

There is a new play heading to the Edinburgh Festival in 2022 about Charlie Williams. It is called *Eh Up, Me Old Flowers!* Williams was an old-school comedian, the sort who would brave the nicotine pea-soupers of northern clubs in a jacket and bow tie. He was typically Yorkshire in that he was born in Royston, a few miles north of Barnsley, worked at a mine and then played football for Doncaster Rovers. One of the lads. The only difference was that Charlie was black. He was funny enough to get on *The Comedians*, the seventies TV show that was the main forum for professionals to reach a broader audience, but he was controversial because he used the audience's prejudice for laughs. He would say things like: 'If you don't shut up, I'll come and move in next door.' Charlie Williams's thing was he sounded like he was from sixties Yorkshire but didn't look like it. He felt his only means to acceptance was to play along and be one of them. It caused hurt for a lot of black people, and some were unforgiving.

Howard gets his laughs by looking like a Yorkshireman but saying things you would not imagine one to utter. Times have moved on, but he knows it's not all good. He was born two beds down in hospital from a boy whose family had done that seemingly apocryphal thing and driven through the night so he could be born in Yorkshire and thus qualify to play cricket for the county. 'My parents were, "How do you know he'll like cricket?" It's hard to believe that was a thing, not allowing people who were not from Yorkshire. I mean, it's racist, isn't it? And let's get onto the ugly side, because racism in Yorkshire is a thing. I have sat at Elland Road and heard people say, "I'm not racist, I just don't like Pakis." I think there's an economic racism too. If you were an immigrant, you had no chance if you didn't work all hours. And a lot of lazy white Yorkshire folk got envious of hard-working Asian folk slaving away every hour God sent.' Of Yorkshire grit, Palin wrote in his letter, 'Now the grit has got caught in the works following the cricket scandal. It could be a long time before the Yorkshire brand recovers.'

It is a concern, because Yorkshire is proud of being proud. And being biggest hits the sweet spot. 'I don't think there is that level of pride in Lancashire for whatever reason,' says Howard. 'It's not as tangible to the outsider anyway. I don't think it's anything to do with history and the loss of industry. If that was the case, it would apply across all the hard-hit counties. It's the moors and the Dales, recognised as essential areas of nature, the diversity of wildlife, the fact that Yorkshire is self-contained, with lovely coastlines, nearly mountains, vales, incredible metropolitan cities, vast areas of farmland – that "we have everything" thing.'

I tell Howard about exhuming my father's ashes and wondering if place matters any more. If we pretend somewhere is superior to elsewhere, are we not just the modern version of the family driving north on a cricketing fantasy? And if it's not where you're from but where you're at that counts, does it not stand to reason that where you finally fall down is just as important?

Howard lives in London and says he is going to have to go back too. 'At some point, when my mum dies, I will have to go back and bury her and put the house on the market. My mum's parents were from Barnoldswick. They were Yorkshire through and through. They were buried in Barnoldswick, which was in West Yorkshire at the time, but then they moved the county line and now it's in Lancashire. So they were buried in Yorkshire but rest in Lancashire. Now that should be bloody illegal. You exhumed your father and drop-kicked him off a cliff in Cornwall, and that's fine, but this was done by faceless bureaucrats. I put that up against anyone's story. Absolutely brutal.'

The story of Howard's grandparents, taken from Yorkshire in 1974, forms part of a wider one about age-old land disputes. In 2016, the *Guardian* exposed one of them. Helen Pidd, the excellent north of England editor, wrote, 'It is more than 500 years since the House of Lancaster won the ultimate battle of the Wars of the Roses, but the Yorkies have finally wrought their revenge. On Monday, despite protests by farmers in the red rose county, a lovely little corner of

Lancashire found itself subsumed by the Yorkshire Dales, after the national park increased in size by 24 per cent.' It was pointed out that the old park boundaries were bureaucratic anachronisms and paid no attention to landscape and beauty. The Friends of Real Lancashire (tagline 'Our county is called Lancashire, not Cumbria, Greater Manchester, Merseyside or part of Cheshire' – it probably needs work) were unimpressed. Exiled Lancastrian Robert Wright wrote in and suggested that 'the only good thing that comes out of Yorkshire are roads into Lancashire'.

Cue a response from the people's epistolary front of Gargrave, up in the Dales. David Handley wrote, 'What has Lancashire done to deserve this? Well, I will tell you. In 1974, Lancashire seized Barnoldswick from the West Riding and made it part of Pendle. This was akin to the recent annexation of the Crimea by Russia.'

I say goodbye to Howard, who is locking Keith in the closet this weekend because he is off to play Bloodstock, a heavy metal festival in Derbyshire.

He is not bumptious and neither is much of Yorkshire. In 1983, Ian Clayton and his wife got home just in time to see the climax of that murmuration as the Featherstone team went down Station Lane on an open-top bus. 'There was so much goodwill, they could have travelled down on breath, like angels,' he says. Station Lane was the town's artery. Once bedecked in blue and white and hope and glory, it is now a run-down affair with a pizza takeaway, tanning salon and mandatory eyebrow threader. Post Office Road leads off it, and was so tethered to the community that people tied their washing lines to the stadium walls, but as Ian says, you lose the ethos and you lose the value. Briefly, after the miners' strike, someone opened a shop on Station Lane selling iguanas. It didn't last, but the shops selling shoes and fruit and three-piece suites also went. Ian has just signed a petition to save the 178 bus to Castleford. Two generations of his family were conductors on the route.

'I saw drugs come into this town on a scale that was unimaginable,' he says. 'Someone said to me, "Ian, my lad's a smackhead, I don't know what to do." I can't imagine anyone here would have said that sentence in the 1980s. Up to then, if you got a different type of tobacco they'd think you were on drugs, but within half a generation there was silver foil all over Station Lane. Yes, there were lots of middle-class dinner parties shoving cocaine up their noses, but if you can afford to feed a habit you're not as likely to get poorly with it. Round 'ere, they end up with all the bad stuff.'

Ian worked at Wakefield Prison. One day an old inmate was getting out and asked how he got to Westgate station. Ian told him. 'No, I mean how do *I* get there?' he replied. 'I've been in 'ere so long, I don't know 'ow to turn left.' Ian sighs. 'It was like that when the pit closed. People who had lit the country's furnaces, fuelled wars and powered trains were now throwing cauliflowers into red racks to feed Asda's profits.'

They get stereotyped up here. 'My grandad was a miner, and not only was he knowledgeable about the history of what he was doing, he was knowledgeable about the world. When *University Challenge* was on, before King's College were buzzing in, he'd say the answer, whether it was English literature, geography or Norse mythology.'

But if the town is not what it was, why would you return? 'There's something here,' says Ian. 'It's not in the water, but it might be in the food and it might be in the gossip and it might be in the colours and the shapes and the roots and the bricks. I saw a documentary once about Henry Moore, and he was touching bricks in the street where he grew up. This was a man who chiselled away at marble brought back from Italian quarries, and he's still talking about the bricks in his street.'

He echoes what Richard Hawley told me. 'I've spent a lot of my life trying to get out from where I'm from and then trying to get back in.' They are a similar age, so maybe this nostalgia is middle-aged catharsis. 'It's like there's a barbed-wire fence. I lift a strand and I crawl through, but there are things pulling me back. Vince Farrar (rugby player) for one, Auntie Alice another, my elderly neighbour telling stories going back to the Boer War. It's like homing pigeons. Is it some kind of instinct, like a magnet in their head, or is it a primitive memory? At the end of the day, we all want to get back home.'

We want to go back to where hope was not tainted by grim reality and where there was endless time. Perhaps it is why we like stereotypes. Some may be mocking, and worse, but some are reassuring. The truth may hurt too much.

9

CHAMPIONS

For a split-second I thought I were all right, then me brain
said, 'Go down, you daft bastard.' I tried me best.

Richard Dunn, boxer, on his fifth and final knockdown
against Muhammad Ali in 1976, quoted in *Daily Mail*, 2009

The story of Yorkshire sport is one of rise and fall, repeat
to fade, encapsulated in a Halifax scaffolder's heroi-
cally flawed 1976 fight against Ali. Reflecting the pride,
ties, ambition and neglect of its communities, Yorkshire's
sporting teams have provided a microcosm of the county's
past. Sport has also shrunk tribal boundaries, so the insider–
outsider conflict is played out as an internecine scrap. Dunn
lost his Ali fight money in a Scarborough hotel and then fell
50 feet off a North Sea oil rig. His ankle was hanging off but
he walked again – in constant pain. That's Yorkshire sport.

Top of the world

In the summer of 2012, there was much ado about puffing.
People painted their faces, forgot to be angry and went down

to London for a knees-up called the Olympics. For two weeks, everybody ignored the national tendency to mock anything that might be fun. The media misjudged this and assumed they would be safe talking about white elephants and whether inner-city London needed a 10-metre diving board when that money could be used to buy some high-grade plutonium or something. But they got to London and were aghast to realise everyone was up for this. It was the mother of all jollies. Make fun of the opening ceremony, which featured Kenneth Branagh seemingly dressed as Abraham Lincoln but playing Isambard Kingdom Brunel, and you were an ignoramus. Instead of default cynicism, we equated the shot-put prelims with a higher state of being, and watched handball mystified but mesmerised and without appealing to the ref. We were all in it together. Unless you came from Yorkshire.

It did not take long for some to point out that if Yorkshire were a country, it would be doing very well in the Olympic medal table. Yorkshire's athletes finished with seven gold medals, two silvers and three bronzes. This was more than Australia, Jamaica or Canada. Indeed, if allowed to be a separate country, Yorkshire would have finished twelfth. Not bad. Yorkshire celebrated Jessica Ennis, the heptathlete given the dubious honour of being the face of the Games, as a proud Yorkshirewoman. Or, if being pedantic, a daughter of Sheffield, as well as of Alison, a social worker, and Vinnie, a painter and decorator from the Windrush generation. The sibling rivalry of triathletes Jonny and Alistair Brownlee was a local affair on loan to the wider public, and when Alistair would later help his stricken brother over the line, in a race in 2016, he was taken to epitomise the hard but fair DNA of teak-tough tykes. Nicola Adams was the ever-smiling boxer mixing grace and violence, no easy task, and in a sport barred from the Olympics until 1996 because premenstrual women were deemed too unstable to beat the living hell out of each other, this black lesbian became a champion for a diverse nation. Except in Yorkshire, where she was just that girl off the Burmantofts estate.

Dorset doesn't do this, but Yorkshire, as is probably becoming clear by now, does like to rate itself. A year after the London Olympics, the Lonely Planet guide declared the county the third best region in the world. In *The Times*, Patrick Kidd wrote, '"Only third?" will come the response from Rotherham to Richmond, from Yorkshire folk aghast not to have beaten Sikkim, a Himalayan state of India, or the Kimberley in Western Australia.' Sam Jordison, co-author of a book called *Crap Towns*, said this sort of accolade would only exacerbate 'how unbelievably chuffing smug' the residents were. His own survey declared that York, the jewel in Yorkshire's crown, was the fifth crappest place to live, primarily due to locals being so very pleased to come from there. While that trait does seem better than a penchant for setting fire to your own town, he had a point. He told the *Guardian*, 'Did you know, for instance, that as well as being the Cath Kidston and net-curtain capital of the UK, Harrogate boasts the most internet porn-watchers in the UK? And that's not to mention the biggest drinkers and the highest concentration of drink drivers. We also shouldn't gloss over the fact that Yorkshire contains a place like Bradford.' Incidentally, the leader of Harrogate council responded to the porn news by saying people could do what they liked as long as it was legal. Perhaps missing the zeitgeist, he said the real worry was that more people were not connected to the internet in Yorkshire.

If we accept that coming from Yorkshire is a tribal thing, then seeing it through the prism of sport is asking for trouble. In his 1981 book *The Soccer Tribe*, zoologist and ethologist Desmond Morris drew parallels between the primeval urge to hunt, the slaying of 5,000 animals on the opening day of the Roman Colosseum, and a routine kicka- bout, adding that church gatherings on a Sunday morning went beyond a need for communal prayer. 'It was also a statement of group identity,' he wrote beneath a picture of a fan kneeling before revered Liverpool football manager Bill Shankly. But now that the dance halls and cinemas were closing, and TV was established as the great social isolator, urban society was being starved of large community gather- ings. Sport was a chance to come together and say how much better you were than geographical rivals. And if your team was crap, then take pride in the spartan ordeal of enduring ninety minutes in a ramshackle stand on a winter's day. Staying loyal to your roots was at the heart of all this, which is why I think football fans prefer to fight over who has the most faithful fans rather than the best players. Or they did when sport was more quasi-religious than show business. One illustration in Morris's book always struck me. It was a juxtaposition of a picture of Liverpool players carrying the European Cup and a line of Amazonian tribesmen carting off a giant anaconda. Take that. Sport was made for Yorkshire. And Brazil, and Merseyside.

The chuffing smugness manifested itself when Yorkshire set up its own international football team, which debuted in 2018 with a home match against the Isle of Man at Hemsworth Miners Welfare FC. Jordan Coduri, a nifty midfielder with Penistone Church, scored Yorkshire's first goal in the landmark game. 'On Ilkla Moor Baht 'at' was the team's national anthem, but alas, this was not aired due to someone double-booking the brass band.

Still, they nearly made the 2020 CONIFA World Cup, different to the FIFA World Cup by being less naff, although some people wondered just what an English county was doing in a qualification tournament for displaced peoples, stateless nations and disputed territories like Darfur, Cascadia and the United Koreans of Japan. 'No one is claiming Yorkshire is like those places or people,' said Phil Hegarty, the man behind the Yorkshire International Football Association. He did not sound convincing. He had gained membership of the international governing body by saying that Yorkshire folk 'overwhelmingly thought of themselves as being from Yorkshire before England'. Hegarty said he would install those 'exclusively' Yorkshire qualities of grit and fight in his team. This was similar reasoning to the Welcome to Yorkshire tourist chiefs making Gareth Southgate, the England football manager and native of Watford, an honorary Yorkshireman. It was his 'insistence on doing things his own way' that made Southgate typically Yorkshire. Or, as his detractors might say, his obdurate refusal to play his best players while simultaneously wearing a waistcoat.

Yet for all the puff and chuff, Yorkshire's history of sport is revealing of wider characteristics. The North Riding is famed for its horse breeding, but the oldest English classic is the St Leger, which takes place at Doncaster in South Yorkshire. However, that only dates back to 1776 and is a mere baby compared with the Kiplingcotes Derby, an annual four-mile race held in the middle of nowhere in the Yorkshire Wolds. This is as quirky as horse racing gets. On the third Thursday of March, since 1519, anyone can turn up on any sort of horse. Former racehorses are often disguised and given false names. Clydesdales, alas, struggle to go incognito. Jockeys cannot weigh more than 10 stone. The winner gets £50 and the runner-up gets more from taking the bulk of all the other entry fees. As for the course, it is a long, straight tarmac road. The Tudor rules state that if no one completes it then the race cannot be held ever again, so when the pandemic struck, two riders walked a horse around the course to guarantee survival. It is old, weird and has been likened to Brigadoon, the mythical village in the Scottish Highlands, in that it is here today and gone tomorrow. It is quintessentially Yorkshire.

The soccer tribe

Back in the real world, Yorkshire is inextricably linked to the birth of football. The game had ancient origins but gained popularity in medieval times when Up'ards and Down'ards contested the Royal Shrovetide match in Ashbourne in Derbyshire and would try to score goals by hitting the ball on mill posts set some three miles apart.

The years passed, even if the greediest psychopaths refused to, and two men from Sheffield Cricket Club, Nathaniel Creswick and William Prest, decided they could do with something to keep them fit in the off season, and so they organised a game of football. Sheffield FC was officially formed in 1857, when matches were generally an in-house thing between marrieds and singles. Creswick and Prest drew up the Sheffield Rules a year later, including definitions of the throw-in, kick-off and fouls, and these became the bedrock of local games beyond the posher rules forged on public school playing fields. Sheffield FC is now recognised as the world's oldest independent club not associated with an institution such as a school or university. Brazilian legend Pelé would later say there would have been no him without Sheffield, which seemed a bit of a leap but was well intentioned.

However, when the Sheffield Football Association finally succumbed and merged its rules with those of the FA, it was the beginning of a long, slow fade into obscurity. The FA introduced the offside rule and football has never stopped arguing. Sheffield FC clung to its amateur status and drifted down the leagues. Now the club plays in Derbyshire, although at the time of writing, there are attempts to bring it home.

Sheffield's role in making football a game of the people was in keeping with the city's status as the capital of the socialist republic of South Yorkshire. During the 1980s, David Blunkett, the leader of the council, pursued policies at odds with the government. The council built streets in the sky and Richard Hawley wrote songs about them. A peace treaty was signed with Donetsk in what was then the Soviet Union. As the miners went back to work, Blunkett was defying the rate-capping policy that wrested more power from the regions. Sheffield wanted to play by its own rules again.

When Sheffield Wednesday, one of the city's two professional clubs, began to get good in the late twentieth century, the manager, Howard Wilkinson, spoke publicly about the miners' plight. Himself the son of one, he would be characterised as an archetypal Yorkshireman – flat cap, joyously dour, living in the past – but his theories on teamwork went far beyond coaching manuals. In Anthony Clavane's book

A Yorkshire Tragedy, Wilkinson said, 'It seems to me that politics is more than about just making good, sound business decisions. It's about the values you want to see represented, and to me, to take away what the miners had and not replace it with anything – that was the crime.'

Wednesday was so named because it, too, was born of cricket. The Wednesday Cricket Club was established in 1820 and took its name from the founders' day off. Under Wilkinson, Sheffield Wednesday was a huge success, finishing fifth in the first division. Wilkinson moved to Leeds and won the second division title in 1990, then, two years later, the last first division crown before it became the Premier League. His ethos was: 'It's amazing what can be achieved if no one minds who takes the credit.' This is at odds with the modern way and the craven need for validation, but Wilkinson was a quiet revolutionary. Leeds United was a malignant club when he took over. Not only was it unsuccessful, it had also been home to a violent cult and a casual acceptance of racism, with the National Front handing out bilious propaganda by the turnstiles. Wilkinson's era did more than any to try to wash away that stain.

Nobody from outside Leeds much likes its football club, and so it is the perfect symbol for Yorkshire pride. The club was dragged up by Don Revie, a Middlesbrough man with a talent for binding tactical acumen to paranoia. One day in around 2000 I met Peter Lorimer, a club legend who could reputedly shoot at 90 mph, in his pub in Holbeck. Long retired from football and moving a little slower by then, he pulled a pint and rolled out stories. 'His lucky suit was so worn out that his arse was hanging out of it,' he said of Revie. Then there were the tomb-like dossiers about opponents. 'The lads would just be thinking, "Let's go out and give this lot a good tanking", but by the end of it all you'd be thinking, "Crikey, these aren't a bad side." You'd end up with a bit of fear, and though it's not a bad thing to have a bit of respect for your opposition, it got to the stage where you'd think you were up against Real Madrid when in reality it was Aldershot.'

Leeds won lots – two league titles, an FA Cup, a League Cup and two Inter-Cities Fairs Cups (the precursor of the UEFA Cup) – but their brilliance was tainted for many watchers. They were hard and not always fair. They merged sublime football with what some deemed thuggery. 'Nazis in Umbro', as Stuart Maconie put it succinctly in his terrific book about the north, *Pies and Prejudice.*

My dad dragged me to my first football game when I was six and not really bothered. It was the 1975 European Cup semi-final between Leeds United and Barcelona, and I was more fascinated by the tallest floodlights in Europe than by Dutch genius Johan Cruyff. Norman Hunter was not playing that night. Born near where the Angel of the North now stands overlooking the A1, Hunter travelled south at 15 and joined Leeds, and although he had a few years playing in Bristol, he never really left Yorkshire again. He was known as Bites Yer Legs, and the moniker adorned Wembley flags and cider ads. This most unassuming of Leeds heroes once recalled that in his pomp, he received an income tax return and was surprised to see a handwritten note enclosed. The two-word message was: 'Keep biting.'

He cringed when remembering the punch-up with Francis Lee that saw both men sent off on a fractious day at Derby County in 1975. 'I'm very embarrassed by the Francis Lee thing,' he told me. 'Nobody should do that on a football field.' By the 1990s, Lee was chairman of Manchester City and Hunter was working for radio. When his team visited Elland Road, Lee quipped: 'Let's finish it in the car park.' Hunter declined.

There was a dualism about Leeds that fascinated, yin and yang, admired and despised. When they played Chelsea, it was a clash of contrasts that breached more than football's boundaries. It was the north–south divide with screw-in studs. Leeds played carpet bowls and bingo. Chelsea had movie stars Steve McQueen in the dressing room and Raquel Welch wearing a T-shirt proclaiming: 'I scored with Peter Osgood'. The 1970 FA Cup Final was considered the dirtiest match ever played. Years later, one Premier League referee watched the game back and said that now there would have been 11 red cards and 20 yellow ones. Chelsea won. Leeds were damned as chokers.

When Revie left for England in 1974, Brian Clough took over at Leeds. He'd also been born in Middlesbrough, but the two men were worlds apart. Possibly the most outspoken figure in British football history, Clough was an anarchist who despised Revie. His first meeting with his new players, who had a slavish loyalty to their old boss, has become folklore. Lorimer told me the story is true. Clough really did greet the league champions with the words: 'The first thing you can do for me is chuck all your medals and all your caps and all your pans into the biggest effing dustbin you can find, because you've never won any of them fairly – you've done it all by bloody cheating.' He lasted 44 days.

In 1992, Wilkinson signed an enigmatic Frenchman called Eric Cantona. Hearing that he liked Rambo, the more ardent Leeds fans gamely turned up to training dressed in full combat gear, only to be told Cantona had actually referenced absinthe-addled poet Arthur Rimbaud. He scored a few goals late in the season, usually as a substitute, and was credited with taking Leeds to the title. It was another untruth and went against Wilkinson's socialist ethos and the side-before-self slogan popularised by Revie's ginger-haired lieutenant Billy Bremner. Later in the year, Cantona went to Manchester United. Where else? 'Eric likes to do what he likes when he likes,' pointed out Wilkinson. 'And then fucks off.'

Sheffield United, the Wednesday and then Huddersfield Town were the pioneering powerhouses of Yorkshire football. Huddersfield had the great Herbert Chapman, who had been with Leeds City, only to resign and take a job at a coking works when trouble loomed. It must have been bad. City were disbanded in 1919 after an illegal payments scandal, although the recalcitrant stance of the directors over an inquiry did not help.

To me, though, one Leeds player summed up Yorkshireness. Here's why. One day in the 1990s, England's players had a day off. Tony Dorigo, the pristine left back who never sweated, went to the golf club, because that was what players did for laughs in a time before nitrous oxide. David Batty went fishing. When he returned to their shared room, he was covered in blood and fish guts. 'Your tracksuit is disgusting,' Dorigo said. Batty did not miss a beat. 'It's not mine,' he said. 'It's yours.'

This was Batty, a blood-and-guts footballer who did not give a fig what you, me or the England left back thought. When Leeds got promoted to the top flight, Batty, then a rising star, spent the summer helping his dad on the bins. He was the ultimate antidote to the pomposity of modern football and is still the cure for the self-regarding egomania of social media. Everyone craves hits and clicks and likes, but David Batty did not give a toss.

As a boy, he once shocked his teacher at Scott Hall Middle School by enlivening show-and-tell with a couple of rotting fingertips that he had lost playing 'war' in a local churchyard and since kept in the back of a cupboard. As a Premier League player, he would go camping at motorcycle races. When he developed a heart problem, his response was a shrug. It was no problem.

As down-to-earth as a subterranean grouter, he lacked ambition and still got 42 caps for England. His approach was summed up in the penalty shoot-out that did for England in the 1998 World Cup. Batty missed, obviously, but there was no pizza advert as with Gareth Southgate, no tears and six-year wait for an exorcism as with Stuart Pearce after his miss in 1990. Batty just poked out his tongue and walked back to the halfway line. 'I thought I'd score,' he said bluntly afterwards. 'I knew he'd miss,' his dad added. We all did. Batty now lives quietly in the Dales. He does not go to football or pitch for jobs on the TV. He has no clothing line. He remains the least preposterous player of modern times.

Dockers and miners

Football is not a parochial passion. From the barrios of Brazil to the dog-fouled parks of Yorkshire wastelands, it is Esperanto with Deep Heat. Pelé might say he would not have happened without Sheffield FC, but he would have still kicked a ball around at Santos in São Paulo; it is just that his genesis would have been traced back to other Victorian football clubs such as the Civil Service FC or Yokohama Country Club. However, had he been a rugby league player, he could accurately have said he would not have been the man he was without the George Hotel in Huddersfield. Rugby league was born there. Rugby union was born in Rugby. To understand the difference, I first go to Rugby School. This is where William Webb Ellis supposedly picked up the ball during a football match and showed what was recorded as 'a fine disregard for the rules'.

The school archivist, Rusty Maclean, tells me the Webb Ellis story may never have happened. 'I'd be surprised if they chose him as their hero,' he says. His suspicion about Webb Ellis – the Rugby World Cup trophy is named after him – emanates from the fact that he was in Town House at Rugby School, which was regarded as the paupers' house. Different game.

The George Hotel is 90 miles from Rugby. By the 1880s, there was concern that northern rugby union clubs were becoming too dominant and were paying players 'broken-time' money as compensation for taking time off work. This north–south schism festered until 1895, when representatives of 22 clubs pitched up in Huddersfield to form the Northern Union. Over the next few decades, tweaks to the game were introduced. For example, the lineout was abolished as being a bit silly. Part-time professionalism was legalised. The Northern Union changed its name to the Rugby Football League. And while rugby union would relish its toffs tag, league settled down as the bastion of miners and dockers. Sport and a nation were split, not down the middle but across its bruised chest.

Like Ian Clayton, I went to the Challenge Cup Final in 1983. My dad took me. Featherstone Rovers' 14–12 victory over Hull was by no means a classic game, but it was an epic result. Featherstone is a small town. The population then was around 14,000. Like many West Yorkshire rugby league clubs, the team often comprised only miners. Featherstone lived off coal, and rugby and mining were symbiotic things, hard, physical labours with a shelf life. Despite the size of the town, Featherstone was a successful club, but that narrow win against Hull marked a turning point. It also underscored the patronising depiction of working-class Yorkshire in the wider media, trumpeting the idea of the good servant, loyal to his town, a bit naïve, obviously unsophisticated. Rugby union was played by RAF pilots in Leicester and doctors in Bath. League was stuck in the past, and its days out at Wembley were its chance to taste the high life and overpriced pints.

A year later, Featherstone was rocked by the miners' strike. Ackton Hall Colliery shut and was then razed to the ground. It was a kind of industrial book burning. The town's identity was tested, but it still had rugby. Yet it was left behind there too. The club's attendances had fallen away during the strike, and that Wembley day was replaced by a procession of groundhog ones. Then rugby league morphed into a glitzier, richer, more corporate version called Super League. A merger of Featherstone, Castleford and Wakefield Trinity was suggested. Wakefield voted for it, but Featherstone was not about to let the other part of its proud history be amalgamated. In the pubs they toasted the decision to stay independent. The club finished eleventh out of 16 teams in 1995 and was effectively dumped to make way for the London Broncos and a team from Paris that could not even be bothered to come up with a nickname.

In time, Featherstone would sell their ground and go into administration. Mining was no longer the common bond of players, but they toiled on. A sport born in working-class culture now had something called the million-pound game, where the top two lower-league sides played off to gain access to the Super League. In 2019, Featherstone finally made it that far. They had to go to Canada, where they lost to Toronto. In 2021, they went to France and lost to Toulouse. Everyone knows it will never be like 1983 again, a time before the strike, before Yorkshire's sport was given a lick of paint and sold off.

In the nineties, I went to work in Leicester, where union was the game. As I sat in the ground down Welford Road and looked at the Barbour jackets, the hip flasks, and ex-policeman Dean Richards sticking the ball up his jumper as his team swarmed around him and trundled down the pitch as an amorphous mess of scar tissue, I wondered what my dad would have thought. My first sporting occasion was a Bradford Northern match at Odsal. It was rough and ready. A family friend played for Halifax. I would see him at our annual Boxing Day party and note the increasing decrepitude. Every Christmas it seemed harder for him to walk without his knees buckling, and harder still to turn his neck as the years and the injuries piled up, but I guessed that, as was the case with many in rugby league, it simply hurt too much to look back.

The XXL cap

Perhaps nothing better sums up the tension between continuity and change, the insider–outsider dynamic and the county's defining stereotypes than cricket. Yorkshire cricket is part of the landscape and holds a totemic place in the minds, if not necessarily the hearts, of millions. And

then in 2021, the county cricket club was accused of insti-
tutional racism. The cricketer who raised the concerns,
Azeem Rafiq, spoke about years of abuse, mental trauma
and dismissal of his pain by the powers that be. It was
initially brushed under the carpet, but the dust gathered
into lumps and nobody could pretend the mountains were
mere molehills when the Department of Culture, Media
and Sport called its own hearing. Famous players were
embroiled. Some accepted their wrongdoing and tried to
make amends. Others denied everything. A letter was sent
to the Yorkshire board from staff complaining that nobody
had fought their corner and talking of 'white rose values'.
In the following months, it became a row about Rafiq, the
club, and the subsequent sackings, but far beyond that there
were plenty of local coaches, parents and players pointing
out that cricket had not been for everyone in the county for
a very long time.

For some, this was the horrible consequence of those days
when Yorkshire proudly refused to pick players born outside
the three ridings, thus discriminating against part of its own
population. That requirement lasted until 1992, and many
people felt that a tribal badge of honour had morphed into
something more sinister in its refusal to acknowledge the
changes going on in Britain at large. Azeem Rafiq would
recall how someone had defecated in his garden, and he
had received death threats. He had been forced to move not
just across the border but abroad. To some, it seemed that
Yorkshire did not just decline to move with the times, it
seemed oblivious to the need.

Evidently not much had changed since 1954, when John
Fairfax-Blakeborough wrote in *The Spirit of Yorkshire*,
'We're essentially a stubborn people, tenacious of our

rights, more impatient with officialdom and interference than most folk, difficult to convert from an opinion once formed, conservative, and not easy to dislodge from well-tried ruts. We are – with some cause – conceited about our country.' That 'some cause' showed the difficulty in avoiding even a gentle boast when owning up. 'Yorkshire folk, as a rule, are cautious, not easy of approach, non-confiding and uncommunicative.'

That was 1954. Geoffrey Boycott was only 13 at the time, so it is safe to assume Fairfax-Blakeborough had not been writing about the teenager from the mining village of Fitzwilliam on the edge of Wakefield. But if the XXL cap fits ...

Ask people of a certain generation for a famous Yorkshireman, and Boycott's name would be close to the top of the list. Resolutely bereft of flamboyance, he was renowned for playing forward defensive strokes in several hours of flatlining entertainment. He was hugely respected, and not only in Yorkshire, but he also played a part in tearing the club apart. The perfect county figure but a monomaniac, synonymous with his side but a bit obsessed with himself. He was from mining stock, his family having left Shropshire for Yorkshire's black gold, and would tell people that various things beat being down t'pit. A relentless, brave batsman, he was also the prematurely balding star who said his life changed when he started to wear glasses. Once he had been carefree, but from that point on he was the withdrawn, distant teenage loner.

Nevertheless, his puritanical work ethic and bottom-less bloody-mindedness took him to the summit. He got a hundred first-class centuries while still living with his mum. He epitomised resistance. And in conservative, stubborn and tenacious Yorkshire, stuck in well-tried ruts, he was just right.

Yorkshire was well established as a behemoth of cricket by the time Boycott pitched up. Dapper greats like Herbert Sutcliffe had passed on the baton to Len Hutton, who famously saddled the county with the epithet 'In an England XI the flesh may be of the south, but the bone is of the north, and the backbone is Yorkshire.' It was an exaggeration fashioned from a truth. Yorkshire did win a lot of county championships from 1893 to 1968, although the forties and fifties produced just one title in each decade. It was the swinging sixties that saw the county dominate. It was another four Yorkshiremen sketch in a way: Brian Close, the skipper; Ray Illingworth, the off-spinning all-rounder and tactical genius in some eyes; firebrand Fred Trueman rattling bones and egos as a one-man hurricane; and Boycott. The 1959 county championship title ushered in seven in ten years. Yet the county's remarkably enduring capacity for self-flagellation saw Illingworth leave when he was told a one-year contract would have to suffice. Close was sacked in 1970, partly because the loyal captain did not wish to be railroaded into picking emerging players. As he drove away from Headingley, he stopped to be sick by the side of the road. It was becoming messy, and while not all Boycott's fault, his tenure as captain from 1971 to 1978 was grimly unsuccessful.

In his book *Geoff Boycott: A Cricketing Hero*, Leo McKinstry recalls a story of a teammate's father giving Boycott a lift to a game in Middlesbrough. Boycott did not offer any petrol money but did ask the father, a miner as it happened, to go off and buy some red cheese for his tea. He didn't pay for that either. This meanness could easily segue into arrant rudeness. One of the saddest stories about him comes from a 1980 Gillette Cup game when an old lady served him potatoes with his dinner. Boycott said he didn't want her 'bastard potatoes', swept the spuds onto the floor and stormed out. This was Boycott the spoilt mummy's boy. As McKinstry said of his relationship with his mother, 'The intense love may have also made him suspicious of the outside world.' He was only at peace at home – or at the crease.

Another story has Boycott and South Africa-born batsman Basil D'Oliveira in Sydney facing spinner John Gleeson. The England team had been struggling to read the unorthodox bowler, but during a long fourth-wicket stand with Boycott, D'Oliveira finally cracked the code. Walking down the wicket, he told Boycott the happy news. 'Oh, I sorted that out a fortnight ago,' Boycott replied. 'But don't tell the buggers up there.' The buggers were the faces in the England dressing room. Boycott denied this exchange ever happened but there was no doubt his primary concern was to win his own battle; the rest would follow.

Boycott's sacking as Yorkshire's captain came soon after his hundredth century and just days after his mother's death. The club was all politics at the time, with infighting, cliques, and former greats unceremoniously discarded. The frustration with Boycott's leadership meant his own players wanted a new captain. Cue a pro-Boycott Reform Group to fight his cause. Boycott, meanwhile, had retaliated in a uniquely Yorkshire manner by going on *Parkinson*, the chat show hosted by his former Barnsley teammate and another son of a miner.

Michael Parkinson spoke of Boycott's fanatical dedication, and he replied that Yorkshire's committee were

small-minded people who could not even wait for him to
bury his mother. 'A lot of people take it the wrong road
about me,' he said on an earlier appearance. 'They think I'm
being very arrogant and conceited. I'm not. I believe I'm a
professional man and I'm very proud of it.' He added that
people were jealous of his publicity and listened to hearsay
from those who didn't like him, but claimed he had changed.
'I think I have arrived at the point where I know I'm a good
player now. Now I realise that if I make 100, I'm not necessarily the greatest player in the world.'

Yet for many, he was. And like it or not, he was
Yorkshire. He had unwavering belief. He said what he
liked and liked what he said. He was clichés made man
and did not champion the good work he did for charity
and for young players. He didn't need to. He was Captain
Bloody Boycott.

He was not like Close, the personification of the stiff
upper lip, taking blows from West Indies pacemen, wincing
but never wilting. Nor was he Trueman, the fast bowler
whose sublime action was that of the purest golf swing but
whose technique was allied to bar-room bullishness, a giant
of a man swapping missiles for pints and generally being the
Yorkshire of the people.

Trueman's no-nonsense approach seeped from his name
to his birth. His grandmother delivered him, presumably in
between peeling spuds for dinner and scrubbing the floor,
and sorting truths from myths has been a chore ever since.
He was born near Doncaster (true), slept in a drawer (probably not), had a year off school after taking one in the groin
(possibly), and was sacked from a job as a bricklayer for
telling the foreman to bugger off (almost certainly). He was
the bad boy who was too good to be true, so a whiff of

apocrypha clings to his shadow. He took a job at Maltby Main Colliery in South Yorkshire, but not as a miner, and when he was granted leave from the RAF to play cricket, one mother complained to the House of Commons that her own son had missed out on a banjo-playing competition.

Trueman was bold and brash, one of the angry young men epitomised by the likes of John Braine, the Bradford novelist whose 1957 book *Room at the Top* touched tangentially on themes of Trueman's career: the idea that you should know your place and adhere to tested roles. Trying otherwise could be bad for you; hence *Room at the Top* ends tragically with a car crash and a guilty conscience.

Parkinson said Trueman was anti-authoritarian from the start, and he certainly refused to accept his given place. On tour with England, he baulked at the decree from his captain and co-Yorkshireman, Len Hutton, not to fraternise with the West Indies players. This was England as colonial masters, and Trueman was buggered if anyone was going to tell him who he could socialise with. Clashes with authority and the suspicion of blazers saw him miss numerous England tours. But where Boycott had his 100 centuries, Fiery Fred was the first man to take 300 Test wickets. In *The Times*, John Woodcock marked this achievement in 1964 with the memorable line: 'On his day he has displayed, to the highest degree, the beauty and skill and the manliness and the terror of his calling.'

For many, Trueman is Yorkshire in sporting form. 'Some of the committee did not like my forthright attitude, which they misinterpreted as being bolshie,' he said. 'These committee men would rather choose a gentleman and a decent chap rather than the best equipped to win.' To Trueman, this was just not cricket.

It was said he softened in older age, and his 2004 autobiography, *As It Was*, includes florid passages in which he
speaks in a way that suggests hidden depths, or at least a
good ghost-writer. 'I've learnt from life that love can take
many forms. There is the grand passion, which is electric,
stimulating and fulfilling. But that sort of love can't be
enduring all the time. There is also another type of love in
a long-term relationship. Though it does not involve grand
passion, it is stronger, in many ways more comforting.' It is,
he goes on, the love that checks the car insurance and doesn't
forget birthdays, knows what colour to paint the bathroom
and decorates the dull facade. This, I would contend, is the
love of Yorkshire.

The course of true love never did run smooth, though,
and Boycott and Trueman fell out. It was inevitable. Maybe
Boycott was jealous. It was said Yorkshire's female physio
believed that God only gave out one perfect physique and
He gave it to Fred. To which Boycott might have countered
that he had no memory of doing so. A female supporter told
Trueman his batting was like making love to her husband. 'It
may not last long, but by heck while it does the sparks really
fly.' The two cricketers both thought they were the best, and
at times they both were. 'T'greatest fast bowler who ever drew
breath' was the title Trueman suggested for his biography.

Trueman courted controversy too, and once had to tell
officials he was 200 miles away from where a perceived
misdemeanour took place. Boycott ended up in court for
assaulting his girlfriend. He denied the charges and some of
the evidence was questioned by case commentators, but his
conviction, in France, led to criticism when he was awarded
a knighthood in 2019. Boycott's response to a statement
from the co-acting chief of Women's Aid at the time did not

help: 'I couldn't give a toss.'

And after Boycott had forged a career as a blunt commentator, Trueman said, 'If Geoffrey had played cricket the way he talked, he would have had people queuing up to get into the ground instead of queuing up to leave.'

In the authorised biography *Fred Trueman*, journalist Chris Waters records a reunion in 2005 between Boycott, Trueman, Close and Illingworth in the Sawley Arms pub in Ripon. By then, much dirty water, flecked with blood and bodies, had flown under the burnt bridges. Trueman is late and bemoans a flock of sheep at Grassington. They talk of the Ashes, bloody Australians, and a younger generation who 'don't know they're born'. Boycott asks Trueman how many wickets he took. Trueman answers 2,304 first-class ones at 18.29, and 307 Test ones at 21.57. The vignette ends with the quartet discussing Ant and Dec. 'Ant and fucking Dec,' says Trueman. 'They're not fit to lace the boots of Morecambe and Wise.'

As Waters walked to the car park, Trueman told him the things that were wrong with Yorkshire. He had to pay towards his own leaving present for one. The anger was undimmed and he moved on to Boycott. 'All that civil war at Yorkshire in the 1980s involving Geoffrey, God bless him, led to me being voted off the Yorkshire committee and replaced by some bloke with a deaf aid from Keighley.' There is, perhaps, no better epitaph for Yorkshire cricket.

God and Beryl

Sport is emotion and meaning, heart and soul, suspect centre halves and no half-measures. It's not fluff, though.

It's a tie that binds and it's a way of showing off, which is a Yorkshire pastime.

This penchant for peacock displays was never more evident than in 2014, when Yorkshire got to hold the first stage of the Tour de France, or Le Grand Depart as cycling folk prefer it. I was there and I saw the aerial shot of an enormous yellow jersey atop York Minster emblazoned with the words 'Allez Alleluia'. The Church's bandwagon jump was symbolic of the success of the Tour de God's Country. Almost everybody had taken the chance to showcase the county's grandeur and their business's wares. It was a Monet-making exercise worth an estimated £100 million to the local economy, even if that sounded like a suspiciously round number.

There were world-weary French miserabilists who believed the Tour had sold its soul in selling Le Grand Depart to the highest bidders, but Yorkshire put on its Sunday best and the sense of commonality had not been felt since the 2012 Olympics. Four million people lined roads, cobbles, moors and pockets. It was, in terms of numbers, the biggest sporting event Britain has seen. 'I had goosebumps,' Chris Froome, the defending champion, said of the crowds.

There was also a more tangible legacy. Plans for the Tour of Yorkshire, a three-day UCI Europe Tour race, had been announced, and nascent tour companies were relishing a new era of stage reruns for MAMILS (middle-aged men in Lycra); you could see the name already – 'The Brontë Sore Arse'. Despite bids from more obviously pouty candidates such as Barcelona and Florence, not to mention the government-stamped Edinburgh entry, Yorkshire won. Among other things, Gary Verity, the boss of tourism agency Welcome to Yorkshire, was a prize-winning sheep farmer. That had been Yorkshire's shtick, playing up to stereotypes while debunking them.

The number of fans was the biggest Tour legend Bernard Hinault said he had seen in 40 years. York University gave Verity an honorary degree, the Queen gave him a knighthood and the French president made him a chevalier of the National Order of Merit. He became deputy lieutenant of West Yorkshire. Then it was alleged he had been creative with his expenses. Nothing was proved and he resigned on health grounds. Welcome to Yorkshire went into liquidation. Yorkshire had to survive without the soft focus and evangelical marketeers.

One of the quirks of Yorkshire's sense of self is that perhaps its finest ever sports star is barely known. Beryl Burton was also a cyclist. She was born in Halton, east Leeds, and had a competitiveness that makes Boycott look like an apathetic jellyfish, but she suffered because sport was sexist. Her spirit seemed to stem from a form of mental breakdown when she took her 11-plus exam, which segued into debilitating physical symptoms. In *Beryl*, her biographer Jeremy Wilson says she spent nine months in St James's Hospital in Leeds and then 15 in a Southport convalescent home run by nuns. Only when she was 12 did she declare herself ready to go home.

She met her husband, Charlie, while working in a clothing factory, and Saturday-morning rides turned into an obsession. Sport likes stats and it needs them for comparison's sake; she won seven world titles and 122 national ones. She was the youngest women's world champion and a serial record-breaker in time trials. 'Anything the lads can do, I can do,' she said, but that was not true. The Olympics did not let women do anything likely to make them sweat, so road cycling was only permitted in 1984 and time trialling had to wait until 1996. Burton's reign lasted decades, but it did not reach the Olympics. Instead, she made do with winning the battle of the sexes.

This was not necessarily something to be celebrated in Britain, and perhaps especially Yorkshire, where traditional familial roles were relied upon. Richard Hoggart, born and educated in Leeds, lest we forget, remarked on this when discussing women who worked up until or after childbirth. They did this not because they were 'revolting against the demands of marriage' but because they wanted the right to pay for little luxuries and have fish and chips twice a week. 'When that goes, it goes,' he wrote in *The Uses of Literacy*. 'Most working-class girls do not much pine for their lost freedom; they never regarded it as other than temporary.'

But Burton pushed parameters. And so one day in 1967, she turned up to a 12-hour time trial run by Otley Cycle Club. There were 99 men competing that day, including Mike McNamara, the previous year's winner. Riders set off at intervals, but Burton reeled them all in. Then she came to McNamara, who was trying to fend her off while nursing an overwhelming need to relieve himself. 'Poor Mac,' she said. 'His glory, richly deserved, was going to be overshadowed by a woman.' As she passed him, she handed him a Liquorice Allsort. With the game up, McNamara dismounted and urinated in a bush. Burton's record that day, of 277 miles in 12 hours, stood for two years.

She carried on working on a rhubarb farm, where two Soviet coaches came to meet her in a quest for her secrets. They left disappointed. Burton did not take drugs, and wearing knitted jumpers and plastic sheets when it was wet was not what Moscow was after. Her secrets were somewhere within, as shown by her almost cruel behaviour to her daughter, Denise, when she grew into a rival. Not shaking hands with her when Denise beat her in the 1976 national road race championship was one thing – 'This is not a story for some romantic magazine,' she explained – but refusing to alter her pre-race routine to check on her daughter after a serious crash was off the scale. She also won tandem races with Denise, kept training like a dervish into middle age, and died of a heart attack in 1966, while cycling to deliver invitations for her fifty-ninth birthday.

The 56

I never knew of Beryl Burton growing up. It was football and rugby league. Hard men ruled. As you get older, you go looking for a softer side, the shimmering edges, so it was nice to hear Yorkshire-born Scouse footballing icon Kevin Keegan tell a story about Norman Hunter. Despite Hunter's reputation as an uncompromising hard man, Keegan praised him for his other side, saying Hunter did not get enough credit for his skill. 'He could flight the ball beautifully with his left foot,' he remarked. A year after the 1974 Charity Shield, a supposedly gentle pre-season kickabout that Leeds turned into a prolonged exercise in goading Keegan, he magnanimously said he would be delighted to play in Hunter's testimonial. 'I drove 100 miles,' he said, 'and the first thing he did was chop me down.'

Revie died in 1989, Bremner in 1997, Hunter in 2020 and Lorimer in 2021. My dad went before them all. For many football fans your club is not really about cups and titles but family ties and heirloom fables. When I think of the Revie team, I think about my dad.

Dad was from Bradford. It gets a lot of stick. It is determinedly not pretty. 'Palpably forlorn,' said Bill Bryson. Some of it is palpably ugly, the obvious product of a drug culture in fifties architectural colleges. Arty buildings with manicured carvings were out, brutalism was in. Luckily, the Bradford Alhambra, a magnificent theatre with Corinthian columns and padded seats in the orchestra pit, had already been built.

But much of the city was indeed forlorn and unloved. On 11 May 1985, some 11,076 people went to Valley Parade to celebrate their football team's Division Three title. It was going to be a good day. Peter Jackson, the Bradford-born club captain, parked his car and passed the steel girders that were lying on the floor waiting for the workmen to arrive in two days' time to start upgrading the archaic main stand. He went into the dressing room and looked at his teammates. One of them was Stuart McCall, the former Bradford schoolboy on the cusp of a glittering career. Just before kick-off, against Lincoln City, Jackson, the local hero, picked up the championship trophy and looked to the players' balcony, where his wife, Alison, held Charlotte, just 18 months old, in her arms.

It was a dull game, but most of the crowd were just happy to have something to shout about. Bradford had suffered as a community: the inertia of its industry, the trauma of the Peter Sutcliffe years and the mediocrity of its football. Now things were on the up. Then, after 40 minutes, a policeman walked up to Terry Yorath, the assistant coach, and asked where the nearest tap was.

The deputy lord mayor, Bill Nunn, had stayed in his seat in the main stand in the hope that Bradford might score before half-time. Bored delegates from twin towns in Germany, France and Belgium had sloped off for a cup of tea. To his left, Nunn noticed a puff of grey smoke near the back. 'I thought it was a smoke bomb,' he said. But then he saw the flames that grew from a flicker to a flare to an inferno within four minutes. The fire started in G block and blazed through the alphabet as the tar roof and the rubbish beneath the stand turned it into a funeral pyre.

Play was stopped. Yorath ran upstairs to his office, where his son, Daniel, used to go for half-time sweets. He tried to spread the word, but the fire was spreading faster. He smashed a window in the players' lounge and leapt to safety. Jackson found his wife and child and escaped, while Nunn got the burgomaster of Hamm out by a rear door.

PC Glynn Leesing pulled the tights off a woman in an attempt to claw her away from the danger. 'My plastic coat had melted and my head and hair had started to burn,' he said. He saw a pensioner dragging an elderly woman over a wall and helped them. John Hawley, the former Arsenal striker, yanked a man over the wall to safety, ignoring the proximity of his own nylon shirt to the fire.

With his club blazer pulled over his sweat-soaked kit, Stuart McCall drove to St Luke's Hospital looking for his father, Andy, who had been badly injured. He was told the more severely burnt had been taken to Pinderfields Hospital, in Wakefield. The 15-mile drive took an eternity. Andy McCall was passionate about football. He had played alongside Stanley Matthews in the great Blackpool side and now loved watching his son perform. When McCall and his brother, Les, walked into the burns unit, they could barely recognise their father through the bandages. Yet Andy McCall would reflect that he was one of the lucky ones.

In total, 56 people died in the Bradford fire and another 260 were injured. The players of both teams assembled in the nearby Belle Vue pub, once a favourite of J.B. Priestley, for a roll call. They watched the mounted television screen in staggered silence. 'They kept saying there might be two or three killed,' Jackson said. 'But later we went back to the ground to get some belongings and I looked out and saw the body bags piled up. I knew it was far worse. It was the most horrible sight.' He got home at 10.30 p.m. and sat on the sofa in his shirt, shorts and socks, arms clamped around his wife, toddler on his knee. 'You never get over it.'

It was an era of cowsheds and fans treated as cattle. That spartan ordeal, as Desmond Morris had it. Heroic stories merged, but in some ways this became football's forgotten tragedy. Years later, John Hendrie, one of the players, said he went into a school to talk to the kids and 'none of them knew anything about it'. Julian Gratton was 11 on the day of the disaster, forever grateful that he persuaded his dad to stand in the Kop rather than take their usual seats in the main stand. Angered by people posting social-media clips of the fire, he would set up a non-profit online resource. 'People don't talk about it much,' he said. 'It's a very Yorkshire reaction in some ways; it's kept insular.' He recalled that when he went to school on the following Monday, 'They did the register and two people were absent. Someone asked, "Were they at the match?" The fire was never discussed after that.'

Martin Fletcher lost his father, brother, grandfather and uncle. He spent years researching and writing a book,

Fifty-Six: The Story of the Bradford Fire. He pointed out that there had been eight other fires at businesses owned or linked to late Bradford chairman Stafford Heginbotham that had resulted in insurance claims. He was accused by some of opening old wounds, but he pointed out what he felt were inadequacies in the investigation. He said the inquiry into the fire by Sir Oliver Popplewell processed up to 15 people a day and the interim analysis was a mere 27 pages long, compared with a report into the King's Cross fire, where 31 people had died, which ran to more than 400. In 2016, the police said there would be no new inquiry. Fletcher, as it happened, was at Hillsborough in 1989 on the day of the tragedy there. He got home and asked his mum why the fences had not come down after Bradford's disaster.

The idea of being let down by authority is a common trauma in the county, from the miners and steelworkers to the victims of Sutcliffe, Acre Mill and Bradford. Yorkshire often feels it gets left behind, even if it does not say it. Sometimes it gets the tragic parts instead of the comedy ones.

Popplewell's remarks in his memoirs now seem barely believable. 'Comparing the reaction of those involved in the Bradford disaster with those involved in some other disasters, one can only be astonished at the wonderful way that the citizens of Bradford behaved. They quietly buried their dead, tended the injured and comforted the bereaved. Not for them the noisy and public whingeing and whining that has been the hallmark of so many other disasters. They did not use their disaster as a weapon of emotional blackmail on the government, nor did they seek to perpetuate publicly the memory of the terrible disaster they had suffered.'

That 'whingeing and whining' and praise for people quietly burying their dead and grievances still shocks.

The campaigners at Orgreave developed links with the
Hillsborough families over their mistreatment by South
Yorkshire Police, but in Bradford, the suffering, for the main,
was kept inside. In 2022, someone desecrated the city centre
memorial with graffiti, just as they had daubed offence on
the grave of Tony Harrison's parents up in Beeston all those
years ago. I think of 'V', and how it's often not for victory.

> *What is it these crude words are revealing?*
> *What is it that this aggro act implies?*
> *Giving the dead their xenophobic feeling*
> *Or just a cri-de-coeur because man dies?*

10

RAMBLERS

It's immaterial.

Dry-stone waller, in answer to a query about
whether millstone grit or limestone is the best material
for building, *The Dalesman* documentary, 1988

Yorkshire is made for walking, and not only because of
cancelled bus routes. The Dales and the North York
Moors are the jewels in the crown, and havens for
wildlife, potholers, farmers, tourists, ramblers and all those
with eyes and ears. Their beauty is deceptive, and life up
and out there is hard. Perhaps more than anywhere, these
are the places that need outsiders while wishing they didn't.
Rambling is also about the gift of storytellers, linking the past
to the present with memories untainted by modern faddery.

Last of the Summer Wine

We are arranging our return to Yorkshire for late 2022
when Mum says, 'I never thought I'd see it again.' It's a fairly

crushing remark, but a practical one. Mum spent 60 years in Yorkshire before she left, and the place has slowly drifted. It feels a bit like the old philosophical question about whether there is any sound if a tree falls in a forest and nobody is there. Things have certainly continued to happen in Yorkshire, but do they rouse the senses if you are not there to see, hear, smell, touch and taste them? You construct a present built wholly from the past, reading the *Yorkshire Post* online and watching the Yorkshire channels: *Our Yorkshire Farm*, *The Yorkshire Vet*, *The Yorkshire Colonic Irrigationist*. That picture is not necessarily wrong, but it is different, like black and white TV with a coat-hanger stuck in the back versus high-res plasma screen with HD technicolour.

Mum does all the things needed for a trip north. She gets her jabs, COVID and flu, and has her hair done. I wonder if she will be disappointed, if memory will prove a bit optimistic. We go through places she wants to revisit – Bradford, where she grew up in that long-gone pub; Leeds, where she shopped in long-gone stores while we watched football in a long-gone league; Tadcaster, where we moved to and lived and where Dad worked and was buried – and raised.

When I was young, I had a deep dislike of *Last of the Summer Wine*. It was a TV show about three old Yorkshiremen getting up to high, or at least elevated, jinks, a sort of *Some Mothers Do 'Ave 'Em* with backache. It was a gentle sort of humour not suited to a generation needing *The Simpsons*, and it felt like people were laughing at Yorkshire and its Norah Battys and dirty old men, but I now realise it was a tribute to old age. Age does not mean having to succumb to expectation and talk incessantly about how the weather is playing havoc with your hip replacement while bemoaning modern life – although there is a place for this.

The producers wanted to call it 'The Library Mob', but Roy Clarke, the erudite writer, went for his emotive title, suggesting the trio of lead characters were past their best-by date rather than their sell-by one. It was still summer even it was throwing it down. Even when two of the lead characters had died it rumbled on, right up until the point when Peter Sallis delivers the last line, which seems innocuous but sums up the fearfulness of old age: 'Did I lock the door?'

Holmfirth, six miles or so from Huddersfield, in the Holme Valley, was the village that had been the setting for the series, and it relished the subsequent tourism boost. It died a little when it ended, although some locals had been grumbling about compensation for the disruption caused by filming. Sallis, not a Yorkshireman, would get to voice Wallace in Nick Park's animated films about a Yorkshireman, his dog (Gromit) and Yorkshire cheese (Wensleydale). Two Oscars followed, and the success led to Steven Spielberg sending a jet for Park's team to travel to Hollywood to discuss other ideas. That became *Chicken Run*, a film about Plasticine birds fleeing a Yorkshire chicken farm. It was a homage to *The Great Escape*, hailed as a feminist, Marxist and revolutionary triumph, and made £200 million at the box office (Sallis had done the first Wallace and Gromit for a £50 donation to charity), but at their heart the films, like *Last of the Summer Wine*, were about freedom, the perils of modernisation and a disappearing north.

Common people

Yorkshire has lost a lot, which explains why we are clinging on for dear life. This is summed up by the way climate

change has baked the Dales and unearthed the past. I head
to a place that Halliwell Sutcliffe, he of *The Striding Dales*,
described as existing between Greenhow and Blubberhouses.
In 1929, he hails the tiny hamlet of West End, in the Washburn Valley west of Harrogate, as a blissful scene bereft of
human life. An old inn stands with a signboard swaying in
the breeze; there are honeysuckle lanes, drowsy bees and
well-masoned stone houses; remnants from the flax trade
when water powered the yarn-making process. He thinks
back to a time when 'the hideous days of child labour were
over' and 'men had scarcely begun to rear the manufacturing
towns that now eat up, like a cancer, league after league of
what was God's country'.

The flax industry died, though, unable to compete with
Russia, and in 1961 the first workmen arrived to begin
building Thruscross Reservoir. Five years later, Yorkshire
Water flooded the area and West End disappeared, sinking
into old yarns. Yet very occasionally, if the summer is long
and hot enough, the old buildings re-emerge. It happened
in 1995, when the summer stretched and the water level
dropped. Yorkshire Water became the first privatised water
company to ask the government to impose emergency measures. A hearing was held in Shipley near Bradford. Labour's
shadow environment secretary, Frank Dobson, ploughed
into the shallows and said Yorkshire Water was losing 100
million gallons a year through its leaky system.

That year, 1995, one old reservoir man returned and
remembered how he had been among the first to arrive
three decades earlier. His home-made film is still buried on
YouTube, the digital date 25.10.95 steady in the bottom
corner as his shaky video camera scans the drained basin
and reveals the bridge, the chapel walls and other ruins.

The voiceover says he is now going to descend the reservoir banks. The film blurs. It restarts with a cautionary tale. 'In no time at all, up to the knees, a wellington gone, swallowing me up, I had to scream for help. I only just got out. A very nasty experience.' He details this near-death escapade in a low monotone. Very Yorkshire. 'Terrifying,' he says, as if describing events at the meat raffle. 'Makes you think.' Then, without any hint as to whether he is joking, he adds: 'I'd been at solicitor's this morning revising my will.' His camera stalls on the same bridge he drove a truck across in 1961. 'Just shows how you can become badly unstuck.' Fade. It's like the Ramblers' cut of *The Blair Witch Project*.

West End used to be home to around 600 people, but it was a ghost town before it became a lost village. There were only six occasionally occupied dwellings by the time it was drowned, four of them rentals. I imagine the last person leaving, bought out and facing a new life after rural institutionalisation. Across the bridge, up the slope and down the Washburn Valley, carried away on the current like degrading peat, stopping only to think, 'Did I lock the door?'

West End was not alone, and the floods came for many. Yorkshire has more than 120 reservoirs. It is not enough. In the 1990s, satirist and comedian Mark Thomas affected delivering a tanker of water to Yorkshire as a gift from the people of Ethiopia. The Yorkshire Water chief protested and said he had stopped having baths, but people still smelt something fishy. In 2022, there was renewed anger over fat dirty cats and a £1.6 million fine for discharging sewage into Bradford Beck. And once again Yorkshire felt the heat, from dale to city. The water level dropped. The north might not be rising, but West End did. The Blair Witch Rambler no doubt went back to look for his lost welly.

When people talk generically about Yorkshire, they are often taking about the Dales. If not that, then the North York Moors. This is what people refer to as God's Own Country, for the beauty and drama of the landscape, although one would imagine He would have put in better waterworks. The bogs up here are in trouble. The government encouraged drainage of peatlands for agriculture in the 1950s and channels called grips were subsequently dug. Natural gullies then formed. The water table dropped and the quality of the peat fell as the land eroded. Peat was also washed into the river system and huge amounts of carbon were released into the atmosphere. It was a man-made disaster. The Yorkshire Peat Partnership has since been striving to save the blanket bogs, which cover more than 50,000 hectares. One way is to bring in thousands of tonnes of local stone and Sri Lankan coir logs to block the erosion channels.

You get commoners here. Not common people like Pulp would sing about. These commoners are custodians of the land. Magna Carta set in law the rights of poor people to access communal land for their animals and to reap some basic materials. Now 'commoning' involves a collective of farmers sharing unfenced land. They gather their own sheep and restore them to their heft, the pasture they become habituated to. Together they protect the land, which is not worth much in terms of agriculture but is valuable for its beauty, history and biodiversity. In *The Shepherd's Life*, James Rebanks explains the importance of the practice in the Lakes. 'Commoner isn't a dirty word here; it is a thing to be proud of. It means you have rights to something of value, that you contribute to the management of the fells, and that you take part in our way of life as an equal to other farmers.' Commoners are part of history, but the withdrawal from the

EU means funding could soon be cut in half. Leaving this land is becoming a reality.

The Dales are hills and river valleys, mainly draining to the east into the Vale of York. This region sits above industrialised West and South Yorkshire, below County Durham (the only county with that prefix) and Cumbria, to the left of plain old North Yorkshire, which includes the vast moors to the north-east and the Wolds below. Beyond that, only the sea and the south.

Broadly speaking, the Dales are where you go to get away from the other Yorkshire. No disrespect, but they have little in common with Sheffield or Doncaster. The vistas vary from dale to dale, but this is the land of deserted barns and dry-stone walls. Of limestone and mudstone and millstone grit. I go there for a fortnight in June, and my plan is to travel from the bottom at Bolton Abbey, through Wharfedale, which is my favourite part, up to Hawes, the market town and heart of Wensleydale, just above the centre, and then bear left to the Three Peaks, climbing one of the great mountains. Trains, trails and turned-off mobiles.

Riding the snot train

It is not long before you start to feel as though you are in a different world as you journey up through Wharfedale. Once I have left the Strid, I head north to the Valley of Desolation, so named because a violent storm in 1836 left great oaks uprooted. The loss of trees changed the landscape and it became a place for sheep to graze. It can be beautiful and it can be savage, which is Yorkshire in a nutshell. Halliwell Sutcliffe, an able guide as the first president of the West

Riding Ramblers' Association, warned that whatever time of year you visited, it was always a bit winter.

Simon's Seat is an imposing millstone grit outcrop, the bull to the Cow and Calf, and is swathed in legends. In one of these Simon was a shepherd who came across an abandoned baby. 'Unwedded, except to Dale, weather and sheep-tending', as Sutcliffe had it, he tugged on his beard and wondered what to do, but was smitten by the blue eyes, and before long, the local shepherds agreed to raise the child between them. The baby became Simon Amangham, as in 'among them', a notable Wharfedale name. Another origin story claims the rock was named after Simon Magus, who was better known as Simon the Magician and unfortunately most famous for his death, which occurred when he tried to show Emperor Nero his admittedly impressive trick of levitation. St Peter and St Paul were concerned, however, and prayed that he would not be carried off by the angels of Satan, whereupon he fell to earth and broke his neck. Be careful what you wish for. Quite how this relates to Wharfedale is anyone's guess.

I plan to drive from Ribblehead to Ingleton. Ribblehead, a spot on the 80-mile Dales Way path between Ilkley to the south and Lake Windermere to the north, has a miraculous viaduct, although it does not go over the top about it. The information board in a room at the little station in Settle, 12 miles south, cannot be accused of bragging, calling it a very ordinary viaduct and nothing special. In terms of marketing, this is known as 'soft', but it is always stunning to see this man-made landscape emerge from its natural one in autumn camouflage. Drive on and don't look back at it or you will miss the sharp turn. Craggy rock faces on either side now grind teeth as you wind along the tarmac tongue. These grey borders are a riot of lines, Yorkshire's Mount Rushmore as imagined by Hockney on an Etch A Sketch.

I park up on the side of a road near a rough track hemmed in by dry-stone walls. Yorkshire's Three Peaks route takes in Pen-y-ghent, Whernside and Ingleborough. Of these, Whernside is the tallest, at 736 metres, but in terms of British peaks, this is pretty modest; Ben Nevis is almost twice that size. Indeed, England's mountains (anything above 600 metres) are generally statistically unimpressive, with Scafell Pike in the Lake District the highest, at 978 metres.

I want to climb Ingleborough, though. Mum has recently let slip that she lived briefly in Ingleton, at the foot of the mountain, when her dad worked as a warden for the vicar. I never got to meet my mum's parents. It's one of those things you wish were different, and the more you edge away from the past and its people the more you realise what you never saw or asked. Meanwhile, Dad's parents lived next door to us in Stutton, a quick jump over the back wall away, but they never got to an age where I wanted to talk family history with them.

I'd never heard the story of Mum living in Ingleton before, but she told me about the mountain's flat top and the six-foot snowdrifts they would battle to make the school bus. And so here I am. On one side of the walls are sheep dotted around the greenery like shanked golf balls. On the other are silhouetted rocks that gently move and merge into cows when you get nearer. For 20 minutes there is no sign of a mountain and it is just a farming idyll. The sun is filtering through half-hearted clouds. I plough on and it occurs to me I have not seen another human being for an hour or so. It is good for the soul. Ukraine, the cost of living and the tragedies and trivia of daily life all fade. All I hear is the wind pushing me on and the tap-tap-tap of my walking pole.

I come to a gate and two men are sitting on the other side of it. Both have cool hiking beards and look jaded. 'It's blowy up there,' says one. 'Caught us by surprise, to be honest.' They are younger than me and I note have no pole. I wonder whether this makes me look more expert or just one of those all-the-gear-no-idea people, the sort who would never borrow a cup of sugar when they could set up a direct debit with a free-trade collective in Brazil via their Hebden Bridge go-between.

'Is it raining?' I ask, because there is a cap of cloud sitting on the pewter peak.

'No, but it nearly knocks you off your feet.'

I smile politely and carry on. *An American Werewolf in London* comes back to mind. 'Stay on the roads. Stay off the moors.'

The route is obvious enough, though, and to my surprise, I come upon a stone house to my left. It is advertising bed and breakfast. This is Crina Bottom, a 400-year-old off-grid farmstead with two rooms available overlooking the fell. It is out of season and nobody is around. I carry on, along rocky trails, grassy interludes and then, as Ingleborough rears up like some millstone cobra, rougher ground.

A descending dog approaches, followed by two women. 'It's nice when wind's behind you,' says one. The other smiles. Possibly smirks. Could be paranoia. I wish them well and crack on. The view is soon bottled mindfulness. Whernside is out there to the north, bigger and bleaker. All houses shrink and then disappear, even Crina Bottom. I realise I am now above the sheep line, with the hardiest some way down there. Swaledale sheep are some of the toughest animals anywhere. They are the David Batty of lambing. Their wool is not high grade and is best for carpets, but prize specimens can fetch mind-boggling prices. Not long ago, King Kong went for £60,000, bought by the appropriately named Flash Farms at the Kirkby Stephen sales in Cumbria. It is best not to mention that around here, not after the bitter row about whether it or Hawes is the spiritual home of Swaledales. Oh the embarrassment if Cumbria had the rights to the logo of the Yorkshire Dales.

The dry-stone walls are a marvel of the Dales. There are 5,000 miles of them. As I look down into the sun, their blackened lines form infantry columns and a forever march. This is no idle metaphor, as the stones do move in the wind. Some of the walls, held together by stone fillings, are havens for tiny wildlife, one side wet, the other dry, a perch for preying birds or a path for lay preachers, some with distinctive tops built to keep out wolves. That practice died out when the wolves did, around 600 years ago. Some were supposedly built by Napoleonic prisoners, some in the days of the Knights Templar. Most are much newer and came about through the various enclosure acts. Some border L-shaped fields worked by oxen, while the S-shaped ones housed more nimble horses.

The craftsmen live on as down-to-earth artists dividing the land as they build five metres a day. Bill Mitchell, the former editor of the *Dalesman* and prolific writer, whose works are found in every railway station on the Settle–Carlisle line and every bookshop in Yorkshire's green bits, loved the wallers. In his 1993 collection *Bill Mitchell's Yorkshire*, he wrote of Dave Hannam being paid half a crown for seven yards after walking from his home in Horton to build on the top of Pen-y-ghent, and of Moonlight Jack, who was so accomplished that he was forced to go out at night to pull down sections to keep himself in work. 'Held together with hard work and common sense and building 'em right,' said one modern waller in a radio interview. 'If one fell down in my lifetime I'd be very upset.'

Onwards and upwards. I am surprised to see a line of colour bleeding the grass. Two teenagers come past first. They are American.

'What's it like up there?' I ask, my concern growing.

'We had to come down on our butts. Good luck.'

My confidence is waning in inverse proportion to the growth of an ache in my ankle. Suddenly the colour bursts into focus and I realise it is a trail of school kids. Some fly past me wearing only shirtsleeves. In contrast, I have an insulated vest, woolly shirt, hoodie and waterproof jacket.

'Keep left,' shouts a teacher as the procession of snot passes by.

'Did you get to the top?' I ask one kid.

'Nuh. Wunt let us.'

There is something heart-warming in this. In these days of health and safety, when certain schools would deem a game of rock paper scissors too fraught with risk, it is edifying to see a child trying to scale the second highest mountain in Yorkshire, in high winds, under an unpredictable sky, armed only with trainers, a Beyoncé T-shirt and a teaching assistant who looks as if he may prefer unnatural highs. I pick up a discarded anorak that is in danger of blowing away to Whernside.

'Is this one of yours?' I ask a teacher.

'Probably.' She grins.

Maybe they are a local school and do this stuff all the time before shearing sheep and skinning wolves. Or maybe they are from London and just haven't got a clue. Either way, I start to look for stray children as I make my way up the steeper climb, and picture the roll call at Toddington services.

High up the hill, the weather seems like a threat now. 'Get off our land.' I see a Yorkshire Dales noticeboard, which is a bit depressing. Not quite up there with Scott finding a Norwegian flag in Antarctica, but close. The board crams in a lot of information. It mentions the Yorkshire Three Peaks Challenge and how two teachers completed its 24-mile route in 14 hours in 1887. Now the record is under three. People even run up this route. Personally, I consider fell running dangerous, with a clue in the title, but if you can do it then it must be hugely satisfying, like communing with sheep via the medium of power socks. The board also claims that in 1830, a wealthy landowner went further and built a tower up here to house grouse-hunting parties. I find this staggering. Traipsing up here with guns while quaffing from silver hip flasks makes Year 7 appear the epitome of good sense. It turns out the landowner even marked the opening with a horse race. My sense of achievement begins to die. Some of the locals got drunk and tore down the tower, and the unamused landowner was sufficiently annoyed to leave the remains there. The rocky detritus is the old equivalent of 3 a.m. in any city centre.

Nevertheless, I stumble and crawl to the top, the wind now strong enough to make me wonder if I'm being foolish, and the views are vast and broadscreen. There is Whernside looking down on us, beyond it Scafell Pike and the Old Man of Coniston. Ilkley Moor is 30 miles to the south east and Pendle Hill is conjuring up spells 20 miles west of that. Even Snowdonia can be seen from up here.

The wind is now positively mardy and I know I need to get down quickly, but it is tempting to linger over the narrowing shafts of golden light. I have been reading a lot of Helen Mort's prose and poetry lately, and one line is swept into my head. She was talking about a different county, but Yorkshire today is also a glass of heat and the sun a slice of lemon rind. I drink it in. Helen likes to climb; I shuffle and scramble a bit. I follow the advice and go down the first bit on my bum. For two hours the wind will now blow in my face, like modern life passing me by in its rush to the top. My hair will be sculpted into a Stan Laurel tribute, but regardless of the fitter, faster, better people who have been here, I feel content. Today I have climbed a mountain and that feels bloody great.

Whernside is now brown-grey to my right and it is definitely raining there, but Ingleton still looks yellow-green. Four seasons in one dale. I see only two people on my way down. Suddenly I feel experienced, able to pass on advice. They have matching expensive North Face jackets and I realise this probably sounded like a romantic idea for at least one of them. But climbing, even shuffling on gentle routes to a summit, is only about you. Forced to focus on yourself, you shut out the worlds of others. Yorkshire looks big up here, but the world becomes tiny. It's just the next step. I see a distant dark bird unfurl its wingspan. I wonder if it is a buzzard, a goshawk or a just a big raven. It turns into the wind and holds its place, like a child's kite on a string. It ebbs and flows in the unseen tide and then banks away sharply and lets the current take it at blurring speed. Then it turns and sits again. It might be hunting but it seems to be playing. And then it twists once more and is catapulted over Ingleborough, traducing a three-hour trek to an adrenalin rush.

The rest of the descent is a race, between throbbing feet and the clouds being shovelled my way from Whernside. A rainbow straddles mountains as a new Ribblehead viaduct. Will I make it? I wipe my nose and realise I am now on the snot train too. The sun doffs its cap and the valley is tinted with closing time. I hope the couple are okay up there and love conquers all.

When I do make it down, I sit on the edge of the open boot and take a swig from a bottle. I remember Helen Mort's line about feeling so alive that your tongue turns water into wine. She's right. But I am looking forward to the conqueror's pint.

Through this skin of light

The next day I drive up to Bainbridge, a village and parish in Richmondshire, high up the Dales, sitting by England's shortest river, the Bain. It is one of those Dales villages that should be in a James Herriot book. There is no nod to over-crowding, no rush, no coffee on the go. There is just a large oasis of green in the centre of nicely spaced homes. I park up by a large building that houses the Yorkshire Dales National Park Authority. The locals don't like the place. It has the look of a well-designed prison and people complain it spoils the view, although you don't have to look far to find a better one.

Andrew Fagg is waiting. He works in the media depart-ment, but was with the BBC for years until he decided, in his words, to commit career suicide by coming home. From a London basement to the top of the world, he looks content with his choice. He speaks in a smooth, calming, Ovaltine voice and tells me about local issues. There has just been an emotional planning meeting where a woman wanted to build a huge new barn. There were complaints. Aesthetics versus survival.

Many of the Dales barns that are near roads have been converted into holiday lets. Tourism is still changing the face of the landscape. Are the locals welcoming, or is it a bit like Cornwall, where Padstow natives smile at people as they head to Rick Stein's and then stick needles into their voodoo dolls of second-home surfers? 'If you ask my brother, tourists can do no wrong,' says Andrew. 'He runs a chip shop in Hawes.'

He shows me an advert in a newsletter seeking dry-stone wallers. 'I've never ever seen that before,' he says. 'You can make a good living from it nowadays.' Farming has changed, though. How do you make it work when the government subsidy is more than your income? The numbers are falling. The intensive practices mean the land changes and wildlife moves. 'If there comes a time when I can't hear the sound of the cuckoo or the screaming parties of swifts then I think I'll cry,' he adds.

The hum of peace can be deceiving. At weekends Andrew says the air is sometimes filled with hunting parties. The money is in the grouse. And that means hen harriers have been killed because they like grouse too. I hear about three hen harrier chicks that have been trampled to death, despite the breed supposedly being protected. The curlew was rated 'near threatened' in 2008 due to all that lost habitat, but happily it is on the way back. The bird, with its mottled feathers and overlong fishing-rod beak, is a success story. Now, like Ted Hughes, you too may hear them lancing their voices through the skin of this light.

In other news, Leeds University have finally got their act together after half a century. That is my interpretation anyway. It was the Romans who evidently put a huge sandstone slab over one of their own near the Park HQ. The writing was on the underside and it is said this was down to some indiscretion carried out during his life. One of the great sandstones discovered in these parts in 1960 weighed 600 lb. The stones ended up in a basement at Leeds University, but now, in 2022, they are going on show again. The media department at the university is hailing one of them as having a superstar inscription about building barracks, although to the uninitiated it seems long and dull, with few highlights, which makes it sound more like Gandalf's beard rather than anything to chisel home about.

One man and his dog

After an afternoon in Hawes, I go back to my Airbnb at Pateley Bridge, a snaking hour's journey to the south-west. Tomorrow's plan is to drive from there to Malham, walk to the cove and then go on to Settle for the sort of train journey that Michael Portillo would roll out the red trousers for. Pateley Bridge is a curious place. It runs down a hill to the auctioneer's, where they sell sheep, which is next to a pub where they probably drink Black Sheep. At the top is a building called Folk Finders, which claims to be the only high street genealogy shop in the UK. This could open up the past. It is closed.

This same stretch was named Britain's best high street in 2016. This begs a couple of questions. What was the competition like, given that most high streets are no-go areas unless you like whitewashed windows, tumbleweed and the stench of slow death? And secondly, how many years after winning such an award does it start to be a thing of jaded glory? 'Look, son, you may think the social club looks about as appealing as Artexing your nether regions with cat litter, but it's won a bleeding prize.' Naturally, in the same year that Pateley Bridge won its prize, Hebden Bridge won both the small market town award and the people's choice gong, with 40,000 votes, the most in the competition's history and roughly equating to one vote for every gluten-free eco loo. A few years ago, artist Jack Hurley produced a series of pithy prints under the banner 'Rubbish Seaside' but catering to inland places too. He said they were backhanded compliments, proof that a place does not have to be good or even average to be loved. The slogan for York was 'Death by Heritage'. Leeds rejoiced in 'At Least it's not Manchester', but when push came to shoving you back in your place, nothing quite had the acerbic bite of the one offered for Scarborough, which simply read 'We're Sorry'. Meanwhile, he nailed Hebden Bridge with 'Free Range Smugness'.

After breakfast I hit the road to Malham. It undulates like a flicked rope. I am not far from Kirby Malham now, which is where Bill Bryson went to live for a while. I've liked Bryson ever since he wrote his first book, *The Lost Continent*, and I went to see him do a reading in a shop in Chester. Being young and not yet having had my confidence whittled away, I approached him afterwards, handed him a brown A4 envelope and asked if he would mind reading a chapter I had written. It was my best Bill Bryson rip-off. Not long afterwards, he sent a hand-typed reply with his address in the top corner, as required by any self-respecting schoolteacher. It told me to keep at it. He probably did not read my offering, but it was a small gesture remembered a lifetime. Thereafter, he has always been a good guy, and I have bought all his books. It pays to be nice.

A white van approaches and stops alongside me. I remember Bill writing of the Malhamdale wave, a respectful kinship deployed by a small extension of the index finger. I try it. The man looks baffled. I wonder if he is torn between Bills Bryson and Caspar and thinks I have given him the finger. I wind down my window. Not long out of the city, I fear the worst. Abuse certainly, possibly swearing, and, if I can't find reverse imminently, a punch.

'You going to Malham?' says the driver, a young man with random stubble like moss on a limestone pavement.

'I was hoping so,' I say.

'Road's closed. Car on fire. You'll have to go back way.'

I park on a verge and go to have a look anyway. I am soon marvelling at the calmness of the police. One walks towards me with some tape. His lethargic approach does not smack of an emergency, and he looks like he probably belongs to the kerfuffle services instead.

'You'll have to go back way,' he says.

'I know,' I reply. 'Any idea how long it'll be shut.'

He looks back up the road as if this this might provide the answer. His radio crackles. 'You there, Rog?'

He puts the tape in his pocket and sighs. 'Can't say,' and I am not sure if he is talking to me or the radio.

I follow the van man's extended directions and quickly realise the truth of what Andrew Fagg had told me, about how the Dales are largely moors. The sky slumps and the bracken browns. Cow, sheep, barn and horizontal rain. I go down a steep incline, pass exposed rock and finally make it to the top of Malham Tarn, the glacial lake that never seeps because of its slate bed. I pass Winksill Stones, a real

limestone pavement bought by the charity Plantlife after
an appeal by TV gardener Geoff Hamilton. In between the
cracks and grikes you'll find things with wondrous names
like brittle bladder fern, green spleenwort and wall lettuce.
I plough on to Malham, park up by the visitor centre and
amble to the cove. It is a curved limestone amphitheatre
made from a fault line and centuries of attacks from water
and ice. It yawns in front of you like grey pterodactyl wings.
Climbers dangle. Somewhere up there a pair of nesting
peregrine falcons sit and plot.

The rain comes again, and I hurry back to the village,
which is a tiny jumble of blacksmith's, pub, chapel, café
and visitor centre. I almost spend £40 on a Yorkshire Dales
cycling shirt, even though I haven't got a bike. Just for the
Swaledale logo. That's what it can do to you. Then I get a
coffee in the café and sit and listen to a procession of people
come in and talk about the closed road. This is proper news,
not some 24-hour ticker and gotcha political interview.

'Road's closed.'

'Aye, car on fire.'

'Fire?'

'Melted intu road.'

It turns out thieves had been stealing quad bikes from a
farm. They were making their escape when they turned the
car over. Then they set fire to it and fled across the fields.

'Two teas. Sugar's on side.'

'Bloody bastards.'

Getting around in Yorkshire has always been a kerfuffle.
The Romans were obviously dab hands at building roads,
and so they established more than 1,000 miles of them
in Yorkshire. The most famous was Ermine Street, which

linked London and York. In Cambridgeshire, Ermine Street would meet the Great North Road, the medieval highway that went all the way to Edinburgh. Old packhorse routes across the Pennines and elsewhere would give way to turn-pike trusts, whereby locals were forced to pay tolls to maintain the roads.

John Metcalf, the son of a Knaresborough horse breeder, took advantage of this and in the 1760s won a contract to build a short section between Minskip and Ferrensby in the Harrogate district. Metcalf had been blind since he had smallpox as a child but would become renowned as Yorkshire's road builder. His life has oft been retold as an enduring romp: his job as a fiddler, saving a drowning soldier, fighting Bonnie Prince Charlie, one particularly gruesome prank involving decapitating birds, and coming up with a decent punchline when accused of fathering an illegitimate child – 'I haven't seen the woman in years.' Nobody has satisfactorily explained how Blind Jack was also a superb card sharp.

For those living the outdoor life, improved transport was a double-edged sword. The Leeds–Liverpool canal took almost half a century to complete. That was 1816, but rail mania, when 263 acts of Parliament were passed to set up new companies in 1846 alone, was the game-changer. Good for business, but the Dales also became a tourist attraction for the first time. Offcumdens flooded in. Writing in 1954 in *The Spirit of Yorkshire*, John Fairfax-Blakeborough highlighted North Yorkshire's opposition to the Access to Mountains Bill of 1939. Ramblers wanted their right to roam, but those owning and working the land favoured trigger-happy gamekeepers and barbed wire. Fairfax-Blakeborough bemoaned the motor-bus

service, the aircraft, the requisitioning of land by the War
Office, flooding of tracts to provide water to outsiders,
and farmers needing chequebooks instead of the perfectly
efficient way of hiding it all under the bed. 'In the Dales
ayont [beyond] the Yorkshire hills some of us thought the
peace of sylvan Arcadia would be preserved for all time.
Their isolation amid guardian everlasting mountains, and
their inaccessibility, we imagined would protect them from
the inroads of iconoclastic commercialism, modernisation
and desecration. We were wrong!' Bear in mind this was the
1950s, when the use of an exclamation mark was considered
the very zenith of grandstanding, and you sense his outrage.

The value and cost of rail travel in the Dales is best highlighted by the 72 miles of the Settle–Carlisle line. This runs
from Settle in the south, a touristy array of hiking shops
and cafés called things like Ye Old Naked Man (possibly
down to a seventeenth-century gibbet and possibly a sales
pitch), and bursts out of Yorkshire's ceiling as a Dahlian
glass elevator. The stations are small brick buildings with
manicured red and white borders. Bill Mitchell, that doyen
of Dales writers, was smitten. 'Settle–Carlitis is an incurable
disease,' he wrote.

I sit down in a near-empty carriage in Settle and note
the lack of people trying to exhibit a sense of exotica by
talking loudly to Colin about their morning meeting, or even
drinking booze because, well, there is no time zone on a
train, is there, or just playing music loudly enough on their
headphones for you to think you have tinnitus.

The trip is too short as you wind through Horton, where
there is a limestone xylophone called a lithophone in the
waiting room, past Ribblehead and on to Dent, England's
highest mainline station at 1,150 feet and a quirky four miles

from the village it supposedly serves. The scenery is all you could want from a train. The hum of slow travel splitting hill and dale, the vast verdant streams running down to stone wall dams, isolated trees thumbing noses on exposed horizons and the velvet sheen of autumn's late kindling.

'You from Settle?' says a voice. The accent in nondescript English. A face peers around a seat.

'No, just visiting,' I say.

'Not much to do, is there? In Settle, I mean.'

'I think people come for the scenery,' I offer.

This is ignored. I think of the installation on the top floor of the old Salts Mill, which comprises eight Hockney video screens forming a moving mosaic of a snow-bound Yorkshire path. Hockney did this by rigging cameras to a 4x4 and said the work was a literal moving picture, an exploration of time, landscape and memory. It lasts 49 minutes.

'Yeah, guess so,' says my co-traveller, unconvinced. He looks at his phone rather than the window. 'Have you got any signal?'

Having people like the outdoors is one thing, but denying others a means to post messages about how dull they are is the end of times. When this person, who lacks hiking shoes, a waterproof or any visible sort of flask, mentions the Conservative leadership contest, I wither a little. The game's gone and, soon after, so am I. I say goodbye and get off at Garsdale to save myself and the rest of the view.

I have another reason to get off here anyway. On the platform over the bridge at Garsdale is a statue of a dog that recalls an extraordinary story of endeavour, monumental folly and community resilience.

In many ways, Settle–Carlitis is the abridged version of Yorkshire, which has managed to stay on track despite industrial disease infecting the nice countryside. The line was built out of political shenanigans in the 1870s. Midland Railway needed access to Scotland via the line run by London and North Western Railway (LNWR). The trouble was, LNWR was a rival, and they made life hard for Midland by terminating trains at the end of Ingleton Viaduct, which meant Midland passengers had to walk a mile between two stations to carry on their journeys. Even when they offered an olive branch, it quickly drooped. Yes, Midland could share the line, but the devious minds of the LNWR ensured their rival's carriages were attached to slow-moving goods trains. The disgruntled Midland top brass developed their own plan to build a line from Settle to Carlisle. Parliament agreed. But then the two companies struck a better deal to co-exist. That might have been that, but when Midland went to Parliament asking for official permission to abandon their £2.3 million project, it was refused, partly due to other rail companies seeking to benefit from a scheme without investment.

The track nobody wanted was thus built by a vast army of more than 6,000 navvies. It was back-breaking, dangerous work done in inhospitable terrain in snow and rain. The camps became huge melting pots akin to Wild West outposts. Drinking was the primary pastime, although fighting was also popular, with a champion for each shanty town. Batty Wife Hole was a particularly huge camp, but others had more decent names, like Sebastopol and Jericho. There were attacks, brawls, and a jail for the man who stole a mackerel and then defended his honour with a pickaxe. People died of cold, dynamite and smallpox. One undertaker at Chapel-le-Dale boasted of toting over a hundred bodies down to the churchyard. Runaway wagons struck the unsuspecting.

Cranes crushed bodies. Preachers sent in by Midland bosses found they could not save souls.

Nevertheless, the line opened to passengers in 1876 and was an engineering wonder. It was also troubled. The boom of rail mania eventually gave way to post-war nationalisation, and by that time there were only four rival companies. There is a laminated article pinned to a wall in Appleby station detailing the story, just next to a 'Vote Helen' flier for the local star now on *Strictly Come Dancing*. The article includes a delicious jibe aimed at Ernest Marples, the transport minister in the early 1960s. 'Mr Marples would later flee to Monaco to avoid prosecution for alleged tax fraud', it reads, although in fairness to anyone thinking this is blinkered fare, it does not mention Marples's alleged fetish for dressing in women's clothes and being whipped by prostitutes.

The fight to keep the line open fell to a bunch of volunteers called the Friends of the Settle–Carlisle Line (FoSCL). British Rail were happy to see it close, and so they bemoaned the cost of repairs. They cancelled trains and spoke of dwindling passenger numbers. This was closure by stealth, but a defiance grew down the tracks. One dissenter was Charles Wallis, whose father, Barnes, had invented the bouncing bomb. He was a British Rail engineer and said the estimated repair cost was wildly exaggerated. However, the decision to close the line was finally taken in 1984, whereupon a concerted campaign by enthusiasts, users, local people and pure fans fuelled a rise in numbers using it. One of those heavily involved was the first secretary of the FoSCL. He was called Graham Nuttall and he had a dog.

Some 32,000 people signed the petition to save the line. There was also one pawprint, belonging to Nuttall's border collie, Ruswarp. It worked. On 11 April 1989, the line won its reprieve. Nine months later, Nuttall and Ruswarp went rambling in the Welsh mountains. A neighbour reported them missing, and a search ensued. Posters and leaflets were distributed, but there were no sightings. The days turned to weeks and hopeless months until finally, on 7 April 1990, when the weather had softened, a walker found Nuttall's body by a mountain stream. Standing over him was Ruswarp. Weak and malnourished, the faithful dog made it to his master's funeral, emitting a mournful howl at the end of the service according to one witness, but died shortly afterwards. Now his statue guards Garsdale station, a tribute to loyalty, lifelines and defying the environment.

Too long a winter

Ruswarp was not alone in staying in the harshest of regimes. It is a heroic act that has been played out over the great Yorkshire outdoors for centuries. The duplicity of a place endures and those figures who stick out the bad continue to fascinate.

The Yorkshire Dales are marked by those who left. The last Dales lead mine closed in 1912 and miners found other work or moved as the industry struggled with cheaper imports. Younger generations now leave for university or better prospects. It can be economically impossible to stay, and the latest proposal is to double council tax on second homes; an average Dales property costs £400,000 and the average wage is £530 a week. But there are always some who remain, and one of them was Hannah Hauxwell.

In 1972, Barry Cockcroft, a film-maker for Yorkshire TV, was rambling out in the wilds of Teesdale. At the time, this barren, weather-beaten land was still in the old North Riding of Yorkshire, and although the boundary changes two years later would drag it into County Durham, it can be regarded as the northern tip of the old Yorkshire Dales. Cockcroft had heard of a mysterious woman who lived on her own with no running water or electricity. He would later tell of how during his search he came across a farmer surveying his grass and asked if he knew where Hannah Hauxwell lived. He did, but added the caveat: 'Tha'll never find 'er.'

Fed up with the weather and the fruitlessness of it all, he was going to give up when he cleared one last dry-stone wall and approached a dilapidated farm building with an ill-fitting slate roof. He spotted a woman in rags and cleared his throat. 'Miss Hauxwell?' He described her reaction as a roe deer startled by a predator. In time, some would feel that was the perfect metaphor.

An article about Hauxwell had appeared in the *Yorkshire Post* two years earlier. In it, she asks the writer if the Reuters journalist Anthony Grey has been released by the Chinese. Grey had been detained for two years and the diplomatic incident was a newspaper sensation, but by the time the reporter sat down with Hauxwell at Low Birk Hatt in Baldersdale, Grey had already enjoyed six months of freedom. Hauxwell's isolation bucked modern trends. She walked three fields to collect bread left by far-off neighbours. Water came from the stream where her cows drank. She lived on £170 a year. Since her mother's death 12 years earlier, she had lived here alone. She often went 10 days without seeing anyone.

You can see why Barry Cockcroft would have been happy to trudge around Teesdale in search of this elusive figure. And what he found was TV gold. Not only did the story stack up, but Hannah Hauxwell was a kind, poetic figure with antiquated manners. She was a loner, rarely leaving her vale, the ultimate insider living outside, tied to place because it was where she was from as much as to the joy she got from it.

The ensuing film, *Too Long a Winter*, was screened in 1973. It featured a few people living in Yorkshire's extremities, and is still moving. The strings on the soundtrack ratchet up the emotion, *Dr Zhivago* with sheep and sleet. The Bainbridges are first up. Brian is seen digging a hog (a young sheep) out of a deep drift. He is a no-nonsense man. When everybody else is invited down to a dance laid on by the rich lady of the manor, he is out in the snow with a dead animal. He lost 350 in the winter of '63. 'Just too long a winter for them,' he says, and thus gives the programme a title. 'Not buried by snow, just too long a winter.'

Hannah does not appear for the first 16 minutes, but when she does, she makes her mark. Some of it is her appearance. She is 46 but looks 66. Her hair is white, her cheeks red, and she speaks in a lilting north-east voice like a harpist tuning up as she explains how little she survives on.

What did you have for your lunch today?

'Butter and bread,' she laughs.

What keeps you here?

She says her family has always lived here. It is enough. 'And the lovely countryside, down the New Road, through the iron gate, I've often thought it's my favourite walk and I've stopped and looked and thought if I haven't money in my pocket it's something nobody can rob me of. It's mine, it's mine for the taking.'

She talks of being 'rather down in myself', which seems an understatement since it had led to eight weeks in hospital. This depressive episode is raced over in the way of the times.

She 'took rather badly' to the quiet when she returned, but that's about it. Marriage is out of her hands, but she says a bad marriage must be a desperate thing. 'There's all difference in the world between a good marriage and being on one's own, but of course if it isn't a success there can be nothing worse than being obliged to share a roof with someone you're utterly at variance with.'

It is a gentle film that hits you over the head with its nostalgia, but it is no worse for that. This is a snapshot of all our yesterdays, the perfect film about how place runs through us. The film ends with her playing the organ and saying, 'That's my picture I see every day. I never tire of it. I think the time might come when I can't stay here. As long as I can, I'm very much attached to the place. It's home.'

Too Long a Winter aired in an unfavourable time slot, 10.30 p.m. on a Tuesday in January. The reaction was phenomenal. More than five million viewers watched, and the switchboards at Yorkshire TV's offices in London, Sheffield and Hull were jammed the next day. The critics enjoyed it too. Hannah Hauxwell became an overnight celebrity for the acceptance of her lot. The message seemed to be: if only we could all endure like this and be grateful for the little miracles that we take for granted. Gifts, letters and money flooded in. When the programme was shown abroad, it elicited the same response. Sacks of mail mounted at TV offices and it was almost all for Hauxwell. Only half a dozen letters expressed any interest in Brian and Mary Bainbridge and their plight. Maybe viewers reasoned they had each other and one of those good marriages.

Hannah was flown by helicopter to a press conference in Leeds. Then she stayed in the Charlie Chaplin suite at the Savoy for the Women of the Year awards. It was a sort of

Pygmalion meets *Crocodile Dundee* as journalists, royalty and Middle England rejoiced in what they assumed was a culture clash.

The first of many cash-in books was illuminating. Where many of the articles in the national media liked to present Hauxwell as a great eccentric living out a sort of nursery rhyme with her beast – she had one cow, Her Ladyship, and sold a calf each year at market – she talked of pig-killing time as a child, of the slit throat draining blood and the carcass being hung up while the entrails were scraped away, brawn made from trotters and ears, and potted meat from the head. She defied stereotype with her love of music and literature. Tchaikovsky was a favourite, but she did not care for the Brontës. 'I consider that the story of the Brontës themselves is more interesting than the characters and situations they created.'

In 1989, the TV crew went back. Hauxwell was 63 now and struggling with rheumatism. Her front room was shrunk by piles of cans, papers, parcels and letters. She confessed to being a hoarder and never throwing anything out, but it was a sad sight. She hung food in bags from the wall so the rats couldn't get it. 'I did not think I would be as happy as I am,' she says. 'Like Edith Piaf said, no regrets.' The film shows her hunched over with a bale of hay on her back, and then hacking in vain at a frozen stream that meant she would need to take her pail to the reservoir she likened to the Mississippi. 'To me there's nowhere like it and never will be,' she says. 'Whatever I am, wherever I am, this is me. This is my life. Nowhere else.'

But there was a somewhere else. When her body could not fend off the worst of Baldersdale, she moved to a cottage in the nearby village of Cotherstone. The clip of her sitting in a removal van, her farm disappearing out of the back window, strums power chords on heart strings. The *Zhivago* soundtrack is turned to 11.

And yet that was not it. The success of the second documentary meant there had to be more. So Cockcroft came up with a plan to take Hannah, the epitome of the solitary Daleswoman, out of her comfort zone. Now she would travel. And she agreed. To Paris, Naples, Vienna and the USA. She met cowboys and the Pope. She finally got to see the world, but some would wonder whether she needed to. It certainly demolished the narrative that she could only live in her familial home in Yorkshire and was forever tied to the land.

The boundary changes meant she was living over the border when she died aged 91 in 2018. Brian Bainbridge, the unsung, forgotten hero who had farmed a meagre existence five miles from Low Birk Hatt, had died in 2006. His wife, Mary, told the *Northern Echo*: 'He always thought the TV programme was a bit of a farce. Neither he nor I ever met Miss Hauxwell. I thought she was rather exploited.'

It was a word that would have concerned Cockcroft, but in truth, seeing Hauxwell outside her natural environment was never as interesting as seeing her in it. Hers was a tale of the strength of roots, but if they can support us, they can probably bind us too tightly, part tourniquet, part garrotte. What was missing from Hannah Hauxwell's life was not really electricity, water or rat poison, but those she had loved, and like all of us, when the men in brown coats arrived to auction off the past, she took the memories of her granda, uncle, mum and Her Ladyship with her.

11

CHEFS

The most exciting piece of excrement I've ever seen.

Dr Andrew 'Bones' Jones, paleoscatologist, on the
20-centimetre coprolite, aka Viking dung, found in York, 1972

We are what we eat, and food tells our history in terms of both our tastes and what was available from the land. Yorkshire is now famous for numerous dishes, cooking up a collective identity through shared and changing experience. Alas, the coprolite was broken when knocked off a display stand, and despite a conservator stressing we could still tell that the Viking diet comprised meat and grain and constipation, it was a faeces-saving exercise. Then, as now, it's about holding it together.

The mystery of Harrogate

Writing about Yorkshire invites salvos from the offended. Walter White knew this back in the 1860s, when he added a self-justifying new foreword to his book *A Month in*

Yorkshire. He complained that he had been 'pelted with animadversions' for the 'scandalous misrepresentation' of a conversation with a villager from Burnsall in Chapter 22. Sheffield had complained too, although White said that if he had his time over again, he would have been even harsher on that particular front. 'A town which permits its trade to be coerced by ignorance, and where the ultimate argument of the working-classes is gunpowder or a knock on the head, should show that the best means have been taken to purify morals as well as the atmosphere and streets, before it claims to be "nothing like so bad as is represented". But the proverb which declares that "people who eat garlic are always sure it doesn't smell" will perhaps never cease to be true.' Have it, Yorkshire.

White did not visit Harrogate. In some ways this is understandable. Harrogate is Yorkshire in fancy dress. It is elegant and unashamedly posh. The 200-acre Stray is a gasp of breath in the halitosis of urban Yorkshire, once a royal hunting forest owned by John of Gaunt, the same king's son who set up the House of Lancaster and thus paved the way for the Wars of the Roses, but it neatly evaded the eighteenth-century enclosure acts, which led to both productive crop rotation and the eviction of tenant farmers and villagers from common land. Instead, wealthy visitors were free to stroll around in fur hats as they contemplated prolonging their easy lives.

Harrogate is a short drive and a world away from industrial Yorkshire. Leeds is 14 miles directly south, Ripon 10 miles north and York 20 miles to the east. The Dales are close by on its western flank. It is mature and classy. If it were a person, it would be Helen Mirren or David Attenborough. Flowers forever bloom and the Stray holds the old town in its cupped green hands, stopping just short of Bettys, the world-renowned café famed for its fat rascals.

It is easy to sniff at Bettys, and not in a garlic-detecting way. You look at the pristine lettering on the crafted iron-work, the spotless windows and the roped-off queue on any afternoon, and you see a place that knows it has got you. The origin story is good too. One night in 1890, there was a fire by the River Aare in Switzerland and Johann Bützer, a miller and baker, evacuated his family. Realising his eldest daughter was still inside, he plunged back into the flames. Alas, both died. Ida went to live with her stepmother's family and five-year-old Fritz was sent back to the mountains down which the family had once bounced Julie Andrews style. He was sold to a farmer, who effectively used him for slave labour. He stayed there until he was 14, whereupon he decided to become a master baker, travelling to Paris and then London. He was given the name of a confectioner's in Bradford and told strangers at the station that he was looking for a place that sounded like Bratwurst. Finally he made it to Yorkshire and found the shop. He was paid the equivalent of 120 Swiss francs a month.

In 1919, now known as Frederick Belmont, he raised enough cash to open a first-class confiserie and café in Harrogate. Thinking big, despite the post-war depression, he furnished the place with grey-blue china, nickel teapots, precious wood and ornate mirrors. He took £30 on the first day but £17,000 the following year. Bettys was up and running and would spread its sugary tentacles across Yorkshire. By the time Frederick and his wife, Claire, were on the *Queen Mary*'s maiden voyage in 1936, mixing with the likes of Lord Burghley, the toff of the track immortalised by Nigel Havers's champagne-swigging turn in *Chariots of*

Fire, it was a happy success story. Belmont disembarked and took the ship's interior designers with him to build a new café in York. During the Second World War, hundreds of Canadian airmen scratched their names on the mirror behind the bar, and many generations returned to look their relatives in the eye. As with Ilkley Moor, the signatures of ghosts are still there.

It was also during the war that Belmont fought to avoid having the Harrogate café requisitioned and carried on making meals from corned beef, spaghetti, powdered egg and fish scraps for a maximum price of five shillings. The cynical visitor might say it was the last time anyone got value for money at Bettys.

I sit in a room surrounded by teapots and, it has to be said, the occasional crackpot. I forgo the afternoon tea, which costs £24.95, and the ham and cheese sandwich on offer for a more manageable but no less extraordinary £8.25. Instead, I go for a scone and consider that people are always happy to spend an inordinate sum on an unadorned bun if it makes them feel warm inside. 'Harrogate is the queerest place,' wrote Dickens. It had 'the strangest people in it, leading the oddest lives of dancing, newspaper reading and dining'. Not much has changed, other than the dancing and newspaper reading. Bettys, for better or worse, has become a Yorkshire icon, a slice of the past with a reassuring cup of twee. It is a pretty dam against progress and all its polluting Starbucks soy chai lattes and hotspotting SEO operatives.

It has not all been bliss, though. Without an heir to his kingdom, Frederick asked his sister, Ida, for one of her sons. Carl Viktor Wild answered the call and, in keeping with tradition, anglicised his name to Victor. In 1957, Frederick collapsed in his office above the original Harrogate café just

over the road from where I now sit. Sad as this was, Victor
did the decent thing and kept the café open until normal
closing time, whereupon the body was heaved down the
stairs and out the front door.

Bettys might have gone under in the aftermath, but Victor
bought C. E. Taylor and Co., and some 15 years later this
joint venture launched Yorkshire Tea. Sean Bean would do
the adverts after killing France in *Sharpe*. The early strapline
was 'Blended in Yorkshire to suit Yorkshire people and
Yorkshire water'. This did not mean full of peat and leaks,
but online trolls have branded them disgusting for not actually growing their tea in Yorkshire. Bettys' riposte was to
point out that tea is grown in 20 places across India and
Africa and you need catchy names for supermarket sales,
which is why oolong keemun lapsang souchong is better
known as Russian Caravan.

In 2022, the *Daily Mail* got hold of Rodney Light, a
former plumber who had married Frederick's adopted
daughter, Valerie, famously part of the family since
being spotted as a toddler by a sympathetic Frederick
on Bournemouth beach. The sanitised version goes that
Victor, then 23, awoke to find the toddler by his bed with
a message pinned to her arm: 'I'm your little sister.' So far
so Paddington, but Light told the *Mail* man that Victor
had marginalised his cousin, aka 'little sister', and it took
a bitter wrangle for her to get £4 million for her 23 per
cent stake in the 1990s. He even recalled taking a secret
tape recorder to a meeting with Victor to gain proof of his
alleged parsimony. 'I'm no bloody James Bond,' he told the
Mail. 'The recorder was stuffed in my jacket pocket and
I was terrified Victor would see the bugger, or it would
suddenly start squeaking.' To cap it all, Light suggested

Valerie was really Frederick's illegitimate daughter, which does make a modicum of sense given that most people were satisfied with marking a day trip to Bournemouth with a stick of rock rather than an extra child.

Harrogate is happily old. The North Yorkshire Joint Strategic Needs Assessment in 2021 predicted that the over-65 population of the town would grow by 25 per cent in nine years. The 85s and over will see their ranks swelled by a staggering 34 per cent, with under-45s declining by 16 per cent. The trend is played out all over North Yorkshire, with the 2021 census giving Richmondshire, which covers the hilly wonders of Swaledale, Wensleydale, Coverdale and Arkengarthdale, the title of England and Wales's fastest-ageing area. Contraception rates are abnormally high here too. Perhaps couples realise there is a dearth of jobs and opportunities for another generation facing a housing crisis. Or perhaps they are sex-craved after all that internet porn.

Harrogate is popular with visitors, old and older. Scone scoffed, I pay up and head down Parliament Street. Next door is the Ivy, where two more women are framed by gilt-edged glass as they mime away and drink champagne or prosecco. I'm pretty sure it's champagne. Next to them a rare teen has his head bowed, probably in prayer or porn. This is a place for ladies who lunch, brunch, breakfast and take afternoon tea before popping into high-end interior design shops. I may be mistaken, but I don't recall seeing a single child here when I have visited in the last 10 years. No swings and roundabouts, it just stays the same.

This demographic makes it surprising that Agatha Christie chose Harrogate as the ideal place in which to get lost. She was a mere 32 during her 11-day exile in Yorkshire, and you would imagine she would have stuck out like a sore thumb. The famous writer of mysteries conjured up a real one in 1926 when her Morris Cowley car was found abandoned with the lights on next to a Surrey Hills chalk pit. Her fur coat and old driver's licence were in the back. It sparked what a brass plaque honouring 'Agatha's Retreat' in the foyer at Harrogate's Old Swan Hotel hails as 'one of the greatest manhunts in history'. This may be so, but she was not hiding away in some stone barn on the moors, merely living it up at what was then the Harrogate Hydro.

She had checked in as Mrs Teresa Neele, the surname of her husband's mistress, and mingled freely with guests, dancing, playing billiards and, according to the hotel manager, going out on the town every single night. Yet in a time before your cat's tea could be globally famous via the internet, nobody recognised the famous author, while down south the greatest minds in sleuthing worked at solving the puzzle and decided to dredge a lake known ominously as the Silent Pool. The Home Secretary offered a £100 reward. Sir Arthur Conan Doyle, creator of Sherlock Holmes, saw a chance to champion his belief in spiritualism by consulting a clairvoyant named Horace Leaf. When Leaf was presented with one of Christie's gloves, he proclaimed that it belonged to someone called Agatha. Amazing. 'There is trouble connected with this article,' he added. 'The person who owns it is half dazed and half purposeful. She is not dead as many think. She is alive. You will hear of her, I think, next Wednesday.'

It was actually next Tuesday. Two Hydro bandsmen – Bob Tappin, a man with a banjo and a monocle, and Bob Leeming, a saxophone player – had gone to the police to say they recognised the author. Rosie Archer, a chambermaid, was also suspicious and kept a diary of the guest's movements.

Alerted to her whereabouts, her husband, Colonel Christie arrived, and Agatha kept him waiting while she dressed for dinner. Christie told journalists his wife was suffering from complete memory loss. They had dinner and got the train home the next day. A search of a 40-mile area in Surrey was called off. Some people claimed this was all revenge for her husband's affair, but in her excellent 2022 biography, *Agatha Christie: A Very Elusive Woman*, Lucy Worsley suggests she was suffering from mental illness brought on by the death of her mother and the collapse of her marriage, and that the sexist nature of the twenties meant she was brutally shamed thereafter by the media. Worsley says she had genuinely crashed the car and been happy to die.

Quite how people did not recognise her, given that her picture had been printed on the front page of the *Daily Express*, or how the police missed the sizeable clue of her having written to her brother-in-law about a trip to Yorkshire, remain other mysteries. We do know that Conan Doyle's involvement was met with no little scorn. 'He says the case has afforded an excellent example of the uses of psychometry as an aid to the detective,' stated an editorial in the *Leeds Mercury*. 'I fail to see it. Sir Arthur called in a psychometrist, but it was the alertness of some people at Harrogate – their Yorkshire gumption if I may use the word – that ran Mrs Christie to earth. They were the Sherlock Holmes this time.'

The sun is washing the white walls of the Old Swan's library, where a Lynda La Plante paperback has invaded the leather-bound collection of Christie hardbacks. Fact and fiction both reside within these walls. I sit down in one of the well-worn reading chairs and look at a photograph of the Old Swan's previous incarnation as Harrogate Hydro, when

each room had a coal fire and it ditched its alcohol licence
for morning prayers, an ambitious move in any age.

I flick through a 2018 report from the British Heart
Foundation that I had come across earlier. It states in bold
type, 'Yorkshire residents more likely to die from heart
and circulatory disease than any other region.' The death
rate then was 10 per cent higher than the English average,
although the most dangerous places were Hull, Scarborough,
Bradford and Leeds rather than Harrogate. The report quotes
a cardiologist, Professor Tim Chico, who was researching
how the zebrafish could help mend a broken heart and
whose investigations included putting drugs into a pool
with embryos, which sounded very rock and roll. Was this
disproportionate level of heart disease down to Yorkshire
living? Was it the result of stress in the cities, rural decay or,
let's be blunt, the diet? What we can say with some degree
of accuracy is that Harrogate would not be what it is today
if visitors had not been so ill.

Harrogate's status as a spa town began when an otherwise
unremarkable figure called William Slingsby discovered a
well in 1571 that gained royal approval from Elizabeth I,
who was trying to stop people visiting the Catholic hotspot
of Spa in Belgium. He named it the Tewit Well, after the
lapwing that frequented the spot on the Stray. Scores of
other springs would soon be discovered, and drinking
the magical, if sulphurous, waters of Harrogate became
a thing. The waters were deemed particularly useful for
flatulence, constipation and hysterical affections. It obviously worked, because Harrogate is still the least hysterical
place on earth.

Lepers used the Royal Pump Room – one contemporary
visitor wrote of their 'putrid rags' and 'besmirched clouts' –

but it later went upmarket and got a Thomas Chippendale canopy from the Otley-born cabinet maker. This whiff of snobbery is recorded in Paul Chrystal's *Harrogate History Tour*, and was summed up by the 1813 *Guide to All the Watering and Sea-Bathing Places*, in which people drank water that 'tastes like rotten eggs and gunpowder' on 'a dreary common'. Visitors were encouraged to drink the water right up until 2012, when an EU directive said it had failed its safety tests. Officially the classification was 'unwholesome'. Resigned tourist chiefs said they wanted to allow visitors to experience what once drew people to Harrogate, but reluctantly conceded they probably should not put their lives at risk in doing so.

And so Harrogate is simultaneously a place of fine and healthy dining, wind and constipation. It is a neat and tidy, messed-up place where the residents seem reinforced against the rising heart disease of Yorkshire. If we are what we eat, then clearly some Yorkshire people are a cucumber sandwich with the crusts cut off. Other, more mortal folk are a bag of scraps.

One of each twice

Fish and chips are synonymous with Yorkshire. They are often sold as an emblem of Britishness, and then Yorkshireness. I drive into Wetherby from Harrogate and stop at a chip shop on the main street. I love these places for their sheer lack of pretension. This one, like a thousand elsewhere, has no pictures on the walls. It's concession to blue-sky thinking is opening the door. There is one of those old calendars with dates crossed off by a convict counting days. No TV, pot plant or picture of an old East Coast trawler. It's beautifully dull.

'One of each, please,' I say as homage to my roots, when Saturday lunchtime exchanges were brief and functional. One half of one of each is a battered haddock fillet. It has always been haddock in Yorkshire and expats look down at cod. The other half is a bag of chips.

'There you go, love,' says the girl behind the counter, who is probably half my age.

I find a bench.

'Nice?' says an old bookend with a tie.

'Very,' I say. The scone is long gone. We dip our heads into an autumn wind as hard brown beech leaves applaud their way across the road. Life is simple.

'What do you think about Prince Andrew then?' the old chap says from nowhere. There is some new newspaper talk about his friendship with American sex offender Jeffrey Epstein. The man keeps looking at the leaves. As ever, I wish they'd shaken out more vinegar. 'Only two things get things done in this country,' he says. He pauses for a bus to pass and, I think, dramatic effect. 'Ballot box and revolution.' I have a chip.

Sometimes when we were young, we would casually amble into the chip shop and ask for a bag of scraps. These were the bits of batter that had not lasted the course and were now little freedom fritters making their own way in that sick light that warms fried fish while you feel fat seep into your skin and wince at the jar of pickled onions on the counter. Ideally, you'd want a clumsy server so they would clip off tufted nuggets when catching one of the dead fish. As you got older and realised you were asking for something for nothing, this request died, but it is a testament to long-gone community – an era when someone was kind enough to give you a bag of dripping-fried rabbit droppings just because you asked for it.

Fish and chips have been mythologised over the years, not least in Yorkshire, where Harry Ramsden is the most famous name of all. Being the most famous does not necessarily mean the best, though, regardless of the branding, and in an unlikely review in the *New Statesman* in 2013, the eminent author Will Self visited one of Harry Ramsden's franchised chains at Euston station to prove this point. In fairness, these places are doomed to failure because fish and chips are not fast food. At best they are medium-paced fare, like Fred Trueman in his girth-gathering dotage, not fine dining but good enough for a plate if you're not on the coast and so missing a battalion of insane seagulls. Self wrote, 'I've eaten in various Ramsden's over the years, hanging on pathetically to the notion that buried in their red-and-white Formica frames there must remain beating a distinctively northern heart. But then, what's in a white rose? A Harry Ramsden's by any other name would probably taste remarkably similar. What I'm driving at here is that the food has not been great – contra Harry's law, I've found soggy chips, pulpy fish in grotty batter, and mushy peas with the flavour and consistency of plumber's mastic.'

In the end Harry Ramsden gets away with it because this is the southern version, the nether regions, and who knows what it's like up there in the unhealthy heartlands? 'I listened to the train announcements and wished I were about to head north out of this cesspit of gourmandising towards a more earthy realm where nowt folk were queer and nowt needed frying for more than three minutes – including bruschetta.'

Yet if we allow ourselves to believe that Yorkshire is the home of the best fish and chips – go with it for a moment – and that the best fish and chips come from Harry Ramsden's – keep on – and that the best Harry Ramsden's is the original one in Guiseley to the north-west of Leeds, the heart of a food region becomes smaller as the arteries to it clog with rush-hour traffic. Anyway, the truth is, fish and chips are not even a British invention.

It was the Marranos in Portugal, Jews who had converted, unwillingly, to Christianity, who brought a form of battered fish to England in the 1500s. Dickens talks of a fried-fish warehouse by the barber, coffee shop and beer house where Fagin exploited young boys and sang about pickpockets. Panikos Panayi, a professor at De Montfort University, who wrote *Fish and Chips: A History*, highlighted a newspaper article from 1848 that said Jewish areas were recognisable 'by the dingy shops of second-hand wares, the clusters of dirty frippery hung from the door posts, the plates of oil-fried fish displayed in the cook shops'. In *The Book of Jewish Food*, cookery writer Claudia Roden said that a Jewish immigrant named Joseph Malin was the first person to sell fish and potatoes together. Alas for Yorkshire's claim, this took place in Bow, in London. As for chips, they came from Belgium and France.

Harry Ramsden was born in 1888, in Bradford. His father, also called Harry because people had little imagination back then, had a shop in a rough part of town on Manchester Road, complete with coal-fired range. The younger Harry worked in a mill and a barber's, drove a taxi and leased a pub. Without a music licence he booked a pianist and installed a lookout on the door. He did his time in the army and finally moved into the fish and chip business. Originally

a wooden hut at White Cross in Guiseley – eventually demolished because of asbestos – this was the place that became
the benchmark and grew into a dynasty. No chip was cooked
unless the temperature of the fat was 350 degrees. Fryers
used rulers to measure the depth of the dripping; 3.5 inches
was the minimum. A list of 100 daily tasks was drawn up. As
the business grew, carpets were put down so nobody would
slip on the rubber and sue. Penny slot machines were bought,
and according to Ramsden's son, Harry 'damn near hugged
himself' every time a punter lost.

A snooker table was installed in the basement. Vinegar
bottles were filled from a cask for added taste. Haddock
was bought from Grimsby, dripping from Bingley. Another
Harry – Corbett – played the piano. One day he went to
Blackpool and bought a yellow glove puppet. He called it
Teddy and did some rubbish magic tricks, but he won a
talent competition. To make Teddy show up on black and
white TV, he applied soot to his nose and ears. Teddy became
Sooty and got his own show. And then opened a new branch
of Harry Ramsden's in Shipley. Elton John wrote 'Circle of
Life' about something similar.

Eventually Harry Ramsden's was taken over by corporates
and the quality waned. In 2012, the owners, Birmingham-
based Boparan Ventures, announced that the oldest shop
was closing. Redundancies were announced. It was a sign of
the times when they took down the sign. Palates had become
more refined. No longer did cooking lasagne at home make
you some sort of barefoot Charles Manson acolyte.

By a quirk, the people who used to run the same Stutton
Road chip shop in Tadcaster where I would ask for scraps
were the ones who saved the original Harry Ramsden's. They
had moved on from Tad and bought other shops under the

Wetherby Whaler name. 'It would be a national scandal if it were to close at this time of economic uncertainty,' Phillip Murphy told the *Yorkshire Post*.

I always remember Phillip cutting up fish in the back at Stutton Road and sweating buckets, while a queue clung patiently to the wall. The next day, I go to see him and his wife, Janine, for the first time in years. 'It was only going to be temporary,' says Janine as we sit over a plate of haddock in Guiseley. 'We were from Bradford and had just got married. I worked in the town hall. I couldn't afford to give it up. Then an uncle from Bridlington called and said the man who owned Stutton Road was packing in. We worked out he was making about the same as our combined wages.'

They drove from Bradford to Tadcaster and learnt how to cook fish. Always beef dripping. Haddock with no bone. I mention a fish and chip restaurant in Bournemouth and they know the owner. Their competitive instinct means they are glad he never made good on talk of moving north.

'Does he leave the skin on?' asks Janine.

They never took a holiday for years, but it worked and they got more shops. They bought a plot of land and built one from scratch on the way into York. A hotel was built on another plot but people coming from Tadcaster saw the Whaler first. 'The lad who bought the land for the hotel got the sack,' says Phillip. 'He'd bought the secondary site.'

The talk of the negotiations involved in their rise is littered with colourful asides. 'Deal with him and you'd count your fingers after,' Phillip says of one wheeler-dealer.

'We fry in beef dripping,' he tells me when I ask the secret to Yorkshire fish and chips.

'Not all beef dripping,' Janine corrects. 'It gives it flavour, but lots of shops use oil now. We have an oil pan. A pan for coeliac. We cater for everyone. Did your grandad have a furniture shop?'

He did, although they know more than me. 'It was on the corner of Killinghall Road,' says Phillip. 'It was a big shop.' The site he means is now opposite Mother Hubbard's fish and chip shop. Phillip and Janine are business people and are interested in family, trees and succession. Their daughter, Caroline, came home after studying and said she would give them two years. Far beyond that now, she is still here. Phillip proudly says she is flourishing in the National Federation of Fish Friers.

Janine's phone bleeps. 'Oh, that man with the modified pig heart has died.'

It seems a good time to tour the kitchen. Old photos of Harry Ramsden are on the wall. He is dapper, a bit Neville Chamberlain, a bit Everygrandad. 'That's from 1952, when they celebrated 21 years by selling at the original penny ha'penny prices.' Unsurprisingly, the picture is crammed to the frame with people after a bargain. The old man was the same. Harry Ramsden grew so disgruntled when people caught the toilet door and so avoided putting a penny in the slot that he removed the locks and installed a turn-stile instead.

The big blue square slabs in the kitchen, like floats you used to get in the public swimming pool, contain the frozen fish. It is Icelandic and it is a problem. 'There were supply issues before the war in Ukraine but it's even more serious now,' says Phillip. 'Russian fish goes through Norway. There's a couple of boats due next week and I don't know if the Norwegians will accept them. If they turn them round it could become the start of something.' Russia had been providing 40 per cent of fish fillets used in UK fish and chip shops. Spiralling fertiliser prices mean potato prices are rising too. Ukraine and Russia also provide 60 per cent of the world's sunflower oil. Small world.

The Wetherby Whaler sells 750,000 portions of fish a year, but there are lots of these sit-down fish and chip restaurants in Yorkshire. They were built as a working-class treat, plain food with a slice of bread and butter and a pot of tea. The sweaty Bettys. Phillip thinks lots will go to the wall in the coming months. The future might even be the drive-through. Bloody hell. Most kids no longer want to go into these family businesses. They process the fish on the boats now, nicking out the bones and skinning them at sea. And the old bones of the fryers are aching. They are a dying breed.

'Say hello to your mum,' says Janine as I let them get back to work and finish my haddock. I thank her for the loan of a season ticket to watch Leeds United battle away the next day. I burn the clutch in a car park adjacent to Beeston Hill. Leeds lose 3–0 to Aston Villa.

Don, Marco

Food is part of us, however briefly. My father-in-law was a chef. He was born in Middlesbrough, a hard old town forgotten by those with geographical altitude sickness, and sent away aged nine to work with his uncle Harry in his guesthouse in Bournemouth. Years later, my future wife would sit in the corner of Don's greasy spoon playing with her dolls and then cross the busy Wimborne Road to get the bread for her dad. She was five.

Don was a character, a working-class eccentric. His fingers were crooked from hiding fags in a fleshy shield behind his back in kitchens. He had an imaginary friend called Malcolm. He bastardised names but somehow you learnt his language, so friends Frank and Bridge became Fred and Betty, and actress Martine McCutcheon became Sheila McNuggetty. He cooked for the Queen and ran a vast industrial canteen at ICI in Manchester, but in later years he was as happy doing the buffet for Winton Working Men's Club or being in the veg aisle at Asda. He was a talented, self-made man with an unfeasible work ethic, and everyone was roped into his world. The first time I met him, I was nervous and had put on my best shirt and shoes, but I ended up washing the kitchen walls at Poole Arts Centre. Friends stood in the back of his beloved blue van, bungee-clipped to the walls, as he took us to another outside catering job. He died in 2016 and I miss the stories and laughter. But it was hot and hard and pressurised, and it was about timing and money as much as food. And loading a hundred red racks into the back of that bloody blue van.

Don did not like fancy restaurants. When my mum went vegetarian, he cooked her fish. Nouvelle cuisine was the emperor's new clothes. But Yorkshire can do posh. And it was the home of the first great enfant terrible of the culinary world, the inaugural rock-star chef and the man who made Gordon Ramsay cry. It takes all sorts.

When Marco Pierre White burst onto the culinary scene in the eighties like a Viking god spewing blood and leftover lamb shank, it was exhilarating. This was a time before being a chef was an easy route to being a celebrity. White was partly just another kid from a troubled Leeds council estate and partly an Italian love god who struck menacing poses and, like Don, smoked fags, and unlike Don, pre-empted a fall-out with Damien Hirst by posing half naked with a shark. He also had a healthy contempt for some people. Even the book that broke the mould for chefs and their recipe lists, *White Heat*, which can be mistaken for a book on the Vietnam war if you squint at the pictures of charred flesh and hopelessness, began with the line: 'You're buying *White Heat* because you want to cook well? Because you want to cook Michelin stars? Forget it. Save your money. Go and buy a saucepan.'

Stories about White quickly did the rounds. There were the times he got so fed up with posh preppy City boys that he would stride into the restaurant after his staff had cleared the table mid meal and whip away the tablecloth. This was known as the Whoosh! In one interview in the *Observer* in 2001, he mused, 'I threw 54 of them out one night. It was an engagement party, but they were far too rowdy, they were dropping cigarette butts on the floor, for Christ's sakes.' When someone asked for chips, he spent an hour making a portion 'hand-cut, blanched, lovingly fried, served up with a little silver plate of sauce'. He charged £25.

He casually dismissed chefs like Jamie Oliver and Ainsley Harriott, but he admitted he was 'a shit' too. His old head teacher said he would amount to nothing, and White agreed with him. Money doesn't make him anything. Money is about survival.

His first job, at the Hotel St George in Harrogate, was as a bookie's runner for the head chef. From there he went to the Box Tree in Ilkley, a pretty sunken corner cottage with stained-glass windows. This place changed eating habits in the north. Once a stop-off for travellers to the Dales, it began serving just dinner in 1962. Its owners, Malcolm Reid and Colin Young, went on reconnaissance missions to Paris, ate all day, and then asked their staff to replicate their indulgences. As White said in his autobiography: 'No one in Yorkshire had ever seen food like this. They didn't know such food existed.' It was expensive, but the restaurant was full. Mill owners would eat there. So did Shirley Bassey, the favourite singer of Marco's father, and, later, Margaret Thatcher. The menu was written mainly in French.

It was here that White says food became an obsession. With a piratical image, he became a force of nature. He was the Muppets' Swedish chef, Heathcliff, Brando, Belushi and the template for every scene about tomato sauce in every gangster film thereafter. A brooding, hulking, hirsute mess of manliness, he was a tortured artist and torturer of others, and not likely to sacrifice his ego on the altar of your wallet just because you were paying through your stuck-up nose for something you couldn't read.

Anyway, he was the youngest chef to have three Michelin stars in the nineties, but ignoring the trend for wholesome cookery books, he went off the rails. 'It was great to be decadent,' he wrote. 'At first, anyway. But eventually I couldn't stand watching another person getting drunk or injecting smack into their veins.' You didn't get this from Delia Smith. Well, apart from that one night at Norwich City.

Who knows why Marco Pierre White became such a maniac? Maybe it was the death of his Italian mother when he was only six. His brother was sent to live with an uncle in Italy after that and his father instilled harsh life lessons at home. One time, two men were taunting a tramp. White's father walked up to them and punched them both in the face without a word. Not subtle, no subtitles necessary, they ate ordinary northern food – fish and chips were 'divine comfort'.

Marco went to London and became famous. Harveys in Wandsworth opened in 1987 and became a thing of wonder, with the chef proudly boasting that you got Yorkshire portions rather than London ones. And then, on the cusp of the millennium, he retired and gave back his Michelin stars. 'I was being judged by people who had less knowledge than me, so what was it truly worth?'

He had answered that years ago in *White Heat*, when he said that any chef who claimed to cook for love was a liar. 'At the end of the day it's all about the money.' It was a very Yorkshire approach. Pragmatism pulled the tablecloth from under the nose of romance. Cookery has since been elevated to a sort of art, and White himself says cooking and eating his perfect tagliatelle of oysters with caviar is theatre, but really you just want something nice to eat. It is a fine line and £20 between a bag of scraps and cauliflower foam.

It always seemed that as well as being a sensory smorgasbord, cooking for Marco was combat. He said Harveys was the SAS of kitchens and he was the drill sergeant spawning a monster by making Ramsay cry as he worked under him. 'He made himself cry,' he corrected in an interview. 'You do that to yourself. Nobody has the ability to make you cry. It's whether you allow it. I cried some nights after a tough service but I did it when I was walking home.' One day at the Box Tree he had cramp in both arms, but head chef Michael Truelove told him service could never be emotional. This was war. With oysters. And really, I see similarities between Don, a pensioner with a shuffling gait and a huge personality that rippled around him, and Marco, looking at the stars from the gutter and then tossing them away when he had reached the stratosphere.

I look at two photographs. One is of Don, at his golden wedding, sitting dead epicentre, a post-carvery fag in hand, surrounded by generations of his family, proud, but a slightly distant look in his eye, maybe wondering whether to sell the house he loved, always half thinking about where he had come from and where the next meal was coming from. And there's Marco, alone in the kitchen, post-service, post-coital cigarette in his fingers, a frown as deep and wide as Malham Cove. They are cut from the same cloth. For both it was about going south to find themselves, bottom lines, living hand to mouth and getting by. And all over the Yorkshire food world, from the farms to the fields and from the sit-down chippies to the great restaurants where carrot purée is not considered hospital food, it is about having enough.

Growing in the dark

The war in Ukraine goes on, and later in the summer of 2022, I pick up the *Yorkshire Post* and read a piece by a farmer near Hull. She says her father grew crops to feed the pigs that became pork to feed the community. 'The government is pursuing free trade deals which don't seem to benefit the UK or its farmers, instead expecting small family farms to go toe to toe with some of the world's major agricultural exporters such as Australia and New Zealand.' We can fight them on Olympic tracks but not in the fields.

The Rhubarb Triangle had been struggling long before Putin's steroids kicked in. It's war, lockdowns, the falling pound, Brexit (Yorkshire was widely pro-Leave), labour shortages, taste. Janet Oldroyd Hulme sits down with a sigh in an office at E. Oldroyd & Sons in Carlton, a village south of Leeds with a name derived from the Old Norse for commoner. The distance from the urban landscape to the rural one is a heartbeat.

Around her are farm buildings and a lazy summer yawn, but this nine-mile West Yorkshire triangle between Wakefield, Rothwell and Morley is famous. Janet used to be a medical scientist at St James's Hospital, but left to have children. Then she joined the family business. Some call her the High Priestess of Rhubarb, but her expression exposes the vacuity of slogans. This is a painful, tiring story, but she helped save the wider business by starting rhubarb tours, researching its history and explaining to visitors from Iceland and Australia just why this vegetable is big in Yorkshire. Or was. There used to be more than 200 growers in this area, but Janet says it is down to 10. It might be nine, but she would have to ask around. In the coal-mining belt, the future has turned its daggers on the farms.

But before the now, the then, and Janet slips into tour mode, pausing only to let the dog in. We start in 2700 BC, when rhubarb was used as a drug. 'A professor came here one day,' she says. 'He was studying arthritis and was really interested in rhubarb. He said in ancient times they believed that when you were ill, evil spirits had taken over the body, but rhubarb had the power to cast them out. When they looked at what was in rhubarb, they found it was basically poison. There was a huge amount of oxalic acid in the leaves, but there were perfect levels in the petiole – the stalk – to cleanse and detoxify the body.' It was particularly handy for dysentery.

We fast-forward to the 1620s when rhubarb seeds came to Britain from the banks of the Volga in Siberia. 'You think it's tart now, you should have seen what they brought back then!' says Janet. It was a prized drug in those days, measured against gold and sold for three times the price of opium. This was the time when you might find a poet like Coleridge off his face on opium and singing songs about big birds and sailors, but even he was not daft enough to eat rhubarb, until 1817, when workmen installing a drainage system at the Chelsea Physic Garden found some dormant roots. It was used mainly as a fruit after that and it quickly made its way to Yorkshire, not by design but as a happy accident because the region was already a big market gardening area.

There are different types of rhubarb but the nicest, more mysterious stuff is grown in the darkness of low-rise forcing sheds. It could be a metaphor for Yorkshire's insularity, secretly enjoying the fruits of its labours and only showing the harsher front to the wider world. Everyone thinks they know Yorkshire because they can see it, but it is a riddle wrapped in a mystery inside a candlelit shed in Carlton.

Janet is in her well-worn flow now. 'A forcing root lives outside happily for at least two years. That's important as it will have access to photosynthesis, and we leave it alone. If you sit here and refuse to do any work and have all the best food brought to you then you will store excess fat and put on weight. At that stage we don't want roots working. We want them storing energy before the glucose gets changed naturally to carbohydrates.' It is the move to the forcing sheds that makes the magic happen; stalks turn red and the rhubarb becomes sweeter and tender. It grows so fast that you can hear it.

Yorkshire was ideal territory because of the Volga-like frost cast by the Pennines and the coal fields that meant the ground was rich in nitrogen as well as providing coal to heat the sheds. In addition, the waste from the mills, mungo and shoddy, was high in nitrogen and used for underlaying.

Urban and rural landscapes coalesced. The business was so successful that special rhubarb trains were sent to London with the mail carriage hanging on the back. It was a good life – but nothing lasts for ever.

The fight for this industry is personal. Janet's great-grandfather was a strawberry grower from Wisbech who lost everything in the Great Depression of the 1920s. He moved north to be nearer his daughter, who had opened a grocer's in Yorkshire, and got friendly with a rhubarb grower. They swapped secrets. Janet's father, Ken, always wondered what was behind the secret door to the forcing sheds, and when he was allowed in, he was mesmerised. Eventually he took over the business, but everybody was sick of rhubarb after the war and its popularity faded. Sugar shortages meant it could not be sweetened; urbanisation and the construction of the M1 and M62 ate up land; clean air zones meant higher fuel costs; school dinners opened lasting wounds.

Another industry teetered on the brink. The trains to London stopped. Ken tried to rally the troops and set up the Yorkshire Rhubarb Growers Association, but some farmers did not want anyone else knowing their business. 'My father said, "We must stay together,"' says Janet. 'He was convinced people would return to forced rhubarb. He refused to give up.'

In 2002, he had to step back when he had his driving licence revoked for failing eyesight. Lost without his work, he remained a believer until his death in 2007. But the hard times have endured. Janet tells of problems between some Romanian and Ukrainian workers, but the real problem is climate change. The long, hot summer has just wrecked schedules and upset the frost pocket. The seasons and super-market demands are out of synch. 'Now is the winter of our discontent' might be the new marketing line.

The newspapers like to say that rhubarb is grown by candlelight in Yorkshire, but it's not true. The candles in the sheds are only there so the pickers can see during harvest time. The supermarkets were worried about wax dripping onto the plants, so the growers went to the blacksmiths and got cup holders. Now health and safety have told Janet she needs to put electricity in her sheds. 'I don't want that.' It takes five weeks of darkness to get to the point of harvest, and then the pickers have around four weeks.

Janet followed her father and attended meetings at Stockbridge House, which is now an agricultural and horticultural centre of excellence. This 67-acre site near Cawood, in the Selby area of North Yorkshire, is effectively a testament to old knowledge and new aids. It was here that new rhubarb varieties were tested after the war and where they did the early experiments about the impact of climate change on tomatoes.

The fight was fought on all fronts. Janet thought they needed to publicise the benefits of rhubarb and not live in the past. They needed to celebrate that, but also shout about the Sheffield Hallam University study that found that rhubarb's polyphenols could kill or stifle cancerous cells. It was easy to see that baking rhubarb to combat cancer could be a media hit. At one meeting she stood up and said all this to growers. She got a standing ovation. The tours started. Other Yorkshire folk didn't want outsiders snooping around, but Janet and her father had always been more outward-looking. And most important of all was Janet's battle to get protected status for the triangle.

In 2010, Yorkshire forced rhubarb became the forty-first British product to be awarded the Protected Designation of Origin mantle, following Melton Mowbray pork pies and Cornish sardines, and joining more celebrated names such

as Champagne and Parma ham. This restricted the use of the
Yorkshire forced rhubarb name to a few growers.

For once, the wider reputation of Yorkshire is crucial to
the survival of natives. Yet, typically, defining place is not
always easy. Just as borders shift and the deceased relocate,
the Rhubarb Triangle has been a source of conjecture. It is
generally considered to comprise around nine square miles,
where once the industry covered triple that. But are the
three points Leeds, Bradford and Wakefield, or Wakefield,
Rothwell and Morley? And where does this leave Carlton, the
home of rhubarb growing, which appears to be just outside
the triangle if you draw a straight line from the centre of
Leeds to Wakefield. I suppose the Rhubarb Pentangle didn't
sound as good and would probably have attracted unwanted
Satanists. What we know for sure is that they have rhubarb
statues up here. That's not normal.

Janet lets the dog out. I have taken up a lot of her time.
She has just invested heavily in new sheds. That's the future,
but its survival is tethered to the past. 'My grandfather came
up here on a horse and cart,' she tells me. 'You think, Christ
almighty. They loaded the roots onto small trailers and that
one horse would pull it all. You know, horses don't damage
the soil structure in winter, but tractors do. Maybe we'll go
back to horses one day.'

Maybe. I think about a passage from *The Striding Dales*
in which Halliwell Sutcliffe champions the idiosyncrasy
of the Dales village school. 'They are taught what other
children learn,' he writes, 'but through their tasks the magic
of a countryside, rich in old-time lore, spins threads of
true romance.' He adds that the schoolmistress is an aider
and abettor who can see fairies in the hollows and goblins
on the moor 'as if the braver medieval times were not yet

deceased'. This, he concluded, was why her pupils were apt to go far in life.

It does not really stack up in hindsight. Sometimes you have to go with progress and adapt, if only to pass your GCSEs and avoid being pilloried in an anti-goblin WhatsApp group. 'It seems indeed to be a truism that there are more fairies in the world than people who can see them,' claimed Halliwell. This is hard for anyone to quantify without modern surveying techniques, but I like to think of an old rambler, pipe in hand, munching on some rhubarb by a stile in the Dales and accosting a burly blacksmith as he stumbles out of the Linton Arms. 'Do you believe in fairies, Arthur?' Thwack.

The unprotected pudding

Halliwell's wistfulness showed how things have changed. Yet in the Yorkshire Society's 2021 report into the future of the region, the answers were predictable when people were asked what best symbolises Yorkshire. The White Rose was most popular, but was closely followed by the Yorkshire pudding, with far more votes than Vikings, terriers, cricket or Wensleydale cheese, which Halliwell pointed out should have been Yoredale. 'Wensley is a village that might have been brought here from some southern shire in its entirety and planted in a sterner setting,' he sniffed. The Yore was a proper river, too, prone to headstrong passion between its gentler moods, like the Wharfe, the same river that would claim the life of the man who sketched the castle on the opposing page to Sutcliffe's huffing in *The Striding Dales*. Yes, cling to those banks and those memories, because life can be a straight line as well as a circle.

The Yorkshire pudding, though, is indisputably symbolic. Hannah Glasse is credited with being the first person to apply the term 'Yorkshire' to the dripping puddings that had been around for centuries. Essentially this was a way of making use of fat that seeped from meat cooking on a fire. In 1747, an identifying symbol was born, on page 190 of Glasse's *The Art of Cookery Made Plain and Easy*: 'Take a quart of milk and five eggs, beat them up well together, and mix them with flour till it is of a good pancake batter, and very smooth; put in a little salt, some grated nutmeg and ginger; butter a dripping or frying-pan and put it under a piece of beef, mutton, or a loin of veal that is roasting, and then put in your batter, and when the top side is brown, cut it in square pieces, and turn it, and then let the underside be brown; then put it in a hot dish as clean of fat as you can, and send it to table hot.'

As a result of this paragraph, people get unduly agitated when the Yorkshire pudding's provenance is tinkered with. The USA, that historically shallow madhouse where high class is having reservations about *High School Musical 3*, has been the worst offender. Hence the anger over the *New York Times* recipe for a variant to be served as a dessert with syrup, preserves and cinnamon sugar. Cue scoffing, and not in an edible way. American writers leapt to their own defence and pointed out this was a Dutch baby or a popover. Anyone who had ever been to the States would have known that Americans like to put syrup on anything, and so it should not necessarily have been taken as a slight.

Some things are inalienable, though, and the modern whim of having round Yorkshire puddings is an affectation. Nowadays celebrity chefs are also always publishing their own unique take on what is a blindingly simple recipe. We are not talking Heston Blumenthal making dodecahedrons of ox cheek from Fuzzy Felt and dodo blood here. It's a prosaic dish that should be cooked in a large baking tray and then cut into squares. Then it should be served as a stand-alone starter with only gravy. The question 'How many Yorkshires?' should never be asked. One is always enough.

Glasse was a Londoner, so why did she use the county's name in the title of a pudding? In *Traditional Food in Yorkshire*, writer Peter Brears suggests it may have been down to miners' eating habits, free coal leading to lots of joints. What we know for sure is that Glasse was a plagiarist, not uncommon at the time, and she took scores of recipes from *The Whole Duty of a Woman*, which was written in 1737. Dubbing itself an 'infallible guide to the fair sex', it contained 'rules, directions and observations for conduct and behaviour through assorted roles as virgins, wives and widows'. In an age before self-awareness had been invented and when misogyny was celebrated, this book merrily mixes advice on the duty of virgins while lamenting a degenerate age in which men were effeminate and women confident. This does sound like a Yorkshire sort of gripe, in fairness. There was also a recipe for dripping pudding. In 2011, a bid from several manufacturers to gain EU Protected Geographical Indication status for the Yorkshire pudding failed. It was being produced widely throughout Britain by the early nineteenth century at the latest, so what was so special about Yorkshire's Yorkshires? The EU felt the pudding was just a bit too generic. This may explain Brexit.

It was in high-calorie company in failing to get protected status. An attempt to gain the mark for the parmo, the Middlesbrough takeaway favourite that basically comprises fried chicken, breadcrumbs, béchamel sauce and melted cheese, was also doomed. Reputedly the parmo was invented by an American soldier who was invalided out of the Second World War and made to put on weight in Middlesbrough. Its chances of special status were undermined somewhat when Tam Fry, chair of the National Obesity Forum, said, 'You would have to be an Olympic athlete to eat it without effect; for the rest of humanity there is an unbelievable risk of obesity.' The personal trainer of a 30-stone local supported that view by distributing leaflets to parmo takeaways with the message: 'Do not feed this man.'

Glasse's own story was also ill-fated. She eloped with a poorly paid soldier, had strained family relations, and after failing to make a living selling quack oil called Daffy's Elixir, she wrote her cookery book for servants, even apologising for not using a high, polite style. Dr Johnson would muse, 'Women can spin very well, but they cannot make a good book of cookery', but it was a hit. It was still in print in 1751, when she was even afforded the honour of having her name on her own book, but three years later she was declared bankrupt. She sold the copyright and was sent to the notorious Marshalsea debtors' prison, made infamous by Dickens in *Little Dorrit*. She died in 1770.

In truth, the Yorkshire pudding is not even Glasse's greatest claim to fame. That came on another page, where she set down the first recorded recipe in English for a curry. It involved two fowls or rabbits, three or four onions, 30 peppercorns, coriander, and a large shovel to beat it all to a pulp.

Sweet pain

I admit it, I am in the Yorkshire Pudding Facebook group, where people spend afternoons showing photographs of

Yorkshire puddings. No recipes, just post and gloat. It's the best thing about twenty-first-century living. But should the plain old Yorkshire pudding really be Yorkshire's greatest claim to culinary fame? Elsewhere, there is Yoredale (okay, Wensleydale) cheese, that oatmeal and black treacle cake called parkin, and the newer cuisines from Yorkshire's Asian population and eastern European immigrants. Building on Glasse's recipe, Yorkshire likes to think of itself as the second home of the curry, with Bradford its capital. Kashmir was one of the first restaurants, a meeting place for those arriving in a very foreign land in the 1950s, and its popularity slowly spread from the immigrant population to the student one, and then, when locals stopped complaining about the garlic, the rest. Some cuisines, such as Caribbean, took longer to filter into general use, initially blocked by a lack of adventure and an abundance of prejudice, while more recent times have seen the emergence of Polish restaurants and stores.

And then there's booze and the fuzzy warmth of Theakston's Old Peculier. Few feeling that peculiar afterglow may know that the Peculier of Masham was actually a court comprising a group of men called the Four and Twenty, set up because the Archbishop of York was too lazy to travel to carry out his ecclesiastical duties. Or he was posting pudding pics on Facebook.

However, if Yorkshire can claim to be the home of any food, it is surely sweets and chocolate. The list of companies that thrived in the county, many of them in York, is long: Bassett's, Thorntons, Terry's, Rowntree's, Mackintosh, Nestlé, Dunhill, Craven et al. In 1899, a Bassett's sales rep called Charlie Thompson was carrying a plate of rejected sweets during a visit to a buyer in Leicester. He slipped, and the sweets became jumbled up on the floor. The buyer liked the colourful muddle, and Liquorice Allsorts were born by chance. Some 90 years later, Bassett's, based in Sheffield, made the news for complaining about a *Doctor Who* storyline in which the pathological Kandyman bore an uncanny resemblance to Bertie Bassett, the company mascot created in 1929. A hallucinogenic plot had Sheila Hancock playing a Margaret Thatcher-style tyrant who employed death squads to clamp down on killjoys. Sylvester McCoy, cast as Dr Who, later came clean about the allegory and mused, 'Our feeling was Margaret Thatcher was far more terrifying than any monster the Doctor had created.' A call for the drones to revolt was a teatime echo of the miners' strike. Bassett's were unimpressed. It was not good for business to have their mascot killing people with his fondant surprise. They complained, and the Kandyman died by additives soon after.

Liquorice first came to Pontefract via knights and then Dominican monks. In 1614, Sir George Savile was stamping his initials on the Pomfret cake, but it was a medicine at that time, used for coughs and stomach ailments, and only chemist George Dunhill's experiment of adding sugar in 1760 transformed it into a sweet. Tradition merged with loam soil, needed for the long roots, and Pontefract became the unlikely hub. It takes all, no stop.

When I was growing up, Rowntree's was part of local culture. Joseph Rowntree was a Quaker philanthropist, building his own little Saltaire and bailing out his brother, Henry Isaac, who had founded the eponymous confectionery business in 1862 but then grown distracted by his role as a newspaper editor. He created a sweet-toothed empire that led to Aero, Black Magic, fruit pastilles and then Kit Kat, Rolo, Lion bar and, of course, the Yorkie.

He also fathered Seebohm, who rose to prominence as a social researcher as well as sweet experimenter. In 1899, Seebohm published *Poverty, a Study of Town Life*, in which he conducted an empirical survey of 46,754 people in York. Defining the phrase 'poverty line', he calculated that 28 per cent of respondents lived below it. His work investigating the causes of that poverty is now seen as fundamental to the rise of social liberalism.

Winston Churchill, who would famously cross the floor of the Commons to join the Liberals in 1904, said *Poverty* had made his hair stand on end. 'Although the British Empire is so large, the poor cannot find room to live in it,' he said. 'This festering life at home makes world-wide power a mockery. I see little glory in an Empire which can rule the waves and is unable to flush its own sewers.'

Two more studies followed over another half-century. At the factory, Seebohm and Joseph produced a template for a better working society, with widows' benefits, pensions and a company dentist. For Seebohm it was not about handouts but creating better conditions to foster improved productivity. Had he been around today, he would still be demanding a living wage, as he did in 1910, but would also be installing beanbags and table football in the office. The Joseph Rowntree Foundation survives to battle poverty. Seebohm is all but forgotten, but he has a decent claim to being one of the greatest Yorkshire natives.

They don't grow much liquorice in Pontefract any more. The Rhubarb Triangle no longer chimes loudly. The future of fish and chips might be the drive-through and Bettys is thriving in the past. The Yorkshire pudding has still not got protected status, and the poverty line is rising along with temperatures. If we are what we eat, this is food for thought.

12

PIONEERS

My desire to get here was like miner's coal dust; it was under my fingers and I couldn't scrub it out.

Betty Boothroyd, Dewsbury-born first female speaker of the House of Commons, on arriving in Parliament, 1973

In her 2021 book *How to Be Hopeful*, Bernadette Russell writes: 'We need our hope to be underpinned by real innovations, inventions, experiences and positive changes.' Yorkshire has always had this inventiveness of thought and deed in spades, and in hydraulic lime in concrete (John Smeaton), commercial steam trains (Matthew Murray), stainless steel (Harry Brearley), board games (Waddingtons) and the floating ballcock, if not the actual toilet (Thomas Crapper). The pioneers ranged from inventors to adventurers and from eccentrics to activists. All were bonded by a willingness to rail against the existing machines, systems or status quo. They dared to be different. They lived in Yorkshire but thought outside the box.

Reclaiming the night

Up on Beeston Hill in Leeds, I make a quick stop in Holbeck Cemetery to look down over the cityscape. Through the gapless rain, buildings huddle together like cattle by a dry-stone wall. Up here tombstones have toppled with age and disrespect. Joseph Harrison, Tony's dad, is over there. A wrought-iron gate with 'V Poem' fashioned in the corner stands nearby. The Harrison grave is now free of graffiti, but others have been daubed with white tags. It is depressing. I walk through the V signs and go down a road of red-brick terraces until I come to my destination. I knock on the door and Al Garthwaite opens it and invites me inside.

She clears away her grandchildren's toys and sits down in a room bedecked by books. She takes a sip of tea and begins. 'The first demonstration I went on was about overseas students having to pay fees,' she says. This was at Durham University, and it was the time of the Vietnam War. Protest was in the air. The first women's liberation march was in 1971. When Al moved to Oxford – the city not the university – a small group began protesting because there was a men-only bar owned by a college. 'We went along, and it was basically old men smoking pipes and playing dominoes, so they were not exactly the bastion of privilege. It was not the Bullingdon Club. They looked at us in amazement when we went to order a drink and someone said they'd have to call the police. We didn't want to get arrested so we traipsed out, but because it was owned by a college it made the papers.' They picketed every week on a point of principle rather than the need for a pint. Terry Eagleton, a young liberal don, said the college should not be funding something with discriminatory rules, but he was outvoted.

Coverage of the nascent women's liberation movement was aggressively unsympathetic. 'It was all about how we looked,' says Al. 'Dungarees were actually very fashionable then, but it was all "dungarees, short hair, big boots, lesbians, lesbians, lesbians". It varied from the outright attacking to the mocking.' She went for one job and was asked what salary she was looking for. When she came up with a figure, the boss said: 'I could get a man for that.'

After a few years in cramped living conditions with some friends, Al and a few others moved to Leeds. And in 1975, the first murder was committed. Wilma McCann had left the Room at the Top club in Chapeltown just before 1 a.m. late in October. She was eating curry and chips and tried to flag down a car for a lift home. Peter Sutcliffe was in his lime-green Ford Capri. Her body was found by a milkman the next morning, around 100 yards from her home. 'They falsely said she was a prostitute,' says Al as she goes back to a time when horrific crimes and systemic abuse were lost in a Victorian fog of true-crime tropes. 'She was a single mother. Her body was found on the Scott Hall playing fields. I used to visit a friend over at Woodhouse and walk back into Chapeltown and I'd do that at two in the morning. I thought, "Gosh, this is quite near." At that point we weren't living in fear because, unfortunately, women get murdered. Life went back to normal.'

Three months later, Emily Jackson was murdered. Then, in 1977, Irene Richardson, followed by three more women – Patricia Atkinson, Jayne MacDonald and Jean Jordan – the same year. And that was when the fear really spread. Until then, a hopelessly inept police investigation was comforted by its attitude that prostitutes did not matter as much as other women. But when MacDonald, a 16-year-old shop worker, was murdered, the police went public with their prejudice. Now he was killing what they would call 'innocent girls'. Later, a detective would see nothing wrong with telling a press conference, 'He has made it clear he hates prostitutes; many people do.'

Sutcliffe later said he was sure he would be arrested the day after he became a killer, but he overestimated the police. They interviewed him nine times and ignored the reports from the victims who survived. One said he was white and bearded. The police told her he was black. The pervasive attitude was that if you were a woman out late then you were 'asking for it'. Survivors were scarred by both their attacks and the police indifference, and a squalid glamour was ascribed to a serial killer. He became the Yorkshire Ripper. The nickname mythologised him. It was something from the penny dreadfuls or Conan Doyle. In her controversial book *The Street-Cleaner*, which came out in 1986, when memories of the murders were still fresh, Nicole Ward Jouve wrote of 'an overwhelmingly seedy, violent, dark industrial north' and how this enabled the rich south to feel complacent. 'Male violence is displaced onto one extreme northern example.' She added that this becomes an 'entertaining but gruelling circus' for the rest of the country.

But not in Yorkshire. Not when everyone's sister seems to have a story of being followed or chased. Not when a bearded neighbour is questioned over the batch of five-pound notes that police think might hold the key because of money found in one victim's handbag. Not when paranoia is running so wild that people start suspecting relatives, and not when the nights close in. 'I'd been to a party just the other side of the road in Chapeltown when Jayne MacDonald was killed,' says Al. 'We walked back very near the scene. At that point the police came and did door-to-door inquiries. My brother had been staying with me but had gone back to Bournemouth. They asked for his address and said they'd have to go and talk to him.' Yorkshire had never felt more claustrophobic. Jayne MacDonald lived on the same street as Wilma McCann, and one of McCann's children, Carl, was convinced the killer was coming for him next.

Al began working for the Women's Information Referral and Enquiry Service (WIRES), the internal newsletter for the women's liberation movement. One day she read an article in feminist magazine *Spare Rib* concerning Walpurgis Night, 30 April, the traditional time for witches to roam freely in Germany. Groups of women in various cities were fed up with being sexually harassed and abused by men, so that year they dressed as witches and marched in Cologne and Frankfurt. Any men who got in their way were pelted with flour bombs and shot by water pistol.

The idea of a similar march in Britain germinated. A proposal put to a women's lib conference in Edinburgh was rejected. 'I thought, "Why don't we do something in Leeds?" There was a serial killer about but if that was the only man we had to be bothered about then we were very lucky. It took time to organise because there was no internet. It was all newsletters and the post then.' But on 12 November 1977, around 60 women marched. One group started from Chapeltown Community Centre, another group from the Peel statue in Hyde Park. 'Woodhouse [a neighbouring district] was – and remains – an area where predators tend to lurk.' Other cities joined in too – London, Manchester, Bradford, York and Lancaster, where Al's daughter would go to university and where she says it is well known that predatory males from rural Cumbria go into town to grab freshers.

Al had ordered flaming torches from Barnum's carnival shop in Hammersmith. They were like the ones used by side-show jugglers. At that time the city centre was near deserted in the evening, but as they walked along North Lane, a group of men stumbled out of the Eagle. 'They were harassing us and said things. We thought they might possibly assault us, but we didn't think they would come at us with cleavers. They were just drunk blokes who saw a load of women and thought we were fair game – 'What are they up to? Let's be having them', that sort of thing. We advanced towards them with our flaming torches and they backed off.'

The women rallied in City Square and handed out leaflets to the few people they encountered. Transport was arranged for those who wanted to go home. Nobody went alone. The rest gathered at a house party. 'I don't think any of us thought it was the start of something that would continue to this day.'

It was six weeks since Jean Jordan had been murdered in Manchester. It was two months before Yvonne Pearson and Helen Rytka would be killed. Ingrained sexism meant these women were ignored.

And the horror continued: Vera Millward, Josephine Whitaker, Barbara Leach and Marguerite Walls. Someone else's bogeyman.

Al sips her coffee. The rain refuses to stop its snare.

Two years later, the Reclaim the Night march attracted 400 people. The media interest grew, especially after the murder of Jackie Hill, a university student, at the end of 1980. The university stopped evening seminars, put on a late-night minibus service and told women not to go out alone after dark. 'Some of the national media wanted to come up and interview us. We said we thought it should be a woman because we felt women journalists deserved a break. Not that it meant we got sympathetic coverage. There were black women on the march but some people said it was racist to go through a mainly black area. But women were under threat in that area and we lived there. I repudiate that criticism. The passers-by we did see were astonished because it was taken that women didn't go out. It was just something that was accepted, like the rain coming from the sky.

'One reporter stood at the bus stop, and as a woman got off he said, "Why are you on your own? Why aren't you with a man?" There was some benefit event in town and at the end they said could all the men make sure they accompanied a woman home. Well, any of those men could have been Sutcliffe. It had a huge impact. Some women left their jobs. Some left their uni courses. Others stopped going to evening classes.

'We felt like we were the ones being scrutinised rather than the fruitless attempts to catch this man. Our phones were tapped. You'd hear these clicks and sometimes you'd be put through to someone. This was before there was a group called Angry Women who went out and set fire to some sex shops. I don't know who they were. Nobody was hurt but arson was a serious crime. Usually it was minor stuff, certainly compared to what men were doing to women. These days you have social media and you don't need to spray-paint a wall, but when no one is listening sometimes you have to do things that are a bit illegal to draw attention.'

In January 1981, Sutcliffe was finally caught. By chance. Five months later, he was convicted of 13 murders and 7 attempted murders, but many people believe that is far from the sum of his crimes. Capturing a killer was a story not a cure, though, and Al and her colleagues in the women's liberation movement continued to demand change.

It came slowly. Al remembers working for WIRES when a woman came in. 'She was in her forties and had been walking back from a party, not in a particularly deserted spot, and a young man dragged her off the street and raped her. She went in to report it and they said, "Why would he want to rape you? You must have wanted it."' There was the time one notable judge said that women and small boys were known to tell lies.

But refuges and rape crisis centres began to appear, and the mocking tone of the media softened. Al and her fellow activists received media training – at least the ones not so alienated that they had vowed never to speak to journalists. The police's idea that these were mad women on the margins, gluing up the locks of sex shops and hissing at bystanders, was now a crude caricature. The mayor of Barnsley, a middle-aged Yorkshireman, greeted 200 women who were campaigning against an unsafe underpass. 'The ridicule went right down in the eighties but then went up again in the nineties,' says Al. 'That was the time of lad culture, men supposedly shaking off the shackles. The early nineties was not a good time for women and no one wanted to listen to people like us who were now the age of their mothers. We were past our sell-by date.'

The mission was not complete, though, and Al began to work for Leeds council. She still does, as lead for the campaign to end violence against women and girls. She cringes when she talks of woman-blaming. Back then, the media suggested that Sutcliffe's wife, Sonia, was a cold, sinister figure. 'But *she* didn't murder loads of women, for goodness' sake!'

In 2014, the Holbeck area of Leeds introduced a pilot scheme in which prostitution was allowed after 8 p.m. if it took place away from residential areas and businesses. The first such project in the UK, the intention was to make life better for locals and safer for prostitutes. A year later, Daria Pionko, a Polish woman, was murdered for her £80 earnings and the scheme was changed, paused and then scrapped. Lydia Pionko called her daughter a 'joyful girl', but it was a life to bleach the joy from any spirit. The *New York Post* referred to Holbeck as the 'UK's seedy dread light district', and locals talked of children being propositioned and of seeing people having sex in broad daylight. By 2023, long after the scheme had gone, people were still photographing car number plates and shaming the 'punter of the week' online. And beyond the 'street cleaning', vulnerable women descended further into drugs and other means of oblivion. Now Al says hotels still let a group of men sign in with a single drunk woman. On another occasion, an older man asked for a room for him and his 'daughter' but demanded a double bed. And got it.

After Sutcliffe died in November 2020, the current chief constable of West Yorkshire Police, John Robins, apologised not only for the mistakes made by Assistant Chief Constable George Oldfield and his team, but also for the 'language, terminology and tone' used by officers in relation to the victims. Oldfield had died in 1985 after a series of heart attacks. Four months after the apology, Sarah Everard was kidnapped by a policeman on Clapham Common and raped and murdered. In the immediate aftermath, police knocked on doors and warned women not to go out. 'This was the same rhetoric used in the seventies during the Yorkshire Ripper,' someone posted on Twitter. #Reclaimthenight began to trend. A huge vigil at Clapham

Common ended with six arrests, and the image of Patsy Stevenson being wrestled to the floor and handcuffed became the picture of renewed struggle.

A year on, Al Garthwaite, pioneer, liberator and defender of women, watched TV reports of schoolgirls in Iran removing their hijabs and defying the patriarchy. She was thrilled. Maybe she was transported back to the smoky rooms where she and her friends used to hold meetings and plan the next battle. Now they can do that in council chambers. It is progress.

She has carried on the activism of the Yorkshire suffragettes from the early twentieth century, women like Mary Gawthorpe, Isabella Ford and Dora Thewlis. The famous names of the movement would hail from the middle classes, but in Yorkshire the movement had strong working-class links and was allied to trade unionism. Ford fought for the mill workers, marched with the Manningham strikers and was the first woman to speak at the annual conference of what would become the Labour Party. Gawthorpe, born in Woodhouse, heckled Winston Churchill and was crudely beaten for her protest. It was not the first time. The hunger strikes and force-feeding that followed caused her lasting damage. Thewlis was dubbed 'Baby Suffragette' when she appeared in a London court after attempting to 'storm' the Houses of Parliament in 1907. She was just 16 when her picture was printed on the front page of the *Daily Mirror*, and the pompous magistrate suggested her parents back at home near Huddersfield sort her out. They wrote back and told him they were proud of her. These were brave women kicking against obvious but accepted wrongs.

'People say nothing's changed, but of course it has,' says Al. 'I haven't wasted my life. Will we ever end violence against women? Probably not. Will we ever end drink-driving? Probably not. But we can try, and we can do an awful lot.'

In his poetic book about life in the Upper Calder Valley, *Under the Rock*, Benjamin Myers posed an unpalatable question: 'To what extent does a place dictate people's behaviour? Can the contours of a county determine the actions of its residents?' He mentioned the other sort of Yorkshire grit, not the stone or endurance, but the grating kind, the stuff that Michael Palin says gets in the works. Myers cited Ward Jouve's polarising book and the masculinity she felt in the area where Sutcliffe killed. 'You feel the violence in the wind,' she wrote in *The Street-Cleaner*. A new myth was forming in the bleak and brown of West Yorkshire, and it was willing her dead.

Myers's book is beautiful, but he does not spare the blood and bone. He mentions Jimmy Savile, who was set fair for a life as a Yorkshire archetype, given that he had worked in a mine and been a semi-professional wrestler, and then gone on to become a TV phenomenon despite an artificial persona of lame catchphrases and gold lamé jackets. It turned out he was also a paedophile and a necrophiliac. It has tainted memories of places he worked, such as the Leeds General Infirmary. Once I thought of Leeds hospitals happily, of my wife working there as a speech therapist, trying to get people to remember words lost to stroke and piece together things they once knew. Now I think of a monster lurking in the mortuary and using a fame based on lies to hide in plain sight.

But as Myers asks, is it bad luck that Sutcliffe and Savile lived in the same pocket of West Yorkshire? Or that Harold Shipman started killing people when he moved to Todmorden on the Yorkshire border? Or that John Christie, the 10 Rillington Place murderer and rapist, was

born 14 miles away in nearby Northowram, and Donald
Neilson, an armed robber and mass murderer glamorised
as the Black Panther, was from Bradford? This is the West
Yorkshire people would rather forget.

A year after Sutcliffe's trial, Barry Prudom shot and killed
PC David Haigh, electrician George Luckett and Sergeant
David Winter in an 11-day period. Ward Jouve wrote of a
vigilante spirit taking over Malton in North Yorkshire where
she lived. The greengrocer told her he had a rifle and was
ready to kill. The solicitor loaded his pistol and put it in the
top drawer. Prudom was eventually shot 21 times by the
police, with the shooters exonerated. 'But the Leeds women
who walked with a can of spray paint in their handbags
were accused of carrying offensive weapons,' she wrote. She
wondered about the support a vigilante group of prostitutes
would have mustered. 'While the Ripper operated, 12 Leeds
women were arrested for picketing the entrance to a cinema
that was showing *Violation of the Bitch*.'

A bizarre memory emerges. It is 1981, and outside the
Madhouse, a small exhibition of novelties and seaside hokum
next to the Princess café in Scarborough, Peter Sutcliffe is
standing tall. The owner has decided to install a waxwork
of the killer on the front, next to shops selling sticks of rock,
commonly known as wife-beaters, and kiss-me-quick hats –
'I'm not the Ripper, love', as the chat-up line went. In 1981
Yorkshire is a confused place.

The Nondescript

Maybe there is something in the old stereotypes that makes
some Yorkshire people daring when it comes to standing

ground or reshaping it. Perhaps the pig-headedness is why the dry-stone waller will climb to the top of Pen-y-ghent for a pittance. Belief, smug or not, is made for pioneering.

Take Charles Waterton. His feats would include encouraging future adventurers and setting up a walled nature reserve to shut out the Industrial Revolution in the 1820s. Part of his shtick was to disguise himself as a dog and bite his guests' legs. When not doing this, he liked to pass himself off as his own butler and tickle his visitors with a coal brush. He dissected a gorilla at home. He rode a crocodile. He invited those considered lunatics from an asylum to watch waterfowl through his telescope because he appreciated the calming wonder of birds. Perhaps most dramatically, he advocated the use of the South American poison curare, used on the tips of blowpipe darts, as an anaesthetic in the treatment of rabies. There was madness in the method, as when, in a move to show the merits of curare to the public, he injected an ageing donkey with the substance in Nottingham. When the poison took effect, seven men lifted the animal onto a table, whereupon Waterton worked bellows to pump air into its lungs for seven hours. Eventually it revived. Hurrah. And then it died. He got another donkey. This time it worked. And then he waited for decades for a rabid human to try it on. He even asked people to telegram him if diagnosed, but annoyingly, they tended to die before he could get there.

Waterton was a remarkable figure by any standards. Sir David Attenborough certainly thought so, and hailed him as the man who created arguably the world's first nature reserve – in Wakefield. Sir David recorded a short paean to Waterton for the BBC, in which he rejoices in his predecessor popping a boa constrictor on its nose and dangling a naked leg from a hammock in a South American jungle in the hope that he could carry out a live study of vampire bats.

Born in 1782, Waterton lived in the family pile, Walton Hall. In 1804, he ventured to British Guiana, now Guyana, encouraged by Sir Joseph Banks, president of the Royal Society and a veteran of Captain Cook's exploration of the South Pacific on HMS *Endeavour*. His role was to manage his family's sugar plantations, complete with their 400 slaves. Waterton would deny ever owning a slave but he did teach one how to stuff birds. This man would be renamed John Edmonstone, after his Scottish owner, Charles Edmonstone. On becoming a free man after travelling to Scotland with his master in 1817, he set up a taxidermy business on Lothian Street in Edinburgh. One regular visitor was a teenager called Charles Darwin, whose enthusiasm for his medical studies suddenly dimmed. Instead, he began to draw birds, and a few years later set sail for South America on HMS *Beagle*.

By then, Waterton's *Wanderings in South America* had been published. Despite a typically eccentric structure and almost biblical writing style, the book was a runaway success, helped by stories such as his capturing of a ten-foot caiman. Insistent that it should not be shot or stabbed – not due to any compassion, but from a desire to get a perfect specimen to hollow out and preserve with chemicals – he hooked the beast. There then followed what sounds like a cross between Indiana Jones and *Carry on Taxidermy* as he climbed onto the back of the animal and grabbed its front legs. Amid the furious splashing, the reptile was overpowered.

You can see how his book might have appealed. It also featured his biggest scam. For a man of nature and science, Waterton did enjoy a puerile prank. And so the frontispiece of *Wanderings* contains a picture of the Nondescript, the head and shoulders of a wild man that Waterton claimed to have killed. He said he had severed the head to make it easier to carry from the jungle – nobody seemed too concerned by such behaviour back then – but this was actually a skilled piece of artistry fashioned from the backside of a howler monkey.

His true significance, however, resided in a small corner of Yorkshire. Alarmed by the smoky onset of industrialisation, Waterton determined to make Walton Hall a sanctuary and spent years erecting a nine-foot, three-mile wall around it for protection. 'Smoke was belching from chimneys,' said Attenborough. 'Leaves shrivelled on trees. Slag heaps and slums were everywhere.' Waterton did not remove fallen oaks, as most estate owners did, but made them havens for birds. He climbed trees and drilled holes. He created a sandbar for sand martins. There were swans and herons and owls and woodpeckers. Other people's vermin were his guests. He paid sixpence for any hedgehog brought to him. In Walton Hall's pomp, he welcomed 18,000 visitors a year, and was happy to show off his double-jointedness, which meant he could put a foot on his head. There was also a bitter legal battle with a neighbouring soap boiler about pollution. 'Charles Waterton was little known not only internationally, but shamefully, in this country too,' said Attenborough.

Times change, though, and new research of old documents has thrown a light on the darker corners of Waterton's tale. Sarah Cobham, a writer and historian, has documented some of this for the Yorkshire Bylines organisation. The evidence is challenging to tourist bosses, who have championed Waterton as a stuffed cash cow. I call Sarah and she explains that Waterton's claim that he had never possessed a slave was made in 1833, the year slavery was abolished and when it was prudent to be on the right side of changing history.

His defenders often point out that he wrote, 'Slavery can never be defended.' Sarah says that is true, but in the same paragraph, he also expanded on how a British colonialist 'cheers his negroes in labour, comforts them in sickness, is kind to them in old age, and never forgets that they are his fellow creatures'. The British plantation owner, then, was portrayed as a kindly old soul, but this can be easily refuted, not least by an 1804 newspaper article describing how Charles Edmonstone's runaway slaves, branded with his CE monogram, tended to get shot or executed.

Waterton is on record paying a fulsome tribute to Edmonstone, and was rewarded by Edmonstone giving him one of his mixed-race daughters, 18-year-old Anne-Mary, as a wife. This was a business deal that provided an instant £625,000 in today's money and would secure the future of Walton Hall. Anne-Mary died a few weeks after giving birth to Waterton's spendthrift son, Edmund, and her sisters, feisty pipe-smoking Eliza and nature-loving Helen, helped raise the boy.

Sarah says the story of the Edmonstone sisters shows the oppressive system of patrimony of that time, but Wakefield would become a hotbed of progressive thought as locals rebelled against injustices. In the early nineteenth century, Ann Hurst became a pioneering newspaper proprietor in the city and used her position to publish anti-slavery propaganda. In 1833, Mary Heaton was locked up in the West Riding Pauper Lunatic Asylum in Wakefield for the crime of heckling a preacher in church for not paying her for music lessons. She was duly told to swallow mercury and had electric shock treatment of the pelvis, but she helped pioneer art therapy when she started making tapestries, often stitched with words detailing her grievances. Fittingly, Wakefield has been home to a mental health museum since 1974, with many of the exhibits artwork by former patients of the same hospital.

Sarah's Forgotten Women of Wakefield project means blue plaques have been going up around the city. This pioneering spirit could also be witnessed down the Wakefield City Club in 1978. Sheila Capstick, who was married to the future vice president of the NUM, refused to be cowed when told she could not play snooker at the club. Outlawing sexism in working men's clubs probably seemed anathema to regulars, but A Woman's Right to Cues became a campaign, and another picket line formed. 'Bigger than snooker,' said Ken Capstick. It took 29 years for clubs to open their doors to all, with a lukewarm welcome and a half a lager.

Waterton was undoubtedly one of Yorkshire's trailblazers too, even if his history can no longer be regarded as a merry, crowd-pleasing jaunt. The footnote is also fabulous. His sisters-in-law, Eliza and Helen, were formidable women who fitted into high society despite their colour – Darwin described them as 'Mulattresses' after a visit – and Waterton left everything to them in his will. When he died in 1865, his wayward son used patrimony laws to overturn that. The sisters chose to go quietly, as long as Edmund protected his father's legacy, and they took up residence in Scarborough, eventually finding their way to Belgium. Edmund, though, had no interest in his father's legacy or in keeping his word. Running up debts, he sold Walton Hall to the son of the same soap boiler his father had fought for so long. It was left to Eliza and Helen to ensure that Waterton's name survived, and they duly became custodians of his letters and the natural history collection that would fuel the interest of Attenborough. It was, then, two unchampioned sisters from Demerara who ensured that Charles Waterton became renowned as a Yorkshire pioneer.

When you have curtains you can't see out

The idea of the pioneer as an eccentric or a mad scientist appeals to Yorkshire quirkiness. All manner of incredible life and society-changing things have been invented in Yorkshire. Joseph Bramah was doing great things with the flush toilet in the eighteenth century, long before Thomas Crapper was hailed as the king of wasteful thinking. Indeed, the word 'crap' made it into the *Oxford English Dictionary* when Crapper was only 10, thus debunking another myth ascribed to the Doncaster plumber. (We should have known his role in toilet invention was overstated from the fact the satirist who first championed it had also said the brassiere was created by a man called Titzling.) John Harrison, from near Wakefield, is credited with solving the issue of determining longitude while at sea. It took him decades, and involved a clock that could keep time to within three seconds a day. His eighteenth-century quest saw him fall out with the Board of Longitude, though, when he did not gain what he felt was his just recompense from the talent competition born of the Longitude Act, designed to stimulate scientific endeavour.

For Yorkshireness, though, it is hard to beat Percy Shaw. His 1968 meeting with Alan Whicker, the much-impersonated broadcaster who helped set up Yorkshire TV and then used it to screen *Whicker's World*, remains a classic of incongruity.

There is Whicker in Halifax, debonair, with his prize slug moustache, talking to a rotund figure in a trilby and a cream suit looking somewhere between Al Capone and the local butcher. 'Anyhow, got to get home, and it's that foggy headlights make it a white sheet,' Shaw says from the back of his Rolls-Royce. 'Are you all reet?' he asks suddenly, when Whicker seems to have drifted off.

The story goes that Shaw saw a cat's eyes reflected in his headlights. The truth is, he saw the equivalent of cat's eyes in a road sign and thought they should be on the road. He found out these lenses came from a factory in Bradford, who got them from what he calls 'Czech-a-sla-vak-ia'. He started making them himself in an old mill in Halifax because 'Percy doesn't really trust foreigners.'

Whicker asks him if he saw himself making money or doing good for mankind.

'Trouble is, I never thought at all,' Shaw says.

The documentary really hits its stride when it joins him at home. He is cooking a joint of beef for a bunch of pensioners lined up in front of four televisions. If he sees something he likes, he turns up the volume on that set. Whicker asks what he enjoys watching.

'Wrestling,' says Shaw. His trousers are pulled up to his chest, failing to hide Big Daddy blubber.

Everyone is smoking. Shaw has no cupboards and stores everything on display shelves. He drinks four pints a night. There are no curtains. Whicker asks why.

'Well, when you have curtains you can't see out,' says Shaw. 'And when it's snowing it's a picture.'

Why is there no carpet?

'Can't see as there's any sense in it.'

Nelly in the staff canteen at the factory is incredulous when this is relayed to her. 'He has some lovely curtains,' she tells Whicker. 'Cost many a pound but he says they gather dust.'

It is 1968 and Shaw has lived here for 76 years. His only luxuries are his two Rolls-Royces. 'Being rich, I forget what I have,' he says, which is a killer line. He has no wife or children, just the line of pensioners. Poignancy and tobacco hang in the air. 'What you going to be doing with your money?' he asks Whicker, before going back to his own world, looking out of the window and on to his Halifax haven.

A thousand miles for freedom

In any list of the greatest Yorkshire people, William Wilber-force invariably features prominently. He was the man whose refusal to be beaten led to the Act for the Abolition of the Slave Trade in 1807, and, not long after his death, the Slavery Abolition Act in 1833. There is no doubt that he had an epic perseverance, and that he paid dearly for his abhorrence of a trade that was a cornerstone of the British economy. Defying norms took guts.

Wilberforce was not evangelical about abolition at first, but he was appalled when he heard the account of James Ramsay, who had lived in the West Indies and had seen the horrors of slaves dying and rotting in the hold of seabound prisons. Ramsay's *Essay on the Treatment and Conversion of African Slaves in the British Sugar Colonies* and *An Inquiry into the Effects of Putting a Stop to the African Slave Trade* were both published in 1784. This was a year after the court case concerning the *Zong*, a ship owned by Liverpool merchants from which 133 slaves were tossed overboard in an insurance scam.

It was another few years before Wilberforce sat down beneath an oak tree on the estate of his friend William Pitt, not yet prime minister, and resolved to take on the slave traders and their paymasters. Others were involved too, notably Thomas Clarkson, though he was all but ignored

when Wilberforce's sons wrote a biography of their father
five years after his death. This was the work that became
accepted truth. Wilberforce was the Christian hero of
choice, despite the fact that many bishops had kept slaves
until it was illegal. This perhaps highlights why he trod
carefully through the political mud even if the ethics were
transparent. In 2007, the bicentenary of the act that ended
the slave trade in most of the British Empire, William
Hague, another Yorkshireman, appeared in the House of
Commons and lauded Wilberforce as 'one of the greatest
campaigners' and 'one of the greatest liberators in British
history'. Heavy can be the head that wears that crown. And
that is why I am driving from Harrogate to Markington,
a small village in North Yorkshire. The sun sweeps the
landscape. I park on the gravel drive. I am here to meet
William Wilberforce.

This one is the great-great-great-great-grandson of the
more famous version, who owned and visited Markington
Hall but never lived here. He welcomes me warmly and
shows me inside. It is a lovely old pile; not pristine, but lived
in, and alive with age and history. By the window is a grand
piano, behind which a painted image of the old abolitionist
monitors the keys; the original is in the National Portrait
Gallery. It is one of the more eclectic rooms I have ever been
in. A Free Tibet scarf sits on a cushion. There is a signed
album by slide guitarist Jack Broadbent on a stand. William's
son, also called William but going by second name Dan, is
here too. He has an interest in human rights law, but other
talents include documentary photography. On the wall is a
tiny locket that I learn contains a lock of Wilberforce's hair,
and I'm handed a black tobacco box that is made from the
shackles of freed slaves.

William, the son of a diplomat, has worked in construction and farming and is now marketing Markington as a wedding venue. He tells me that it was not until the advent of the bicentenary that he began to get back in touch with his roots. Being the descendant of someone portrayed as a moral hero is, he admits, a lot to live up to.

'I felt unworthy,' he says. 'It took me a long time to understand that. In the end, I realised all you can do is live your own life according to the creed you believe in, but my whole thinking has been coloured by what he managed to achieve in his life. We're still on the left of centre in politics, we believe in freedom of speech and that it doesn't matter what colour you are. That's ingrained in us.'

And yet, perhaps because of the perceived wealth that comes from living at Markington Hall, people think they know him and he is pigeonholed. 'It constantly amazes me that people don't take you at face value,' he says. 'You come from a house like this and you are automatically labelled. I had a Conservative MP come round here and he said, "Well, I take it I can count on your support." I said, "I've never voted Conservative in my life and you'll never get my support." He was quite mortified.'

Similarly, when culture wars are in the spotlight, journalists sometimes call. Dan, piercing eyes, and a tattoo seeping from beneath his T-shirt sleeve, says, 'It blew up on Twitter. James Cleverly [the Foreign Secretary at the time of writing] said Wilberforce was a Tory. I took issue with that and said there was a reason he was an independent; he wanted the freedom to say what he wanted and not be whipped to vote against his conscience.' Dan is an eloquent speaker and I imagine he will become a fine lawyer. His dad is softly spoken, ruddier-faced, and likes to laugh.

William Wilberforce the famous was born in 1759 in Hull. In 1768, his father died and his struggling mother, Elizabeth, shipped him off to London to live with his uncle William and aunt Hannah. It was here that he was introduced to the Methodist movement, which was challenging the hypocritical, nepotistic and looser strands of Christianity. It was also here that he heard a sermon from John Newton, who had been both a slave in Sierra Leone and a slave master at sea before undergoing a spiritual conversion. However, when William's mother heard that he was being seduced into Methodist life, it was as if he had joined the Moonies. Wilberforce was taken back to Yorkshire, where he was able to monitor more normal Christian practices such as gambling, dancing and flirting. He went to Cambridge, noted the 'licentious' habits of idle students, and decided to become an MP. If you were rich, that was not hard in those days, but those Hull freemen who had a vote expected to be reimbursed for using it, so when Wilberforce was elected at the age of 21, he had a bill that would be the equivalent of £1 million today. History would regard it as money well spent.

While William and Dan are respectful keepers of the flame, they do not try to peddle Wilberforce as a strait-laced paragon of virtue. 'Oh, he used to take the piss out of Lord North [former prime minister],' says William. 'He was quite a laugh. He would have the House of Commons in fits.'

In those days political speeches could last for hours, unlike today where they just seem to. 'There was a lot of social hypocrisy back then and Wilberforce was good at pinpointing that,' says Dan. 'He pushed through these moral reformations. He was saying, "What about innate human dignity?" Kant and Hobbes were the thinkers who gave birth to these ideas, but he championed them.'

It took its toll. The slave trade was fundamental to British wealth and power. In his biography of Wilberforce, Hague noted that when Pitt became prime minister in 1783, some 80 per cent of income flooding into Britain from overseas came from the West Indies slave trade. Innate human dignity was one thing, but in purely monetary terms, Wilberforce was asking the turkeys of the British elite to vote for Christmas.

His health suffered and he took opium three times a day for most of his life. 'He had six nervous breakdowns because he got a lot of flak,' says William. 'There's a caricature of him in *Punch* with a big black woman sitting on him. That was all because Haiti had become independent, and he invited the ruler and his wife to visit.' There were death threats, and plenty of anti-abolitionists ready to challenge him to a duel. Even national heroes appeared to line up. Admiral Horatio Nelson has been damned for a letter purportedly written from his desk on HMS *Victory* in which he pledged to fight the 'damnable and cursed doctrine of Wilberforce and his hypocritical allies'. The difficulty in judging old heroes was shown in 2020 when a former director at Sotheby's, Martyn Downer, said the letter was an anti-abolitionist forgery and the original wording was 'against the damnable cruel doctrine', which was a reference to concerns that Wilberforce's bill would lead to violence and more bloodshed.

Nelson would hit a career peak, albeit a mortal one, with the Battle of Trafalgar just two years before the act to end the slave trade was passed. His punishment for questioning Wilberforce was being made to live with pigeons on a plinth in a London square; incidentally, the original lions that had been intended for Trafalgar Square can now be found in Saltaire after being judged too small for London.

Fuelled by his friends in the social-reforming Clapham Sect, Wilberforce began to besiege Parliament over the slave trade in 1789. Initially, abolition of slavery seemed too high a hope, and while his approach has been criticised, it was the most likely to succeed. And ultimately it did, despite being hampered by the French Revolution, which provoked distrust in any radical thinking. Bills were introduced and votes lost, but over time the 'doctrine' became normalised.

Yet there was enough nuance for people to review Wilberforce's actions. That has never been more evident than with the creation of an abolitionist colony in Sierra Leone. Stephen Tomkins, an author who has written widely and admiringly on Wilberforce, said that after the 1807 act had passed, slaves seized from now illegal ships were taken to the colony. 'They were called "apprentices" but they were slaves,' he wrote in the *Guardian* in 2010. 'The governor of Sierra Leone paid the navy a bounty per head, put some of the men to work for the government, and sold the rest to landowners.'

It was another man from Hull, Thomas Perronet Thompson, who would free these men. He had become the first crown governor of Sierra Leone, due to knowing Wilberforce, but was shocked by what he saw and made the seemingly heretical claim that the great abolitionist and the Sierra Leone Company, the body that founded Freetown as a settlement for freed slaves, 'had by means of their agents become slave traders themselves'. Thompson, who would serve as an MP for Hull and Bradford, was an interesting figure, a teetotal vegetarian who backed the suffragettes, wrote a book called *Geometry Without Axioms* and also found time to pen a 30-page pamphlet with the title

'Instructions to my daughter for playing on the enharmonic guitar: an attempt to effect the execution of correct harmony, on principles analogous to those of the ancient enharmonic'. She must have been thrilled.

But why did Wilberforce allow these 'apprenticeships' in Sierra Leone? One theory is it may have been a means to a humanitarian end, a sad but necessary concession to get the Abolition Act through Parliament. When Thompson asked for an explanation, Wilberforce said, 'I wish I had time to go into particulars respecting the difficulties which forced us into acquiescing in the system of apprenticing.'

I expect William and Dan to be defensive when I mention this, but they are not. Wilberforce was clearly a moral man who saw the dehumanising horror of slavery, but perhaps he had to make sacrifices for the greater good. What William is particularly keen to highlight is that others deserve credit too. Hague gives an exhaustive list of the bodies set up by the Clapham Sect, which shows how Wilberforce was not a lone voice in his reforming life. These included the Society for Superseding the Necessity for Climbing Boys in Cleansing Chimneys and the Friendly Female Society for the Relief of Poor, Infirm, Aged Widows and Single Women of Good Character Who Have Seen Better Days. It makes you wonder how anyone got anything done.

Foremost among those wronged by history, though, was Thomas Clarkson. It was Clarkson who spent two years travelling around the country gathering information on slavery. He reportedly interviewed 20,000 sailors – although that seems a mind-boggling number – and some of them tried to kill him. He collected the tools of torment, the shackles and handcuffs and thumbscrews. He became an expert, effectively a detective, collating information, talking to witnesses and gaining the knowledge with which Wilberforce could petition Parliament. They were a powerful double act, but Clarkson's involvement, which included gaining signatures of support, has diminished. By the time the Hollywood film about the campaign against the slave trade, *Amazing Grace*, hit the screens in 2006, he was portrayed as something of a drinker to boot.

'Clarkson was incredibly important,' says William. 'He was critical to the fight, but he got shunted aside. At a ceremony at Westminster Abbey in 2007, I met some of his descendants and they said "thank you very much" because I had stressed his role in a few interviews. I wanted to correct that as much as I could. I also wanted to highlight the work of people like Olaudah Equiano [a slave from what is now Nigeria who bought his freedom in 1766]. He went around the country with Clarkson. He was a large man, and when he went into town halls you can imagine them thinking, "What's he doing here?" Then he would begin to speak, and for the first time some people realised that these were sentient human beings.'

Being the descendant of a historical figure has unexpected consequences. Dan has had hundreds of Facebook requests from Wilberforces in West Africa, because many people took the campaigner's name. 'I'm only a quarter Wilberforce, but that's what people want to talk about. Sometimes it's a bit much. Sometimes I'm like, "I'm not him."' William went to Antigua for his fiftieth birthday and was in a taxi one night. A friend told the driver he was in the presence of William Wilberforce. The driver told him not to take the great man's name in vain, and it ended with William having to show him his driving licence. 'He refused to take any money,' he says. 'I find that embarrassing and very humbling. I didn't do anything.'

The family history is now interwoven with global history and the past of this small village in North Yorkshire. The future of Markington clearly concerns father and son. The cricket team has folded. So has the football one. The pre-school has shut and the big school has only two classes. A cluster of seven farms has dwindled to three. 'I think university has had a big impact on villages,' says Dan. 'It was pushed by the government, and my generation went away to the cities. House prices went up and so it's just the parents left. This is becoming a retirees' village.' Cocaine is becoming the scourge of rural villages too. 'Eighty quid a gram. All as high as kites. And then you see the aggro.'

Dan would like to leave his mark by doing something for Yorkshire. That may come from changing the landscape, and this highlights a parallel between Wilberforce and environmental campaigners. 'The powerhouse of the British Empire was the slave trade, so he was applying a moral perspective that would have huge economic consequences. That is very transferable to environmentalism and our dependence on fossil fuels. There is a lot of vested interest, a lot of people lobbying to keep the status quo, and a lot of people approaching it from a radical perspective are getting a lot of grief. Wilberforce lived that life.'

Not long ago, Dan says, he went canoeing down the River Ouse in the Vale of York. He had a spinning line going for 20 miles and did not get one nibble. 'Pesticides and fungicides and nitrates. There is nothing there.'

Farmers generally get the blame for this, but Dan says that is unfair. 'The buck stops with them because they chose to do it,' he says 'but freedom to starve is no freedom. Community is about making sure you have systems that regenerate, but we've become this industrialised parasite. And the farmers are being forced into it by economic circumstances. They have to be allowed to treat the land delicately and favourably.'

He sounds passionate and political, and I wonder how much of this comes from being a descendant of Wilberforce. Dan admits he was 'almost ashamed' of his heritage growing up because he, too, wondered what he had done to deserve it. He is aware of his privilege and the inequalities of life in Yorkshire, and the need to act. 'This isn't a dress rehearsal,' he says. 'You only get one life. I'd like to build a better community here.'

I ask William if he thinks Yorkshire influenced Wilberforce. Clarkson was from Cambridgeshire, Equiano from Igboland. Inevitably, circumstances helped form their arcs and opinions, but was there anything peculiar to Yorkshire that could be seen in Wilberforce?

'Well, he was described as the Yorkshire terrier because when he got his teeth into something he would never give up,' says William. 'And as a Yorkshireman he was incredibly deter-mined and proud.' Indeed, when his son ran up huge debts, he rejected all offers to help. 'He said, "I'm a Yorkshireman, I will pay my own debts,"' adds William. Then a bassoon laugh. 'I've always been terribly sorry about that!'

We talk about Yorkshire and other places William used to live, including Huddersfield and Sheffield. Reputation can be a challenging thing, both for people and places, and some-times we choose to remember things as we would like them to have been. Harewood House, in a village north of Leeds, is a prime example, recalled fondly by generations of schoolkids who went on trips to the bird garden there, with few knowing that the house was built by the Lascelles family with the proceeds from the sugar plantations they owned in the West Indies. And often missed out, but not by the Wilberforces, is the role of black people in the abolition movement.

*

In 1850, an American couple named Ellen and William Craft were living in Britain. Barely two years earlier, they had been slaves in Georgia. Ellen's mother had been raped by her master, and Ellen's skin was light enough for her to pass as white. Hence Ellen and William devised a way of plotting a remarkable escape. Ellen cut her hair short and posed as a man, with her husband as her manservant. It was one of the most daring departures of the era. Ellen sat in first-class train carriages with her hand bandaged, lest her lack of education and her inability to write be exposed. You can imagine the fear of being found out on that journey as she tried to survive in the company of white men and women. Later, in their landmark 1860 book *Running a Thousand Miles for Freedom*, she recalled a well-to-do lady seeing William and shouting that he was Ned, her slave, whom she referred to with the N word. Ellen had to convince the woman that he belonged to her.

The pair made it to the free black community in Boston, but the introduction of the Fugitive Slave Act meant Southern slave-owners were now entitled to travel north and drag their 'property' home. Bounty hunters were sent to find the Crafts, who were staying with a former slave who had become an established figure in the underground. When the hunters arrived, William told them the door was primed with dynamite and they would rather die than surrender. It provided some respite, but they were now in danger and abolitionists arranged their passage to Britain.

Once they had landed, they travelled around the country and gave talks about the reality of slavery, adding music and dramatic flourishes for the paying audience. Wilson

Armistead, a notable Yorkshire Quaker, who wrote *Tribute for the Negro* in 1848, invited the Crafts to stay when they came north. Significantly, in an act of quiet protest, he registered them in the 1851 census as residents of Leeds, with their occupation listed as 'Fugitives from Slavery'. The simple act of protest attracted widespread attention, and the *Illustrated London News* wrote, 'This is a startling entry, perhaps more extraordinary than any in the new return of our population.' Some 170 years later, a paper by Dr Bridget Bennett at the University of Leeds hailed it as a 'guerrilla inscription' that sharpened the British focus on the Fugitive Slave Act.

William tells me his godfather was Lord Wilberforce, the great-great-grandson of the anti-slavery hero. This Wilberforce was regarded as one of the more civilised judges, and was the president of Anti-Slavery International. 'He was the man who ruled in favour of the miners,' says William, referencing the 1972 strike. He chaired the government inquiry into the seven-week strike and recommended that miners get a 27 per cent pay rise. Politicians were aghast. His response was: 'We know of no other job in which there is such a combination of danger, health hazard, discomfort in working conditions, social inconvenience and community isolation.' He got his way, but he was never called on to chair another inquiry after that.

'When [eminent judge] Lord Denning died, he practically got a state funeral, but my godfather got nothing,' says William. 'I'm positive it was because he'd pissed a lot of people off. He was also the guy who ruled champagne had to come from Champagne. Two weeks later, he could not get into his house for crates of the stuff. I once asked him, "Did these come before or after?"'

The final frontier

Meeting the Wilberforces has made me think about how knowing your past becomes more important as it gets further away, and I wonder about the people we would like to know but never can. Another person who has been looking into her family is Diane Mckaye, a Yorkshire expat working for a global communications firm in London. One day she came across an obituary for her grandfather, David Makofski, in the *Jewish Gazette*, dated 4 January 1974, in which it said he was responsible for saving '700 Jews from the same fate as their parents' during Hitler's reign. She did not know much about him. Big voice, small man, a keen golfer who helped set up the Moor Allerton Golf Club in Leeds as a safe haven for Jewish players when anti-Semitism was a barrier to established clubs; a young Marco Pierre White would also work there as a caddie and sell off the personalised balls of the Leeds United football manager Don Revie.

Born in Yorkshire to Baltic immigrants, Makofski was wounded on the Somme battlefield. Back home, he set up a tailoring business and would travel to Karlsbad in the Czech Republic to soothe his war injuries and arthritis. The Jewish Refugees Committee was set up in 1933 to aid refugees move to Britain from Germany, and Makofski was moved to help. He would head up a branch in Yorkshire, setting up a trainee scheme and using his contacts to place escapees from across Nazi-occupied Europe in jobs.

The refugees had to find money to pay their way. The rules also stated that only those under 35 could come. Diane's grandfather thus found himself with lives in his hands. One application letter from 1939 reads, 'You surely will know about the bad situation in which we German Jews are in, and especially we young people. We have no possibility to learn or to get education. Neither are we allowed to go to universities nor to museums nor to the theatre. Every educational establishment is forbidden to us. We also have no possibility to study a trade. The factories are not allowed to have Jewish apprentices and the small establishments which are arranged by the Jewish congregation are not at all able to satisfy our desire of learning. The life itself is full of sorrows.'

And from all these stories, others are born. Plot lines cross, doors slide, it's where you're from and where you're at. One of the firms Makofski used was Montague Burton, where he had trained. Born Meshe David Osinsky, Burton came to England alone in 1900 when only 15 to escape the anti-Jewish riots in Lithuania. He bought suits from a wholesaler and set up in Chesterfield before moving to Yorkshire and creating the Burton clothing empire. Almost 20 years earlier, a Russo-Polish Jew, Michael Marks, had preceded him by leaving his home in what is now Belarus. He began selling goods in Yorkshire villages and then set up a penny bazaar in Leeds market. Fast-forward to 1894, and he teamed up with Thomas Spencer, a bookkeeper from Skipton who paid £300 to come on board. Fast-forward again to 2008, and when one of their stores opened in Tripoli, it was reportedly subjected to a virulent smear campaign by the Libyan government, which said Marks & Spencer was a Zionist entity that supported killing Palestinians. It was quite the change.

Yorkshire cannot look down on other places' bigotry and has been as guilty as many of anti-Semitism. Diane remembers swastikas being painted on the walls of Jewish clubs in West Yorkshire and bricks being hurled in her youth, but for her grandfather, in an age hurtling towards genocide, and Oswald Mosley's home-made fascism, the risks were far worse. Diane now lives in London. Her family has digitised the correspondence between her grandfather, the authorities and refugees, and she wants to find the families he helped. She is wary of the Schindler analogy, given that her grandfather was not risking his life, but she imagines what it was like trying to deal with decisions that could prolong lives and lineages.

Imagination is the start of pioneering. You need to be able to look beyond the status quo, the TV news on the four sets, through the open curtains and beyond Halifax.

Yet of all the pioneers, the one who went furthest was a small, thin woman from Sheffield called Helen Sharman. Her path initially seemed unlikely to be particularly unusual. She was born after the big freeze in 1963 into a normal suburban family, with a lecturer as a father and a nurse as a mother. She shared a bedroom with her sister and went to Jordanthorpe Comprehensive. After school she did not move far, choosing to study for her chemistry degree at home in Sheffield, and her career highlight seemed destined to be as part of the team that developed Mars ice cream. Then, one day in 1989, she was driving back from her job as a food scientist with Mars Wrigley Confectionery in Slough – later immortalised by Ricky Gervais in *The Office* as the most crushingly dull town on earth – when she heard an advertisement on the radio: 'Astronaut wanted – no experience required.'

She applied and was invited to an interview. And then another. There were medical and psychometric tests. The aim was to gain a golden ticket to Project Juno, a privately funded mission created by Jewish refugee and TV scientist Heinz Wolff to get a Briton into space. The 1986 *Challenger* disaster, when the space shuttle disintegrated 73 seconds after take-off and killed all seven crew members, had led to astronauts being sent home from NASA, and a lack of will. But now the Russians came calling.

Britain had no space programme, but the Soviet Union was approaching Western countries seeking pay-as-you-go cosmonauts. The space race of the early 1960s was a distant memory now; Russia was open to foreign astronauts and had even forged a partnership with NASA. However, PM Margaret Thatcher was not keen on throwing money at a romantic notion of exploration. 'It was the eighties,' Sharman would recall. 'The government wanted a quick return on investment before they got re-elected. It was a me-me society.'

Nevertheless, this was also the age of *glasnost* and *perestroika*, and Thatcher and Mikhail Gorbachev, the president of the Soviet Union, were savvy enough to work together despite their ideologies. The cost was £7 million, and companies like British Aerospace, ITV and, more bizarrely, Interflora dug deep.

The plan was to pay for someone to go and train in Star City, the mysterious Soviet space enclave not found on any maps, and then voyage to the Mir space station. More than 13,000 people applied. That was whittled down to four, and then two. Sharman was one of them. She was given four days' notice to quit her job.

The quiet lab worker craved excitement. Slough will do that. She had the science background and practical job that the Soviets demanded, as well as falling within the right age range. Going into space in a Soyuz T rocket was one thing, but what also thrilled her was the prospect of going to the Soviet Union and learning Russian.

She arrived at Star City, with its ugly tower blocks and perimeter wall, and its communist-style monuments to Yuri Gagarin and, later, Laika. Gagarin was a god to cosmonauts, having beaten the Americans to become the first man into space, in 1961. Laika, a stray terrier, had gone four years earlier to prove that a living being could withstand the micro-g environment. *Sputnik 2*, and Laika's remains, disintegrated on re-entry five months later.

Helen was not scared, though. In Star City, she got to know Valentina Tereshkova, who in 1963 became the first woman into space. Gagarin himself would say that Tereshkova had 'a special unobtrusive feminine beauty', and her looks would feature prominently in stories thereafter. Her hairstyle became a fashion craze, and she was well placed to advise Helen when the head of the programme suggested women truly belonged in the kitchen. Fellow cosmonauts said women were 'uniquely Earth creatures'. Yet even the trenchantly sexist knew that women were prized in space because of their size and need for fewer calories.

By the time 18 May 1991 came around and Helen was sitting in her seat, with its four-centimetre gap at the back to allow for her spine to expand in space, Thatcher was no longer prime minister. Three months later, an attempted coup would spell the end for the Soviet Union. Helen had spent months in Star City and felt she was more aware of *glasnost* than the people she had met. Now she braced herself for lift-off from Baikonur Cosmodrome in a desert steppe in Kazakhstan, with the 99 exams, 72 measurements for her suit and 4 centimetres behind her. She had said the launch was a mundane thing, but she was aware that she could be killed at any time, and an oxygen leak tested her nerve.

Back at her old comp in Sheffield, the head teacher spoke to two reporters from the *Evening Standard*. They asked him for 'the dirt' on Briton's astronaut, but Ken Cook said there wasn't any.

Helen spent just under eight days in space. The money for British scientific experiments had run out, but she did some for the Soviets instead, agricultural ones looking at the growth of roots in different magnetic fields and medical ones looking at the effect on the blood and the loss of potassium from muscles. For two-thirds of each orbit of the earth there was no contact with mission control. She and her fellow cosmonauts, effectively Mir repairmen, were on their own. As the blood drained to their heads and cold set in, they took turns warming their feet on tiny fluorescent lamps. Quirkily, there was a musical keyboard for entertainment.

The day quickly came when she said goodbye to Anatoly Artsebarsky and Sergei Krikalev and came home with two others from Mir. Krikalev would become known as the last Soviet citizen, because his country ceased to exist while he was in space and he was told there was no money to bring the flight engineer home. His only option was to use the Mir re-entry capsule, but that would mean there would be nobody to look after the space station. Landing back at Baikonur Cosmodrome was also complicated by Kazakhstan becoming an independent state. Even the formerly one-eyed Soviet newspaper *Pravda* called him 'the man who is sick of flying'. Krikalev spent 311 days in space and only made it home when Germany paid for one of its citizens to fly to Mir. A report in *Russia Beyond*, a state media outlet, described him on his return as being 'pale as flour and sweaty, like a lump of wet dough'. The USSR badge was suddenly a relic. It is easy to imagine his mixed feelings of belonging: a hero, but to whom? He came from Leningrad but that was now St Petersburg. His country was no more. He was an alien at home.

Helen was in demand on her return to earth. She visited schools, TV studios and newspaper offices. She felt an obligation to explain what it was like to be the first Briton into another world. Then she disappeared.

Some said she was fed up with being asked about how you go to the toilet in space. *She* said she was fed up with being asked where she bought her clothes. Fame was the dark side of the moon. Interviews were declined. Then, in 2015, Britain lost its collective head when Major Tim Peake was trumpeted as the first Briton in space. Helen was being slowly written out of history. The UK Space Agency indulged in semantics by calling Peake the UK's first official astronaut. She asked them what 'official' meant. It grated, but she was not bitter. She handed Peake a copy of *Road to the Stars* by Yuri Gagarin and told him to look out of the window.

She went back to working as a scientist and took a senior job in the chemistry department at Imperial College in London. She preferred talking about science than space. No Briton had ever gone further, but even she is tethered to the past and roots. 'I love the whole way in which people in Yorkshire seem to operate,' she told the *Yorkshire Post*. 'It's very practical, very pragmatic. I don't like having to pussyfoot around people or trying to second-guess what they might be thinking. There's also a tenacity that goes with the Yorkshire spirit – the idea that we will make it, come what may. I think that wherever I live, that bit of Yorkshire comes with me.'

Helen was the end of a Yorkshire line of pioneering aviation that started close to Scarborough, where Sir George Cayley conducted numerous experiments on his family's Brompton Hall estate. In the eighteenth century, he designed a glider with fixed wings, and in 1849 he sent a 10-year-old boy off in a triplane glider. That managed only a few yards, but in 1853 he claimed to have flown a triplane more than 900 feet with his coachman, John

Appleby, on board. The elderly Appleby's reported quip that he wanted to quit as he had been hired to drive, not fly, sounds like old-time PR, but Cayley was an innovator and the pioneer of heavier-than-air flight. Of course, Orville and Wilbur Wright have places cemented in history for flying the first motor-operated aeroplane, but that was 1903 and they knew the debt they owed to Cayley. In 1909, Wilbur Wright said: 'About 100 years ago, an Englishman, Sir George Cayley, carried the science of flight to a point which it had never reached before and which it scarcely reached again during the last century.' Cayley and Sharman were the opposite ends of a fantastic spectrum.

At the end of 2022, Richard Hawley played a series of gigs at the Leadmill in Sheffield. The old venue was under threat of closure. Jarvis Cocker, his old mucker, joined him on stage to save the former warehouse. Pulp had started out there on 16 August 1980. 'They might own the bricks but they don't own the feeling,' said Cocker. Two days later, it is Helen's turn.

The crowd is raucous. Hawley is deferential as he introduces her, but I wonder if they have any idea who she is. She is still small and thin, dressed in a purple jumper, and bounds on enthusiastically.

'It was only after I returned to earth that I realised that what I had not thought about when I was in space was the material stuff I had owned,' she says. 'What astronauts think and talk about is family and friends, who and what we care about, our passions, the issues and causes.' The crowd is listening now. 'That's what makes life beautiful.'

And then she goes to sit behind the keyboard, and the band play 'Space Oddity'.

13

LEGENDS

Here lies she who never lied

Epitaph on the lost grave of Mother Shipton, Knaresborough
prophetess, died 1684

One of the peculiarities of Yorkshire is the feverish desire to appropriate and reimagine the deeds of figures such as Robin Hood and Dick Turpin and wear them as proof of just how interesting the county is. This ownership of legends, and the simultaneous erasing of home-grown heroism, is a sort of inexplicable FOMO, while the willingness to cling to the utterings of witches, soothsayers and con artists shows there has always been a need for something above Yorkshire pragmatism. Suffice to say, the apocalypse could be now, then or a week next Tuesday, but the need to believe in the unbelievable would go on.

The myth and madness of Robin Hood

We need to talk about Robin. For many, the outlaw legend is the heroic charmer synonymous with Errol Flynn's portrayal on film. Discerning truth from fiction is hampered by time, which is probably good for Flynn, a notorious gambler, drunk and sex addict whose jovial 'in like Flynn' tagline overlooked the underage rape trials, but less so for those confused by Robin Hood's origins.

Flynn, who was acquitted in 1943, was saying huzzah to Olivia de Havilland in Sherwood Forest in Nottinghamshire, or so we are told. This is now home to a tourism industry. You can meander from the visitor centre, where there will often be a disaffected student posing as an anaemic Robin Hood, and find the Major Oak, with its wildly sprouting branches like electrified hair. Reasoned to be at least 800 years old, it was chosen as one of the United Kingdom's 70 most significant trees as part of the Queen's Platinum Jubilee celebrations. In the olden days, the royals were supposedly less enamoured by it, as this was reputedly the base for Robin Hood and his band of merry thieves who robbed from the rich and gave to the poor. Only the reality is that Robin Hood is more likely a hero of Pontefract, in the borough of Wakefield, or at least that nondescript bit of turf now dissected by the A1.

That is if he existed at all. Nobody knows for sure. At least not in the way we like to know him. He might have been a Robert of Locksley in Nottinghamshire, or Robin of Loxley in Yorkshire, or maybe even Robert Hod of York, but he was more likely an amalgam of ideas about the benevolent outlaw, a figure plucked from ballads, doctored, tinted, touched up, exaggerated and purloined.

One of the first references came in *Piers Plowman*, a religious allegory written by William Langland sometime in the fourteenth century, but things gathered pace with *A Gest of Robyn Hode*, which combined a number of stories into a single text in the early sixteenth century, although many believe it is much older. There were other ballads, such as the fifteenth-century 'Robin Hood and the Monk', originally untitled but later given this heading as a reference point, and these gave folklorist detectives enough leads to claim him as a Yorkshire figure rather than a Midlands one.

For a start, the ballads' Robin Hood operated in Barnsdale, which is a real place between Doncaster and Wakefield. In medieval times, the forest would have been rich with game and deer, albeit sparsely populated with trees, and certainly no self-respecting outlaw would have been donning Lincoln green and swinging through the fauna as a bucolic Tarzan. Nevertheless, Barnsdale fits neatly with the forest law brought in by the Norman kings to protect the rich's hunting rights, and the subsequent legend of Will Scarlet killing a deer before telling Robin Hood that his family has just been evicted. A 1306 report also talks of increasing guard in Barnsdale due to its reputation for banditry.

From there, Yorkshire references ripple through the yarns, although we should note that hundreds of years had passed since these events were said to have taken place. Nevertheless, weaving threads from the main sources can reasonably lead us to the conclusion that a fictional Robin, at least, was declared an outlaw in Pontefract. Friar Tuck might have been a monk from Fountains Abbey near Ripon, cast out for his demonic ways and thereafter living in a cabin in Eldritch Oaks, somewhere in Barnsdale Forest. Loxley is three miles south of Sheffield and is where John Harrison, admittedly writing in the seventeenth century, claimed that our hero was born on a 'little haggas croft' in 1160. In 2020, the local primary school said this was round the back of the playground.

One of the teachers, Dan Eaton, teamed up with Sheffield University's Centre for Contemporary Legend and produced a book called *Reclaiming Robin Hood*. For people in Nottingham, this was as inflammatory as saying their river was not named after Terence Trent D'Arby or that there were only six girls for every boy in the city in contradiction of the urban-mythical seven. Dr David Clarke, an academic at the centre and a contributor to the book, said, 'It shouldn't be taken too seriously. All we're saying is, there is a lot of evidence that someone who called themselves Robin Hood was born in Sheffield, not necessarily *the* Robin Hood, because there is no such thing as *the* Robin Hood.' Which does somewhat beg the question: why reclaim him? The Sheriff of Nottingham – yes, there really is one – responded by saying, 'Robin Hood is as much from Sheffield as Jarvis Cocker is from Nottingham.'

Robehod and Robbehod were common names long before historians started pinpointing individuals. The Sloane manuscripts are an eclectic collection of works gathered by Hans Sloane, an Irish physician and president of the Royal Society, who funded his 71,000 purchases via marriage into wealth. Five of these pages, dating back to around 1600, comprise a rough pooling of ballads and offer a basic 'Life' of Robin. Before long, even Shakespeare, a notorious rewriter of history, was mentioning Robin Hood, Will Scarlet and Maid Marion, in *Henry IV Part 2* and *As You Like It* among other works, but by then the legends were already, well, legendary.

If the identity remains a perpetual mystery, the whereabouts, as detailed in the ballads and legends, do not. Wentbridge, to the south of Pontefract, has a plaque declaring it as a place that can be located in *A Lytell Geste of Robyn Hode* (1492–1534). Robin disguised himself as the potter of Wentbridge in order to travel to Nottingham, and it was also there where some claim he fought Little John, who probably never existed, in a scene prominent in every retelling.

And then there is our hero's demise at Kirklees Priory, near Brighouse in Calderdale. In later life, Robin was visited by his cousin, Alice of Havelond (no relation to Olivia de). He agreed to make a return trip to see her at the abbey in Kirklees. Indeed, he went every six months and had his blood let to offset the ravages of old age, after which he spent several days recuperating. On one of these visits, his aunt, the abbess, Dame Ursula, told him Alice had died. Robin paid his respects in the churchyard before Ursula invited him upstairs for some pick-me-up bloodletting. Alas, she drugged him and allowed the blood to flow into a jar while she welcomed Sir Roger of Doncaster, an avowed enemy of Robin and crony of Guy of Gisborne.

Having been paid off, Ursula at least begged Doncaster to put Robin out of his misery, but he refused. A blow on the hunting horn from Robin, and Little John – who probably did not exist, remember – came running. He got there in time for Robin to take out his bow and fire off one last arrow. It landed some 600 yards away, and the imaginary Little John carried him to that spot, where he was buried. Or so they say. Nobody knows. There is a tomb with an inscription, but some experts suggest the language used is a nineteenth-century imagining of the correct English. All of which makes you wonder why it matters so much to people to know where a thousand-year-old will-o'-the-wisp is buried anyway.

In *The Robin Hood Handbook*, Mike Dixon-Kennedy makes a convincing case for a Yorkshire Robin before concluding, 'Nottingham may always remain the city most commonly associated with Robin Hood and his men, but I shall never be able to consider it the home of the outlaw, for to me Pontefract and Sheffield have equal claim to his name, and to the association with one of the most enigmatic figures of British folklore.' He says he believes Robin was a real person living and operating in South Yorkshire. He mentions the Yorkshire villages of Robin Hood, Stanley (sounds like Stane Lea, which may have been the site of Robin's camp) and Outwood (Robert of Locksley's manor), not because of any documented links but because he believes they were so named to preserve a memory of a historical figure and not some legendary character already appropriated by Nottinghamshire.

Robin Hood is now remembered in all manner of ways, including an old black and white BBC clip that shows the Robin Hood Society in full flow in Nottingham.

'I am Robin Hood, sir,' says a man too serious about his hobby.

'They want to preserve the legend of the city's most famous bandit,' the presenter tells us, adding that Robin is called Steve and works as a teacher.

Maid Marion (Eva) says, 'Well, he does have some strange habits.'

The unspoken undertone of the report is one of incredulity. 'The usual kicking, gouging and bashing,' says the presenter, who has loosened his tie and embedded himself between two medieval wenches. 'It seems to send the crowds ecstatic at the public displays,' he adds as Little John and Much the Miller engage in armed combat that is as terrifying as under-fives origami.

'Go for 'is head,' shouts Maid Marion.

'Not very ladylike, is it,' says the BBC man, who adds that the only thing that seems to upset them is 'a certain indifference' from the city of Nottingham.

What we do know for sure is that a lot of people want Robin Hood to be real. Brigadier General Sir George

Armytage, who used to own the Kirklees estate, said he had sifted through all the evidence before concluding that he was buried nearby. Others have pointed out that he could have boosted Yorkshire's Olympic record if he could really fire an arrow 600 yards.

By the Doncaster bypass, up in Barnsdale, you will find Robin Hood's Well, which may be so named due to a connection with fountains mentioned in a ballad called 'Robin Hood and the Curtal Friar'. Robin Hood's Bay, that stunning vista on the North Yorkshire coast, cleaved from ancient shale, sandstone and mudstone, slowly eroding away and slip-sliding into the sea, bears the name of a man who seemingly never visited. There is a legend of him fighting French pirates, but he was almost a forest sprite by then and something of a good-luck charm.

Dr Clarke said Sheffield was not indulging in cultural theft, but noted that the fact people were getting so irate about it all, some 800 years after something probably didn't happen, showed it mattered to them. Why? Maybe because in the twenty-first century, with cities changing at blitzkrieg speed and technology scaring older generations, we need stories to bookmark our places. Or maybe because we want an excuse to wear green tights.

Witchery

The need to believe so fervently in good and bad often seems a modern innovation, with shouty debates in Parliament and people fighting to out-capitalise each other on Twitter. Middle ground is for wimps and the rational. However, it has actually been this way for centuries. Witness how Yorkshire has long loved a good execution. Pocklington is a small town between Hull and York with a population of around 8,000. It is the sort of place that has a Flying Man Festival in honour of a bloke who died trying to walk a tightrope from the church to the pub in 1733. More worrying still is the tale from 1630, when a mob that was described as angry – to be honest, you rarely get an even-tempered one – carted off Old Wife Green and burnt her at the stake. Back then, more benevolent psychopaths merely hanged witches, although this was an age when having a beard could be enough to sway public opinion. Old Wife Green's demise may well have been the last witch-burning in England, which lends added credence to the idea that Yorkshire is not always the most tolerant of places. Isabella Billington, also from Pocklington, was bang to rights after crucifying her mother and offering a calf and cockerel as a sacrifice, but even she was sentenced to death by hanging in 1649. Mind you, they burnt her afterwards just to be on the safe side.

People were within their rights to believe that the eggs delivered by Mary Bateman's hen really did have 'Crist is coming' on them. Quite why they would believe Crist would signal his arrival in such a mysterious way or with such careless spelling is up for discussion, but Bateman, born near Thirsk in James Herriot country, was a con artist and fake fortune-teller who in 1809 would also be hanged when it was discovered she had fed poisoned pudding to a client as part of an elaborate fraud. The daughter of a North Yorkshire farmer, she seemed to progress from being a mere conniving thief almost by chance. Initially she would tell stories to aid her thefts. At one point she pretended to be a nurse, collecting linen from the hospital, but she then sold it for her own good. After a fire at a factory claimed many lives, she asked a benevolent woman called Miss Maude for linen to lay out a dead child, but sold it at a pawnbroker's shop instead. More often she was a go-between who could contact a mysterious Mrs Moore. She could clearly spin a web, telling one suicidal woman that her husband was in jail and she needed to produce four pieces of leather, four pieces of blotting paper, four gold coins and four brass screws. The screws were for screwing down the guards, the money for old rope, and the rest just dramatic fluff. When the woman said she had no gold, she was surprised to hear Bateman suggest she steal it.

In 1803, she was ingratiating herself with more gullible prey, the Kitchin sisters. Nobody knows when she decided to start killing, but it seems it may have been an expedient whim. One of the maiden ladies fell ill. Bateman hastened her on her way and said it was the plague. Within 10 days two sisters and their mother were dead. Bateman helped herself to their possessions. Five years later, she was scamming William Perigo and his wife Rebecca, who was told she was under an evil spell and should sew money into her sheets. When Rebecca died after eating herbal puddings, Perigo became suspicious and found the money in the lining had been replaced by coal and halfpennies. Bateman produced a letter from a mysterious Mrs Blythe that suggested it was his wife's fault for not licking the required amount of honey, but the game was up.

The living did not come out of this unblemished either. She was convicted of murder but it was the witch moniker that drew 20,000 to her execution, despite the 1735 Witchcraft Act having banned witch hunts. Bateman's body was put on display by Leeds General Infirmary, with people paying threepence to see it. Slivers of skin were sold as lucky charms. You could still see her skeleton at the Thackray Museum of Medicine in Leeds until 2015. They/we are a gruesome lot.

Dick Turpin v. John Nevison

Bateman is routinely referred to as the Yorkshire witch, although she was more accurately a fraudster-cum-killer. But we shape villains as we want. For many years I had been fascinated by the cell that held Dick Turpin at York's Castle Museum. This is a wonderful place and, like the best museums, marvellously eclectic. There is a Victorian cobbled street with an apothecary, Ernest Shackleton's cocoa tin from his 1909 Antarctic expedition, and displays of soft toys and vintage bras. It sits next to the motte-and-bailey castle known as Clifford's Tower. Each summer tourists climb the steps to that and eat their ice creams, not giving undue thought to the horrific atrocity that took place high on the grassy mound. It was here in 1190 that around 150 Jews committed suicide or burned to death or were murdered in other ways by another angry mob. At the time, anti-Jewish sentiment was rife, fuelled by the Crusades and by the moneylending activities of some prominent city figures. After a group broke into the home of a moneylender named Benedict of York, killing and stealing on their way, wider chaos ensued. The Jewish community, led by Josce of York, sought refuge in what was then York Castle; it was another 140 years before Roger Clifford was executed there for rebelling against the magnificently named Hugh Despenser the Younger, thus giving the tower its nickname. The mob formed around the castle, roused by the rhetoric of a nobleman named Richard Malebisse as he sought to avoid paying his debts, and demanded the Jews convert to Christianity. There was no acceptable way out, so fathers killed their wives and children before taking their own lives. Josce began the slaughter. The wooden tower was set on fire so the bodies could not be mutilated. The next morning, any survivors were put to death.

In Yorkshire that dark day gets less attention than Dick Turpin, who spent his last days in a cell that was part of the debtors' prison and is now part of the museum. He was not a hero in any way, shape or form. Having spent his early life as an Essex butcher, he joined a local band of reprobates dubbed the Gregory gang and broke into the house of a wealthy farmer, forcing him to drop his breeches and dragging him around the house by his nose before merrily pouring boiling water on his head.

After the rest of the gang had been shot, executed or deported, Turpin turned to highway robbery. *The Gentleman's Magazine* told how he did 'barbarously murder' Thomas Morris, describing him as '30, 5 feet 9 inches high, brown in complexion, vert much mark'd wit Small Pox, his visage short' and, perhaps the clincher for those seeking portents, with a 'face thinner towards the bottom'. He stole two horses from outside a pub in Essex. Then he bragged about shooting a man's fighting cock, which in those days was fighting talk. He was moved from Beverley House of Correction to York and was accused of horse theft. By now going under the decidedly unsexy alias of John Palmer, he was undone by a letter he sent to his brother-in-law that ended up in a post office in Saffron Waldon, where a James Smith, his old schoolteacher, recognised his handwriting. Smith travelled to York, identified the thief and got his £200 reward from the Duke of Newcastle.

Turpin had no defence. Literally. Erroneously thinking he would be tried in Essex, he had not bothered to appoint a lawyer. He was found guilty of stealing horses and sentenced to death. His hangman was a fellow highwayman who, in accordance with custom, had been pardoned on condition he do a stint as the city's executioner. Turpin paid for a few mourners and was described as behaving in a brash manner, but this was not a crime that captured the imagination of either a city or a nation. He was hanged on the 7 April 1739 at York Tyburn on the Knavesmire, the most popular of the city's four execution sites, and his corpse was stolen by body-snatchers. It was recovered and now lies in Fishergate, just down from Wetherspoon's.

Fact soon became fiction again. Much of this was down to William Ainsworth's 1834 Gothic romance *Rookwood* in which Turpin is cured of the pox, has a face of normal dimensions and rides his mighty horse, Black Bess, from London to York in pursuit of an alibi. Basically, he becomes Errol Flynn.

If Yorkshire wanted a really bad outlaw with a bit more murderous panache, it could have celebrated Owney Madden. Unknown to most folk, the Yorkshire-born Madden went to New York in 1901 as a 10-year-old, where he joined the Gopher gang, killed lots of people, courted Mae West, bankrolled her play *Sex*, got described as 'sweet but oh so vicious' in her memoirs, became a bootlegger and puppet-master for world heavyweight boxing champions Gene Tunney and Max Baer, owned the Cotton Club, was feted by the club's strippers when doing time in Sing Sing, opened an Arkansas hotel where Al Capone was caught, and finally died peacefully in his sleep aged 73. But no, we still harp on about Turpin.

Far more popular than Turpin in real life was John Nevison, and he actually had the credentials that should have maintained his status through the decades. For a start he was born in Yorkshire, probably in Wortley, and had served with some distinction in the Duke of York's army during the Battle of Dunkirk in 1658. He spent several years looking after his elderly father before, like many ex-servicemen faced with poor job prospects, taking to the life of a highwayman. Records claim that he really did rob the rich and redistribute some of his spoils to the poor, and refrained from violence and, worse, impoliteness.

Nevison, who used the old Robin Hood hideout of Wentbridge, had true tales to tell. Details vary, but the consensus is that he was the man who, having been seen robbing a man at Gads Hill in Kent, made an overnight flit to York on a bay mare. He crossed the Thames and found his way to the muddy, mired Great North Road. The claim that he travelled 220 miles in around 13 hours is surely exaggerated, but he made sure that he was seen in York by attending a bowls match, where he struck a wager with the Lord Mayor. When arrested, he called upon the mayor to prove he could not have been in two places at once. Such was the ingenuity and bravado of all this that it made Nevison a well-known anti-hero. King Charles II demanded to be told the story first-hand, and on hearing Nevison boast that even Old Nick could not catch him, the king dubbed him Swift Nick.

The story of his escape from Leicester jail could have come straight from the pages of Alexandre Dumas – who instead wrote about musketeers (and Robin Hood) – and involved having a friend paint plague-like blotches on his skin and eventually escaping from a coffin after being confirmed dead by a doctor who did not wish to get too close. However, he shot and killed a constable who tried to arrest him and was finally turned in by a landlady at a pub in Sandal Magna, near Wakefield. Half a century before Turpin, Nevison was also taken to the Knavesmire and executed. A blue plaque in Sandal hails him as a latter-day Robin Hood, and he lies in St Mary's Church, just down from the York Dungeon, a tourist trap that mixes frights with loose history.

Nevison seems a better outlaw to keep alive, but Yorkshire has allowed him to disappear, an oddity given the county's natural urge to shout about anything. Storytellers and even historians have been more concerned with stalking myths and legends than flesh and blood, which is probably a poor reflection on our partisan need for ownership, celebrity and basic desire to be special. John Nevison could have been Yorkshire's leading man, rather than an Essex butcher with smallpox, a real-life Robin Hood, but nobody is writing ballads about him or getting dressed up for the BBC. His fate is to be forgotten, and that is as Yorkshire as it gets.

14

SEASIDERS

Scarborough is where my heart is. It's where I start and finish.

Alan Ayckbourn, playwright, www.alanayckbourn.net, 1980

The seaside holiday in Yorkshire began after the 1626 discovery of spring waters in Scarborough, which quickly became a posh holiday resort. As if it were a dusty room, globalisation and modern life slowly swept the old ways from the middle of Yorkshire to the edges, and the seaside became a place of lumpy nostalgia. The Yorkshire coast links the Tees and Humber estuaries, contains three sections protected by Natural England, towns including Whitby, Bridlington and Filey, with the city of Hull some 20 miles up the Humber, and has been the stage for great industrial, military and ecological struggles. It has been a vital part of Yorkshire but feels other-worldly, remote and separate. In short, distilled Yorkshireness.

Between a rock and a hard place

If you want to know how Yorkshire explains the world, then you are probably best off heading to the seaside. This may sound counter-intuitive. After all, the decline of English seaside towns has been decades in the making. Few places highlight this quite like bits of Scarborough. This was once Harrogate-on-Sea, a spa town for the well-to-do, with fresh air and graces, the habitat of Anne Brontë, party political conferences and locals like Alan Ayckbourn, who staged scores of plays at the Stephen Joseph Theatre but only one set in Scarborough, which perhaps tellingly, as his archivist points out, was an adaptation of an adaptation.

In *The Uses of Literacy*, our old friend Hoggart explained how Scarborough once operated for the masses: 'Here again the same clutter, the same extraordinary Bartholomew Fair of a mess, but even messier.' It was a walk past the shops, a drink, deckchair, ice cream, mint humbug, Mrs Johnson paddling in her bloomers, Mrs Henderson pretending she had got off with the deckchair attendant, meat teas, and crates of beer in the back on the way home.

People still go to the coast, but Scarborough, the jewel, knows its glory days are gone. I still love it, and Bridlington and Filey – go even higher to Saltburn and the beach is vast and beautiful – but the package holiday and the slow realisation that the North Sea is about as welcoming as Wharram Percy at its most paranoid have taken their toll. The Grand Hotel is a barometer of change. The largest hotel in Europe on its opening in 1867, it was fashioned around an elaborate theme of time, with four towers to represent the seasons, 12 floors, 52 chimneys and 365 rooms. Seven million lovingly placed bricks provided a show of power and timeless elegance.

And yet in 2021, *The Times* was reporting bloodstains on the walls, skid marks on the bed sheets and condoms in the hallways. They quoted a customer, Zena Breckner, as saying, 'Don't stay there unless you enjoy self-flagellation.' There was also sympathy for the Afghan refugees being housed there. 'I feel sorry for them,' said one guest. 'As if escaping from the Taliban wasn't bad enough.' Quite what Anne Brontë, who died in a house on the site of the hotel, would have made of it is open to debate. There might have been a decent book in it, though. Around this time I turned on the TV to find travel expert Simon Calder mounting a vigorous defence of the Grand. He had a point in saying there is nothing wrong with budget hotels, and maybe it is simple snobbery, but it is still hard to sit in the foyer of the Grand, by the bleep of the arcade games, and not feel the sting of progress.

The pandemic was all it needed. Millions stayed away from the seaside and businesses were pushed to the limit. Families frayed. Yet along the coast are signs of more seismic change. This is a strip of land that tested biblical creation theory and paved the way for Darwin's *On the Origin of Species*. If you want to look out, you need to get your feet wet.

There are not many parts of Yorkshire that have remained untouched by the need to dig, excavate and remove anything worth money. Coal, ironstone, jet, limestone, lead, peat and alum have all been harvested. The Dales countryside still betrays its lead mining past and some of that industry's stone ruins are mistaken for disused farm buildings. Working conditions there could be just as brutal as in the coal fields. Over on the coast, alum, used to fix colour in the dyeing process among other things, had been mined since the start of the seventeenth century, when landowner Thomas Chaloner realised the rocks on his estate at Guisborough resembled those he had seen in the Tolfa hills outside Rome.

Previously, there had been a papal monopoly on alum production, but Chaloner was granted a patent, whereupon it is said he combated the Italian dominance by sailing into Civitavecchia, some 40 miles from Rome, and persuading two prominent workers to be smuggled back to Yorkshire in barrels. The truth of that tale has been questioned, but thus began an elaborate, long-winded process that required working quarried shales, nine months of burning great pyramids on the beaches and then adding human urine to the extracted aluminium sulphate liquor in the alum houses. Urine was used because it is an ammonia and thus created the crystals. Buckets were left for urine collection in city streets to aid this process. New toilet blocks were even built in Hull for the job, but the industry grew so large that ships from London would sail northwards with a cargo of wooden tubs. These were then returned containing butter. All that was then left was to deduce when the solution was the perfect temperature for alum to be formed without being polluted by ferrous sulphate. The method for determining the right time was to add an egg. If it floated it was ready. If it sank, at least it wasn't a witch.

The Lower Jurassic shales stretched from Saltburn in the north to Robin Hood's Bay in the south, and alum mining became big business. But the alum excavations would also reveal another form of treasure. In 1758, Captain William Chapman and John Wooler found some fossilised bones set in what they called a 'kind of black slate'. They wrote to the Royal Society, and their haul would find its way to the British Museum and the Natural History Museum. Given the popular faith in the Bible, the notion of a prehistoric animal being preserved in rock was hard to fathom. God created the earth before animals, so how could this be? The answer was that a huge event must have taken place and washed the rocks over the animals: Noah's Flood.

Times were changing, though, and so was accepted wisdom. In 1815, Oxford's William 'Strata' Smith had published his ground-breaking geological map of England and Wales, as well as bits of Scotland. This humble man, whose father was a blacksmith, had ruffled the feathers of the toffs of the Royal Geological Society with his curiosity and foresight.

He was the first to recognise that fossilised remains in rock layers were an effective way of dating strata in different areas of the country. It was one thing seeing the layers in a canal cutting with the naked eye, but if these layers were replicated all over the country, it had implications for mining and agriculture, where the quality of the rock and soil were obviously hugely important. According to writer and fossil expert Roger Osborne in *The Floating Egg*, Smith once ascended York Minster to prove his point. 'From the top I could see that the Wolds contained chalk by their contour,' he said. Pleased with himself, he had 'a good dinner and a pineapple at the Black Swan' and then journeyed north to find that the Hambleton Hills had the same features as the Cotswold ones. The country was not as different as it might have thought.

A year before Smith published what author Simon Winchester called 'the map that changed the world', a boy named Lewis Hunton was born in Loftus, a few miles north of Whitby. His father was an alum-maker, and Lewis spent his time trawling through the detritus of that life. Naturally, he became interested in fossils.

When he was just six, there was an astounding discovery around 20 miles away, at Kirkdale in the Vale of Pickering.

Workmen at a limestone quarry came across a cave and
found a collection of old bones. They guessed they were
from cattle, but a local naturalist was alerted and quickly
surmised they were wrong. Before long, William Buckland,
a fellow of the Royal Society who liked nothing better than
to hang around geological sites while dressed in his academic
gown, was on the scene. His verdict was that these were
the remains of animals now extinct in Britain, including
mammoth, elephant, hippo and bison.

Buckland would outrage some by suggesting there was
more to the Creation than we could possibly know from
literal interpretation of the Bible because these exotic animals
were not from far-off lands. Instead, he hypothesised that
they had lived in Yorkshire in a different climate for a long
time before Noah's Flood. The entrance to the cave was too
small for it to have washed them inside. His explanation
came from the teeth marks on the bones, which he said was
evidence that hyenas had dragged the carcasses into their
cave. He later amended his theories and suggested that
God was a progressive creationist, who came up with new
animals from time to time, but Buckland was a one-man
representation of the struggle between religion and geology.
The Dean of York Minster was aghast, but Buckland was no
heretic; he believed in the Universal Deluge, just not quite in
the way he once had. This eternal conundrum may have been
partly responsible for him living out his days in a Clapham
mental asylum. Not for the last time, Yorkshire was causing
people to question their very existence.

In truth, it was an odd age. One of Buckland's stated aims
was to eat his way through the entire animal kingdom, and
so he extolled the taste of panther, puppy and mice on toast,
but baulked at mole with a bluebottle garnish. At one typical

Victorian dinner at the Archbishop of York's residence, he even swallowed part of Louis XIV's mummified heart, which had been in a locket owned by his host. Clearly, he had a voracious appetite and a thirst for knowledge – or, on the occasion he bent down to disprove the claim that a damp patch in an Italian church was caused by a martyr's tears, bat's urine.

Hunton, meanwhile, had gone off to university, and in 1836, at the age of just 21, he published his solitary scientific paper. The title bore the bloated character of the age: 'Remarks on a section of the Upper Lias and Marlstone of Yorkshire, showing the limited vertical range of the species of Ammonites, and other Testacea, with their value as geological tests'. The key phrase was 'limited vertical range'. Hunton's examination of Easington Heights on the North York Moors took Smith's work up a notch, honing it and showing that while a certain type of fossil could be very common in a layer, it would also have a limited vertical range. Hunton had revolutionised the science of biostratigraphy by showing that fossils could be restricted to narrow bands of rock.

He also noted that some animals had been unable to change, and some, like ammonites, had. This was still two decades before Darwin became truly famous by explaining how this happened. Yorkshire, that backward wasteland of pig-headedness, was on the cusp of the theory of evolution but could not quite join the dots.

Many of these pioneers fell into history's gutter. Smith was aghast to find that George Bellas Greenough, president of the Geological Society, had produced his own map, which Smith would say was a 'ghost' of his own. The level of skulduggery involved is debated, but Winchester is convinced Smith was wronged. Smith certainly had to sell his collection of 2,657 fossils to the British Museum, and was still cast into the same debtors' prison Dickens wrote about in *David Copperfield*. He would muse that his fate mirrored that of his collection, which languished unseen in a dusty museum basement.

When he got out of prison in 1819, however, he found a more willing audience in Yorkshire. He moved to Scarborough and was enthralled. 'Everyone here is very fond of talking of geology,' he wrote. After his exclusion from the higher echelons of geological and philosophical society, and the attendant shame of his imprisonment, it was refreshing to find that these people had no side. His map of Yorkshire followed in 1821 and he became a geologist-for-hire, travelling around the county to give talks and evaluations. At last he was content, and he designed Scarborough's Rotunda Museum, with its spiral staircase offering access to fossils as if stored in strata.

Finally the Geological Society recognised him too, with Buckland one of those now championing his work. Why this would be is unclear. Perhaps it was pressure from overseas geological developments. Perhaps it was the change of president. Certainly people could change their thinking on scientific and spiritual matters, and in 1831, Smith was awarded the Geological Society's highest honour, the Wollaston Medal. President Adam Sedgwick described him as the father of English geology.

Seven years later, poor Lewis Hunton died. A Francophile, he was going by the name Louis when he succumbed to tuberculosis near Nîmes, aged 23. Most people have never heard of him, but geologists abide by his advice to only collect fossils in situ, not from detritus, which will give false conclusions. This is the coast of Yorkshire. It pointed to the future then. It does now.

At length did cross an albatross

The albatross is the loneliest bird. It is a real bird made fiction by Samuel Taylor Coleridge's 1798 poem *The Rime of the Ancient Mariner*, in which a sailor is haunted after shooting one with his crossbow, but it is fabulous all on its own. There are 22 distinct kinds, ranging from the wandering albatross, with its 11-foot wingspan, to the small and sooty light-mantled albatross, which is half that size. Most are endangered because of trawler and long lines, as they feed on fish and squid and waste from boats. Warmer waters down in the South Atlantic mean they are flying further from home to find food, which means more of these monogamous couples are splitting up. As the hunter stays away from home for longer, scientists have found stress hormones are rising. Chicks are struggling to survive. The human desire for anthropomorphism can be easily satisfied by the albatross. It's faithful, it commutes, it struggles to put food on the table. It sums up hard times.

The albatross lives in colonies, largely on far-off islands, which is why the chalk cliffs at Bempton, between Bridlington and Flamborough, are besieged every year by a battalion of binoculars. Nobody knows why, but a single albatross is here, the only one in the northern hemisphere. It is thousands of miles from home. They had to give it a name. Albie. Buckland would have tried to have it for breakfast.

Abbie Ferrar has a background in marine biology and now works for the RSPB at Bempton. 'The first time it was sighted was 2017,' she says as we walk to the barren cliffs. 'It was not here for very long, but it's been seen most years since then. Last year [2021] was the first time it had stayed so long, hanging around with the gannets from May to September.'

Was it emotional seeing something so rare?

'I almost cried, let's put it that way. It was overwhelming. A gannet is a big bird with a six-foot wingspan, but the albatross is bigger. The gannet is my favourite.'

Why?

'They are just magnificent, they are so clever, they are beautiful, they have personality, they know they are big and can do what they want, so seeing an albatross next to a gannet is amazing. It looked like a puffin in comparison.'

Birdwatchers travel from far and wide to see the albatross, and many do cry, but it is a bird out of synch. According to the bird census, which involves people sitting in boats and counting, there were 13,400 pairs of gannets at Bempton in 2017, up from 2,550 in 2000. Since that previous count, guillemots had risen from 31,000 to 57,000 pairs, razorbills from 5,700 to 19,000 pairs, and there were 1,440 pairs of puffins. The cliffs had become a haven, but this is an anomaly, as the numbers of seabirds have declined elsewhere. Habits are changing too, and Abbie tells me about the plight of the kittiwakes, the sea-loving gull. 'The main reason is climate change,' she says of their decline. 'Puffins will dive and swim and gannets will dive deep, but kittiwakes are surface feeders. When the water gets warmer there is less plankton and so there's less fish.' It means that ingrained behaviour changes, and now you will find kittiwakes, a marine bird lest we forget, nesting along the Tyne in Newcastle. I cannot help thinking of Hannah Hauxwell being forced to move. 'Seabirds are a key indicator of climate change,' says Abbie, to underline the point.

Albie, a black-browed albatross, likes to hang out with the gannets too. Maybe it is a size thing. Nobody knows for sure what sex Albie is. The experts at Bempton would like to track it and see where it goes when it leaves, but they have no intention of catching it. The chances are it is lost. It went too far in search of food, or something went wrong with its radar. The albatross has an ability to lock its wings in place and use its surface area to glide, but flapping them to combat light equatorial winds is not its forte. It can cover 600 miles a day. Distance is not a problem, but there is no going home.

The black-browed albatross is easy to spot. It belongs to the procellariiformes – or tubenoses in lay terms – and its underwing has a black border, its eye a smudge of mascara. It is the goth of birds. On the day I visit, Albie is long gone, drifting slowly on its sad northern loop, but there is a short-eared owl getting mobbed by crows, a few lazy gannets refusing to leave, and out there on the sea, bobbing around, two black and grey puffins, shorn of high-season colour and clown faces. These are the cliffs as an empty stage, swept of a quarter of a million birds. Yesterday, 35 dolphins came past the various lookout points. Sometimes the spotters see a minke whale. Once a humpback swam by. On another occasion a dead one drifted past with its own funeral cortège.

Later in 2022, an Arctic walrus will turn up in Scarborough harbour. Locals will be delighted by the three tonnes of tusk and blubber – and name it Thor. Buckland is thankfully no more. The New Year's Eve fireworks will be cancelled out of respect for the sleeping giant, and Scarborough College will get 41 applications from overseas students seduced by the tale and evidently not realising Thor had buggered off by New Year's Day. Council leader Steve Siddons will opine that 'any publicity is good publicity', and conservationists will again warn that seeing Thor is evidence of melting ice, warming seas and a chilling future.

It is bloody freezing. I am staying in a shepherd's hut

down a farm track opposite a petrol station. I arrive late in the pitch black and spend an age trying to get enough charge from my phone to illuminate the laminated directions on a gatepost. Inside the hut I try to light a candle so I can read the instructions that say, with some condescension, I feel, that a few idiot guests have tried to light the LED candles. I hide the burnt-out match and flick the switch on the base. The midnight shutter has come down on the sea view, and at length do consider an albatross winging its way across the Baltic, condemned to a solitary, off-grid life and an endless quest for home.

The whalers

The next day I head back up the coast to Whitby. There are plenty of reasons to visit Whitby, where quirky shops are interwoven with whaling and Captain Cook attractions. It has managed to mix populism with prettiness and has not given in to the crowd that once wanted Peter Sutcliffe waxworks and still needs fairground rides run by people who look like they may lack an engineering background.

But the best place of all is the Whitby Museum. It is not the biggest museum, or the most renowned, and it is short on the interactive exhibits now mandatory elsewhere, but it is a wonderful kaleidoscope. It opened in 1823, when exhibits included the horn of a unicorn fish, a tattooed head from New Zealand, an African elephant's tail, the lower jaw of a Kirkdale Cave hyena and a confessional stone made from the mud of the Ganges. Best of all might be the Tempest Prognosticator, an ornate contraption comprising bottles of leeches wired to a bell. When the weather was going to turn, the leeches climbed, the bell rang, and you knew to wear a coat. George Merryweather – yes, his real name and not a hobbit – took it to the Great Exhibition but unsurprisingly failed to convince the government to install one in every port.

Alison Roberts is the Whitby Museum chair. Like most of the people here, including the collection curators, she is a volunteer; the place survives on hard work and goodwill. It is hard not to be stopped in your tracks by the juxtaposition of exhibits in a relatively small place, many in their original mahogany-lined display cases with gold-leaf lettering. Alison shows me behind the scenes at the museum, where, down in the basement, there are antlers, model ships, a caiman, medals, umpteen serious-looking figures in gold frames, this and tat. There is an extensive collection of birds' eggs in varnished wooden drawers that may go back on display soon. In another vault by the library, where they are holding a book sale, is a complete collection of the *Whitby Gazette*. Some are signed by famous visitors. Bram Stoker, author of Whitby-inspired *Dracula*, is one of them. But Alison's real love is the costume collection, and she likes to hide in a back room with years of clothes in sewn covers. A highlight is a black Victorian wedding dress. The groom must have suspected the worst.

The items on display exude possibility. There is Captain Chapman's marine crocodile fossil, bought for £7 in 1824. At one point in the museum's history, they contemplated hacking a bit off the tail because it didn't fit the space on the wall, which seems a very Yorkshire thing to do. You can picture the Victorian tradesman sucking in his cheeks and saying, 'I can make it fit, but it'll cost you.' They displayed it diagonally instead. And here is an assortment of stuffed birds, which shows that long before they did puffin cruises from

Bempton, the Victorians were masters at killing animals. In Adam Nicolson's book *The Seabird's Cry*, the lustrously named sea commander Hugh Horatio Knocker, who literally died on the *Fly* in 1868, recounts how 107,250 birds were destroyed in the vicinity of Bempton in four months of shooting parties.

There are dinosaur footprints, a chessboard carved from a single piece of jet, and a witch post, which is a cross carved on wood to stop Mary Bateman flying down the chimney. Sceptics might point out that the flip side of this was disappointing the kids at Christmas, but they were a devoutly superstitious bunch back then. There are also items from Captain James Cook's expeditions, and Whitby loves Cook, even though you could argue he did not discover that much apart from islands where people already lived and things that did not exist, like the great southern continent. Okay, that may be harsh. In 1770, he was the first known European to land on the east coast of Australia, but this was 164 years after Willem Janszoon had landed up north. The fact is, being a skilled navigator and avoiding scurvy was not as sexy in historical terms as 'discovering' Australia. Still, he was born in Middlesbrough, lived in moors village Great Ayton and, in his late teens, cut his sea teeth in Whitby. Tourism was not about to let him slip through the net.

There is also an exhibition about whaling. Whitby has no qualms about celebrating its destructive past, hence the whalebones that are the town's enduring postcard. 'We have people saying it's a bit gruesome,' says Alison. 'But you don't have to come in here. I mean, it's whaling – what do you expect?'

Indeed. Whaling was a cruel enterprise of blood and blubber and bone, and the father-and-son duo of William Scoresby Snr and Jnr were its kings. Where Snr would be responsible for the deaths of 533 whales and sated his conscience with the notion that this was God's will, his son seemed slightly more equivocal, but then, as now, oil ruled. Only this kind was boiled from blubber in metal vats in four yards in Whitby as whales lit Britain's lamps for nigh-on 100 years and bones were scraped and cleaned for corsets. Whitby, then, literally made a nation gasp. It and Hull were the industry's twin peaks, with Whitby bringing home 2,760 whales in all, as well as 25,000 seals.

The first whaler left the town in 1753, and Scoresby Snr made his first trip to Greenland three decades later. His rise through the ranks enabled the family to move from Pickering to Whitby, whence he set sail onboard the *Dundee* in 1800, only to find that his 10-year-old son had stowed away. Father left son with a friend on Shetland, but the boy hired a boatman to take him back to the ship, and the secretly pleased Scoresby Snr thus took his son on a dads-and-lads Arctic adventure when he should really have been at school. It did not take long for trouble to rear its head, when a French ship drew alongside and its captain demanded to know their nationality. Scoresby reportedly responded with a dismissive wave and the unveiling of six cannons. The French fled, but the voyage was dogged with setbacks. The *Dundee* would later spend eight weeks encased in ice, and would kill only three whales.

This was a time when the quest to find the Northwest Passage was in full flow, as explorers sought a trading route between the Atlantic and the Pacific. Scoresby Snr came as close as anyone when master of the *Resolution* in 1806, reaching a latitude of 81°30' north with his 16-year-old son as his first mate. Whaling, though, was his income, with up to £600 on offer per voyage, and his religious zeal meant the pursuit of the whale was a righteous mission. It did not end well for him. Long retired, he shot himself in the chest in 1829, but his legacy was his mighty haul of blubber, inventing the crow's nest, his habit of getting his crew to run from one side of the ship to the other to free it from pack ice, and, most importantly for the future, his son.

The Scoresbys are also responsible for the plastic polar bear that sits on top of Holland & Barrett in Whitby town centre. This is a tribute to the time William Snr was the commander of a ship when a mother bear was shot dead. Two cubs survived and were taken on board, with one making it all the way home. Scoresby Jnr would recall, 'These animals, though at first evidently very unhappy, became at length, in some measure, reconciled to their situation and being tolerably tame, were allowed occasionally to go at large about the deck.' One bear disembarked in Whitby and was occasionally spotted swimming in the harbour. Scorseby Snr famously proved that he knew his ursus from his elbow when one of these animals escaped its tether and was pursued into a nearby wood by a posse of bloodthirsty men, armed with guns and aided by a pack of dogs. The captain arrived to save it, and the bear licked his hand. He arranged for its transfer to the Tower of London, the zoo not the prison although the line was fine, and when visiting a year later, confidently put his arm through the cage to pet his old friend. It is a nice story, at odds with his belief that all animals were put on earth for man's use, and the bit in his son's memoirs when he talks enthusiastically about how a bear makes a nice rug but eating its liver can make your skin fall off.

Despite that, Scoresby Jnr was an innovative man and a deep thinker, whose legacy, it could be argued, matches that of the more venerated Cook, although it is Cook's replica boat *Endeavour* that still dominates the harbour, and his old lodging house that wins tourism awards.

At 21, Scoresby was in charge of his father's old ship, the *Resolution*, and when not killing whales, he made some discoveries that would trickle down the ages. One of his most notable feats was designing the marine diver, an instrument that could be lowered into the depths, where it could trap water in a chamber and thus measure the temperature. This showed that the water in the Arctic was sometimes warmer the deeper the diver went, while the wire gauze attached to the top snared a shrimp and provided proof of life at 750 fathoms. Scoresby sketched and theorised and wrote. His ideas were laid out in his 1820 book, *An Account of the Arctic Regions and Northern Whale Fisheries*, which would cost the equivalent of £90 in today's money and for which he was to be paid the equivalent of £14,500. It contained his detailed drawings of snowflakes, observed under a microscope, which showed their variety for the first time. His enthusiasm for studying ice, water, temperature and fauna meant he even suggested using a dog-drawn amphibious craft for travelling to the North Pole.

Scoresby also told an astonishing anecdote. The master of another Whitby whaler had shown him part of a stone lance removed from the fat of a whale. The wound had healed, and Scoresby noted that this type of lance was in common use by the 'Esquimaux' 'on the northern face of the American Continent' a century earlier. He was the first to realise not only the longevity of whales, but also, and more importantly, that this stone lance meant there must be a Northwest Passage.

Eleven years after Scoresby's book was published, Darwin took a copy with him on the *Beagle*. A man enthralled with links must have been impressed with how Scoresby had first recorded the idea of a food chain. When on board the Arctic whaler *Esk*, he had noted that the sea was ultra-marine but whales tended to feed where it was green. There was nothing he could see to account for the variation, but noticing that the ice was tinged orange-yellow around the edges, he deduced there must be something in the water. His answer was to take some snow from the ice and let it dissolve in a wine glass. This examination revealed a 'great number of semi-transparent spherical substances with others resembling small portions of hair'. This was plankton, or whale food.

Scoresby noted the feeding habits of whales, dolphins, seals and medusae, and wrote about the concept of a connection. 'Thus, the whole of the larger animals depend on these minute beings which, until 1816, when I first entered on the examination of the seawater, were not I believe known to exist in the polar seas. And thus, we find a dependent chain of existence, one of the smaller links of which being destroyed, the whole must necessarily perish.'

Scoresby was honoured in extraordinary fashion in 1991, when Jack Lammiman, a craggy, crotchety, pipe-toting Whitby sea dog, declared that he was off to erect a plaque on Jan Mayen, a Norwegian volcanic island in the Arctic Ocean. He spent £3,000 on publicity to drum up backing, but nobody was very interested. Authorities said his ancient fishing boat, the *Helga Maria*, was not up to the job, and refused permission until he made a plethora of upgrades. Captain Jack eventually grew so frustrated that he set off anyway, barking: 'I've had enough of this silliness.' His crew had also worried the authorities. It comprised a vicar who had grown up on the North York Moors and worked as a psychiatric nurse, an elderly ex-MI5 clerk from Wormwood

Scrubs, a drifter, a welder and a 73-year-old romantic painter. It was the oldest, and probably oddest, crew to head to the frozen north.

They spent their two outbound weeks avoiding detection, and then Captain Jack ordered two of his charges to take a bag of cement and the plaque, donated by the local butcher and inscribed with his name, and build a cairn halfway up a mountain. Not bloody likely, they said. There might be bears, and anyway, this was Norwegian territory. You couldn't just start building monuments wherever you fancied. After making Captain Jack radio for permission, they eventually set off for home, repainting the boat to confuse spotting planes or boats. Fourteen countries joined the search. Finally the crew arrived at Whitby to a hero's reception and 43 charges under the Merchant Shipping Act. Captain Jack was fined £400 and served four days in jail when he did not pay.

I reluctantly leave Alison to her museum and its stories. Later, I pop into the Captain Cook Museum, which provides details of his voyages across uncharted seas. Out of the window in a room where the introductory video plays, I spy a woman in black with raven hair and a snowy face. She stands out but is a familiar sight around here. The goths gather in Whitby each October and the streets are filled with jet black and alabaster, Victorian corsets and a new wave of Siouxsie Siouxs. Goth Weekend is a bit of fun and a boon for the tourist trade. It also means Whitby becomes a safe place for another marginalised subculture. One goth called Dan tells *Dazed* magazine, 'Living in Scarborough you can't really be yourself without being judged.'

Inevitably, Whitby has ravished its Bram Stoker connection too, and it now has a Dracula Experience. It is fair enough. He did stay there in 1890 after touring Scotland as the manager of actor Henry Irving. Some scholars believe Irving was the inspiration for Dracula, who was going by the slightly pathetic working moniker of Count Wampyr until Stoker nipped into Whitby library and read William Wilkinson's account of Vlad Tepes, aka Vlad the Impaler, who used the infamous name. He excitedly noted that it was Wallachian for devil. He also scribbled down names from headstones to be reborn as characters, although not that of Anne Brontë, which is probably just as well given that the wording on her grave was riddled with errors, the majority of which were fixed by Charlotte, but not the age at death, which remained defiantly as 28 until corrected 164 years late. Stoker also called the boat that carries Dracula to Whitby the *Demeter*, possibly an artistic version of *Dmitry*, a boat wrecked under the town's East Cliff five years earlier. *Dracula* was a flop as a play and then a hit as an epistolary novel. It has been analysed to undeath, but it is easy to see how it played to Victorian (and Yorkshire) fears about outsiders. It gave birth to hundreds of films, pastiches and fancy-dress outfits, as well as a notice posted on the door of St Mary's Church in the town that read: 'Please do not ask staff where Dracula's grave is as there isn't one.'

To Hull and back

Jimmy Hodgson was meant to be on holiday from his job as a messenger with the Auxiliary Fire Service, but on that black night in 1941, lit by the lightning flashes and white noise, he went out to work. He was only 17, just 4 feet 7 inches tall, fresh-faced with naturally raven hair. He walked into the street, and maybe it was the naïvety of youth, but he ignored the random violence in the air and just set about helping. 'First of all, I put out some incendiary bombs and then went to a wrecked house under which I heard that a number of people were trapped,' he would later tell a journalist from the *Hull Daily Mail*. 'A tunnel was being made under the wreckage and I volunteered to crawl through it. At the end of the tunnel, I could see Beatrice Dove, a 15-year-old girl who used to go to the same school as myself and lived in the same street.'

It was close to home, but Jimmy did not ponder that it could have been him. He just thought about her. 'She was pinned under the debris with only her face and a hand showing,' he said. 'She was laid on a couch with a dead three-year-old child alongside and her dead father laid over her. Below this wreckage was a blazing inferno, so hot in fact that I had to take a stirrup pump in to cool the bricks and other wreckage around Beatrice. She was crying out for water, so I fed her through a baby's bottle. As she complained of pains in her back, I tried to make her forget her troubles by chatting to her about the pictures we had seen at local cinemas. "Have you been to the Regent tonight?" I enquired. "I will not be going to the pictures any more after tonight," she replied. A few minutes later she was dead.'

Jimmy got out just before the building collapsed. Ten people died in total. When he went back to work at the depot, his boss asked him how he had injured his hand. Jimmy made light of it and said it had just been air raid work.

He got the British Empire Medal for that, but it was only one human story from the Hull Blitz. Few other British cities were as badly damaged as Hull by the Luftwaffe in the Second World War, with 95 per cent of houses destroyed or damaged, 1,200 people killed and 152,000 made homeless.

Yet much of the country never knew just how badly it had been charred and eviscerated. In dispatches it was referred to as 'northern coastal town' to prevent the Germans knowing what and where they had struck. As a result, much of the heroism and carnage has never really forged its way into the public consciousness in the way of the Blitz in London. And this is Hull all over, the last place in Yorkshire, out there on the end of the cold, bleak M62, with the Humber Bridge and its suicide barrier as the last line of defence.

The devastation wrought in the Second World War is highlighted in Frank Shaw's *We Remember the Blitz*, published in 1990. One man recalls the city centre being ablaze and a German parachutist disappearing into the flames of Hammonds department store. Another saw the body of his cousin coming down to earth after treading on a mine. 'They later found his head and shoulders separated.' A man's shop was destroyed, and he decided his family had to leave the city. The nights of sleeping in an air raid shelter and never getting undressed had taken its toll, taut senses firing at every sound or vibration. The only trouble was, the man's son, unlike Beatrice, had gone to the pictures that night. The father took a torch and searched every row of seats, but finally realised he was in the wrong cinema. When he found him, the train to Doncaster had long gone. His sister recalled, 'If we all get killed tonight it will be our Eric's fault.'

You don't get bombed if you're not important, and Hull's status has stretched and strained from the days of the monks at Meaux Abbey who used the prime location near Beverley to export wool. The place was called Wyke before Edward I gave it a royal charter in 1299 and it became King's Town upon Hull, named after the river bleeding into the Humber estuary. It grew as a port, fortified itself and flexed its muscles during the English Civil War. Wilberforce gave it a moral compass and aviator Amy Johnson its spirit when the home-town heroine flew solo to Australia. This was Hull. Lots to shout about and much that it would rather forget.

Ever since those monks fished the Humber, Hull has been an important centre for fishing and whaling. Hessle Road was its hub, and hundreds of trawlers were based in the port. Then came the Cod Wars, from 1958 to 1976, with Britain and Iceland locked in a bitter row about fishing rights, exclusion zones and, mainly, survival. Ultimately, Iceland won out after it threatened to close a NATO base and forge stronger ties with the Soviet bloc. After two decades of conflict, jobs went and it took another 36 years to get an apology and proper compensation from the government.

One trawler sums up Hull's plight. The *Arctic Viking* was launched in 1937 but was converted into an anti-submarine vessel during the Second World War and patrolled the waters off Dunkirk before being sunk near Portsmouth in 1942. She was salvaged, refitted and went back to post-war fishing. Then she sliced into another British vessel in Icelandic waters and had to rescue that crew. This eventful life continued into the Cod Wars, and in 1959 she was again spotted in Icelandic waters. Enter *Thor*, which followed up warning shots with ones aimed at the mast in an effort to cut off radio communications. The British response was to send in HMS *Contest*, a C-class destroyer. *Thor* was suitably chastened. The following year, *Contest* was decommissioned and sent to a breaker's yard in Essex, but the *Viking* kept going, and in 1961 suffered her lowest moment.

As she neared home one October night, an enormous wave battered her and she began to take on water. The skipper paused to allow a pipe to be fixed so water could be pumped into a starboard tank to correct the list, but she was then struck by two vicious assaults from demented waves. The terrified men saw the funnel and mast sink into the water, but two of the crew managed to free one life raft. 'Some got in, but others hadn't a chance,' said one survivor. 'I jumped into the sea without life jackets from the side of the bridge as the trawler was turning over. I swam to the raft and was lucky to surface about 20 yards from it.' After an hour, a Polish vessel, the *Derkacz*, rescued the survivors, and its crew gave up their bunks for them, but now the *Derkacz* was stranded in the gale. It took them two days to make it back up the Humber, with the flag at half-mast for the five men who'd been lost. Among them was Arthur Waddy, the 47-year-old bosun. Sixty years later, Waddy's son, Charlie, was still working the sea on the *Kirkella*, a £40 million vessel that was the last of the Hull deep-sea trawlers. It had a cinema and a sauna, but Waddy pointed out that the temperature could still drop to minus 30 even if he no longer had to do 18-hour shifts as he had as a boy.

Fishing was a hard enough life anyway, but in 1904, the Russian Imperial fleet mistook Hull trawlers for Japanese torpedo boats in the Dogger Bank, a shallow area 100 kilometres off the British coast. As the Russians opened fire on the fishermen – and, inadvertently, themselves – two trawlermen and a Russian Orthodox priest died. Walter Whelpton, skipper of the *Mino*, explained that he was initially thrilled to see these mighty boats. 'I thought it was going to be a brilliant spectacle,' he said. Then the *Mino*'s funnel was hit. 'Good God!' he shouted. 'Lie down, lads, and look after yourself.' The tsar apologised and

Russia paid £65,000 in compensation. It meant nothing to Whelpton, who died seven months later; it was put down to the shock.

The air did not offer a haven either. Amy Johnson had become a celebrity when she flew her second-hand Gipsy Moth to Australia in 1930. The Hull-born granddaughter of the mayor, she had that same pioneering spirit and fearlessness later shown by Helen Sharman. Having worked as a secretary in London, she had a refined accent that made her wander instead of wonder when she recounted her dream of flying to Australia. 'The idea obsessed my mind day and night. No one had faith in me except myself and who could blame them? Where could I find hundreds of pounds? Two kind-hearted Englishmen. Now the rush began. May 5 is ringed in red as the last day I can make a stop. Ten days before I am due to start and I have not got an aeroplane but then I am introduced to *Jason*. It's glorious to be off at last. Now I have time to think. Where am I bound for today? Vienna, am I really bound to see this city of dreams? *Jason* is a dear. I'm very frightened really, but *Jason* isn't. India. Poor old *Jason* was so upset he ran his nose in a ditch in Rangoon. We cheered up a wee bit when we saw a rainbow over the Java Sea.'

It took 19 and a half days and she never needed the sheath knife she carried in case she crash-landed and came across any sharks. In 1941, she parachuted into the Thames Estuary while piloting a wartime plane to RAF Kidlington. Reports claimed she had overshot her destination and ran out of fuel. HMS *Haslemere* went to her rescue and threw out a rope, but she was unable to reach it. The captain, Walter Fletcher, dived in to save her, but he was unsuccessful. He was unconscious when the lifeboat reached him and died days later in hospital.

That is one story but some say she was killed by the ship's propellers, and more than half a century later, a retired gardener called Tom Mitchell, aged 83, tried to clear up the mystery. He had been a soldier stationed at Iwade on the Thames Estuary when he saw the plane, and after Johnson twice cited the wrong identifying code according to military protocol, he was told to shoot. 'Sixteen rounds of shells were fired into the sky and the plane dived into the Thames Estuary,' he said in 1999. 'But on the ground, we couldn't see that at the time. The next day, when we read about it in the papers, the officers told us to keep quiet and never tell anyone what happened.'

The following month, 20 people died as bombs fell on Hull in a horrific preamble. By March, the Germans were targeting St Andrew's Dock but killing people indiscriminately. And Jimmy Hodgson decided to go outside.

In all, there were more than 80 raids on Hull, but it often seems that it is still an anonymous northern coastal town, not expunged from memory because for much of Britain it was never there. In 2015, when the BBC screened a documentary series called *Blitz Cities*, Hull was notable by its absence. That angered locals but probably did not surprise them. For a place the Germans could not miss from on high, Hull has remained good at being overlooked.

After the devastation of the war came the rebuild. The plan was grand. Patrick Abercrombie was a dapper town planner who came up with a scheme that Will Alsop would have been proud of. Hull would get the city its suffering population deserved after the war, with a village scheme with private gardens, a tree-lined boulevard running from the station, and blissed-out parks. It was ambitious, a bit utopian and fatally flawed. Discussions, public meetings and artistic maps segued into frustration, objections and inertia. Hull people wanted their town back, but any town would do. Many were homeless at the time, and needs must. So prefabs were built and some families lived in Nissen huts. The sprawling Bransholme estate would go up in the late 1960s and become home to tens of thousands of people. Routinely dubbed Europe's largest council estate, a disputed claim, it inevitably gets picked on by people who have never been there.

You can make an argument for saying other British cities were forgotten after the war and that some of them also went unnamed during it. But what is clear is that the belief that Hull was marginalised and not given due credit was real and heartfelt. And so when they throw other things at Hull too, it does not take much to scrape the scabbing from old wounds.

For a start – syphilis. It had long been thought that Christopher Columbus's crew had brought the deadly venereal disease to Europe from their New World shenanigans in the late fifteenth century. Then, in 2018, they dug up the site of the old friary in Hull and found hundreds of skeletons, many betraying signs of the disease. The battered bones were from between 1300 and 1450, backed up by dating the wooden coffins, which was significant because it showed that the disease was present in Britain long before Columbus was 'discovering' places. Hull had a new claim to fame that naturally made people wonder just what the monks had been getting up to. Finding short wooden rods next to some of the bodies was taken as evidence that the Augustinian friars had been a self-flagellating sect who would whip themselves into a frenzy and thus create open sores on the skin that facilitated infection. Add gallons of wine shipped up the Humber from Spain, and you can see how the disease could have spread. Hull, then, had rewritten history.

A year later, Oxford University killjoys carbon-dated the bones to between 1410 and 1530, meaning syphilis in Hull might have been post-Columbus after all. Hull's fish trade was to blame for the confusion. Experts said the high-fish diet meant the bones appeared older because of all that ancient sea carbon. It meant Hull's new-found status as being pivotal to the understanding of syphilis was under threat. I suppose you need to pick your fights, but this malaise has spread like, well, you can imagine.

Philip Larkin has also been part of this re-evaluation. Born in Coventry but a librarian in Hull for ever and rewarded with a statue, his reputation as the greatest post-war poet, as appraised by *The Times* in 2008, has been overtaken in recent years by discussions about his bigotry. The arm of the statue outside the station has been snapped, and even toads created in homage to his poem of that name and positioned in the city to mark the twenty-fifth anniversary of his death were vandalised. Larkin had not even liked Hull much to start with. 'What a hole, what witless, crapulous people,' he wrote soon after arriving in 1955, but he came to love it and did nail its appeal for some. 'I like it because it is so far away from everywhere else.' About 34 miles from York, anyway.

The great rugby league teams waned too. Hull and Hull Kingston Rovers both won the league title in the early 1980s but have not done so since. Hull fans still sing 'Old Faithful', a slightly bizarre tribute to a rock-steady kicker from the 1930s based on singing cowboy Gene Autry's paean to his horse, and faith has often been all they have.

Back in the 1920s, attempts to repatriate black seamen in Wilberforce's city fuelled one-eyed violence. In 1976, prisoners destroyed much of Hull prison in protest at staff brutality. Three years later, a 19-year-old man poured paraffin through the letter box of a house in Hull. One of the boys inside managed to get his mother out, but he and two siblings died. A troubled pyromaniac who had changed his name to Bruce Lee was responsible. He admitted to other acts of arson that had led to 26 deaths and was convicted at Leeds Crown Court of manslaughter in January 1981, but even being Britain's worst mass killer did not really infiltrate the wider public consciousness, because it was barely a fortnight since Peter Sutcliffe had been charged with the murders that had dominated the headlines.

The good, bad and ugly of Hull were, then, often local matters, but there is much to like about the city. J. B. Priestley got this way back in 1934. 'Hull is out of your way,' he said. 'You cannot pass through it to anywhere.' He added, 'It is not really in Yorkshire, but by itself, somewhere in the remote east, where England is nearly turning into Holland or Denmark.' This did not sound an overly promising beginning, and Priestley also said he had never known 'such a place for ice rain', but among manifold references to the sleet and cold, he maintained that the city had a 'cleanish, red-brick look' and not the usual 'down and out' face and thick gloom of London or Liverpool. As for the people: 'They are so queer because they are not quite Yorkshire and yet not quite anything else.' He concluded that Hull was 'a sound and sensible city, not at all glamorous in itself yet never far from romance'. Like the man in Tadcaster Cemetery all those years and pages ago, Hull is the city on the edge with people ignoring the disappearing borders.

That might be Yorkshire. It is attacked and ignored but alive and proud, brilliant at some things but last to be picked. At various times Hull has not been in Yorkshire; it became part of Humberside and then, when that was carved up, its own unitary authority. You could not get more quintessentially Yorkshire than being so peculiarly Yorkshire that you get ignored by Yorkshire. It's the county in microcosm – out there, quirky, not much liked by some and with a distinctive whiff. And it likes itself, even if God sometimes forgets. It's self-contained but it looks out too, to Europe and, in less wistful moments, Lincolnshire, if it can remember what any of these places are called with all the shifting name tags.

And it also offers a reminder that time is short. Out there in the mouth of the Humber estuary is Ravenser Odd, the prosperous port town that was swallowed up by Grote Mandrenke, or St Marcellus's Flood, in 1362. In 2021, a team from the University of Hull thought they had located it and suggested it could be vital for our understanding of the climate crisis and coastal erosion, but in truth this coast already is. From Hull to Flamborough Head, at least 25 villages have been lost to the sea. This stretch of coastline is losing up to 15 feet a year from erosion. Yorkshire, big and brash and bloody-minded, is getting smaller by the day.

15

NOW

Is God in?

The time for our family trip to Yorkshire with Mum is fast approaching. Maybe it's why I'm getting nostalgic. I'm listening to the Wedding Present, reading Barry Hines and wondering if any of those snails that we used to paint nail varnish numbers on and then tempt across a paving stone with lettuce while we wagered 10ps made it out of the seventies alive. There are a few people to see first, though.

One is Sharon, the smiling, helpful media chief at York Minster. She used to work in London, which might explain her ebullience now. She has put me in touch with a colleague, and that is why in October 2022 I find myself on a Zoom call with the current Archbishop of York, Stephen Cottrell, who tells me he is an Essex boy who rented a cottage in the Dales for his honeymoon and then took his bride to see the aftermath of the fire at York Minster. 'I know how to show a girl a good time,' he says. I had not expected that. 'I'm very proud of my Essex identity and Essex is a really persecuted place,' he continues.

More than is normal during these Zoom events, I find myself trying to spot the titles of the books on his shelves, hoping for something inappropriate, but I am soon wholly engaged by his forthright candour about identity and the north–south divide.

'Essex is the butt of everybody's joke. I moved north in the 1990s to Huddersfield and two of my children were born there. They did their growing up half down south and half in Yorkshire. They don't have a Yorkshire accent, they've not lived here for a long time and their parents did not press the identity thing, but if you asked where they came from, they would say Yorkshire. Down south regional identity is alive in the West Country and it's alive in Essex, but the Home Counties have become one homogenous region.

'I was a vicar in Chichester and I observed the dying-out of an accent. They used to say Chidester but you'll no longer find anybody who speaks like that. It's been taken over by that Thames Estuary way of speaking. So I love the sense of identity in Yorkshire, that there's an accent and a sense of humour. I think that is very precious.'

The archbishop is not about to champion one place above any other – although he comes closer than I anticipated – and he places this love of regional identity within what he calls the ecosystem of humanity. 'It's really important to celebrate and cherish your identity because that's how the ecosystem flourishes,' he says. 'Diversity is not just about colour and ethnicity – it's about the regions. There's a common humanity, and rich differences should not blind us to that, but at the same time differences should not be a problem. If we pretend that we are all the same, that extinguishes variety, and if a species becomes extinct, you cannot get it back again. But there is also a danger that it becomes hard and inward-looking and even damaging.'

He is not a politician, but he has views. He wrote a book during the pandemic called *Dear England*. It is a powerful thesis. There are clearly manifold religions and millions who are irreligious, but he talks of Brexit, COVID, 9/11, genocide, and says he became a priest because he felt the human race needed a heart transplant. And if he is not political, he does believe more power should be devolved to the regions and that the geographical divide is becoming a chasm.

'I do think the north is being left behind,' he says. 'Since returning to Yorkshire I have been shocked by some of the changes. I'm thinking about the poorest communities in Hull and Middlesbrough, some of the poorest urban conurbations in the UK. There is a widening gap between wealth and poverty and now we're in a cost-of-living crisis and winter is starting to bite. It's not my responsibility to point the finger and blame people but somebody has to say it how it is. Of course there is poverty and deprivation in the south too, but it's on a greater scale up here. Whole communities have been left behind.

'My personal view flows from my world view. I think the best way to exercise responsibilities is to build up local and regional identity and give agency to local and regional government. One of the best ways to strengthen our unity as a United Kingdom is to give greater power to Yorkshire. I'd like to see that accelerated.'

He takes me to task when I suggest the influence of the Church is diminishing and mention all those oversized churches closing in the Dales. He says that 40 years ago the pub, post office and church were the foundations of each village. The post office is gone and the pub is following, but 'We're still here. And who is running the food banks and the homeless shelters? Where's the one place you can go to this morning without an appointment and someone there will welcome you? My plan is to open more churches, but it's just the new ones tend to have flat roofs rather than spires.'

I feel reprimanded as he gathers momentum. 'We have 1,600 parishes and we have some historic assets, but mostly it's all funded by people putting their hands in their pockets. Excuse me, Rick, but it's a bloody miracle.'

We all need bloody miracles, now as then. The archbishop talks about post-war community and how sad it is that it takes tragedy to bring us together as one. It was the same in the pandemic, when people really felt they were in it together, until politicians started flouting rules and people peddled cruel theories that ignored a war-like death toll. They stopped banging pots and pans and instead became trolls and tub-thumpers.

'If there's a hard-working mum in Hull who can't feed her children, something has gone wrong in the whole ecosystem of society,' he says. 'I would say I carry big responsibilities and I have great sympathy for political leaders, but if I have a criticism, it is that they don't dream. As a nation we need vision.'

He tells me about his favourite bit of York Minster. It's by the west door and is a list of all the archbishops. It starts in the top left with Paulinus in 627, and the last name, in the bottom right, is Stephen Cottrell, but it does not end there. 'I received the baton from these guys,' he says. 'It puts me in perspective. You're just the latest. Do your best. One day there'll be another name. That's York Minster to me. In a rapidly changing world with all the challenges we face, it represents the security of the presence of God.' He says the Church's real role is not in pleading with people to come on Sunday; it's out there in the community. He gets it and then he says it. 'God loves Yorkshire.' Of course he does. It's where he's from.

A walk in the park

In November, I go to Bradford for one more solo visit before I return with Mum. I'm here to meet Mohammed Qasim. He will soon get an MBE for services to academic research and to young people. In 2018, he wrote a book, *Young, Muslim and Criminal*, that is a fascinating read, even if a lot of people would rather ignore it and stick with their preconceptions. In it he mentions the claim that British Muslims have become regarded as 'the enemy within', the same term once applied to British miners.

A few yards up the hill from the house where I meet Mo is Lister Mills, but it is underused nowadays. Where Salts Mill, in another part of Bradford, is a pristine arts venue and exhibition space, here there is a boarded-up gate, and rubble nestling uncomfortably against a desolate football pitch where crows crowd the sagging crossbar. Birds and balls. I think of Brian Glover. Lister's Pride is still there, though the chimney looks like it's trying to escape upwards. Fancy penthouses were part of an ambitious scheme, but those who bought them now struggle to flog them.

I have lunch with Mo and then we go for a walk, with his young kids and nieces and nephews, down to Lister Park by Manningham Lane. This was voted Britain's best park in 2006. It houses Cartwright Hall, with its Hockney room, and has Lister and Titus Salt statues bookending Bradford Grammar School, just over Frizinghall Road, in the middle. Not long ago, Mo and a journalist called Max Daly wrote an article for *Vice* magazine that recalled the 2001 riots. It was a searing piece that used Mo's contacts to get recollections from some of the 200 people who were jailed for a combined 604 years. It showed how a city was split wide open and divided. Bridges were burnt and stolen cars pockmarked the chasm. Now Mo tells me that Bradford, the UK City of Culture, is also a segregated city.

'After the Second World War there was a need for people to come here and work in the textile industry,' he says amid periodic warnings to the kids. The building of the Mangla Dam in the early 1960s in Mirpur, Pakistan, led to hundreds of villages and towns being flooded. It is a northern echo that should reverberate through Yorkshire, where old towns were flooded in the Dales and villages are being lost to the North Sea. 'These people were displaced, and many came here to work in the mills. The mill owners knew they did not have long, and they needed to work at maximum speed to be competitive, so this was the first time that the country saw night shifts.' The immigrants worked long hours for low pay, but it was still better than what they had, and much of the money was sent home. Eventually, when the Immigration Act changed, families followed.

'But it all goes wrong in the seventies because these textile industries collapse. The local economy starts to blame the ethnic minority for its problems. Enoch Powell makes his "Rivers of Blood" speech. Tension flares, skinheads, Paki-bashing.' The Pakistani community had already grouped together, because of the low-cost housing near the mills and the need to share homes, but now it became a case of safety in numbers. 'That external aggression from the locals made this community very insular,' says Mo. 'Comfort was sought. Mosques were set up and there became this mosque-going culture; I don't mean that in a bad way. Fast-forward to '95 and that road there is Oak Lane. That riot started when the police turned up to the house of a family I know. They were there to arrest one of them for something, but in the process, they pushed his mother to the floor. Many of these young Pakistani men had fought off white racist groups, so they were already united and had big numbers.'

It got worse. In July 2001, Nick Griffin and his far-right BNP were allowed to stage a rally in Bradford. The Anti-Nazi League met in Centenary Square and the National Front also gathered at a pub. 'Nobody stopped them coming into Bradford and they beat up a handful of Pakistanis. One person was stabbed and they pulled the headscarves off a few women. I'm anti-technology but I remember receiving a text message saying, "Your community is under attack." And loads of Pakistanis came together to defend themselves. When the white racist groups disappeared, their anger turned to the police, so we had three days of street battles. We were young kids. It seemed cool and fun, people driving BMWs out of the car showroom, but they did not recognise the long-term damage the riots would do to the community. White flight. People putting their houses up for sale. It became like Detroit. Look at Bradford now – the Asian community is not further than one mile outside the city centre. Bradford is a big city, but three miles out and you will not see an Asian person. The riots really damaged Bradford. It was seen nationally as a problem city. For many it still is.

'It's just won the capital of culture but the community is very inward right now. They cater for themselves, with the shops and food places. It *is* a very segregated city. Other than you and me, it's very rare to see white and Asian people together in 2022. Look at this park. You see some Europeans, but the white British are almost non-existent, and if they come, they come early in the morning or on Friday when everybody goes to prayer.'

He rescues his son from too ambitious a climb in the playground and we walk past Bradford Grammar School.

He remembers wealthy kids being dropped off from fancy
cars in his youth, and perhaps another seed of them-and-us
resentment was sown. The school is now more mixed, but
the portrait of Bradford as contentedly divided is depressing.
'When communities are divided you can't see the problem,'
says Mo. 'I want my kids to do well in education, I want my
kids to interact with their surroundings whether it's white
people, black people, whatever, and I would question sending
them to a school that is 99 per cent Pakistani. How would
that serve them in later life? What you learn as a child stays
with you.'

A white man approaches us. Mo nudges me and asks me
to watch. He says the man will refuse to make eye contact.
His kids run off, blissful in their pursuit of fun. The man
walks on by, his gaze straight ahead. 'How can you do that?'
Mo asks with a sigh. 'You're telling me something – either
you don't like me or you're not confident enough and you
don't want to create conflict.'

The Bradford riots ended on 9 July 2001. On 11
September, two planes flew into the World Trade Center in
New York. Six years later, the two hundredth person was
jailed for his involvement in the Bradford violence.

'I never used to think that if you didn't like me it was
because of my religion,' says Mo. 'Only after 9/11 did
Islamophobia start to be thrown around. People began to
look for comfort again, and the history of Islam, fighting
against the Crusaders, is a story you can tap into. Before that,
I felt my cultural identity was Pakistani.'

Attitudes and images changed. The first wave of immigrants, those who worked in the mills, are gone now. Do the
imams and the MPs now speak for the local youth, or do
some of them just harden the dividing line?

'The community does not live in fear any more,' says Mo. 'The racism has become more subtle. But we are not preparing our young people as we should. The identity is more Muslim now. The Pakistani identity is still there but it's on its way out as the elders pass away. This is a safe place, but there are issues with drugs, heroin, depression, anxiety, the cost of living.'

There were 10,000 British Pakistanis in 1951. Sixty years later, the figure had risen to 1.1 million. In Bradford, the youngest city in Britain in terms of the age of its population, Mo earned the trust of a group of youths called the Boys, and his account of their lives, crimes and injustices cuts to the heart of the city's problems. It was not the case, as one local MP said, that 'sheer criminality' was the root cause of the 2001 riots. Michael Mansfield QC, the man who had defended the miners, led an appeal against the sentences and said the rioters were living under 'a matrix of fear'. In 2005, the Joseph Rowntree Foundation would report that young Asian men were 'disempowered and disenfranchised' and frustration had fuelled the riots. This was a generation used to police harassment and the hopelessness of unemployment. In his article in *Vice*, Mo quoted one anonymous rioter from 2001 talking about what he faced when he had served his sentence. 'It was hard. I got out and I was a man. Things were different, life was not the same as it was before I went in. Lots of people my age got locked up. We were an embarrassment when we came out, our community had turned on us.'

Back in 1989, around 1,000 people gathered in Bradford to burn *The Satanic Verses*, Salman Rushdie's allegedly blasphemous book, but Mo says that was a case of Asians protesting against an Asian man, so the white community did not get involved. But it was the start of the shift in terms of how some

people thought of British and Muslim identities. By the time of
9/11, it was easier for some to portray Braford's Asian men as
the sort who might endorse a negative form of Islamic funda-
mentalism. And in the twenty-first century, a string of horrific
scandals involving grooming gangs and child sexual exploita-
tion, from Rotherham to Huddersfield, increased suspicion and
reinforced cultural barriers between the innocent on both sides.

As generations passed, the mill worker was replaced by
the taxi driver, the halal food store owner and the curry
house entrepreneur. Yet the young were still disempowered
and disenfranchised, sometimes stifled by their communities
but too close to them to leave. 'The second group who came
over didn't work in the same industries as their parents,' says
Mo. 'I think if the first generation was still around, they'd
be shocked.' He wrote about how the Boys were now on the
cusp of being displaced by a new, younger group called the
Kids. And how both groups referred to Pakistan as 'back
home', although none of them had ever lived there. He didn't
think any of them would leave Bradford. They probably
wouldn't leave Manningham. 'The Boys were trapped by
fear, provincialism and by cultural tradition.'

I notice another white person pass a group of Asian
walkers. It is as if both shrink to opposite sides of the path,
perhaps unconsciously. 'Parallel lives,' says Mo.

We walk and talk cricket. The scandal is still winding its
way to the latest hearing. Mo laughs and says Asian kids
were always fielding when he was a boy. Then he points
out a huge house by the top of the park. It is, he says, the
last white house on that road. He knows this because of
the Christmas tree. His kids hold hands and cross the road.
Lister Mill still stands up the hill, its disused tower a totem
to the past.

The dancing girl

Stu Hennigan parks his van on an estate in Seacroft, Leeds. It is 2020, mid pandemic. He has been volunteering to deliver food parcels to the most invisible areas for more than a month now, and has seen the dystopian underbelly that is not shown on the Yorkshire porn shows: the rubbish entrails, dogshit yards, shopping trolleys, two youths brazenly selling drugs from their Corsa, the needles, the needy, the withered faces, the gnarled ones, the stench of weed and vodka, smashed TVs, the 10-year-old kid telling the copper he'll bite off his nose and spit it back in his face, the man in Armley who bursts out the front door with a look to kill, the woman who says she's tried to kill herself, again, the man urinating by the kids' playground in the middle of the day, the kid with the thousand-yard stare. This one, though, will stay with him for ever. A six-year-old in purple leggings and a dirty top opens the door. And shuts it. The mother in her red trackie comes out on the defensive but ready to attack. Stu says he's from the council and has food. The mood softens. When he brings the bags up, the girl is beside herself. 'Is that food?' she asks. Stu will write that he feels like Father Christmas. And the ecstatic girl starts to dance.

Stu is an author, poet, musician and library worker. He will write up the experiences of his time working as a delivery driver for the food distribution centre and call the book *Ghost Signs*. It is an essential read for anyone who cares. By the time I have read it and we talk, he has sent the book to a few politicians. Some have said they are interested, but many will not like what they see. It's a Yorkshire that looks unfixable, and it's a world away from safe seats and Commons benches.

'There's this Hovis-advert Yorkshire and then there's this Yorkshire that's actually there,' he tells me. He has just been down to London for an event with some politicians and bigwigs. 'They literally think it's flat caps and whippets and they did not know what the fuck to make of me,' he says. 'But just because I'm a scruff-bag who sounds like Sean Bean doesn't mean I don't know what I'm talking about. I guess the myths still perpetuate, but I've lived it because that was my youth. I grew up in Skipton. We were a couple of steps removed from this extreme poverty, but my mam and dad were living wage to wage, and get to Wednesday and the money would run out and my mam and godmother would go to town and split a loaf and a bag of spuds. I go to events and readings and people say it must have been hard for you working in those places, but I'm a lot closer to that than I am to the people asking that question.'

Money came to Skipton, if not to Stu's family, but the number of second homes hurts locals. It is like this all over North Yorkshire. People visit Richmond in the Dales and they see one kind of Yorkshire. It's the one that's got the Georgian Theatre Royal, an exquisite old playhouse with the oldest set of scenery in the world, and the racecourse, with the oldest stone grandstand. It rejoices in its thenness, but even that is not everything. 'Behind all this I know what's there,' says Stu. 'And in rural areas there's even less support services and the suicide rate in young men is through the roof.

'I was shocked by the scale of what I saw. I'd already been in most of those communities, because there are 34 libraries in Leeds and I've worked in all of them. I've done literacy support for kids aged three because they've already been ID'd as falling behind in speech and language skills, and I've worked in a primary school with a drug problem, which is insane. But it's a different ball game when you're standing at someone's doorstep and there's not a single pane of glass intact in the building and you can see through the door that there's mould on the walls, no carpets, broken furniture, and you've got a woman with a six-month-old baby saying, "Thanks for the food, have you got any nappies?"'

Stu talks of ghettos and mentions the Leeds suburb of Gipton. There's a poignant article on a local website about a woman too scared to go out because of the violence, so instead she sits in her flat watching *A Place in the Sun*. Stu says, 'It's not particularly big as far as city areas go, but there's nothing there, not even a school, just some houses and tower blocks. It's ghettoised to the point people from the north don't go to the south – even though you can walk it in ten minutes.

'Poverty is a trauma that's handed down through the generations. There's this Malthusian bollocks that they should have less children, but one less mouth to feed is not going to make any difference; they'll still be working shit jobs for shit pay and living in shit housing.'

It has become so bad that 'shit life syndrome' is now an accepted professional medical term for the effects that endemic poverty can have on people. 'You look at what you're up against and shrug your shoulders,' explains Stu. 'In Seacroft, for example, there are now fourth generations of families that exist with benefits as their sole means of survival. There is no aspiration. And there is this ridiculous fallacy that anybody who applies themselves can get where they want to go. The trouble is, that assumes there is a level playing field, but these people are so far behind the game that they would need to perform miracles just to get to the point where most people are starting from. I tried to explain it to the MPs in London. One of them told me the problem was the disappearance of the great institution of Sunday lunch. I mean, look, pal, you've spent more on that meal than these people have in a month. They talk about social mobility, but that implies movement, and if you're elevating someone then you're still happy for people to be left behind. The endgame should be that nobody needs to be lifted up.'

Stu does good work, but he is just shining a light on the dark alleyways where most people don't want to tread. In *Ghost Signs*, which is beautifully written and relentlessly sad, Stu writes of Leeds, 'I started to see the city as a palimpsest, juxtaposing the layers in my mind in a kind of pseudo-archaeology.' Strata of Hovis and coal pits and flat caps and brass bands sit beneath seams of unemployment, drug addiction and teenage pregnancy. No wonder we mine the past.

He tells me he used to talk about the dancing girl at readings but found himself crying on stage and so he stopped. 'I thought, I can't actually do this,' he says. 'To see a little girl, around the same age as my daughter, reacting in that way to a bag of pasta and a packet of cornflakes, it's madness in this day and age.'

This book has been about leaving Yorkshire and trying to find out what it is all about. I now realise this is a luxury. The Boys of Bradford cannot leave, stifled by systemic prejudice and hand-me-down fear. And the poverty-stricken of Leeds cannot move upwards or outwards either. Some people do not have the choice to stay or go. That's Yorkshire behind the curtain. Better to throw it back, just like Percy Shaw said. Look harder, like David Hockney. Most of the stereotypes don't matter, but this one is true: it can be bloody, horribly, heartbreakingly grim up north.

16

THEN

It is a long drive from Dorset to the Dales. It is December 2022 and there are five of us: me, Mum, my wife, Debs, and her mum, Sandra. And a dog called Dougie. Past Southampton, Winchester and Oxford to the M40 and the M1. Up to the toes of Yorkshire, around Sheffield, Meadowhall, the John Nevison route between the Yorkshire Sculpture Park and to the east, Grimethorpe one way, Wentworth Woodhouse the other, skirting Leeds and on to Otley and Ilkley Moor, and finally Addingham, where the Airbnb awaits opposite the old Methodist hall.

It does not take long to tiptoe back to the past. There is a mandatory James Herriot book on a shelf. Nobody has romanticised the Dales and the North York Moors better than the world's most famous vet. The new TV series is partly filmed in Grassington, that quaint Dales town where locals navigate cobbles to quibble about the traffic in the square. At the top of it is the Stripey Badger, an oasis of a bookshop that becomes a grocer's on the small screen. Things change here, but scratch the surface and it's the same old song.

That night we go down to the Swan in Addingham, stone floor, fragrant fire, dark ale. 'It's so nice to hear the Yorkshire accent again,' says Mum. And it is. It's like a warm aural cuddle, but when we get back up the hill there is water seeping through the roof. Mum saves the James Herriot. It shouldn't happen to an expat. An upstairs tap is loose and water is flooding through the light fittings. A dark patch is spreading across the kitchen ceiling. We wonder if the roof will come down. Call the host. When we say we've turned the water off at the stopcock, he shrugs down the phone. 'Don't worry about it, I'll come over tomorrow.' It's an admirably nonchalant approach to a portentous stain.

Over the next few days, we travel around and then back. Through the Dales from Bolton Abbey, where we talk about how terrifying the Strid was in the mind of a 10-year-old. People from the past are fleshed out during conversations. We recall F. H. Somers, the furniture store in Shipley where my grandpa worked. I show Mum a notice I have found in an old red suitcase in the loft, filled with black and white photographs and occasional newspaper clippings. It says that Walter Broadbent started at Somers as a message boy aged 13 and became the managing director. The Yorkshire dream? I have some old papers about an extension at the original Somers, which is listed as being on Westgate in Shipley, but it is long gone, just a dog groomer, a Spud Hut and a solicitor doing the Grassington grocer thing now.

Mum loves York, and this is the more recent past for her. The Minster is always evolving, but it never changes. Bettys is still there too, on the corner of Stonegate. So are some of the pubs that Mum drove my brother to when he was a teenage drummer in a band. I picture her standing at the back while bands called things like Dodgy sang about summer. It's where I stand now when I watch my own son play guitar.

We drive to Ilkley and have a drink in the Cow and Calf hotel. I think of that man with his drone and his bird feeders, and the one curtain-twitching at Jimi Hendrix fans. And we go to Salts Mill, which is a highlight for Mum. An entire level is lined with Hockney paintings and filled with books and art. Sandra buys a Hockney print for my mum. It's called *Fish and Chip Shop*. He did it in 1954 when he was at Bradford College of Art and my mum was 14. He gave the original to the owners of the Sea Catch chip shop in Eccleshill in return for a bag of scraps. They hung it above the deep fat fryer.

'I think this is my favourite place anywhere,' says Mum. She dashes around the tables stacked with books and calendars and art materials. And for a moment, she seems 14 rather than 82.

These places are the props holding up the past. They force you to at least try to remember. Travelling around Yorkshire, talking to people and sitting in libraries for days on end has been a joy. After all that, what is Yorkshireness? Well, there is definitely something in the water and the bricks and the vowels, but I think part of its DNA comes from being ravaged, wrecked, neglected and eroded. Royal and political rulers turned their backs on the place, and pride in its industries, in doing a hard, probably dangerous job for the common good, was replaced by a bitter pride in giving the Billy Casper Vs to the ravagers and wreckers when those industries went. I remember something that John Giles, the hard-as-nails footballer, told me: 'Being Leeds United we always have to defend ourselves.' That is Yorkshire too. Sometimes we get our defence in early and it can come across as studs raked down the back of a calf. The straight-talking stereotype is in the DNA as well, but the boastfulness also comes from being, as suggested by Adelle's poster, pissed off.

Now we are into generations that can barely remember the mines and mills, and old bits of community are clinging to things like the brass band and Sam Smith's pints. These are things that tether us and help us grow, the roots in our forcing sheds. We are the mum in the red trackie in Seacroft, ready to attack.

Everything is not brilliant in Leeds, Bradford, Grimethorpe and the Amazon warehouses. Mo and Stu know this. And the news coming out now is that much of Yorkshire has been ignored by the government's levelling-up fund. Six Leeds bids for money have been rejected. Hull has got nothing. Nor Bradford. Catterick, in Prime Minister Rishi Sunak's Richmond constituency, has got £19 million for the high street. It will probably win an award.

Yorkshire does look outwards, but group identity, now more than ever, provides comfort, or at least a perception of safety. That can lead to problems if, as the Archbishop of York said, it becomes too hard and too inward-looking, but it might explain why many want devolution, or a republic, or even a Robin Hood. Stiff-necked, wilful and obstinate perhaps, but Yorkshire is needy too.

There is still pride in being proud. And there is prejudice. Tanni Grey-Thompson, the multiple Paralympic champion, has just become interim chair at Yorkshire County Cricket. I know Tanni. I helped her with her autobiography. She came to my house, got out of her wheelchair and dragged herself upstairs to the loo. She is empathetic and pragmatic. On a childhood trip to Lourdes, she asked a priest what the water was like. 'Freezing,' he said. 'I don't think I'll bother then,' she replied. She'd get ignored at checkouts while assistants waited for the carer that never existed. Tanni is Welsh with a Yorkshire husband, and for years lived in Redcar, that old steel town by the seaside, beyond Middlesbrough, in the far corner, home to the world's oldest surviving lifeboat. I wish her well.

Yorkshireness can be crucial. It is needed to protect its rhubarb and its borders even if bits are toxic and the historic rivalries often have blurred edges. I once read a quote from Sir Ranulph Fiennes, who said he could not have people from Yorkshire on his expeditions because they were dour and nursed a grudge, but Captain Cook and William Scoresby did okay. Charles Waterton travelled and nursed a grudge, but Yorkshire knows it can't lock itself away behind a wall. This is not *The Trueman Show*, Fred or otherwise. It needs its neighbours, if only for comparative purposes, and it has a right to be suspicious. Indeed, it seems fitting that just outside Harrogate is Menwith Hill, the top-secret spying base with its huge golf ball domes. Some researchers are adamant this is the US National Security Agency's global surveillance HQ, monitoring millions of emails and phone calls, and even planning drone strikes. In the protesters' eyes, Yorkshire was just the perfect front. A cover story.

What's really going on in there? In the domes and the palaces and the back-to-backs? The Archbishop of York told me, 'There are nuts and bolts and practical things that need to be attended to.' But he wanted 'great vision' from leaders. And in the stonemasons' room at York Minster, where they are planning for the next 100 years, they have it. If you can't look harder at least look again. All those who have made their mark in this book tried to do just that – William Wilberforce, Richard Hawley and Helen Sharman; Anne Lister, Charlotte

Brontë and Al Garthwaite, who has just been named Lord Mayor of Leeds. Yorkshire is bigger than the rest and not always best, but size does matter. Look at Yorkshire and you look at much of Britain. It is a funhouse mirror on the wider world. It gleams and is cracked in places, but in those distorted images you can see what was or what might be.

But after digging up the past, I think what the real quality of Yorkshireness can be reduced to is a sense of difference, as the art expert Michael Paraskos suggested. It is an old-fashioned place, forever championed by its heroes and sun-dappled cobbles, but it is radical and revolutionary in its conservatism. It has its own distinct culture and is proud of being different. Hence the paeans to the Dales and the moors and the food and the accent. The chuffing smugness can become exclusionary and dangerous, leading to extremism and what Hawley called thigmotaxis if there is no air vent to the outside world, so Acre Mill, that poisoned industrial building, becomes a metaphor as well as a scandal.

And as Yorkshire gets left further behind, that sense of difference become stronger. Without it, what else is there? Englishness? What's that? Britishness? A homogenous hotchpotch? There are a hundred Yorkshires and we should celebrate them. And at the same time maybe there are just two – us and them.

Did I feel I had got closer to my dad? Well, it made me think about him more, and how times change, and the things that were normal then but not now. This journey backwards has dusted down old boxes locked in the mind's attic. Place matters when it comes to digging, but I didn't go back to Tadcaster Cemetery, even if some of the ashes might have slipped the coffee jar. I and L and A. You take your history, with all its grit and ash and earth with you, and I don't feel I have to knock on the door of that sooty black office to call a spade a spade.

On our last day in Yorkshire, we go looking for Mum's old house. She was born in that demolished pub near the canal, but she conjures up the name Redcar Road in Greengates. This is where she lived after the Alma. It is not a place that has a great press, more like the Alamo, in fact, and has recently made the news for antisocial kids hanging around and throwing bricks at buses.

'I think that's the house,' she says as we drive up the road. It's a basic, functional place. Houses go for less than £100,000 here. 'I remember walking up this hill to school.' A few roads down, she says, was the warehouse where her dad used to work. Later we will look through the red case and the hundreds of people in there. Lots of them are Mum and Dad as different people. Mum with a beehive and then a pram. Dad as a four-year-old urchin and then a man in army uniform during national service at Kingsley Barracks. I suddenly remember him telling me he was up to his neck in mud and bullets, and Mum laughing because he never was. Seeing makes you able to disbelieve again.

You should ask older people about their lives before they too are locked in a red case or left in a triangular plot of weary grass between a graffitied wall and a road to breweries.

'Thank you so much,' says Mum as we head back down the M1.

Thank you, Yorkshire. For the memories. Good, bad, buried and exhumed. Its myths and legends and figures and fantasies have shaped its people. They are blunt and they are friendly, with the Calderdale village to prove it. Independent whether devolved or not. Passionate whether evolved or not. It is a remarkable county, swathed in world-stopping beauty and practical magic. It is stunning in positive and negative ways, but it's like the Hotel California – you can check out, but you never leave. It's where you're from and where you're at, even if you're somewhere else with a wandering mind.

There is no better place.

And then Mum says:

'Do you think we can go to Cornwall one day?'

BIBLIOGRAPHY

I dipped into too many books to mention, but for varying reasons these were particularly useful.

All Points North – Simon Armitage (Viking, 1998)

The Brontës – Juliet Baker (Abacus, 2010)

Ted Hughes: The Unauthorised Life – Jonathan Bate (William Collins, 2015)

The Sheffield Gang Wars – J. P. Bean (Sheffield D&D, 1981)

Marching to the Fault Line: The Miners' Strike and the Battle for Industrial Britain – Francis Beckett (Constable, 2009)

The British Brass Band: A Musical and Social History – edited by Trevor Bennett (OUP, 2000)

Charles Waterton, 1782–1865: Traveller and Conservationist – Julia Blackburn (Bodley Head, 1989)

On Ilkley Moor: The Story of an English Town – Tim Binding (Picador, 2001)

The Corridor of Certainty: My Life Beyond Cricket – Geoffrey Boycott (Simon & Schuster, 2015)

Traditional Food in Yorkshire – Peter Brears (Prospect, 2014)

Notes from a Small Island – Bill Bryson (Black Swan, 1996)

Richard III: The Maligned King – Annette Carson (History Press, 2008)

Learning to Breathe – Andy Cave (Arrow Books, 2006)

100 Years of Leeds United – Daniel Chapman (Icon, 2019)

Confectionery in Yorkshire – Paul Chrystal (Amberley Publishing, 2012)

Harrogate – Paul Chrystal (Amberley Publishing, 2016)

A Yorkshire Tragedy: The Rise and Fall of a Sporting Powerhouse – Anthony Clavane (Riverrun, 2016)

When Push Comes to Shove: Rugby League the People's Game – Ian Clayton (Yorkshire Arts Circus, 1993)

Mother, Brother, Lover – Jarvis Cocker (Faber & Faber, 2011)

The Story of Sheffield – Tim Cooper (History Press, 2021)

Dear England: Finding Hope, Taking Heart and Changing the World – Stephen Cottrell (Hodder & Stoughton, 2021)

Running a Thousand Miles for Freedom – William and Ellen Craft (W. Tweedie, 1860, republished by University of Georgia Press)

The Kings and Queens of England – Ian Crofton (Quercus, 2006)

We'll Get 'Em in Sequins: Manliness, Yorkshire Cricket and the Decade that Changed Everything – Max Davidson (John Wisden & Co., 2012)

Secret Wakefield – Paul L. Dawson (Amberley Publishing, 2015)

Coal is Our Life: An Analysis of a Yorkshire Mining Community – Norman Dennis, Fernando Henriques and Clifford Slaughter (Eyre & Spottiswoode, 1956)

All the Year Round – Charles Dickens (Chapman and Hall, 1859)

The Robin Hood Handbook – Mike Dixon Kennedy (History Press, 2006)

Rita, Sue and Bob Too – Andrea Dunbar (Royal Court Theatre, 1982)

The Conditions of the Working Class in England – Friedrich Engels (Otto Wigand, 1845)

Life in a Yorkshire Village – J. Fairfax-Blakeborough (Yorkshire Publishing Co., 1912)

The Spirit of Yorkshire – J. and R. Fairfax-Blakeborough (Batsford, 1954)

Fifty-Six: The Story of the Bradford fire – Martin Fletcher (Bloomsbury, 2015)

Amy Johnson – Midge Gillies (Weidenfeld & Nicolson, 2003)

The Art of Cookery Made Plain and Simple – Hannah Glasse (London, 1747)

The Miners' Strike – Geoffrey Goodman (Pluto Press, 1985)

Fatal Colours: Towton, 1461 – England's Most Brutal Battle – George Goodwin (Orion, 2011)

Charlotte Brontë: A Life – Claire Harman (Viking, 2015)

V – Tony Harrison (Bloodaxe Books, 1985–1989)

William Wilberforce: The Life of the Great Anti-Slave Trade Campaigner – William Hague (Harper Perennial, 2008)

Innocent Abroad: The Travels of Miss Hannah Hauxwell – Hannah Hauxwell with Barry Cockcroft (Random Century, 1991)

Seasons of My Life: The Story of a Solitary Daleswoman – Hannah Hauxwell with Barry Cockcroft (Century Hutchinson, 1989)

Ghost Signs: Poverty and the Pandemic – Stu Hennigan (Bluemoose Books, 2022)

A Kestrel for a Knave – Barry Hines (Michael Joseph, 1968)

The Price of Coal – Barry Hines (Michael Joseph, 1979)

Leviathan or the Whale – Philip Hoare (Fourth Estate, 2008)

David Hockney: My Early Years – David Hockney (H. N. Abrams, 1988)

The Uses of Literacy: Aspects of Working-Class Life – Richard Hoggart (Chatto & Windus, 1957)

The Yorkshire Beer Bible – Simon Jenkins (Great Northern Books, 2017)

A Short History of England – Simon Jenkins (Profile Books, 2011)

The King of the Ferret Leggers: And Other True Stories – Donald R. Katz (Random House, 2001)

On Ilkla Moor Baht 'at: The Story of a Song – Arnold Kellett (Smith Settle, 1998)

Know Your Yorkshire – Arnold Kellett (Dalesman, 1980)

Yorkshire Battles – Edward Lamplough (William Andrews and Co., 1891)

The Secret Diaries of Miss Anne Lister: I Know My Own Heart – Anne Lister, edited by Helena Whitbread (Virago, 2010)

Pies and Prejudice – Stuart Maconie (Ebury, 2008)

How Leeds Changed the World – Mick McCann (Armley Press, 2010)

Geoff Boycott: A Cricketing Hero – Leo McKinstry (Willow, 2005)

The Brontë Myth – Lucasta Miller (Vintage, 2002)

Bill Mitchell's Yorkshire – compiled by David Mitchell (Dalesman, 2016)

Settle–Carlisle Railway – W. R. Mitchell and David Joy (Dalesman, 1979)

The North – Paul Morley (Bloomsbury, 2013)

The Soccer Tribe – Desmond Morris (Jonathan Cape, 1981)

Division Street – Helen Mort (Chatto & Windus, 2013)

Harry Ramsden: The Uncrowned King of Fish and Chips – Don Mosey and Harry Ramsden Junior (Dalesman, 1989)

The Gallows Pole – Benjamin Myers (Bluemoose Books, 2017)

Under the Rock: Stories Carved from the Land – Benjamin Myers (Elliott and Thompson, 2018)

The Seabird's Cry: The Lives and Loves of Puffins, Gannets and Other Ocean Voyagers – Adam Nicolson (William Collins, 2017)

Wild Thing: The Short, Spellbinding Life of Jimi Hendrix – Philip Norman (Weidenfeld & Nicolson, 2020)

The Road to Wigan Pier – George Orwell (Victor Gollancz, 1937)

The Floating Egg: Episodes in the Making of Geology – Roger Osborne (Jonathan Cape, 1998)

Fish & Chips: A History – Panikos Panayi (Reaktion Books, 2014)

Black Gold: The History of How Coal Made Britain – Jeremy Paxman (William Collins, 2021)

The Damned Utd – David Peace (Faber and Faber, 2006)

The Bell Jar – Sylvia Plath (Heinemann, 1963)

An English Journey – J. B. Priestley (Harper and Brothers, 1934)

Young, Muslim and Criminal: Experiences, Identities and Pathways into Crime – Mohammed Qasim (Policy Press, 2018)

The Romans in Yorkshire – Arthur Raistrick (Dalesman, 1972)

The Meaning of Art – Herbert Read (Pelican, 1931)

To Hell with Culture – Herbert Read (Routledge & Kegan Paul, 1963)

The Shepherd's Life – James Rebanks (Allen Lane, 2015)

The King's Council in the North – Rachel Robertson Reid (Longmans, 1921)

Looking North: Northern England and the National Imagination – Dave Russell (Manchester University Press, 2004)

We Remember the Blitz – Frank and Joan Shaw (Ebury, 2012)

Old Yorkshire – William Smith (Longmans, 1881–1884)

Prince Rupert: The Last Cavalier – Charles Spencer (Weidenfeld & Nicolson, 2007)

Never the Same Again: Women and the Miners' Strike – Jean Stead (Women's Press Ltd, 1987)

William Scoresby: Arctic Scientist – Tom and Cordelia Stamp (Caedmon of Whitby Press, 1975)

This Sporting Life – David Storey (Longmans, 1960)

Black Teeth and a Brilliant Smile – Adelle Stripe (Fleet, 2017)

Ten Thousand Apologies – Adelle Stripe (White Rabbit, 2022)

The Striding Dales – Halliwell Sutcliffe (Frederick Warne & Co., 1929)

Hockney: A Rake's Progress – Christopher Simon Sykes (Century, 2011)

Hockney: The Biography, Volume 2 – Christopher Simon Sykes (Century, 2014)

The Clapham Sect – Stephen Tomkins (Lion Hudson, 2010)

As It Was: The Memoirs of Fred Trueman – Fred Trueman (Macmillan, 2004)

Fred Trueman: The Authorised Biography – Fred Trueman (Aurum Press, 2012)

The Streetcleaner: The Yorkshire Ripper Case on Trial – Nicole Ward Jouve (Marion Boyars, 1986)

Fred Trueman: The Authorised Biography – Chris Waters (Aurum, 2011)

Wanderings in South America, the North-West of the United States, and the Antilles – Charles Waterton (1828, republished by Cambridge University Press, 2011)

A Month in Yorkshire – Walter White (Chapman and Hull, 1861)

Hearts, Tarts & Rascals: The Story of Bettys – Jonathan Wild (Bettys and Taylors Group, 2005)

The Real James Herriot: A Memoir of My Father – Jim Wight (Ballantine, 1999)

Strike: Thatcher, Scargill and the Miners – Peter Wilsher (Cornet Books, 1985)

Beryl: In Search of Britain's Greatest Athlete – Jeremy Wilson (Pursuit Books, 2022)

The Map that Changed the World: The tale of William Smith and the Birth of a Science – Simon Winchester (Viking, 2001)

Agatha Christie: A Very Elusive Woman – Lucy Worsley (Hodder & Stoughton, 2022)

ACKNOWLEDGEMENTS

I couldn't cover everything. There, that's the disclaimer. Every time I got close to finishing the book, I would come across another nugget, or someone would suggest something new. It's been a thrill to write about something so close to my heart, and the hardest bit was deciding what to leave out. In the end, I chose subjects that I thought added to the broad theme of people and place, and the relationship between the two.

It is not a political book, but inevitably politics inform some of the stories, and while it is a love story, there are shades of *Kramer vs Kramer*.

A lot of people have helped along the way. Among those I am especially grateful to are William and Dan Wilberforce, Richard Hawley, Simon Rix, Ian McMillan, Dr Mohammed Qasim, Dr David Forrest, Dr Michael Paraskos, Adelle Stripe, Benjamin Myers, Andy Cave, John David, Al Garthwaite, Stu Hennigan, Sarah Cobham, Abbie Ferrar, Stephen Cottrell, Janine and Phillip Murphy, Alison Roberts, Ian Clayton, Simon Clifford, Janet Oldroyd Hulme, Diane Mckaye, Andrew Fagg, Matt Lewis, Laurie Shannon, Howard H. Smith, J. Willgoose, Esq., Neil Sanderson, Sharon Atkinson, Elizabeth Addy, Jack Simpson, Dan Broadbent, Richard Whitehead, Tom Palmer, and from older days, Jessica Ennis-Hill, Peter Lorimer, Martin Fletcher, Jack Charlton, Howard Wilkinson, Josh Warrington, Nicola Adams and David Batty.

Two brilliant poets, Helen Mort and Tony Harrison, gave

permission for me to quote their work, which was immensely kind, as did the Kaiser Chiefs.

I have endeavoured to credit people's work within the text or in the bibliography, and apologise if I have omitted anyone. I looked at hundreds of papers, letters and documents, realising again what a brilliant resource our libraries and archives offer. If you are ever bored, just go and find one. The same goes for museums, and Yorkshire is blessed with some eye-popping palaces. Some of those I most enjoyed visiting were Whitby Museum, the Castle Museum, Yorkshire Museum, Kelham Island Museum, the Brontë Parsonage, Thackray Museum of Medicine, the National Coal Mining Museum, the Rotunda and the Peace Museum.

The British Newspaper Archive was a valuable resource, and I made extensive use of material from a wide range of national and regional papers, magazines and online resources. These included the *Yorkshire Post* (a brilliant example of just how important a quality regional paper can be in an age when the industry has been savaged), the *Yorkshire Evening Post*, the *Press* (always the *Yorkshire Evening Press* to me, after doing my first work experience there), the *Whitby Gazette, Sheffield Star, Telegraph & Argus, Hull Daily Mail, Huddersfield Daily Examiner, Barnsley Chronicle* and a number of defunct publications such as the *Leeds Mercury, Leeds Intelligencer, Harrogate Herald* and *York Gazette*. There are so many great journalists covering the north of England, and among others, I have long enjoyed the work of Helen Pidd, David Collins, Martin Wainwright and Tom Ball.

Online: Yorkshire Magazine, Yorkshire Bylines and The Yorkshireman are great online resources for those interested in Yorkshire both now and then. The Grimethorpe brass band story is told in detail on the band website – www.grimethorpeband.co.uk. My knowledge of Acre Mill was

enhanced by reading www.richardcreasney.net. I have
long enjoyed www.alanburnett.com ever since reading the
author's take on Tadcaster's brewing brothers. And the
history videos posted by Catherine Warr are witty and wise.
Look her up @HiddenYorkshire.

The books of Simon Armitage, Stuart Maconie and Bill
Bryson remain inspirations (thanks for that letter, Bill).

I watched numerous films, fact and fiction, to help my
understanding and for pleasure. Among those I found particularly useful were *The Battle for Orgreave* (Yvette Vanson),
Henry Moore: recollections of a Yorkshire childhood (Colin
Nutley) and *Too Long a Winter* (Barry Cockcroft).

Huge thanks to Ed Faulkner, Kate Ballard and all at
Atlantic. Ed's enthusiasm and editing have been vital to
getting this book over the line in coherent shape. Copyeditors
are often unsung heroes, so thanks to Jane Selley too. And a
firm handshake for my agent, David Luxton. We have been
working together for pushing 20 years now, and I am hugely
grateful for his ideas, advice and friendship.

Most importantly, I am lucky to have Debs, Erin and Sam
on my side. The last time I wrote any acknowledgements, I
thanked them for letting me live with them. Since then, Erin
has buggered off to Tooting and Sam is in Birmingham, but
times change. They are still the best people I know, even if
Debs is from Manchester.

Finally, Leeds United were a constant drain on my enthusiasm throughout this project, but geography is unforgiving
and you are what you are. I live in Dorset, but Yorkshire is
where I'm from and, more often than not, where I'm at. It's
a state of its own and a state of mind.

That'll do.

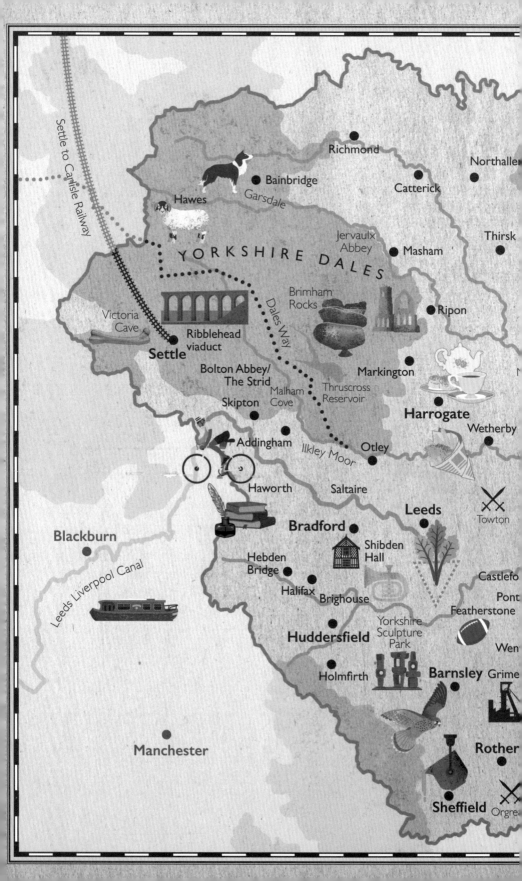